A Rabbi Reads the Torah

A Rabbi Reads the Torah

Jonathan Magonet

scm press

© Jonathan Magonet 2013

Published in 2013 by SCM Press
Editorial office
3rd Floor, Invicta House, 108–114 Golden Lane,
London EC1Y 0TG

SCM Press is an imprint of Hymns Ancient
& Modern Ltd (a registered charity)
13A Hellesdon Park Road, Norwich,
Norfolk NR6 5DR, UK

www.scmpress.co.uk

British Library Cataloguing in Publication data

A catalogue record for this book is available
from the British Library

978-0-334-04913-5

Typeset by Manila Typesetting Company
Printed and bound by
CPI Group (UK) Ltd, Croydon

Contents

Introduction

In theory, rabbis don't give 'sermons'!

Though, truth to tell, we have been influenced by the forms and terms of the wider society – including some of the worst aspects: A late-arriving congregant asks another who is just departing: 'Has the rabbi finished his sermon?' 'Yes,' comes the answer, 'but he is still talking!'

Instead of a sermon, traditionally the rabbi, or indeed any lay member of the congregation, might give a *derashah*, a commentary on the particular passage from the Torah, the Five Books of Moses, that was being read on Shabbat morning that week in the synagogue. (Actually the Hebrew text is not 'read' but chanted according to a traditional set of melodies whose musical divisions also form a kind of commentary on the text.) *Darash* means to seek out, to search out, to delve into the many potential meanings within the biblical text itself, often aided by commentaries composed by rabbinic scholars over the past two thousand years.

The word 'Torah', from a root word '*yarah*', meaning to shoot arrows at a target, is best translated as 'teaching', containing as it does both the narrative parts of the Bible and the legal aspects, everything that points the way towards a spiritual life. Though initially the term referred to the Five Books of Moses alone, understood traditionally as the direct revelation of God to Israel through Moses, Torah developed over time to include the rest of the Bible and indeed all the laws, teachings, opinions and personal examples derived from it.

The *derashah* allows the rabbi to make his or her own contribution to the accumulated wisdom derived from the Torah.

The Five Books are divided into 54 units or *parashiot* so that the entire collection is covered in the course of a year – actually a leap year (one in which an extra month is added because the Jewish year is about one week shorter than the calendar year and has to catch up every few years). In non-leap years, of 50 weeks, some of the *parashiot* are joined together. Texts from Genesis are read in the autumn; from Exodus from the beginning of the year till about March; from Leviticus through to May; from Numbers till July, and from Deuteronomy over the summer months and into the autumn. The entire cycle of readings is completed in the autumn after the Jewish New Year at a festival called *Simchat Torah*, the rejoicing in the Torah, when we read the end of the Book of Deuteronomy and immediately begin again with Genesis. The cycle never ends, and with it the responsibility of rabbi and congregation together to seek out, to search for, the message embedded in the text by God with its lessons relevant for today.

Following the passage from the Torah in the synagogue there is a reading from the second division of the Hebrew Bible, the 'prophets', *nevi'im*. This prophetic reading is called the Haftarah, meaning conclusion. The passage for the week was chosen by the rabbis to echo some aspect of the Torah reading, but at various times of the year it is used instead to introduce or reflect upon the current Jewish festival. In addition, certain biblical books, the five *megillot*, scrolls, are read in conjunction with five key festivals and one fast during the course of the year: Esther at *Purim* in early spring; the Song of Songs at Pesach, Passover; Ruth at Shavuot, Pentecost; Lamentations on *Tisha b'Av*, the fast day during the summer commemorating the destruction of Solomon's Temple by the Babylonians; Ecclesiastes during the autumn harvest festival of Sukkot. So all of these texts may be drawn upon for comment.

The various chapters in this book were not delivered in the conventional location of a synagogue on Shabbat morning. Instead, like those in *From Autumn to Summer*,[1] they are a second collection of broadcasts given on German radio over a number of years during a Friday evening programme welcoming the Shabbat. Though ostensibly aimed at Jewish listeners, their real audience was a far broader one of people who were interested in matters Jewish. So the comments had to reflect some aspect of the Torah reading but also address a far wider community, as part of a broader commitment to interfaith dialogue. The 52 chapters in the book do not follow completely the cycle of the year, but may offer something for a personal weekly dip into the Bible. Some readings relating to specific festivals are to be found towards the end of the book.

Whether called a *derashah* or a sermon, it is a difficult art – to compress into a limited time enough information to explain the context within the Bible itself, and then translate it or open it up to address the expectations and needs of the congregation. Few rabbis can be sure that they have been faithful both to the Torah text itself and the listening congregation even once, let alone week after week. Perhaps the best one can hope for is the kind of positive response I experienced once at a civic service in a small synagogue in south London. At the end, the visiting non-Jewish mayor, said: 'That wasn't a sermon. You spoke to us!'

1

The Call to Abraham

Genesis 12

We begin the cycle of stories about Abraham, the founding figure of biblical faith. He is a most unlikely hero for such an extraordinary achievement. He is 75 years old. Nothing in the previous references to him in the Bible has suggested that he will be a religious pioneer. Indeed, so little information is given that the rabbis are forced to fill in his earlier life with stories that explain how he came to the belief in the one God.

This biblical silence encourages us to enquire about beginnings in general. For example, why does Abraham's story begin here in Genesis 12? Or rather, what are we to make of the few tantalizing glimpses of his earlier life in the chapter before?

There is already something of a puzzle about the opening verses of our chapter. God speaks to Abram, as he is then known – only later will his name be changed to Abraham. God invites him to depart from his land, his family and his father's house to go to a land that God will show him. God's two words in Hebrew, *lekh l'kha*, are actually an invitation to go, not a command as many translations suggest. The two words mean 'go to yourself', 'go for yourself', or 'go for your own sake'. This suggests that Abraham is free to accept this task or not. For God's plans for humanity to have any meaning Abraham has to be a free agent. He must willingly choose to place his life and future in the hands of this God who calls to him.

Nothing is said about how Abraham considered the matter and came to the decision to go. Instead, we are simply told that

Abraham went and took his extensive household with him. These include the servants he had acquired during his stay in a place called Haran. This is an important city on the main route from Abraham's birthplace, Ur, on the Euphrates river, to Aleppo. But at this point something becomes a little unclear in the biblical story.

To understand the problem we have to go back to the previous chapter, Genesis 11. It introduces Abraham's family and the cast list of people we will need to know something about as the story unfolds. Genesis 11 consists of a genealogy extending over ten generations from Shem, the son of Noah, down to Terach, the father of Abraham. We are told that Terach has three sons, Abraham, the oldest, Nahor and Haran. Haran dies, and his son Lot becomes Abraham's ward. He will accompany Abraham on his journey and cause him considerable trouble in the future.

We learn that both Abraham and Nahor marry. Nahor has children who will also feature in later stories about Abraham's family. But Abraham's wife Sarah, we learn, is barren and cannot have children. So much for the background.

But next we learn that it is actually Terach, Abraham's father, who originally set out on a journey away from his homeland, from the city of Ur. Terach's destination is the Land of Canaan, the unnamed land that Abraham is invited by God to visit. Under the name, the land of Israel, it will forever be associated with Abraham and his descendants. Under Terach's leadership the family only get as far as the city of Haran, and there it seems they become settled and remain. So here is the problem. Terach has already set out from the family homeland for the land of Canaan. So what is the meaning of God's invitation to Abraham to leave his homeland, if he has already long since done so accompanying his father? In fact, whose initiative is the whole journey, Terach's or Abraham's? Was Terach also obeying a word from God? Was Abraham merely following a path established by his father?

One thing this apparent contradiction illustrates is the difficulty of pinning down where exactly something begins. Events always have a previous history. What factors might have led to the present moment? A chance encounter, a personal experience, an entire lifetime spent in a certain way, may all turn out to be the preparation for something entirely new and unexpected. Something out of the past, perhaps long forgotten, has had its quiet effect that only now bears fruit. Like the ripples that spread out when a stone is thrown into water, they will touch many other places and have effects that could never have been anticipated.

Our lives are part of a web of endlessly developing results of events from our past, only some of which we may remember. We are held in a matrix of cause and effect, of actions and consequences, of infinite complexity. Perhaps we catch an occasional glimpse of how things came about in a particular case. Mostly we simply try to make sense of what is happening to us now, at this precious moment.

What was it that made Abraham particularly open to the call he received from God? Was it something about the city of Haran that disturbed him? The rabbis assumed it was a place of many gods and many idols that Abraham became unable to tolerate. They tell a story about how he came to worship the one God.

As a child, Abraham began to worship the stars, but when he saw the moon he worshipped that instead. However, when the powerful sun arose the following morning, he became convinced that here indeed was the true God. But then the sun was hidden by a cloud, and he realized that behind all these natural phenomena was a greater power that controlled them. In this way, be came to discover the one God. Once he had made this discovery, he found it difficult to remain in a place of idol worship. So this inner journey explains his need to break with the past and make the outer journey to a new land.

But perhaps there were other factors that made Abraham ready for such a move. Maybe we have to look more closely at the information given us in the previous chapter. The death of his uncle brought new responsibilities as his nephew Lot entered his imme diate family. Abraham became suddenly the possessor of two households, not one. Later in Genesis, we will learn that there is friction between the two families so that they have to separate and each has to settle in a different territory. Perhaps this was a factor that opened Abraham to new possibilities. The need for additional pasturage for his cattle helped break the bonds that kept him tied to his father in Haran. When the call came from God he was more than ready to hear it and to move.

But we know of one other factor that must have weighed heavily upon him – the barrenness of his wife Sarah. A man with no children in that biblical world was a man with no future. Though it is the wife who is assumed to be unfruitful, it was nevertheless a poor reflection on the man who was incapable of producing children. It would have been a source of embarrassment and shame in his immediate society.

We will learn that Sarah is beautiful. Perhaps Abraham is torn between his love for her and the need to find another wife, if his wish to procreate is to be fulfilled. Maybe his departure was not intended as a journey of discovery but rather an escape from an intolerable domestic situation.

All the above reasons suggest some factors that might have predisposed Abraham to make such an extraordinary move at an advanced age. But none of them quite explain the power of his call or the willingness with which he responded. Feeling ill at ease in an alien culture, struggling to support a growing family, or torn by a painful domestic situation – all of these have led throughout history to population migrations. But few have led to a vision that has transformed humanity. Abraham may have thought the call was an invitation to go for himself alone, for his own benefit – but it became a journey not simply for himself but for us all.

2

Etiquette and Hospitality

Genesis 18–22

This passage from the Torah begins with Chapters 18 and 19 of Genesis and provides us with a mystery and some lessons in etiquette. First the mystery! We are told at the beginning of the chapter that God appears to Abraham while he is sitting in his tent during the hot time of the day. Yet, it is not God that Abraham sees but instead three men. In the conversation that follows, it is not certain whether Abraham is speaking to all three of the men, or just one of them, or simply to God. Indeed, does Abraham know that he is speaking to God at all? Who are these three mysterious men, or what are they? Is the whole episode simply a figment of Abraham's imagination? After all it is the hottest part of the day. Perhaps they are a mirage, or he is dreaming. Or are they some kind of supernatural beings, sent as messengers by God?

The more we try to understand the passage, and the chapter that follows, the more our confusion grows. For it seems that one of the 'men' either stays with Abraham or disappears, because in the next chapter there are only two of them. Moreover, in the next chapter, they are no longer referred to as 'men' but as 'angels'. Now they are visiting Abraham's nephew Lot and will rescue him when the towns of Sodom and Gomorrah are destroyed. From the sequence of chapters, they would definitely appear to be two of the original three. But if so, why are they called something different in the chapter about Abraham than they are called in the chapter about Lot?

First, we need to clear up a problem in the Hebrew language. The word translated as 'angel' is *mal'akh*, which actually means 'messenger', someone fulfilling a particular task. When the word was translated for the Greek version of the Bible they chose the Greek word for messenger, *angelos*, from which comes our word 'angel'. It is only later traditions that turned these messengers into the supernatural angels that we think of today with wings and feathers.

So on one level of the story, it is three men who encounter Abraham bringing him a message from God. Two of them will then continue their journey to Sodom and Gomorrah to rescue Lot.

The rabbis were a bit critical about Lot, and in this they were following the biblical evaluation of him. His wealth is all derived from Abraham, but that very wealth leads to the two men quarrelling and separating. Lot, it seems, was a bit too much concerned with his financial situation, which made him forget certain other values about family loyalty and respect. This leads to the rabbinic explanation of why the mysterious visitors are sometimes called men and sometimes angels. Although Abraham only saw men approaching him, strangers, probably idol worshippers, he was such a generous host that he went out into the heat of the day to greet them and showed them great hospitality. But Lot, on the other hand, was so mean that if he had only seen two men coming he would have ignored them. However, because they appeared to him looking like angels, supernatural beings, he was willing to greet them and look after them!

Rabbinic tradition develops the story a bit further and identifies the angels. They pointed out that this story occurs just after Abraham has circumcised himself and his first son Ishmael. Since this was a major operation, no wonder Abraham was lying down in his tent recovering from the trauma. So the first messenger was Raphael, the angel appointed to look after the process of healing. He was there to help Abraham recover. The second was the angel Michael, whose task was to give Abraham's wife Sarah the good news that she would have a child. The third was Gabriel, whose task was to destroy the wicked cities of Sodom and Gomorrah.

The rabbis derived a number of important lessons from these stories about how we should behave. From Abraham's actions, they taught the importance of hospitality, for Abraham went out of his way to look for, welcome and feed his guests. In the same way we should also be generous hosts.

From God's behaviour, we learn the *mitzvah*, the commandment, of *bikkur holim*, visiting the sick. We too should imitate the actions of God and visit those who are ill and support and comfort them.

The rabbis also noticed a difference between the behaviour of the visitors in the two chapters. When Abraham offered them food they ate it at once. When Lot offered them hospitality at first they refused and only accepted when he insisted. From this, they derived the responsibility of guests. Abraham was clearly a rich man and could afford to feed them, so they did not refuse. But it was not clear whether Lot was wealthy and could afford to be so generous, so they refused hospitality at first so as not to embarrass him. Only when he insisted did they agree.

If these are the lessons in etiquette to be derived from the chapter we are left with the mystery of these visitors and how to understand them. One approach is to see them as normal human beings who happen to be messengers for someone else even if they are unaware of it themselves. This means that any encounter with another person contains a message for us, some kind of spiritual lesson, for everyone is made in the image of God. If we behave like Lot, we will never learn this, or recognize the message when it comes to us, because we will always be looking for the extraordinary, for the supernatural, for angels with wings and feathers. But if we are like Abraham, then we will treat each person we meet as a potential guest and will listen out for the special message they have for us, the message that only we can hear, the message that is meant for us alone.

3

Mourning for Sarah

Genesis 23

This reading from the Book of Genesis presents us with one of the recurrent puzzles about why certain passages were chosen to be included in the Hebrew Bible. Genesis Chapter 23 tells of the death of Abraham's wife Sarah and the arrangements he made to purchase a burial place for her. The previous chapter is the powerful story of God's call to Abraham to sacrifice his son Isaac, one of the most difficult and challenging stories in the whole of the Bible. From the major religious questions this raises about God we are suddenly returned to a very everyday practical problem. So why is such a chapter included?

Let us look at it in detail. The chapter itself is a fascinating account of how negotiations were conducted in the Ancient Near East. Abraham and the sons of Het behave with great formality and politeness, but under the surface we can see them working towards an agreement that is acceptable to all parties.

Abraham points out that he is only a resident alien among them. This means that he has only limited legal rights and must rely on their good will if he is to be allowed to purchase land in which to bury his dead. The men of Het, being equally polite, point out that Abraham is an important and celebrated person, indeed a prince of God! His legal status does not matter and it would be an honour to them to give him any piece of land that he desired.

The German Jewish Bible commentator of the last century, Benno Jacob, points out that nowhere in the negotiations do they talk of buying and selling. It would be inappropriate for great leaders of their society to use the crude language of commerce. Rather they talk about exchanging gifts with one another – though it is clear that such gifts have to be of equivalent value!

Abraham asks for the cave at the end of the field of a man called Ephron. Since Ephron is present, and permission has now been given for such a transaction, he is equally generous in offering it to Abraham as a gift. However, while Abraham only asked for the cave, Ephron includes the entire field in the sale as well. Naturally, this adds to the purchase price and probably disposes of a piece of unproductive land at the same time. When the price is finally named, Ephron presents it once again in a gentlemanly style: 'A land worth 40 shekels, what is that between you and me?' The price of 40 shekels, according to biblical standards, is exorbitant. Nevertheless, Abraham pays without a murmur and the transaction is formally witnessed and completed. Thus the cave of Machpelah, in Hebron, will become the burial place of Abraham and Sarah, and their family after them.

So what is the point of the story with all of its details? Perhaps it was seen as important since it was the one part of the land of Israel actually purchased by the first patriarch, Abraham. It symbolizes the rootedness of his descendants in the land. Perhaps for the biblical author such domestic incidents in the lives of the patriarchs were also of importance. Here Abraham acted in a proper fashion and the reader could note how well respected he was in the eyes of his non-Israelite neighbours. But we might also see another dimension in this simple event.

To explain this dimension I have to tell the story of a very special man called Eugene Heimler. Born in Hungary, he was a survivor of Auschwitz Concentration Camp. After the war, he became a psychiatric social worker in Britain and worked particularly with other survivors of Concentration Camps and their families.

He once experienced a brief psychotic episode himself, when his whole world suddenly fell apart. This came as a particular shock, because he had thought that years of personal analysis and therapy had helped him overcome the effects of his experiences in Auschwitz. Nothing seemed to help. Then one day a friend asked him if he had undertaken a process of ritual mourning for the members of his family, who had been murdered in the concentration camps. When Heimler thought about it, he realized that he had not done so. As he explained, many survivors kept up the hope for years after the war that missing loved ones would reappear, long after they knew that this was impossible.

So Heimler decided to go through the formal Jewish mourning procedures, which include reciting the memorial prayer, the *Kaddish*, daily for a full year. In this way, he, too, could finally say goodbye to those he had lost and 'bury' his own dead. Shortly after undertaking this practice the psychotic episode ceased. So he began to explore with his clients the extent to which they too had unfinished business to work through because of some great loss in their life that they had never really come to terms with.

The story of Abraham mourning for his wife and then making the formal arrangements for her burial describes the normal way in which we face such an experience of loss. Tragically, like survivors of the Shoah, or indeed the surviving families of any major natural catastrophe or war, some people may never learn the fate of their loved ones who were killed. As long as the hope is there that the missing person may still one day return, this possibility can sustain them. But at the same time it may prevent them accepting the reality of their loss. Eugene Heimler was able to understand the great damage this had done to his own emotional state. For many the wounds of some such terrible experience, and the unreality of the sudden disappearance of someone so close to them, may have effects long into the future.

The mourning traditions of Judaism aid the process of facing the death of a loved one. The different stages support the mourner in the healing process from the time of the initial shock and pain of loss through the period of recovery and a gradual return to life. Unlike so many who have lost those they love through natural disasters or human violence, at least Abraham was able, in both a physical and emotional sense, to bury his dead, and begin to rebuild his life.

4

The Servant's Test

Genesis 24

This reading from the Torah is rather surprising. All it contains are a couple of domestic stories from the end of Abraham's life. They are far removed from the drama of God's call to Abraham in Chapter 22 to sacrifice his son, which is so often singled out as a central biblical story. In Genesis 23, we learn of the death of Abraham's wife Sarah and the negotiations he undertook to find a burial plot for her and his family. In Chapter 24, he sends a servant back to the land of his birth to find a wife for his son Isaac. But these domestic events, personally important to Abraham but not obviously of wider significance, could have been described in a couple of sentences. So why the need to go into such great detail?

Beneath the surface we can see something of Abraham's insecurities as an immigrant in the land of Canaan. To acquire a burial place requires not only the approval of the owner of the cave that he needs, but also of the leading citizens of the society. The negotiation is conducted with great civility on both sides, with expressions of respect and even flattery. But Abraham's success depends on his ability to pay whatever price they impose on him. Some of the prejudice against immigrants tends to disappear or at least be ignored, if they can more than pay their way. Abraham is forced to buy not only the cave he needs but also the surrounding field, and probably even then at an exorbitant price. The deal is agreed and Abraham buries his wife. One day, he himself will be buried there by his two sons, Isaac and Ishmael.

But the story in the following chapter reminds us of other aspects of immigrant life. However much Abraham has established himself in the land, in one respect he still feels himself to be an outsider. Like so many people who come from a traditional society, when he looks for a wife for his son, he wants to bring over from his homeland someone from his own family and people and tradition. In the biblical world, marriages were arranged by the family, because they concerned more than just the two people. A marriage was also a merger of two families, two sets of property and complex inheritance rights and issues. But beyond these practical and material aspects, all families are concerned to ensure the happiness of their children. So in a traditional society one checks out the family background of the proposed spouse: the respect it has in its society, the stability it has displayed over the generations, the absence of any disturbing behaviour, its piety, and in Jewish society especially, the religious learning and study of its members. It is assumed that these qualities have been passed on to the prospective bride or groom, and so the family can feel assured about the marriage. Today is very different, because the couple alone usually make all those decisions about the suitability of their partner. If the family ask questions, it is likely to be about the groom's financial prospects. Traditional societies look to the past for guidance and reassurance; modern societies look to the future.

But Abraham's situation is complicated. He has left this task to find an appropriate daughter-in-law very late. From the opening of the chapter we learn that Abraham was already very old, and perhaps he was now simply unable to make the journey to his homeland himself. Instead he entrusts the mission to his trusted servant, who has control over his household. The servant is never named in the chapter, but rabbinic tradition identifies him as Eliezer. The basis of this seems to be the earlier reference to a certain Eliezer of Damascus (Gen. 15.2), who would become Abraham's heir, if he was without a son. If the servant is this same Eliezer, it becomes

13

clear why Abraham asks him to make a solemn oath to God at the start of his mission to make sure he does his duty. It would also explain the servant's immediate response – what happens if the girl refuses to accompany me back here, should I take Isaac there? Abraham is very quick to forbid him to take Isaac back to his homeland. No reason is ever given. Perhaps Abraham is worried that Isaac is not strong enough to resist the temptation to stay in the family land rather than return to Canaan. But perhaps he is also worried that a convenient accident might befall his son on the way, as would happen to Joseph in a later generation. So he tells the servant that if the girl refuses to come, then the servant is released from his vow. If the servant is indeed Eliezer, and likely to inherit, then he is faced with a huge temptation. All he has to do is make it impossible to find the right girl or prevent her accompanying him, and he will increase his chances of inheriting.

Does the servant fall into this trap? He travels to the land, leading a huge camel train bearing evidence of the wealth of his master. He stops beside the well, which is the centre of community life. But instead of enquiring about the family of his master and meeting with potential brides, he makes a wager with God. If the first girl he asks for water offers to give water to his camels as well, she is the right one, and God is indeed looking out for Abraham his master.

At first glance, this seems like a reasonable bargain to strike with God. It would show the hospitable nature of the girl, an important virtue in the ancient Near East. But there is a catch that was pointed out by a great Bible teacher, Nechama Leibowitz. She asked the simple question: How much does a thirsty camel drink? Of course, it depends on what kind of camel and doubtless many other factors. But it is something like 120 litres. And the servant has ten camels. We usually picture Rebecca as a pretty little girl with a water jar on her shoulder. Happily she pours a little water into a trough. But this must have been a major, back-breaking undertaking, going back and forth to the well.

The Bible records that the servant simply stood and stared at her, as she managed to achieve it. Any ideas he might have had to avoid finding a wife for Isaac have now been destroyed. He gives her a golden ring and places two expensive bracelets on her wrists, but only then asks whose daughter she is. When he learns that she is indeed from Abraham's family, he bows to the ground to Abraham's God.

There then follows the negotiation with the family to let the girl undertake the journey to marry Isaac. The servant uses all his persuasive powers, though he has to be careful how he explains the fact that he picked Rebecca before knowing who she was. So he tells the story of the well and God's intervention, but changes the sequence slightly. In his version, he asked who her family was before giving her the gifts! He is successful, and with the family's agreement, Rebecca gives her consent to go with him.

This chapter, with its 67 verses, is the longest in the Book of Genesis. So why is so much space devoted to this story? True, it describes the hand of God directing the destiny of Abraham and his future family. It is also a fascinating tale of negotiation and diplomacy. But it also shows that the Hebrew Bible is not just about politics and the great affairs of nations. It is concerned with the practical realities of daily life. How we handle these basic domestic responsibilities within our family is a reflection of our core values and hopes. And, as in the case of Abraham, they give us qualities and credentials for acting with responsibility and compassion in the wider world.

5

A Failure of Communication

Genesis 25.19—28.9

As we read the biblical stories in the Book of Genesis, it is clear that it is men who play the dominant role. Simply naming Abraham, Isaac, Jacob and Joseph conjures up the main stories and events. Yet, the women are clearly there behind the scenes. And sometimes they even come to the forefront. It is Sarah who insists that Abraham sends away his son Ishmael and Ishmael's mother Hagar. Rachel and Leah, in competition with one another for the love of Jacob, will produce the twelve sons who will become the twelve tribes. It is as if the women in these stories concern themselves with domestic issues, especially about who belongs to the family and who will inherit. Though this seems to be a minor role, in the Bible, it is significant. An old joke puts these issues in perspective. A woman explains to her friend how she and her husband divide up their responsibilities: 'He deals with the large matters, and I deal with the small ones. So he sorts out international politics, world peace and the problems of the environment, and I decide where we live, how we earn our money, what careers our children should have!'

In one of the biblical stories, the domestic concerns of a woman have a far wider significance. It is the story that we read in the section of Genesis called '*Toledot*', which means 'the history of the generations' (Gen. 25.19—28.9).

The story begins by telling how Rebecca, the wife of Isaac, became pregnant with twins. This was an unusual experience, and since the twins always seemed to be moving around in her womb as if fighting, she went to consult God. The Bible does not explain

16

how she did this. Did she go to some holy place to consult an oracle, or a priest or a prophet? That is certainly how the rabbinic
tradition understood it. The rabbis suggested that she might even
have consulted Abraham who would still have been alive at this
time. But while the text leaves that possibility open, the obvious
sense is that she herself has direct contact with God, and God
gives her a direct reply. But the rabbinic tradition is again quick to
suggest that the answer came through a messenger, indirectly.

Why this need on the part of the rabbis to find an intermediary?
It does seem to be part of a rabbinic discomfort with the idea that
God might have spoken directly to a woman. The Bible itself will
name other women as prophetesses, notably Miriam the sister of
Moses, Deborah and Huldah. But the culture of the early rabbinic
period had a different view of such things. Religious authority
was in the hands of men. It is only in the past few centuries, and
especially the final decades of the twentieth century, that this has
been challenged.

What is it that Rebecca learns from God? Just as the twins are
struggling with one another inside her, so they will continue to struggle after their birth. Indeed, the older will come to serve the younger.
What seems to be at stake here is who will be the one to inherit the
particular religious tradition of Abraham. Just as Isaac was chosen
and his brother Ishmael was not, so Jacob and Esau will compete for
the blessing that was given by God to their grandfather Abraham.

The twins are born. The first to emerge is Esau. But when his
twin, Jacob, emerges, he is holding onto this brother's heel, as if
trying to get out first. This will give him his name, Ya'akov, from
the word for heel, '*ekev*'.

We learn that Isaac loves Esau, but that Rebecca loves Jacob, so
the seeds of conflict are already being sown in their childhood.
Since Rebecca has learnt from God that the older will serve the
younger, perhaps she tells Jacob about his destiny and awakens his
own ambition. That would explain the first negotiation between
the brothers, perhaps when they are still children. When Esau

returns hungry from the fields, he asks Jacob for some of the food that he is cooking. Jacob sells it to him, but in exchange for Esau's rights as the firstborn child. It is as if Jacob is trying to live out the prophecy told to his mother.

But it is later that Rebecca herself takes a direct hand in the story. She hears Isaac tell Esau that he wishes to bless him before he dies. This blessing would be the equivalent to a final testament in which everything is handed on to Esau. Rebecca is so convinced of the prophecy that she goes to extreme lengths, even deceiving her blind husband, so that Jacob will gain the blessing instead of Esau. Jacob disguises himself, pretends to be Esau, betraying his father and brother in a shocking way. But the blessing that he steals, the one that Esau should have had, seems to be different from the one that Abraham would have handed down. It is for good harvests and success and power in the world. It is the kind of blessing that any father might wish for his firstborn son. Because of this deception and Esau's hatred for him, Jacob is forced to leave home. But on his departure, his father gives him another blessing (Gen. 28.3–4). This time Isaac speaks explicitly about the blessing that he had received from Abraham, the special blessing about becoming a large nation and inheriting the land.

It will take Jacob 20 years of exile and suffering, before he can finally return home to claim that blessing. On the journey back, he sends a gift to his brother, some of the vast herds and flocks that he has acquired during his time away. It is as if he is repaying Esau for the material blessing that he had stolen. Jacob tries to correct the wrong that he had done in the past to his brother. Esau refuses to accept Jacob's gift, which is referred to with the Hebrew word 'minchah', and it is only when Jacob explicitly calls it a b'rachah, blessing (Gen. 33.10) (a distinction that is sometimes lost in the translation!) that Esau accepts it.

As for Rebecca who had sacrificed so much for the sake of Jacob and the prophecy, she died before Jacob returned. She never saw again the son whom she loved and for whom she risked so much.

Was Rebecca wrong to act in the way that she did? She had had the experience of a direct word from God with the prophecy about her two sons. So how could she stand by and see her husband make what she thought was a serious mistake, to give God's blessing to the wrong son?

It is not clear whether she had told her husband about the prophecy. Even if she did, she seems to have assumed that Isaac chose to ignore it. Perhaps in his time as well, women had a very limited say in religious matters. Or maybe it was simply the nature of that family that men made decisions by themselves without consulting their wives or sharing responsibility with them for such important matters. It was only by chance that Rebecca heard Isaac speaking to Esau, the event that started the whole tragic history of deception, conflict and exile.

Could the story have turned out differently? If Rebecca had asked Isaac what blessing he was going to give Esau, she might have learned that there was no problem. Isaac intended to give his older son the blessing that he needed to succeed in life. But he was saving Abraham's blessing for Jacob. Jacob would never have had to go into exile, and the family could have spent the next 20 years together.

There are lessons here about communication, and about sharing responsibility within a family: who makes the large decisions and who the small. There is also a serious challenge posed to any society or culture that ignores the role and spiritual importance of women. These chapters are also about power and the lengths to which people will go when power over their own lives is denied them. The roots of conflict begin in the family, but their consequences can reach around the globe.

6

'Surely God is in this Place'

Genesis 28.10–22

This reading from the Torah contains one of the most famous images in the Hebrew Bible. The young man called Jacob is destined to become the father of twelve sons, the founders of the twelve tribes of Israel. But all of that is in the future. Now he is in disgrace. He has deceived his father Isaac and stolen the blessing that should have gone to his twin brother Esau. He has to leave home and journey to a distant land. On the first night of his journey, he lies down to sleep in a place he does not know. But when he sleeps, he dreams of a ladder rising up to heaven. Angels ascend and descend the ladder, and standing over it is God. God promises him that there will be a great future for him and his descendants and that God will protect him on his way. Jacob wakes up with a start and exclaims: 'Surely God is in this place and I did not know it!'

These words of Jacob have surely been repeated in thousands of sermons. For they correspond to a familiar human experience. We encounter a place where something of enormous importance happens to us, perhaps something that radically changes the course of our life. Before it happens we may have paid no attention whatsoever to our surroundings. But afterwards we realize that the place itself must have contributed in some indefinable way to our experience. We will remember that place and maybe return there, for it has become a special part of our life.

There are places that attract the attention of people. Sometimes the reasons are disturbing. Hundreds of thousands of people each year make the journey to Auschwitz concentration camp, to mourn those who died there, or to try to understand how so much horror and destruction could happen. The burial places of notorious people can also become places of pilgrimage for their loyal followers, or for curious tourists.

But there are places that have acquired a reputation as being special in a spiritual way. Sometimes we call them holy and build a shrine or a temple there. Sometimes they are famous because of a miracle that happened there, and people come to be healed in body or in spirit.

But are such places holy because of their very nature, or because of the emotions and hopes that have been brought to them by successive generations of visitors? If anyone but Jacob had come to the same place, would he or she have had a similar experience of the presence of God? If Jacob had not been in such an emotional state and so vulnerable, would he have had such a dream? Is it the place that is holy or is it the people who bring holiness to a place?

One year, I encountered two places that in very different ways seem to me to have a kind of holiness. I had the privilege of conducting High Holyday services in Berlin. Some of the time I served in Oranienburger Strasse, in the beautiful Synagogue that has been partly restored and is used by a new Jewish congregation. One day, I walked around the area near the Hackescher Markt and found a small alley leading off Rosenthaler Strasse. It had still been untouched despite all the rebuilding and beautifying that is going on all around it. Not knowing what I might find, I wandered down the alley and passed a door. The notice on it indicated that it was related to the Jewish Museum, so I went in. It was the 'Workshop for the Blind' (Blindenwerkstatt).

It consisted of three small rooms. During the war, the owner Otto Weidt had employed Jewish and non-Jewish blind and deaf people producing brooms and brushes. By selling them to the military, the business was classified as 'important for the war effort'. In order to protect his Jewish workers, he maintained that they were indispensable. He bribed the Gestapo, the employment agencies and informers. He arranged false papers for those most under threat. He hid four members of a Jewish family in a room behind the workshop. He even went to Auschwitz in order to get one of his workers released from there. He is counted among the 'Righteous Among the Nations' at Yad Vashem in Israel.

The rooms that make up the Museum contain a few simple documents and photos of life in the workshop. It is preserved more or less as it was during the war.

I was very moved to be there. The generosity of spirit, the quiet heroism, the exceptional activity of Otto Weidt created this tiny safe haven in the midst of hatred, fear and destruction. No miracle happened here, no supernatural event, no act of revelation. But by any definition, this was and is a holy place because of what was achieved there. And if any place deserves to be a place of pilgrimage, this should be one because of what it can teach us of human courage, dignity and integrity.

I know personally one other 'holy place' in Germany but of a very different kind. Sadly I had to say goodbye to it after 35 years. I was a student rabbi at Leo Baeck College when I first visited the Hedwig Dransfeld Haus (HDH) in a town called Bendorf, nine kilometres from Koblenz. It was a conference centre and a *kurort*, a spa, for mothers, established by Catholic women. After the war, the director was an extraordinary woman, Anneliese Debray, who had opened it up to new directions. She was committed to all kinds of reconciliation work. She organized conferences where German families could spend time together with French and Polish families in an attempt to build a new kind of relationship despite the War. In the same way, she began to work for reconciliation between Germans and Jews. It was in that context that I first visited the HDH. Out of that visit came an annual Jewish–Christian Bible Week, unique in its mixture of textual study and personal encounter. Even more challenging was the Jewish–Christian–Muslim Student Conference that ran there for 30 years. This has been an extraordinary pioneering activity that has influenced generations of theology students, rabbis, social workers and teachers from Europe, America and the Middle East. The Conference was honoured with the Hermann-Maas Medaille.

Frau Debray managed to preserve the independence of the Haus so that it could continue to explore new areas. Despite her retirement and death some years ago, it managed to preserve this ethos, among other activities hosting mixed groups from the Middle East and from Northern Ireland. But the finances were always precarious, and it finally went into receivership, and has now closed. The two conferences that were established there, and which contributed to the ethos of the HDH, managed to find new homes and have continued to flourish. Somehow that particular spirit was able to be carried over to inspire new generations.

The Hedwig Dransfeld Haus had a number of useful physical qualities. There was a swimming pool, and it is located in beautiful woods, with a friendly little stream running nearby. But none of these elements gave it its special quality. Rather this came from the generosity of spirit and the personal dedication of those who worked there. It came from the commitment of those who attended over the years, from their hunger to learn and their willingness to take risks in opening themselves to others. It was these that gave the place its special ethos and the love that could be found there.

Is it the place that is holy, or is it the deeds that are performed there that make a place holy? The answer probably lies somewhere between these two possibilities. But of both of the places I have talked about, we can say with Jacob: Surely God was in this place and all who came there knew it.

7

Jacob's Ladder

Genesis 28.10—32.3

The biblical patriarch Jacob is an extraordinary character. Two of the most famous images to be found in the Bible belong to his personal story.

One of them is Jacob's midnight struggle with the mysterious man or angel. It led to his name being changed from Jacob to Israel, though the struggle left him limping.

But the other image comes from this reading. Jacob has stolen the blessing that belonged to his brother Esau. Now, in fear of his life, he has to leave home on his way into exile. He cannot know at this moment that it will be 20 years before he returns to his homeland, years of suffering but also years of great material success. Since the blessing he stole was all about material success that is not surprising, but Jacob cannot have realized at the time what a price in pain he would have to pay.

But all that is ahead of him. Now he is simply alone. Later he will speak of this moment and remember that all he took with him from home when he crossed the Jordan river was his shepherd's staff. He arrives at a place where he will stay the night. Jacob falls asleep and dreams the famous dream of the ladder, the other great biblical image that comes from his life.

And he dreamed and behold! there was a ladder set up on the earth, and the top of it reached to heaven; and behold! the angels of God were ascending and descending on it! And behold! the Eternal stood above it . . . (Gen. 28.12–13)

The Rabbis were puzzled by one aspect of this dream. If angels are heavenly beings then surely they should be coming down the ladder from heaven and only then going up it. But the biblical text specifically puts it the other way round. First they are described as going from the ground upwards towards heaven and only then coming down. The Rabbis found one explanation that fits very closely to Jacob's personal situation at this time.

In this interpretation, these figures on the ladder were the guardian angels that protected Jacob. But the ones that had been looking after him throughout his life till now were restricted to the land of Israel. Now that he was about to leave the land, their task was completed, and they were returning to their base; other angels would now take over to protect him on the journey to other places. Jacob had fallen asleep at the border post at the edge of the land of Israel.

In his dream, Jacob does not try to climb the ladder himself. He remains earthbound. Even when God speaks to him Jacob fails to understand the full implications of what is said.

I am the Eternal, the God of Abraham your father and the God of Isaac. The land on which you lie I will give to you and to your descendants; and your descendants shall be like the dust of the earth, and you shall spread abroad to the west and to the east and to the north and to the south. And by you and your descendants shall all the families of the earth be blessed. Behold, I am with you and will keep you wherever you go, and will bring you back to this land, for I will not leave you till I have done that of which I have spoken to you. (13–15)

God spells out the entire vision of Abraham's blessing and the destiny of the Jewish people; to spread throughout the world but also to live in this special land; to become a blessing for all the peoples of the earth. It is a dazzling and challenging destiny. But Jacob is not ready yet to comprehend what he has heard. His personal situation is too frightening and his immediate needs too great – they overwhelm any long-term ambitions he might have. So when he responds he makes no mention at all of the promise of Abraham. Instead he offers a vow of his own to God, but one that only speaks about his personal needs:

> If God will be with me, and will keep in in this way that I go, and will give me bread to eat and clothing to wear, so that I come again to my father's house in peace, then the Eternal shall be my God, and this stone which I have set up for a pillar, shall be God's house; and of all that You give me I will give the tenth to you. (20–22)

'Just get me home safely,' he asks, 'with food to eat and clothing on my back – that is my only ambition at this moment.' It is partly a promise to God, partly a kind of bargain. Jacob is still Jacob and not yet Israel. Till now all that we know of him is that he is tricky and willing to be dishonest. He seems to be the least likely person for God to want to choose to carry on Abraham's task of bringing blessing to all the peoples of the world. But this same Jacob can also dream dreams, can have a vision of a ladder rising to heaven. So there is also within him the promise of a greater quality to his life that could emerge. He could become two quite different people: the Jacob who steals and cheats or the Israel who wrestles with God and on behalf of God. That is why his name keeps changing back and forth in the different stories about him – Jacob becomes Israel, Israel becomes Jacob.

Before his spiritual self can fully emerge, all of his trickiness and practicality will also be tested. Ahead lies the meeting with Laban his future father-in-law who is more than a match for Jacob when it comes to being tricky and dishonest. Jacob will see in Laban, as if in a distorting mirror, all of the worst of his own qualities. That must make him reconsider his own actions. But he will also meet angels on other occasions in his life, and with one he will struggle all night. But is Jacob trying to pin the angel to the ground, to bring him down to his own level; or is he trying to force his way up the ladder to heaven and overcome the angel who stands in his way? These two key pictures from Jacob's life, the ladder and the struggle, actually belong together.

Today we meet fewer angels, or if we meet them we do not recognize them for what they are. But we can understand the struggle, for we each contain within us a Jacob and an Israel, the material and the spiritual, the earthbound and the heavenly, the part of us that manipulates other people and the part of us that has the potential to bring a blessing to the whole world. And just as Jacob keeps changing to Israel and back again, so the struggle within us is never over till the day we die.

8

Jacob meets Esau

Genesis 32.4—36.43

Because we read the same biblical stories year after year on Shabbat morning, they become a part of our personal lives. They offer us lessons in how to behave and, more often, in how not to behave. Because of this familiarity, we know from the very beginning of each story what will happen to the characters. But just when we think we have learned all there is to know about them, something changes our perspective and we discover a new dimension.

Here we read about the dramatic moment when Jacob finally confronts his twin brother Esau. Twenty years earlier, Jacob had stolen the blessing that belonged to his brother. Out of fear of Esau's hatred, and on the excuse of going to find himself a wife, Jacob had left his family home and country to go into exile, to the homeland of his mother's family. After much success but also bitter hardships, Jacob was now returning. He had God's promise of protection, but before him stood the figure of Esau, coming to meet him with 400 men. For Jacob this could only mean the possibility of conflict as his brother took revenge for Jacob's crime of all those years ago. He took all the possible steps to appease his brother, sending gifts on ahead. But he also took precautions to protect his family, in case it came to a fight. In the night before the encounter, Jacob had another fight, with a man who wrestled with him till dawn. This unknown man, elsewhere called a *mal'ach*, the Hebrew word used for a divine messenger, might have really been someone sent by God. But he could also represent an inner struggle within Jacob himself, as he wrestled with his fear and guilt about the past. But after all these events and preparations, the stage is set for the meeting of the two brothers and the conflict we anticipate.

To our surprise, and certainly to Jacob's, Esau greets him with a hug and a kiss. It is as if the past about which Jacob must have felt so much guilt, had never happened. Esau had simply accepted it and gone on to lead his own successful life. He was even prepared to greet his long-lost twin brother with affection and joy. What Jacob felt at that moment is not recounted. We only know that he took precautions to keep the two families, their possessions and their retainers, apart for the long term. Perhaps he did not trust Esau's friendliness, or felt that it might not last as old memories came back. Perhaps Jacob, a complex character, could never understand someone like Esau who may have been as open and generous as his response to Jacob suggests.

But there is another factor that must have stood in the way of Jacob's ability to understand his brother. For the 20 years of his exile, he had retained in his mind the memory of his brother's anger and despair. This image of Esau, the powerful hunter, had grown in his mind to almost overwhelming proportions. Jacob's guilt made it impossible to see his brother as he was. Esau had put aside the burden of his anger; Jacob was still carrying the burden of his guilt.

The rabbinic tradition was suspicious of Esau's apparent forgiveness and generosity of spirit. In part they based this on a far later historical situation. When living under Roman occupation, the Jews needed a kind of code language through which to express their feelings about the regime. They used the figure of Esau for this purpose, reading into the details of the references to him in the Bible hidden allusions to the misdeeds of the Romans. When the Roman Empire became Christian and Jews found themselves persecuted by the new regime, Esau could continue to stand for this power as well.

Nevertheless, however much the rabbis may have been justified in using the name of Esau for this purpose, we must note a problem with it, at least in terms of the biblical narrative itself. Making Esau somehow the villain of the story is a serious displacement of Jacob's responsibility for what happened. Today we are more aware of the danger of such displacement, whereby the victims are made to seem responsible for their fate, as if that somehow exonerated the perpetrator. The rabbis argued that the biblical text never loses its plain meaning, however much later tradition may read into it. In this case, Esau's innocence is a key to the story itself. That is the particular perspective that I want to bring to the familiar story this time.

Long before the rabbinic interpretation, the story of the conflict between Jacob and Esau had further echoes within the Hebrew Bible itself. When Esau learnt that Jacob had cheated him out of his birthright, 'he let out a loud, bitter cry', 'vayitz'aq tz'aqah g'dolah oomarah!' (Gen. 27.34). The exact same words reappear only once in the Hebrew Bible, this time in the Book of Esther. When Mordechai, the hero of the book, learns that Haman, the villain, plans to exterminate the Jews, he walks about the city crying out with the identical loud, bitter cry: 'Vayiz'aq z'aqah g'dolah oomarah!' (Esther 4.1). For the biblical author of the Book of Esther, Esau's suffering needed to be matched by that of Jacob's descendants, as if to balance out the misdeed of the past and thus finally cancel it. But the linkage between the two passages is even stronger, due to one of those underground connections that run through the Bible.

We learn from one of the genealogies in the Book of Genesis (Gen. 36.16), that one of the grandsons of Esau is called Amalek. When the Israelites are wandering in the wilderness, the weak and the older people who are at the rear of the encampment are attacked by a people called the Amalekites. For this unacceptable act of violence Amalek will be portrayed as an enemy of God and of Israel. Generations later King Saul will fail to destroy them after a battle, sparing their King, Agag. For this, Saul forfeits the throne. But to return to the Book of Esther, the Haman who wishes to extermi-nate the Jews is called an Agagite, a descendant of King Agag of the Amalekites. That ancient battle is refought in the pages of the Book of Esther. It is as if a family dispute that began in the distant past has never entirely disappeared. Indeed, history is littered with family feuds that may lay dormant for generations only to spring to life when some change of historical circumstances triggers vio-lence once again. These stories offer little comfort, but they do present us with certain unpalatable truths about human conflict.

But all of this is in the biblical future. We are poised now at the moment when Jacob meets Esau. As readers, we have followed until now the detailed story of Jacob, because he will be the direct ancestor of the nation. Moreover, the Bible is interested in explor-ing the complexity of our relationship with God and the ways in which an individual changes and grows over time. Jacob's journeys and struggles give us much to consider. But the focus on Jacob should not blind us to the significance of Esau. For it is Esau who manages to transform his justifiable anger into something else; to make a successful life for himself and even, 20 years later, to be able to accept with generosity, and maybe even with love, the brother who had wronged him. As is so often the case in the Hebrew Bible, it is the secondary characters, the ones who appear to provide a mere background to the main events, who help us understand the significance of the story before us. Jacob may be the focus of our attention, but it is Esau who offers the hope that despite conflicts and betrayals of the past, forgiveness and reconciliation between people are always possible.

9

Rivalry among Brothers

Genesis 44.18—47.27

The story we consider here reads like an episode from a soap opera. An elderly man has a number of sons, but his special love is reserved for the youngest. The older brothers are jealous and when the opportunity arises, they kidnap the youngest and sell him to slave traders who take him to another country. They deceive their father into believing that his beloved son is dead. Years later, the young man rises to power in his new country. When his brothers experience a severe drought in their homeland, they come on a visit to the same country to buy food. They meet the man who oversees its sale and distribution, but do not recognize him as their long-lost brother. However, instead of revealing himself, their brother pays a number of distressing tricks on them some of which may be deliberately intended to hurt his father. For if his father truly loved him, why did he not come looking for him all those years ago when he disappeared. In the end, the youngest son does reveal himself to his brothers, forgives them, meets up with his father, and they all seem to live happily ever after. Just to spice up the story, there is also an attempted seduction of the young man by a beautiful woman. And to add to the tension, he spends some time in prison and just when he is about to be released, his hopes are dashed. He is doomed to wait another two years, before his fortune finally changes for the better.

Of course, the story is the biblical account of the life of Joseph, son of the patriarch Jacob. It takes up most of 14 chapters of the Book of Genesis. The story is so dramatic and attractive that

Thomas Mann expanded it into a vast novel, and it was even turned into a successful musical. Describing it as a soap opera seems perfectly reasonable.

Here we read a section of the story which is one of the major turning points. During it, Joseph resolves one of the mysteries that must have haunted him throughout his time of exile. Joseph has forced his brothers to bring his younger brother Benjamin down to Egypt, even though he knows it will cause great pain to his father. He has had Benjamin arrested on a false charge. Now his brother Judah who has played an increasingly more important role in the biblical stories of Genesis, offers himself as a substitute for Benjamin. In doing so, he recounts the impact these events have had upon his father Jacob. But he also reveals something that Joseph did not know, why his father did not try to find him. Also how the brothers could have got away with their plot of selling him to traders bound for Egypt. For the first time, he learns that Jacob had been deceived into thinking that Joseph had been killed by a wild animal. This may have confirmed his worst suspicions about the deceitfulness of his brothers, but at least it meant that his father had not known the truth. It was only because his father believed that Joseph had been killed that he had not searched for him. Joseph had not been abandoned by his father, who truly loved him.

The fact that Joseph did not know the truth also explains why he had never tried to visit his family or even get in touch with them in all the years after he had come to power. Now he weeps. Perhaps they are tears of joy at having been able to reunite with his family. Perhaps they express bitter regret at all the wasted years and the added pain he has caused his father. The brothers will never be absolutely certain that Joseph has forgiven them. Such pain and suffering may never completely disappear, even though he can see that the brothers have changed.

We have to remember that the Book of Genesis is full of stories of rivalry between brothers. It starts with Cain murdering Abel, and it includes the tensions between Isaac and Ishmael, Jacob and Esau. At least here, at the end of the book, some kind of reconciliation between brothers does take place.

So is it legitimate to describe the story of Joseph as a soap opera? Does that not diminish something that is part of the Bible itself? Or rather, what distinguishes a biblical story from a soap opera? Perhaps biblical stories are the equivalent of the soap operas of an earlier age. That is to say they fulfil some of the same purposes. Biblical stories carried the memory of the people's history and of the personalities who had created that history. By telling those stories the characters remained alive. It has been said that we are not truly dead until there is no one left to remember us. But telling the stories also provided some kind of teaching for the present time. How the great figures of the tradition had dealt with events could be a model for how to deal with them today. Though sometimes the lessons might be how not to make the same kind of mistakes this time. So the stories offered a sense of continuity with the past of the family or tribe. But they also provided a link to others within the family or tribe who lived elsewhere. What we share as a family or community helps unite us.

Bible stories are not read so often today, nor in the same way as in the past. Certainly a simplified version may be taught to our children, but the biblical stories need to be read through adult eyes. There are large breaks in continuity between past generations and today's open and largely secular society. Old bonds between families have disappeared. People live far apart from each other in our European society. Moreover, our secularized culture no longer views the Bible with the same awe, respect and authority that it had in the past. In a fragmented world, the television soap opera that reflects more immediately today's reality is more powerful. And indeed, it often contains morality tales about human struggles, successes and failures. Nevertheless, one difference is important. Soap operas come to us as passive observers in words and pictures on television. We are robbed of the opportunity of using our own imagination to picture what is happening. We do not even need the discipline of reading that forces us to think about what is being told to us and what is going on between the lines.

At least, our Jewish tradition of reading from the Torah on a weekly basis keeps both the stories and the written text before our eyes. So it remains our responsibility to try to understand these stories, and ourselves make the interpretation that relates them to our lives. This activity of interpretation seems to be mirrored in the Joseph stories themselves.

There is something in the cycle of Joseph stories that is different from the previous stories of the patriarchs. In the accounts of the lives of Abraham, Isaac and Jacob, God is very much present, in direct contact with them and members of their family. In the Joseph cycle, God never appears directly and is only spoken about. In many cases we learn about God's actions through the words of Joseph himself. For example, it is Joseph, looking back on his life, who sees a pattern that reinforces his trust in God. As he says to his brothers to reassure them after the death of Jacob: 'You meant evil against me, but God meant it for good, to bring it about that many people should be kept alive, as they are today' (Gen. 50.20). Joseph understands that his faith in God in the darkest moments of his life is vindicated by his later success.

As we move out of the legendary world of the patriarchs towards the recorded history of the descendants of Jacob, God is less obviously present. The word of God will come now through specially appointed people, the prophets. Or else, we turn to those who claim to interpret for us the actions of God.

The Joseph story shows how God may intervene in the lives of individuals and entire peoples, sometimes visibly, sometimes in a hidden way. It asserts God's presence, but also the tantalizing mystery of that presence that is only sometimes glimpsed. A certain innocence has been lost. Like Joseph it is now up to us to discover if we can find it in the ups and downs of our lives the presence of God. We are our own soap opera, or we can become our own Bible story.

10

Joseph and Pharaoh

Genesis 41.1—44.17

The Joseph story reads at first like a fairy tale. The handsome young hero, poorly treated by his family and unjustly accused and imprisoned is suddenly summoned before the king. His talents are finally recognized and he is elevated to power. It is an archetypal story and each society produces its own variation. In the Hollywood version, the understudy takes over when the leading lady breaks a leg and becomes a star overnight.

Of course, the Bible version has its own nuances and emphases. Joseph's destiny has been signalled all along. He is the favourite son of Jacob. Although he is an outsider in Egypt, he becomes the favourite of his Egyptian master, Potiphar, because of his administrative abilities. He is also liked by Mrs Potiphar, but for other reasons. When she accuses him of attempting to rape her and he ends up in prison, he becomes the favourite of the captain of the guard.

The biblical story of Joseph's final rise to power is familiar. Pharaoh, king of Egypt, has two dreams. In the first, seven fat cows come out from the Nile to be followed by seven thin ones that devour the first but remain unchanged. In the second dream, seven fat ears of corn are similarly devoured by seven lean ears. Surprisingly, Pharaoh's wise men seem unable to explain the dreams. Or perhaps no one was willing to explain the dreams to Pharaoh – rulers do not like to receive bad news and may shoot the messenger!

The applause for Joseph's interpretation is also puzzling since the dream is rather transparent. The Nile, from which the cows emerged, was the source of Egypt's food supply and grain was part of their staple diet. A warning about a famine to come was an obvious interpretation. Joseph has waited two years for such an opportunity and wastes no time. He goes beyond the task of simply interpreting and suggests that Pharaoh appoint a man to collect a portion of the grain harvest during the good years so that it is available during the years of famine.

Interestingly, the audience that approves this advice no longer includes the 'wise men'. Instead Pharaoh is joined by his 'servants', presumably his political advisers. This project calls for different kinds of skills for it has serious political consequences. Joseph's solution amounts to imposing a major new tax on the people, one fifth of all their produce, justified by a possible famine many years ahead. Whether the prophetic dream turns out to be true or not, Pharaoh will do well out of it, but at the possible cost of alienating his people. Pharaoh declares that Joseph is just the man for the job – presumably his previous success in gaining prosperity for Potiphar is on record. Joseph has successfully overcome disasters and risen to power as was promised long before in the dreams he told his father and brothers.

But is there a catch in all of this honouring? Joseph becomes the first of many Jewish individuals who will rise to high position in the service of a ruler. The dangers of such a position are clear. For despite the appearance of power, the situation is very precarious. A whim of the king can appoint him and another whim dethrone him. Moreover, Joseph is at risk in another way. For, effectively he is the intermediary between the regime and the people. He is the man overseeing the major new tax imposed on the people during the seven years of plenty and likely to be the target of their anger. He will be the one who controls the distribution of food during the time of famine so subject to further resentment. He is the visible face of the regime and therefore the potential object of popular unrest. He can be dropped by Pharaoh at any time if it suits his policy needs or to offer the public a scapegoat. The rabbis warned:

> Be careful of those in power! For they draw no one near to them except in their own interest. They seem like friends when it is to their own advantage, but they do not stand by people in their hour of need! (Sayings of the Fathers 2.3)

And yet, in this case it works, and does so exceptionally well throughout Joseph's lifetime. With Pharaoh's blessing, he is allowed to bring his entire family down to Egypt to settle there with him. Though Joseph and his family became integrated within Egypt they did not totally assimilate. Joseph was given an Egyptian name by Pharaoh, but retained his own Hebrew one. Though he married an Egyptian wife, his children will be counted among the ancestors of the twelve tribes. The Egyptians respected the fact that Joseph had different dietary requirements and allowed him to make separate arrangements. There was no attempt to impose Egyptian culture on this group of immigrants and their children. But the Egyptians were self-confident and proud of their culture and did not feel the need to impose it on others.

Because of Pharaoh's willingness to accept Joseph as he was and welcome the qualities he brought to the land, he has gone down in biblical history as a person of wisdom and tolerance. But there came a later Pharaoh who 'knew not Joseph'. That one stirred up his people against these foreigners, playing on popular fears that they might be dangerous. It was only a small step to enslave the Israelites and begin a secret campaign that would lead in the end to attempted genocide. For all his skill at political manipulation, this later Pharaoh will always be remembered as an evil man and a fool. The net result of his schemes and activities was to bring death and tragedy to his own society and to himself.

Playing on fears and prejudices for political purposes is always dangerous because the emotions released cannot easily be controlled.

Those who play that political card end by losing their reputations and the respect of their own people. Pharaoh became utterly isolated and his people lost forever the contribution that the descendants of Joseph might have brought to his nation. What a tragedy that after all the destruction in Europe in the past century, caused by fomenting hatred of the 'other', the lesson still does not seem to have been learned.

11

Daily Miracles

Exodus 10.1—13.16

This reading from the Torah takes place in the middle of the struggle between Moses and Pharaoh to secure the release of the Children of Israel from slavery in Egypt. Against the military power of Pharaoh's Egypt, Moses comes with the power of the word of God. This power is expressed through a series of plagues and disasters that befall the Egyptian people, each one worse than the one before. At the climax, the firstborn of the Egyptians are killed in a single night, a punishment that corresponds to Pharaoh's act of murdering the male Israelite children.

The ten plagues belong to a series of miracles that mark this stage of biblical history. The exodus from Egypt is followed by the miraculous crossing of the Sea of Reeds, when the waters part to allow them to cross on dry land. But then the waters return to destroy Pharaoh's army. After this they journey through the wilderness, fed by manna, food that comes each day from heaven. As a climax, the Israelites encounter God at Mount Sinai.

Yet how are we to understand these miraculous events today? Does God really intervene so directly in human history with supernatural miracles? And if God sometimes does so, why not at other times? Sadly, there are always people who claim to see the hand of God in any disaster that befalls somebody else and explain precisely what they have done wrong so as to deserve it. The rabbis argued against such an approach with the saying: 'Do not judge someone else, until you have stood in their place!'

A different, but fairly common, approach to the problem of miracles is to ask the question: were events like the ten plagues really miraculous or simply a series of natural catastrophes that were later interpreted as miracles? There have certainly been attempts to explain the Egyptian plagues as a logical sequence. A large mud slide polluted the waters of the Nile turning it red – the first plague of blood. Because the waters were poisoned, frogs were forced to leave it for the shore in large numbers, the second plague. When they died on the dry land, their rotting bodies attracted insects, the third plague. This, in turn, caused the disease that affected the cattle. And so it goes on. Similarly the crossing of the Sea of Reeds could be explained by an unusual tidal surge.

But for most of the past 2,000 years, those who have turned to the Bible as the revelation of God, have viewed these events and many others as miracles. They had to be accepted as divine interventions and a true believer would never question them.

Yet, there is a strand within the Bible itself that reflects a kind of scepticism – not about miracles themselves, but about their significance and lasting effect. Elijah the prophet conjures up a major miracle when he challenges the prophets of the pagan god Baal to a competition between the gods. Two altars are built, and slaughtered animals are laid upon them as a sacrifice. But instead of the worshippers setting them alight, fire is supposed to come down from heaven, directly from Baal or from Israel's God, to consume them. The Baal fails the test. And even though Elijah covers the animals with water, God sends down fire and they are consumed. It is a genuine miracle, and all who saw it were impressed and praised God. But one chapter later, Elijah is complaining that the people have abandoned God, and he alone remains faithful. In fact he is ready to give up his vocation as a prophet. Miracles may be dramatic but do they have a lasting effect on people? A few days after encountering God at Mount Sinai, the Israelites worshipped the golden calf.

The rabbinic tradition tried to limit the belief or expectation that God was always prepared to intervene with a miracle. They taught that a number of miraculous events, like Balaam's talking donkey, were created by God in the twilight between the end of the sixth day of creation and the beginning of Shabbat (Sayings of the Fathers 5.6). Similarly, miracles like the dividing of the Sea of Reeds, and the occasion when the sun stood still for Joshua, were prepared at the time of creation and stored up for the moment when they would be needed. Having created the world and the laws of nature, God was not going to disturb things in an arbitrary way.

A medieval rationalist like Moses Maimonides could suggest that the donkey that talked to Balaam did so in his prophetic imagination, not in an outer reality. As is often the case in Judaism, our tradition divides between those who favour the pious, mystical interpretation of events and those who prefer the rational and logical understanding.

There is a nice story that illustrates the different consequences, depending on which of these two approaches you follow. A town is about to be flooded with water, and all the inhabitants are warned to leave for safety. All of them do so, except an elderly pious Jew, who insists on staying in his home. When a police car comes to evacuate him, he refuses to go with them saying: 'I have faith that God will save me!' The police car leaves. Then the flood comes, and he has to move up to the first floor of his house. A rowing boat comes past with a rescue team and invites him to climb out of the window into the boat and go to safety with them. But again he refuses, saying: 'I have faith that God will save me!' Finally, the waters rise so high that he has to climb onto the roof. A helicopter comes along and they lower a rope to pull him to safety. But once again, he shows his trust in God and says: 'I have faith that God will save me!' And then the waters rise higher, and he drowns. When he gets to heaven, he is most angry and insists on lodging a complaint to God. 'I have been a faithful and pious Jew all my life, so I assumed You would be there for me when I needed You!' 'It's strange that you're here,' God answers, 'I sent a police car, a boat and a helicopter to rescue you!'

So, what are miracles? Jewish tradition sees a kind of miracle in the fact that we wake up each morning. That the world continues in its normal way, that seasons come and go, that life is ended in death but renewed by the birth of the next generation, these are astonishing events that we should acknowledge and celebrate as evidence of God's daily concern with the world. It only takes a breakdown in some of the basic organization of our lives that we are used to for us to realize how dependent we are on the regular ordering of the universe, be it nature itself or human society. As if to remind us of this way of looking at reality, a text in our daily prayers spells it out: 'In every generation we thank You and recount Your praise for our lives held in Your hand, for our souls that are in Your care, and for the signs of Your presence that are with us every day. At every moment, at evening, morning and noon, we experience Your miracles and Your goodness.'

As the great teacher Hillel expressed it: 'The process by which we get our daily bread is a greater miracle than the splitting of the Sea of Reeds!' (Pesikta Rabbati 152a).

12

Stubborn Pharaoh

Exodus 6.2—9.35

This reading is about one of the best known events in the Bible – the ten plagues that were inflicted by God upon the Egyptians during the struggle to release the children of Israel from slavery. Each plague builds on the last leading to the horrifying climax with the death of the Egyptian firstborn.

We read the story from the standpoint of Moses and the children of Israel. Pharaoh has gradually reduced a people who were guests in his land to the level of slaves. He has eroded their rights by a series of laws, brutalized them by the work he has forced them to do and instituted a policy of secret genocide that only the heroism of the midwives has postponed. He has given his people licence to destroy their fellow citizens, the Israelites. Standing against him is the lone figure of Moses, seemingly powerless against the might of the leader of the greatest empire of the time.

We the readers know how it will turn out. We know that Israel's God is more powerful and can call into play the whole of nature to defeat Pharaoh. By the time the plagues are well advanced, we feel sorry for the Egyptians – not Pharaoh who stubbornly maintains his position, but his people who are the ones who suffer directly as the plagues get worse. But of course that is part of the power of the story – this reversal of a situation where it seemed at first that Pharaoh held all the cards. How many movements of liberation from slavery have turned to this story for support and inspiration in their struggle against oppression!

But if we know from the very beginning that God is bound to win, we read the story with somewhat different eyes. For, in effect, the struggle between Moses and Pharaoh is a prolonged negotiation between those seeking liberation and justice for themselves and a dictator who is not prepared to relinquish any of his power whatever the consequences. Read in that way we find ourselves in very familiar territory. Human rights, ethnic cleansing and the struggle to combat totalitarian regimes are central issues for Europe facing a new century.

God's intention is not only to force Pharaoh to let the Israelites go but to establish God's power in the eyes of the Egyptians and with it the principle of justice (Exod. 7.4). To do so, God is prepared to be just as manipulative as Pharaoh in the process. That is why Moses is to start the proceedings with a sign that is bound to be unconvincing. When Moses throws down his rod that turns into a snake, he is merely performing the kind of conjuring trick that Pharaoh's magicians can easily reproduce. Pharaoh is led from the beginning into a false sense of security that will ultimately prove to be his downfall.

For the same reason God insists that Moses performs the first plague, turning the water of the Nile into blood, using the same rod (Exod. 7.15–17). Pharaoh sees this as a further trick that his own magicians can do just as well. His heart becomes harder and his resistance grows.

It is only with the plague of frogs, even though his magicians can reproduce it, that Pharaoh seems to change his mind and give in to Moses' request to release the people. But as soon as the plague is removed, he hardens his heart again. If we translate these events into today's political realities, the first two plagues are the equivalent of imposing sanctions on a country as a way of forcing its government to improve their human rights record. When the first two sanctions begin to have an effect on the economy, the government is ready to open negotiations. This is the phase in which both sides are testing the other, trying to see how strong is their willpower in the short and long term. So it is no surprise that as soon as God has cancelled the plague of frogs Pharaoh 'hardens his heart' once again (Exod. 8.11). True, Pharaoh has shown weakness in asking for the plague to be removed, but he is still very much in control. As far as he is concerned, he is the winner of the first round.

His apparent success gives him the strength to resist the next plague, the gnats, even when the magicians cannot remove them. They say it is the 'finger of God', which presumably means a natural disaster beyond any magic they can control. Pharaoh is not impressed.

The plagues continue in groups of three. Before each group Moses warns Pharaoh, and each plague is more severe than the previous one. With the next plague, boils, Pharaoh is ready to make his first concession. Yes, the Israelites may worship their God, but only in the land of Egypt. Moses negotiates further, insisting that the Israelites have to leave the territory and Pharaoh agrees – only to change his mind once again as soon as the plague is lifted.

Again the analogy with sanctions is clear. For there is always a major debate – should one let up on sanctions, when the oppressive government offers to negotiate seriously, or keep up the pressure until the matter is completely resolved? In this case, Pharaoh once again sees the lifting of the plague as a sign of weakness, or at least as an opportunity to reassert his authority and control, and he backtracks on his promise.

This pattern leads to certain inevitable results. It is not Pharaoh who suffers but his people as crops fail, disease affects the livestock and the people themselves. Long before Pharaoh is prepared to listen, his people have acknowledged the power of Moses' God, and his advisers have warned him to surrender before everything is destroyed. Only Pharaoh holds out till the ultimate sanction, a brutal act of war, the killing of the firstborn children of Egypt.

By this reading, there are ten stages to such a negotiation, and at each stage, there is the opportunity for agreement and resolution.

Direct physical violence is only the last resort, when everything else has failed. As usual, it is the common people who suffer, while their leaders take their calculated risks, hold onto their power and become increasingly autocratic and isolated.

The biblical account offers no comforting solutions. It presents us with the reality of human folly and conflict, leaving it to us to learn from it what we can and do what we must. Again, we are haunted by the victims, visions of the death of children – the Israelite babies thrown into the Nile, the Egyptian firstborn slain in the darkness of night. What better a reminder could there be of our responsibility to the next generation. What better a text to challenge us at the start of a new century, and new millennium.

13

Moses' Secret Identity

Exodus 13.17—17.16

This *parashah* begins in a curious way. After the successful defeat of Pharaoh by the ten plagues, the children of Israel march triumphantly out of Egypt. One of the opening sentences seems to emphasize this – the Children of Israel went up '*chamushim*' from the land of Egypt. What is the meaning of this Hebrew word, *chamushim*? It seems to derive from the number *chamesh*, five, and it is generally assumed that they went out in some kind of military formation based on the number five. Hence, some translations read that they went up 'armed' or 'equipped for battle'. But the previous sentence conveys a very different impression. It explains God's perspective on this exciting moment: 'God did not lead them through the land of the Philistines, which was the nearest route, for God thought that when the people saw the possibility of war they might change their minds and turn around and go back to Egypt!' (Exod. 13.17).

So we have here a kind of tragicomic picture. The Israelites themselves go out brandishing weapons, suddenly feeling heroic because they have been given freedom. But God knows that beneath this bravado, they are still slaves at heart, their spirits broken by their past experience. At the first sign of trouble, their courage might collapse. This had happened once before in Egypt. When Moses first asked Pharaoh to let the people go, he had not only refused, but he had made conditions worse for the Israelites. In this way, he succeeded in driving a wedge between the people and Moses. At that time, they had confronted Moses and said: 'You have made us stink

48

in the sight of Pharaoh and you have put a sword in his hand to kill us! You have given him a pretext to destroy us.' But Pharaoh was already killing their firstborn sons, and hardly needed an excuse! For a slave any change is somehow threatening and dangerous.

There is an ironic little joke that exactly describes this kind of fearful mentality – it is literally a case of gallows humour. Two men are standing in front of a firing squad waiting for the command to shoot them. One of them turns to the other and says: 'Do you think I could ask for a cigarette?' The other replies: 'Shhh – don't make trouble!'

God sees through the apparent courage of the Israelites marching in formation out of Egypt and decides not to take a risk with their newfound confidence. In fact, as the story develops, we know that almost all of this generation that has come out from Egypt will not enter the Promised Land at all. Instead, they will die in the wilderness during the 40 years of wandering.

The great medieval Jewish commentator Abraham Ibn Ezra explained the reason why that generation could not enter the land. In their hearts they were still slaves and lacked the kind of courage needed to conquer the land. Instead, the children of Israel had to wait till a new generation had been born in the desert as free people, able to face hardship and tackle difficult situations, before the next step could be taken.

Only Moses was truly free. He had been brought up in the court of Pharaoh, so he had lived a life of independence and freedom. Moreover, he had been groomed for leadership. Yet, he could have simply stayed within his Egyptian palace and led the life of an Egyptian prince. What led him back to his people and a very special destiny?

An episode in his early life reveals something of his character and helps explain why he acted as he did. In the familiar story, when Moses grew up he 'went out to his brothers and saw their burdens and he saw an Egyptian man striking a Hebrew man, one of his brothers' (Exod. 2.11).

We tend to assume that when he went out to see his 'brothers', it is the Israelites that are meant. But again Abraham Ibn Ezra forces us to look more carefully at the passage and asks why the word 'brother' comes at the beginning and again at the end of the sentence. Moses has grown up as an Egyptian. His last contact with his Jewish origins ceased when he was weaned. Later, at the burning bush, he will not even know the name of his ancestral God! So, when he goes out to see the burdens of his brothers, it is as an Egyptian Prince that he goes out to see the burdens of his Egyptian people. For the Egyptians are indeed burdened with their huge building projects. (Compare Exodus 2.11 with 1.11, where the burdens are those of the Egyptians, not the Israelites.) But at the moment when Moses witnesses the brutal striking of a slave, despite all the assumptions of his royal upbringing, he intervenes on behalf of the victim. At that point, he identifies who is truly his 'brother', whoever is the victim of oppression. Moses becomes an Israelite only after he has discovered his compassion and sense of justice.

At the beginning of the *parashah*, Moses has succeeded in the first part of his task. The children of Israel are setting out on their way to freedom. But there is a major contrast between Moses and the Israelites at this moment. For Moses takes the time to collect the bones of Joseph and ensures that they are taken with the Israelites, when they depart. He was fulfilling the promise that Joseph had extracted from his brothers. That when Israel left Egypt they would take his bones with them for burial in the Promised Land. Moses makes sure that this promise to Joseph is fulfilled. While the Israelites are acting as if they were warriors, Moses, the only real warrior among them, remembers their spiritual responsibilities.

Perhaps we see here a further sign of the slave mentality. Once freed, slaves can remain trapped in the violence that has been done to them. So they in turn may do violence to those in their power and not even recognize or acknowledge what they are doing. They may also come to believe that brandishing swords and making threatening gestures is the way to show their authority, that aggression and force can resolve conflicts. While the Israelites think of weapons, Moses thinks instead of Joseph. He was sold as a slave by his brothers, but he had the inner strength to seek reconciliation with them. Joseph had been treated as a slave but never became a slave.

So filled with these inner tensions, torn between slavery and freedom, at once outwardly triumphant, but fearful within, the children of Israel set out on their journey to the Promised Land.

14

Who is Jethro?

Exodus 18

This reading from the Torah is known by the name of Yitro (Jethro), the father-in-law of Moses. He appears in the first section, Chapter 18 of the Book of Exodus, and advises Moses on how to give a better legal structure to the Israelite society. Jethro is described as a priest of Midian, which means that he is not an Israelite nor does he worship Israel's God. So it is surprising that the whole Torah reading should carry his name since it contains two major events that seem to be exclusive to Israel – the revelation at Mount Sinai and the giving of the Ten Commandments. This raised a number of questions for the rabbis about the character of Jethro and the role that he played.

One view of him was very negative. The rabbis listed him, together with Balaam the foreign prophet who tried to curse Israel, as one of the advisers of Pharaoh, king of Egypt. So Jethro would have helped plot the murder of the male children born to the Israelites. But a contrasting story has him saving Moses' life. When he was still a child, Moses once sat on Pharaoh's lap, and tried to take the crown off Pharaoh's head. Pharaoh wanted to kill Moses at once as a possible usurper of the throne. But Jethro devised a test to show that, like any child, Moses just liked glittering objects, so his actions were completely innocent.

What about Jethro's religious status as a Priest of Midian? Again the rabbis had radically opposing views. One rabbinic text suggested that he was not just the worshipper of one idol alone, but that he was a real enthusiast, trying out every conceivable form of idol worship available in the world! But again there is a contrasting opinion suggesting that he was so inspired by Israel's God that he converted and then converted all his people as well to the worship of the One God.

There is a possible position between these extremes that would see Jethro as at best a pragmatist and at worst an opportunist. When Pharaoh was powerful he worked for Pharaoh. When Moses became successful he joined himself once again to the winning side.

The Bible itself raises none of these questions and shows Jethro in a positive light. Jethro was willing to give a refuge to Moses when he was fleeing from Egypt. Indeed, according to the Midrash, Jethro hid Moses for ten years and his daughter Zipporah went every day to feed him till it was finally safe to emerge from hiding. On the other hand, the biblical text hints at a very different possible reason for Jethro's warm welcome to the stranger. After all, he had seven unmarried daughters who needed husbands! As to the religious differences between them, when Jethro advises Moses on how to structure the Israelite society, he is careful to conclude his advice with the words: if God so commands you. In fact, the relationship between the two men offers one possible model for interfaith dialogue – the sharing of practical advice and mutual support.

At the end of Chapter 18, it says that Moses sent Jethro away and that he returned to his land. Since the very next chapter tells of the preparation for the revelation on Mount Sinai, this would suggest that Jethro had already left, before it happened. But, as the rabbis noted, the Bible is not always arranged chronologically, so he may well have been present at that turning point in religious history. If he was there, this would confirm that the revelation was not confined to the Jewish people alone. Indeed, the rabbis insisted that the Torah was given in the wilderness of Sinai precisely because it belonged to no particular people and no one could claim exclusive ownership of it.

The Bible itself is not clear about Jethro's presence at the revelation at Mount Sinai. However, by calling this reading by the name of Yitro, he is forever associated in our minds with that key event that determined the spiritual task of the Jewish people. This means that we must try to be partners with all who consider themselves to be the spiritual descendants of that moment.

15

Choose Judges

Exodus 18

This reading from the Torah offers us an opportunity to reflect on the kinds of people that we entrust with leadership roles in our society. When Moses' father-in-law Jethro visits the Israelite encampment in the wilderness, he finds Moses sitting all day judging cases brought to him by the people. It is clearly an inefficient system that wears out Moses and frustrates the people. So Jethro suggests that Moses seek out men to act as judges and create a system of lower and higher courts. In that way, all legal matters can be dealt with quickly and effectively. Moses will retain his position as the final court of appeal for cases that cannot be dealt with at a lower level. Thus one of the first institutions to be established in the new Israelite society is to be an independent judiciary, one of the key elements in any democratic society.

But how does one select the judges, who will have so much responsibility? Jethro puts forward a list of ideal qualities for potential candidates (Exod. 18.21). He includes four categories, each of which requires some analysis. The first phrase he uses is '*anshei chayil*', meaning something like 'men of power'. The word '*chayil*' includes anything from physical strength, to wealth, to spiritual strength or virtue. Modern translations suggest that it means 'able' or 'capable' men, those with the necessary qualities to undertake such a major responsibility. The medieval Jewish commentators had more practical suggestions. If they are already rich men, then they will fear no one and be objective in their judgement.

The second quality that Jethro lists is '*yir'ei elohim*', which literally means 'people who fear God'. Here one has to look at the meaning of both of these words. The Hebrew verb '*yarei*' has two senses:
'to fear', but also 'to be in awe of'. Someone who 'fears God' is not
simply frightened, but full of respect and wonder at the power
and nature of God. But even the word '*elohim*', one of the regular
Hebrew words for God, has wider meanings. On two occasions,
Abraham pretends that his wife is his sister so as to protect her
from possible kidnapping by a foreign king. When challenged he
explains that he thought there was no 'fear of God' in that society.
By this, he meant the absence of basic moral values. It was a society where the rule of law did not operate. So it would seem that
Jethro's second quality is a strong sense of morality in someone
who will have so much power and authority.

Next on the list is the phrase '*anshei emet*', literally 'men of truth'.
'*Emet*', 'truth', is derived from a familiar word '*amen*', which basically means that something is 'firm', that you can depend on. So
this quality is about people whose word is reliable, who are known
to be trustworthy. They do not lie.

Jethro's final quality is absolutely crucial given the temptations
of the office of judge. The right people should be '*son 'ei vatza*',
literally those who 'hate bribes' or any other illegitimate way of
obtaining money. The early rabbis explored this idea even further. They felt that the true judge should not only hate bribes,
but not be overly concerned about his own personal wealth. They
taught that a judge who has to be taken to court to force him to
pay money that he owes to a plaintiff should not be a judge at all
(Baba Batra 58b)!

Moses accepted these suggestions of Jethro and set about finding such people. But the Bible reports a rather surprising result. It
is reflected in another change of language. Jethro's suggestion to
Moses is that he *seek out* men, and the Hebrew verb is one that is
used of prophetic visions. Moses is to see beyond the outer appear-
ances in this exacting selection process. But shortly afterwards

(Exod. 18.25), the biblical text simply states that Moses *chose* '*anshei chayil*', 'capable men'. This word 'choosing' is not the prophetic act that Jethro had called for but instead a more pragmatic one. Moreover, instead of listing all four of Jethro's qualities, the verse only mentions the first one on Jethro's list, capable men. So what about the other three? There are a number of possible explanations. One is that the Bible, rather than bother to repeat the same list, simply refers to the first one and includes in it all the others. It is even possible that this was what Jethro intended. The general term 'capable men' would have included the three qualities that he mentioned next.

But there is a deeper problem in Jethro's suggestion. No one, not even Moses, is able to look into the heart of another and know who truly 'fears God', whether in the religious sense or in terms of true morality. That someone has proved to be reliable and trustworthy can probably be assessed. But most people can be tempted by a bribe if the circumstances are right. And a bribe need not simply be about money, but about the abuse of power or giving in to some personal desire. All three qualities open up too many uncertainties, so Moses settled for something more practical.

Another interpretation suggests that once Moses set about applying all four criteria, he simply found no one who could live up to all of them. Or perhaps he realized that it was only by exposing people to the responsibilities of office that one could discover their true qualities. So he was forced to compromise and at least choose people whom he felt would do an effective job.

Elsewhere in the Bible, the responsibilities of a judge are further elaborated. The judge should neither show favour to the poor nor give honour to the great (Lev. 19.15). The judge should not let either his compassion for those in difficult circumstances nor his wish to please the powerful and wealthy affect his judgement. Elsewhere, the judge is warned against simply yielding to the pressure exerted by a majority if this would lead to a false judgement (Exod. 23.2).

These biblical instructions and warnings were reinforced by later rabbinic teachings. One rabbinic passage gives an awesome description of the pressure on a judge to act with integrity. 'A judge should consider himself as if a sword was held above his shoulders, and the underworld was open below him, and he was suspended between them. If he proved to be worthy, he would be rescued from both of them, but if he did not prove worthy, he would be handed over to both of them' (Sanhedrin 7ab) (q. Rabenu Bachya).

Perhaps the most awesome statement about the responsibility of a judge is summed up in the rabbinic teaching: 'Any judge who judges truly, even for an hour, the scripture reckons it as if he had been a partner with God in the work of Creation' (Babylonian Talmud Shabbat 10a).

Perhaps Jethro had too high expectations about the abilities of his son-in-law Moses and the quality of the people he was leading. The Israelites were like any other people, with a mixture of strengths and weaknesses, good and bad qualities. That was why it was important at least to create a system that would offer the best hope for ensuring that justice governed the way they behaved towards one another.

Jethro's four criteria may be too idealistic for choosing judges or other leaders. Nevertheless, they represent a useful way of evaluating over time those who take on significant positions in society. They should be capable of the task they undertake. They should demonstrate moral qualities. They should be reliable and trustworthy in what they do. Above all, they should be seen to resist the many temptations that come with power.

16

Ten Commandments and Human Rights

Exodus 20

The year 2008 was significant for anniversaries. The seventieth anniversary of the *Reichskristallnacht*, night of broken glass, when synagogues throughout Germany were burnt to the ground, Jewish shops were looted and individual Jews were attacked was marked on 9 November. But on 10 December, in stark contrast, another kind of event could be celebrated, one that offers hope for many people throughout the world. On that day in 1948 the United Nations published the Universal Declaration of Human Rights.

The main architect of that document was Rene Cassin, a French Jew, a jurist, a humanitarian and a man with a deep commitment to universal values. Born in 1887, he fought in the First World War and was severely wounded. This led him to found an organization to support disabled war veterans and to work for war orphans. He had a distinguished career teaching law until the German occupation of France. In 1940, he was one of the first to follow General De Gaulle to England. There he drafted all the legal agreements between Winston Churchill and De Gaulle that defined the status of the Forces Françoises Libres. After the War, he held high offices in France, which he represented at the United Nations during 1946–58. He was one of the founders of UNESCO. For his work in drafting the Universal Declaration of Human Rights, he received the Nobel Peace Prize in 1968. He died in 1976.

Cassin wrote an article comparing the Universal Declaration to the Ten Commandments. He noted a major difference between them. The Ten Commandments are religious in their orientation, with God at the centre. They define human 'duties', and human 'rights' can only be derived from them indirectly. In contrast, the Universal Declaration is essentially a humanist document, and those who drafted it consciously excluded any reference to God. It begins: 'All human beings are born free and equal in dignity and rights.'

Nevertheless, its humanist values owe much to the principles established already in the Hebrew Bible and taught by the three great monotheistic religious traditions of Europe. The Bible begins with the creation of a single human being which also asserts that all human beings, whatever their colour, race or belief system, are ultimately equal. That Adam was created in the image of God underscores the inestimable value of each human life. As Jewish and also Muslim teaching express it, whoever takes a single life it is as if he had destroyed an entire world.

For the Hebrew Bible, the future of humanity is bound up with the life and example of the patriarch Abraham. In a key sentence, God explains that Abraham has been chosen so that he may teach his descendants the way of God. This way is defined by two key terms: *tz'dakah umishpat*, righteousness and justice (Gen. 18.19). Abraham is immediately put to the test by God who informs him about the imminent destruction of Sodom and Gomorrah because of their evil acts. Abraham is so shocked that innocent people might be killed alongside the guilty that he challenges God directly. 'Will the judge of all the earth not do justice?!' In a biblical world, where gods dominate all human actions, this is an extraordinary reversal and a tribute to Abraham's courage.

This challenge to act on the basis of justice has been addressed to rulers and leaders throughout history. In its absence the world falls into chaos and destructiveness. The Universal Declaration of Human Rights is the logical extension of that biblical call for justice for all human beings, whether it is based on a divine command or a response to the agonized cries of suffering human beings.

The name of Rene Cassin has been given to a Jewish human rights organization that 'uses the experience of the Jewish people to promote the human rights of all people'. In this sense, Cassin and his legacy are a direct heir of the biblical charge given to Abraham, to exemplify and to teach righteousness and justice to the world.

When receiving the Nobel Prize for Peace, Rene Cassin said: 'The time has come to proclaim that, for the establishment of peace and human dignity, each of us must work and fight to the last.'

17

The Rule of Law

Exodus 21–24

The Ten Commandments are among the best-known passages in the Hebrew Bible. Beyond their important place within Judaism and Christianity, they have helped shape our Western values. They are a kind of checklist against which to measure the state of our society. The image of the two tablets on which they were written, and of Moses holding them aloft, are familiar symbols of the law as a basis for human life in community.

The Ten Commandments were so important that they appear twice in the Hebrew Bible, once in Exodus when they are given to Moses on Mount Sinai and once again in Deuteronomy, when Moses repeats them to the community. Yet, for all their significance, it is necessary to point out that in the Book of Exodus they are only a preamble to the laws that follow. It is the laws that come afterwards that are to provide the basic rules for community life under God. Even the term 'commandments' is not an accurate translation of the Hebrew word. The Hebrew text speaks of them as the 'ten words' or 'ten sayings', and that is how they are known in Jewish tradition. In that sense, they are not exactly commandments. Rather they describe the kind of behaviour which will naturally follow as a consequence of the covenant with God. Once you accept it, your behaviour will change so that you simply will not do anything that might damage your relationship with God or with other people.

Perhaps this will come as a surprise, but Jewish tradition is rather cautious about the prominence that should be given to the

Ten Commandments. At one time they were publicly recited in the Temple service. However, some groups came to believe that only these Ten Words were the direct revelation of God to Israel. Since the rabbis believed that the entire Five Books of Moses were the words of God and therefore equally significant, they gave them less prominence. So Jewish tradition insists that the passages we read from Exodus 21 to 24, are just as important. These chapters contain the laws that Moses presented to the Israelites as the basis of how they were to build their society. So if we are to be true to Jewish tradition, we should study them as a whole and in detail.

But this is not so easy. We have to enter into an unfamiliar world and a very special way of organizing legal materials. The very first laws in Exodus 21 establish an important principle. They are about releasing a slave who works for you after six years. In the seventh year he is to be set free. The freedom of the seventh day, the Shabbat, is also to apply to the counting of years as well. Since the children of Israel have just left behind the slavery of Egypt, this law clearly establishes a new basis for the society they are about to build, a society where slavery is to be regulated and in effect abolished.

But after this opening section, we enter into what seems to be a strange mixture of different subjects. They begin with a series of laws which deal with murder, manslaughter and kidnapping. They also describe situations in which a man hits another man or a slave, or when two men fight and accidentally hurt someone who gets in the way. In all these cases, the law is concerned with the punishment of the perpetrator or with the compensation that has to be paid to the victim. But quite unexpectedly they are interrupted by a law forbidding people to curse their parents.

The next section is about what happens, when the ox that you own gores the ox of your neighbour. The penalty depends on whether this is the first time such a thing has happened, or the ox has been known to be dangerous. In this same agricultural setting are laws about the danger of digging a pit that an animal falls into, about the penalty for stealing animals and about what happens if your animals graze in someone else's field. A later section deals with the responsibility you have for objects or animals that are left in your care and are stolen or damaged.

But after that the series of laws seems to be increasingly more random. There are laws forbidding sorcery or idolatry followed by the command not to oppress strangers, a law that comes several times in the Bible. In between are to be found the prohibition on charging interest when you lend someone money and the command to return an animal that belongs to your enemy if you find it lost somewhere. These are just a few of the different subjects that are covered. So what is the connection between these very different kinds of law?

There does not seem to be a single principle that holds them all together. It may be that there was originally a core of laws about a particular theme. Over time additional laws were added so that the original intention was lost and the collection became a kind of anthology. Nevertheless, there is one factor that runs through most of them. They are about the problem of what happens when there is a breakdown in relationships between people. They range from the most extreme cases of murder and feuding to the everyday problems that arise when something is damaged and a judgement has to be made about who is responsible and who has to compensate whom. So most of them are about resolving conflicts between neighbours and the legal basis for making a correct judgement. The overarching question is how you restore the relationship between people when it has broken down because of conflict. These laws assume that without a comprehensive legal system to regulate such matters society can very easily fall apart. This is very practical law making, with a limited set of concerns, even though they cover a wide range of areas.

It is also obvious that these laws are not comprehensive. There are any number of areas that are not covered. Perhaps the particular ones collected here are included because these represent major differences from the legal codes of the societies surrounding ancient Israel. It was sufficient to indicate here the special concerns of Israel's God. For example, Israel's laws do not demand the death penalty for stealing property, even though that was the norm in other ancient Near Eastern codes. Life is more important than property.

The biblical concern with protecting the stranger is a good example of how law can function in a broader way. Fear about other people, in particular about new immigrants, can lead to prejudice, discrimination and violence. It is hard to change people's attitudes and emotional states. That may take years of education and positive steps to develop understanding, trust and respect. But the law can provide a safeguard for those who might become the victims of prejudice. More than that, the law can indicate that certain kinds of behaviour against other people are simply not acceptable to society as a whole. They form the minimum basis of a shared commitment to justice on which positive relationships can be built.

All the laws in these chapters start from this negative standpoint. Something has gone wrong, so how do we fix things so that normal life can be restored? They tell us nothing about how positive relationships between people are to be cultivated. For this we have to turn to Leviticus 19, which leads up to another very familiar biblical statement about how we are to move from the negative to the positive.

> You shall not hate your brother in your heart, but you shall reason with your neighbour, lest you bear sin because of him. You shall not take vengeance nor bear a grudge against the children of your own people, but you shall act in a loving way towards your neighbour as you would towards yourself. (Lev. 19.17–18)

18

Shekels, Swords and Altars

Exodus 30.11–16

Throughout the Jewish year, the regular cycle of readings from the Torah is amended for special reasons. On those occasions, additional readings may be included that reflect the particular theme of that Shabbat, such as *Shabbat Shekalim*, the Shabbat of the Shekel.

The name comes from an event that occurred during the time when the Israelites were wandering in the wilderness. Moses undertook a census of the population, counting the men from the age of 20 years and upwards. This suggests that it had a military purpose. The Israelites have escaped from centuries of slavery in Egypt. They are on their way to becoming a nation, but must learn how to defend themselves. Producing a register of available fighters is clearly an important step. But there was a problem. In the biblical world, there seems to have been a taboo associated with counting people. In a later period, King David will be severely punished for undertaking a census without taking some kind of precautionary measures. The additional passage from the Torah that we read in synagogue this Shabbat from Exodus 30 (11–16) shows how this problem was overcome.

Each of the men to be counted was to bring a half-shekel. This was not a coin but a piece of silver of a particular weight. It is possible that when everyone had given their half-shekel, these were counted or weighed instead of counting the men themselves. In this way the problem of counting actual people was resolved. This donation is described as a 'ransom for his soul' (Exod. 30.12), suggesting that each person was protected from the dangers of the census by making the donation. The moneys that were raised would be used to help build the sanctuary. Although our passage in Exodus suggests that this was a one-off event, it later became institutionalized as a head tax which would be used to maintain the Temple. The money was collected during the Jewish month of Adar. For this reason the tradition arose of reading the passage from Exodus about the half-shekel on the Shabbat before the month of Adar began to remind people of what was coming.

However, it is possible that there is another purpose behind the idea that the half-shekel was to be a ransom to save the soul of each of the men. If the census is to discover how many able-bodied men were available for military purposes, their lives would be at risk. But also soldiers must inevitably shed blood. The Hebrew Bible is very concerned about taking the life of another human being. Even in the case of a war, where killing may be justified as self-defence, it does not change the fact that a life has been lost and blood has been shed. Some kind of acknowledgement must be made to oneself and to God that another human being, made in the image of God, has been destroyed. That would be another explanation of why the half-shekel donation is said to be a 'ransom for his soul'. It is a way of acknowledging that taking life is against the will of God and an admission of responsibility must be made. According to King Solomon, his father King David was not allowed to build the Temple, because he was a man of war and had shed blood.

Nevertheless, it is strange that the shekels collected in connection with warfare and killing should go towards the maintenance of the Temple, the spiritual centre of the Israelite nation. Indeed, there is another biblical passage which suggests that the exact opposite should be the case. In Exodus 20.24–6, there is the description of the building of the altar on which the Israelites are to make their sacrifices to God. It is to be a simple one made of earth. However, if they wish instead to make one of stones a special directive is given: 'If you make Me an altar of stone, you shall not build it of hewn stones; for if you wield your tool upon it you profane it' (Exod. 20.25).

The rabbis were puzzled by this idea that cutting the stones with a metal tool would make the altar 'profane' and unacceptable to God. They found the following explanation:

> The altar is created to lengthen the days of human beings, but iron has been created to shorten the life of human beings – because iron can be made into a sword. It is not fitting that an object which shortens human life should be lifted up above that which lengthens it. Also the altar makes peace between Israel and their father in heaven, and so nothing should be used in fashioning it that cuts and destroys. (Rashi quoting Mechilta, Middot 3.4)

So it seems we are faced with two contradictory teachings. The soldiers who might have to shed blood make a donation to maintain the Temple. But the metal with which they might do their fighting should not be used in building the altar which stands in the centre of the Temple. There is no comfortable way of resolving this contradiction. At its heart is the awareness that conflict, even war, is apparently an inevitable part of human reality and behaviour. Or rather, that the dream of human beings is a world without conflict and war, but we are still a long way from realizing that dream.

The Hebrew Bible already suggests that limitations must be placed on one's freedom to wage war. When attacking a city, the opportunity to surrender peacefully must be offered (Deut. 20.10). There are laws about the treatment of captives (Deut. 20.11). No scorched earth policy is allowed (Deut. 20.19). These are early steps which helped pave the way towards modern conventions about the conduct of war. According to the Hebrew Bible, only certain people were obligated to fight. Those who are in the process of establishing their families, homes or farmlands were exempt (Deut. 20.5–7). Maintaining life and values, building human society, these are the things for which we should dedicate our lives. War is a sign of our failure to understand our true human priorities.

On the basis of this biblical distinction between those who were legally obligated to fight and those who were exempted, the rabbis developed the idea of two kinds of war. In a war of self-defence, everyone was needed and duty bound to take part, because their very survival was at stake. This was called an 'obligatory war'. Wars started by the king for political purposes or for expanding his realm were called 'permitted wars', but in those cases the general population was under no obligation to take part. However, such clear-cut distinctions are not always possible. When is a pre-emptive strike an act of self-defence and when is it a disguised act of aggression? Such questions are alive and played out today on the world stage.

These distinctions were largely hypothetical for the Jewish people for the best part of 2,000 years. The rabbis who formulated them in the past had no army and no say in the wars of the nations around them. The Jewish re-entry into history as a nation, through the creation of the State of Israel, has radically changed that situation. The brutal fact of war or the threat of war is an everyday reality in the Middle East with no simple solutions.

Whatever the justification, war means the killing and maiming of human beings made in the image of God, people like us, people who, in other circumstances, could be us. The tradition of the half-shekel reminds us that war is not glorious but disastrous, not a sign of human greatness but of human failure. Counting people for the purpose of fighting a war is but a step away from counting body bags. In death, there is no distinction between the two sides of the conflict. All of the dead are made in the image of God, as are all who are maimed by it, all who call for war and all who fight it. All need a ransom for their souls.

We need to return to the story of King David's census. According to the biblical account, he undertook it even against the advice of Joab, his commander in chief. It is not clear why he did so, but there is one significant difference between the count David undertook and the one we are reading about. In Exodus, it refers to counting men of 20 years and above. In the case of David, he counted all the people 'capable of bearing arms' (2 Sam. 24.9), old and young alike. In one explanation of the difference, David was not only concerned with those who were able to fight at the present time, but was anticipating future wars as well, so he counted the young men and boys below the age of 20 years. He was condemning the next generation to war, instead of trying to build a future of peace.

The half-shekel of our Torah reading is meant to save lives, not destroy lives. It is not to be used to manufacture swords, but to help build a Temple for God. It is not for creating stock-piles of weapons, but for a far more difficult task, for creating stockpiles of mutual understanding and respect, of reconciliation and peace.

19

The Absent Congregation

Exodus 35–40

During a visit to America I went to a variety of synagogues to learn at first hand how they address the needs of the Jewish community. Like Jews everywhere Americans are aware of major changes taking place in their community. Up to 50 per cent of American Jews marry non-Jews. So, despite the relatively large size of the community, people have been increasingly concerned about its long-term future. Intermarriage and assimilation are the price we pay for being part of an open society. We may regret it and do all we can to strengthen Jewish identity and loyalty, but very few people want to return to some kind of closed-off Jewish ghetto. Instead communities, especially in America, have begun to seek ways of encouraging Jews to participate more in Jewish life. When there is an intermarriage, some congregations actively try to find a place for the non-Jewish partner. Their hope is that he or she will be supportive when it comes to raising their children as Jews and may possibly even convert to Judaism one day.

The synagogue has become one of the most active agencies in America trying to reach out to Jews. For example, the last few years have seen major investments in resources, personnel and ideas to make synagogue worship services more attractive, as well as offering other activities for people who attend.

These thoughts are sparked off by our Torah reading, *vayakhel-pekudey*, 'he gathered' – 'this is the sum . . .',[1] which describes the building and setting up of the sanctuary in the wilderness. Here was a temporary building, later to be replaced by the Temple, that was to be the centre of the religious life of the community. The main religious act was the sacrifice of animals to God. This would be accompanied in Temple times by the reading or singing of Psalms. A Psalm would be chosen that described the situation of the person bringing the sacrifice, either asking God for help or thanking God for rescue from some kind of trouble. Whatever the reason for coming to the Temple, the central intention was to come nearer to God by this means and to hope that one's particular prayers would be answered.

At a later period, after the Temple was destroyed, our prayer life became more formalized. The three services a day became part of our religious obligation as individuals and as members of a community. Since we had to have a *minyan*, a minimum of ten adult males, for the full religious service to take place, Jews were obligated to support their community in a very practical way. There has always been room in Judaism for private prayers, both within the service and spontaneously. But coming to the synagogue was seen as a duty and a natural part of the rhythm of daily life. Moreover, you did not ask what you got out of the experience, but hoped that you had put the right amount of concentration and sincerity into reading the prayers.

While that still remains true for many Jews today, there has been a major shift in our spiritual concerns. We live in a secular society where belief in God has become a more private matter. The open society has changed our sense of community and raises questions about which group we feel we belong to and for whom we take some kind of responsibility. Above all we live in a consumer society and we judge everything in our lives by the price we have to pay for it and what we get in return. Religion, too, comes to be judged in the same way. This has particular consequences in America and other countries where, unlike Germany, there is no church tax and people have to pay directly to support their synagogue. If the synagogue does not meet the needs of its members, they can simply leave and go elsewhere. That causes a certain level of insecurity but it does make the leadership of the synagogue sensitive to the needs of its members.

Which brings me back to the synagogues I visited in America. They all belong to the American Reform movement. In the past, this was the most radical Jewish organization because of the changes it made in Jewish ritual. Today, it is the largest Jewish religious movement in America and includes a wide range of different religious practices. Some congregations still have so-called classical Reform services, with organ music and a shortened liturgy. But others have returned to more traditional forms, restoring rituals, prayers and practices that previous Reform generations had removed. Of course, one thing they all have in common is that they are completely egalitarian, with men and women playing equal roles in leading the prayers.

At one morning service I attended, almost everyone was wearing *tallit* and *tefillin*, the ritual garments of tradition, and the service itself included most of the traditional prayers. The next day the same group was experimenting with a service for 'healing', selecting a few prayers from the traditional liturgy and interweaving them with new songs and leaving time for meditation. At one Shabbat evening service, the three rabbis and cantor standing in front of music stands and microphones looked more like a pop group. They led a service made up of popular Hebrew songs built around a few traditional prayers. It was almost like a concert, but the atmosphere was very welcoming. More important, some 500 people attend that service each week, and most of them stay on in different groups to study Jewish texts or to socialize or to learn together with their children. In other synagogues, several different Shabbat services are held at the same time catering to the very different needs and wishes of members of the community.

Will such experiments have an impact on the Jewish community of America? Will they slow the rate of intermarriage or bring more people back to Judaism? No one can tell what the long-term effect will be. But, from the tabernacle built in the wilderness of Sinai to the synagogue on the West Coast of America, there is a tradition of prayer and worship that defines the spiritual life of the Jewish people. And as long as Jews gather together to pray, whatever the form it takes, there is hope for our future.

20

On Hats and Hijabs

Exodus 38.21—40.38

Here we complete the reading of the Book of Exodus. It ends in an unexpected way. The Book starts with the arrival in Egypt of the patriarch Jacob and records how his family flourished and grew. They became so many that a new Pharaoh, in order to consolidate his power, built his political platform on fear about these Israelites as a potential fifth column. He laid secret plans to destroy the male children as they were born. But this was prevented by the actions of the Hebrew midwives, the first recorded act of civil disobedience against the misuse of political power. When Moses challenged Pharaoh, a series of plagues seriously damaged the country. The Israelites finally left Egypt, ending their period of enslavement. At the Sea of Reeds, the Egyptian army was utterly destroyed. The end result of Pharaoh's scaremongering policy was exactly the thing that he had wanted to prevent.

In the desert at Mount Sinai, the newly formed nation received its constitution. It contained laws formulated in deliberate contrast to the slave state they had left behind. Theirs was to be a society built on individual freedom within a system based on the rule of law and mutual responsibility.

But the narrative part of the Book of Exodus comes to a sudden halt. The last 16 chapters describe in enormous detail the plans for the building of the sanctuary, a religious centre, where they are to meet their God. The same details are even repeated almost verbatim as the sanctuary is actually fashioned and built.

The change of emphasis between the beginning and end of the Book of Exodus reflects a transition in the life of the people. After the extraordinary experiences of liberation, wandering and nation building, they needed a new kind of stability in their lives. The sanctuary with all the regular sacrifices that took place there provided just this kind of continuity and security. The detailed and repeated description of every element that went into the building of the sanctuary helped provide an awareness of the presence of God in their lives. Each element had meaning and significance.

Almost an entire chapter is devoted to the fashioning of the clothing of Aaron, the High Priest, and his sons who were to serve God in the sanctuary. Each piece of the clothing of the priests had significance in itself, but also as part of defining the role and purpose of the one who wore it. Clothing, especially clothing associated with a religious tradition, can be an essential part of identity building for those within the faith.

But things change over time. With the destruction of the Temple in Jerusalem, the entire institution of the priesthood and sacrifice disappeared from Judaism. Nevertheless, other forms of distinctive dress have become part of Jewish tradition in different times and in different cultures. Some form of head covering has been an important part of Jewish religious identity since the early rabbinic period. Though changes of clothing are often caused by outside influences, they can also reflect inner debates within the Jewish community itself. For example, the issue of whether or not to wear a hat became a source of contention with the emergence of the Reform movement in Judaism in the nineteenth century. In America, where the movement was more radical than in Europe, many Reform Temples insisted that no one should wear a head covering during services.

These thoughts, about the nature and significance of clothing, have been raised by the current debates in Europe about the public wearing of the hijab by Muslim women and other outer symbols of religious affiliation.

The bitterness of the debate reminded me of an experience described by the late Rabbi William Braude, a great Jewish scholar and the spiritual leader of a Reform Temple in Providence, Rhode Island. He told about an evening arranged by his Temple in 1938 a week after the *Reichskristallnacht,* 'night of broken glass'. It was to be a service of grief and sorrow because of the synagogues in Germany that had been destroyed. The congregation invited all the Jewish refugees in Providence to attend. On the Friday night, as he was preparing for the service, one of the members of the Temple rushed into his office and asked: 'Did you give permission to these people to wear hats?' The Temple belonged to the classical Reform tradition, where hats were removed on entering the synagogue. But this would have been surprising, even shocking, to any Jewish refugee from Europe with a more Orthodox background. Rabbi Braude writes:

The fact was that until that instant I had given no thought to the headgear of our guests – the refugees. I did not know whether or not our guests chose to wear hats, to put on Yarmulkes, or not to wear either. And so my response to the question ... was indirect. I began to say: 'But these people are our guests. They have suffered so much. Whether or not they choose to wear their hats, surely we do not wish to add insult to the injuries they had already suffered.' But my interrogator was implacable. 'Answer my question. Did you or did you not give permission to these people to wear their hats?' To this day, I don't know the outcome of the battle of the hats. I was too choked up with pain. Involuntarily I thought of comparable demands – of Cossack officers saying to Jews: '*Shapka doloi*', 'Off with your hat', of SS men saying: '*Hut ab, Jude*.' So when I walked into the Temple I did not look. My head was reeling; my eyes were filled with tears. To this day I do not know whether ushers took it upon themselves to tell our guests to remove their hats and whether some of the refugees left in protest. Whatever happened to the hats worn by our guests, that service for me at least was indeed a service of grief and sorrow.

This story says much about the nature of intolerance. The congregant was so blinded by what he considered to be the tradition of his Temple that he lost sight of the larger picture, the experience of the refugees who were their guests for that evening. He allowed convention to overcome compassion, and dogma to deaden sympathy for and sensitivity to the needs of others.

That is why we need to juxtapose the beginning and the end of the Book of Exodus. To wear or not to wear a hat, or any other special clothing, may carry with it an enormous weight of emotions and historical experiences for the wearer. To prevent any individual or group from expressing their own religious or cultural identity through their clothing is a disgrace to any civilized society.

Pharaoh used the perceived difference of the Israelites for his own political ends. He stirred up anxiety and hatred to consolidate his power, but ultimately he only damaged and almost destroyed the very society he wanted to preserve and protect.

Everywhere today we experience the growing coexistence of a multitude of different cultures, races and religious traditions within any given society. This is a difficult and challenging reality that needs courage, mutual respect and generosity of spirit. We do not need new Pharaohs trading on people's fears for their own purposes. Instead, we need sanctuaries for all the different religious traditions within our society. We need to create and defend a public space where the clothing or symbols that reflect our own religious tradition, and that of others, can be worn with confidence and without fear.

21

Introducing Leviticus

One of the keys to understanding the Book of Leviticus is Genesis 1, the account of the creation of the world. The world that God creates comes into being through a series of separations: between light and darkness, between the waters above and below the firmament, between the sea and the dry land. In the end, there are three major divisions, the heavens, the earth and the waters beneath the earth, each with its own distinctive features and inhabitants. As the Psalmist explains, the heavens are the domain of God, but the earth has been given to human beings to inhabit. However, because of God's experience with human beings, there will be one further act of separation, the choosing of Israel from among all the peoples of the world to be a 'kingdom of priests and a holy nation'.

The Book of Leviticus is about how the collective life of Israel is to be regulated so as to fulfil this task as a kingdom of priests. A key term is '*kadosh*', usually translated as 'holy', but basically meaning 'separate', 'distinctive', and in this particular context, 'set apart' for God. Being set apart for God, one has to exist within certain boundaries and divisions that should not be crossed. Effectively, Israel is to align itself with the pattern laid down by God for creation.

This translates into the language of 'clean' and 'unclean'. The food you eat must conform to certain categories. The animals you eat should be herbivores and neither hunt nor scavenge. Animals that live between two domains, between sea and land, like shellfish, or between land and sky, are explicitly forbidden – they cross boundaries. Clothing made from different kinds of materials should not be worn together. Different kinds of animals should not be mated together. Certain physical or pathological states of the body make one temporarily 'out of alignment' with the normal, and this state must be remedied. Certain human relationships are seen as conforming to an acceptable pattern and others not. Even time must be contained within a divine pattern of weekdays and Shabbat and a festival calendar governing the entire year.

Furthermore, the behaviour among the 'kingdom of priests' must be correct. Yet, inevitably things go wrong. Mistakes are made, boundaries are crossed, human realities, rivalries and needs constantly threaten to destroy the idealized pattern of existence. So an elaborate system is needed to constantly monitor and correct these lapses. The legal system is to ensure that wrongdoing is dealt with, punishment is meted out and the correct human relationships are re-established. But the sacrificial cult fulfils the role of restoring the relationship with God which has been damaged by these activities. The blood of the sacrifice formally washes away the 'uncleanness', in the immediate situation, and once a year on Yom Kippur for the priesthood and the people as a whole.

It is a remarkably coherent and comprehensive system. It assumes that God is a desired presence in their midst, but also a dangerous and barely containable force. It requires an entire population to understand their responsibilities and a priestly hierarchy able to service the system, but with safeguards also to prevent the abuse of their power. As a system it served effectively for more than 1,000 years.

But there is also another possible perspective on the Book of Leviticus. The first word of the Book is 'Vayikra', literally, 'He called'. But if you look at the Masoretic text you will see an anomaly. The last letter of vayikra, the 'alef', is written small and raised above the line. It looks as though it was squeezed in as an afterthought. Without it, we would read the word 'vayikar', 'it happened'. This led to a midrash, a rabbinic commentary. Moses was a very modest man and was embarrassed to write that God specifically called to him, so instead wrote 'vayikar', as if God simply happened to come across him. But God insisted that he add the 'alef' – he was really called by God! The two verbs, though pronounced the same, '*kara*', have diametrically opposite meanings: one is about a calling, a vocation, the other is about chance. And therein lies the problem within the Book of Leviticus. For the entire system is about eliminating chance, of ensuring a rigorous control over every aspect of life, and over everything that happens, within an isolated and hermetically sealed environment. It includes no real relationship with other peoples around, no political dimension, leaving that up to God as the guarantor of their safety. It may be true to the designation, 'holy nation', but takes no account of the responsibility as a 'kingdom of priests', for just as priests mediate between the people and God, so a 'kingdom of priests' bear the same responsibility to the other kingdoms of the earth. It is other strands of biblical thought that address these wider issues.

The Book of Leviticus itself brings us into a remarkable world, far more complex than this superficial introduction suggests. Though it requires a leap of imagination to enter, nevertheless it poses real questions about how a religious society and community should operate; how people should interact with one another, and how, as individuals and collectively, to mediate the encounter with God.

22

Martyrs and Sacrifices

Leviticus 16

Here we read two sections from the Book of Leviticus. The first takes its name from the dramatic opening words: *'Aharei-mot sh'nei bnei aharon'*, 'After the death of the two sons of Aaron'. To understand its significance it is helpful to imagine we are watching a film. At a crucial point in the story we learn about an event that happened some time before but which continues to impact upon one of the characters. In a flashback, we see this event as it happened and relive it together with the person who had the experience. In the case of the opening words, we will need to look back at two particular scenes in the Bible to understand the significance of our opening words, 'After the death of the two sons of Aaron'.

Aaron the High Priest, the brother of Moses, had four sons. The first two were called Nadav and Abihu. In a mysterious story in Leviticus 10.1–2, we are told that the two sons brought 'strange fire' into the sanctuary, the holiest part of the encampment in the wilderness where the sacrifices were made to God. The text adds that they had not been commanded to do this. Suddenly, fire comes down from heaven and burns them up. That is all we are told. Our first flashback establishes the background scene in which this occurred. From the verse before (Lev. 9.24) we learn that it took place at the precise moment that the sanctuary in the wilderness was completed. At that moment, fire descended from heaven and consumed the sacrifice on the altar. This was the proof that the sanctuary, and all that took place within it, was accepted by God. But that same fire seems also to have consumed the two sons of Aaron but no one else.

Much of the crucial information we would need to understand the story is missing. What was the nature of this 'strange fire' that they brought? What was so wrong with it that it led to such a tragic loss of life? Many of the commentaries try to establish some kind of wrongdoing by the two young men to explain their shocking fate. The passage in Leviticus is followed at once by a command to Aaron that the priests should not enter the sanctuary when they have drunk wine or strong liquor (Lev. 10.9). So perhaps Aaron's sons were actually drunk at the time and hence this new commandment. In another view, they were simply impatient young men who wanted to take on the role of their father Aaron instead of waiting till they inherited his task. But if they were simply impatient to serve God in the sanctuary, perhaps their motive was not such a bad one. If so, is there another way to understand what happened?

In order to explore this possibility, we need to look at a second flashback. This time, we return to the moment when the children of Israel stood at Mount Sinai and entered into the covenant with God. The Bible describes an elaborate ceremony, which sealed the agreement between God and the people. At the end, there occurred a unique event. Till now, only Moses had been allowed to climb the mountain to meet God. But now a small group was invited to share that experience. They included Aaron and his two sons Nadav and Abihu as well as 70 elders of the people. In a text unique in the Bible, all of them saw the God of Israel (Exod. 24). This mystical experience seems to have had a profound effect on those who took part. In a later passage 70 elders, presumably the same ones, began to prophecy. So what must have been the impact on the two young men, the sons of Aaron?

Perhaps they became overwhelmed by the direct experience of God and as a result burned with an inner passion and zeal to serve their God. It was this enthusiasm to participate in the sacrifices in the sanctuary that led them to break the rules and enter that special place at the wrong time. On this interpretation, what happened to them was not a punishment. But rather it was a kind of fulfilment of their desire to offer themselves to God. They themselves became a kind of sacrifice, literally burnt up with their own inner fire.

Such passion is the special quality to be found in young people. It fuels feelings of devotion and love, whether directed at another person or a cause. It is single-minded and often uncritical, simply because it is not constrained by the breadth of experience or the weight of responsibilities that come with age. It can lead to great achievements or equally great disappointments. But it is also the driving force that leads to self-sacrifice for a cause, whether it be a religious tradition, or a nationalist movement or a political ideal. It is the energy that creates martyrs and saints.

This story about the death of two young men consumed by fire is not a comfortable one at the best of times. Their passion to serve their God cost them their lives. But any tale about martyrdom has challenging echoes today in the aftermath of 9/11 and in the ongoing cycle of violence in the Middle East. Young men and women are prepared to blow themselves up in public places for the sake of their cause.

Jewish history has its own list of martyrs who were willing to die for the sake of their faith. The Talmud recalls ten rabbis who were executed by the Romans for continuing to teach the Torah to their people when such activities were banned. A passage from early rabbinic teachings asks: 'Why are you brought out to be killed?' 'Because I performed the rite of circumcision on my son.' 'Why are you to be stoned to death?' 'Because I have observed the Shabbat.' 'Why are you led out to be burned by fire?' 'Because I studied the Torah.' (Tanchuma Toledot on Genesis 6 (Buber edition)).

Throughout the Middle Ages, Jews chose to die rather than convert to Christianity or Islam. Tragically, even whole families would voluntarily choose death, the last survivor killing himself. And yet, the rabbis recognized that such self-sacrifice contradicted a fundamental religious value – the preservation of life. So they tackled the problem in the way they knew best. They created laws which set strict limits on when and in what circumstances it was permitted to offer one's life for the sanctification of God's name.

The rabbis often turned to biblical figures to provide models for ideal behaviour. But there is one obvious martyr in the Bible, whose example they did not seek to follow – namely Samson. When Samson killed himself by pulling down the pillars of the Philistine temple, he killed thousands of his enemies at the same time. This could have provided an example to emulate – a self-sacrifice that also served to kill other people. But this never became legitimized in Jewish law. Nevertheless, in times of war, Jews have also been willing to offer their lives and take their enemy with them into death.

It would be nice to make a neat distinction between martyrdom and murder. In such a distinction, the death of the true martyr is an act that only harms directly the person who undertakes it. It is an act of individual resistance and dedication to one's religious faith. On the other hand, deliberately to set out to kill innocent bystanders at the same time as taking one's own life, is an act of murder. For Judaism, Christianity and Islam alike, such an act cannot be considered to be a genuine service of God. And yet, at different times and places, such destructive acts have taken place in the name of any number of religions and in the service of any number of gods.

Religion is also about what people actually do in its name, just as much as it is about what the teachings declare that people ought to do. True religion is always about the struggle between the values it seeks to promote and the sins it all too often commits. So an essential element of religious faith has to be the willingness to admit such sins and seek out the roots within the religious tradition that make them possible. Without such courage and honesty, the sin itself becomes the new truth, and religion becomes its own victim.

This does not change the further duty of religious believers when caught up in conflicts, especially those made more complicated or bitter by religion itself: the duty to remove the causes that lead to such desperate acts of martyrdom; to seek justice where it is absent, pragmatism where there is fanaticism, compromise where there is dogma. Only then can one hope for the possibility of reconciliation and the beginning of the long, long journey to peace.

To paraphrase a dialogue from Bertolt Brecht's *Life of Galileo*: 'Unhappy the land that has no martyrs.' 'Unhappy the land that needs martyrs!'

23

Mysteries of Sex and Death

Leviticus 21

There is a certain wisdom in the Jewish tradition of reading a passage from the Torah each week, sections from the Five Books of Moses. They contain such a mixture of material: stories, laws, poetry, cultic information, that we never know what is going to turn up or what will strike our imagination. So each reading challenges us in a new way to try to discover significance within it. However obscure or difficult the passage may be, this is a word of revelation to be explored, interpreted and applied to our life.

The beginning of this reading from the Torah is an example of such a challenge. It introduces us to a world as remote and bewildering as any we are likely to meet in the Hebrew Bible. It describes the rules of mourning for the priests, the *cohanim*, the descendants of Aaron. But it describes these rules in terms of a puzzling set of restrictions. The priests are only allowed to undertake a mourning ritual for their immediate family: mother and father, son and daughter, brother and sister. But this last case, that of the sister, is even further circumscribed. The sister of the priest must still be a virgin at the time of her death. If she has married, he may not perform the rituals associated with death. Why impose these limits that seem so unnatural on the priests? And why this special distinction in the case of the sister alone?

The very language is also problematic. The priest who comes into contact with death becomes '*tamei*', variously translated as 'impure' or 'unclean', words which carry a negative connotation in our Western culture. But this is actually misleading, as *tamei* only applies to a symbolic status. It makes no value judgement. The priest who functions in the holiest part of the sanctuary, in intimate contact with God, has to remain ritually pure.

It is rather like a surgeon in an operating theatre, who has to wear sterile clothing and wash in disinfectant before he operates. Moreover, everything and everyone around him must also be prepared in the same way. If he does not do so, then any bacteria he carries may infect the patient. The sanctuary was seen as a holy place, set aside for God's powerful presence. So nothing must contaminate it, in case God's anger be aroused and disaster strike the community.

The price paid by the priest for his privileged position of directly serving God was the extra precautions he had to take. Contact with the dead caused ritual impurity, so in theory he should never be in the presence of one who has died. But the Torah at least allows him to be in attendance, when those of his closest family have died and are buried. It is a concession to his natural grief.

The verses we read specify some of the details. He is forbidden to shave his hair or make cuts in his skin as signs of mourning. Physical damage of any sort would also disqualify him from functioning as a priest.

But why may he not mourn for his sister, if she is no longer a virgin? Having opened up this subject, the same text adds that he may not marry a woman who has been a prostitute or a divorcee. Obviously, these are all cases where the woman in question has had sexual intercourse. The priest is to be 'holy', which means that he is 'set aside', 'dedicated' to God alone. Presumably any woman who plays a significant part in his immediate family must be similarly set apart and special, for she is either born into or has married into the priestly caste. Once the sister has had intercourse through marriage, she has left that special domain. The wife of the priest must similarly have an exclusive relationship with him.

I noted at the beginning that this aspect of the biblical world is remote from us. In Judaism, for almost 2,000 years, we have had no Temple, no sacrifices and no officiating priests. Nevertheless, something remains of this past world. There are families who preserve the tradition that they are *cohanim*, descended from the biblical priests. They still have certain limited ritual functions in Jewish life. They are given the honour of being the first to be called up to read from the Torah in Synagogue. In services, they recite the priestly blessing over the community. Moreover, according to traditional Jewish law, they still may not marry a divorced woman or a convert to Judaism. They are not allowed to enter a cemetery, though there are no other limits placed on their ability to mourn members of their family who have died. These are restrictions that are taken very seriously by some who consider it to be an honour to be descended from the biblical priests. But others may simply ignore the tradition which they find has little meaning.

So what do we make of such biblical laws? After all, they do not even apply to the majority of Jews, who are not descended from these priestly families?

The passage touches on two of the great mysteries of life – human sexuality and death itself. Sexual intercourse binds two people physically together, however temporarily, and however casually it is undertaken. They become one. On the other hand, death tears people apart, however intimate, deep or prolonged their relationship might have been. The biblical priest is somehow to remain almost untouched by these experiences, dedicated exclusively to God, to an intimacy that is total, though completely non-physical. Nevertheless, he is expected to marry and have children like anyone else. He is bound to a kind of eternal life beyond the normal boundaries and limitations of human existence.

The biblical priest by his otherness points to the normal dimensions within which we actually conduct our lives. These texts remind us of the extraordinary varieties of human intimacy, the limitless relationships we experience in our lifetime and the many losses we will suffer and have to mourn. The responsibility for how we conduct our lives, how we cope with death, and how we live in the presence of God today no longer depends on the ritual acts of a priestly caste. Those responsibilities and opportunities are in our hands alone.

24

Against Cruelty

When a word only occurs a few times in the Hebrew Bible, we need to compare the different contexts for clues as to its meaning. An example is found in Leviticus 25.39–46. The context is the treatment of Hebrew slaves. These are fellow Israelites who have fallen into debt and earn their way out of it by working for someone. The Torah insists that they are not to be treated as slaves, but rather as paid workers, to be released from their debts in the Jubilee year. They cannot be bought and sold like non-Israelite slaves, and above all they are not to be treated harshly. The word variously translated as 'with rigour', 'ruthlessly' or 'harshly' is '*b'farech*', and it comes twice in this section (Lev. 25.43, 36).

Slavery brings with it memories of the bitter experience of the Israelites as slaves in the land of Egypt, and here, too, we find *b'farech*: 'The Egyptians made the children of Israel serve them *b'farech*, with rigour' (Exod. 1.13). It occurs as part of a gradual escalation of the harshness of the treatment of the Israelites, embittering their lives and forcing them to do the most difficult physical labour. Israelite society is to be different from that of Egypt, though still willing to use non-Israelite slaves.

The rabbis were curious about the meaning of this word. As a verb it means to crush or break down, and they understood it here in two possible senses: to crush the body but also to crush the spirit. They played with the word, breaking it into two syllables: '*peh*', 'mouth' and '*rach*', 'soft', suggesting deceitfulness. They told how Pharaoh deceived the Israelites. He too started making bricks as if setting an example. The Israelites, keen to show their loyalty, immediately set to the work with energy and enthusiasm. At the end of the day, Pharaoh stopped, but insisted that the Israelites fulfil the exact same quota from then on!

The harsh treatment described in Exodus could be understood simply as arbitrary cruelty, performed by those who enjoyed tormenting the Israelites to demonstrate their power over them. But such cruelty can be a deliberate policy of breaking the spirit of the victims, destroying their independence, making them seem less than human and so easier to regard as disposable. In the concentration camps, people were set meaningless tasks, like carting loads of bricks from one end of the compound to the other and then carting them all the way back.

If these are the extreme consequences of such a policy, Rashi, following the midrash, draws attention to the implications within a domestic setting. On Leviticus 25.43, he explains:

'Do not rule over him with rigour, by making him do useless work just to oppress him. Do not say to him, "warm this cup for me", even though you do not need it; or, "hoe beneath this vine till I come" [when he does not know when this will be]. Do not say to yourself, no one will know whether this is meaningful activity or not, so I will tell him that it is necessary. This matter is concealed in his heart, hence the verse (Lev 25:43) concludes: But fear God in your heart!'

By focusing on domestic violence and the abuse of those who work for us, actions that are often concealed from the public gaze, we are forced to examine our own behaviour and the way we use the power we hold over others. An unusual word and a remote verse, are suddenly brought uncomfortably close to home.

25

The Small Print in the Contract

Leviticus 26.3—27.34

With this reading we come to the end of the Book of Leviticus. It is an exploration of the theme of holiness and contains one of the central commands and values of the Hebrew Bible and of Judaism: 'You shall love your neighbour as yourself.' Holiness is about the relationship that exists between people and the care with which they maintain that relationship.

But Chapter 26 comes as something of a shock. There seems to be very little about holiness here, instead it is made up of a series of blessings and curses: blessings that will come to Israel if they obey God; but curses if they do not.

Behind this language is actually a legal document. These 'blessings and curses' correspond to the small print at the bottom of any business contract. Both parties agree to work together, and then set out in the contract the conditions of their partnership. But suppose one or other of the partners fails to live up to the terms of the contract – then the contract contains a list of sanctions and penalties that come into force.

The curses in Leviticus are just such a section in the contract, the covenant between Israel and God. And they are very disturbing to read. If Israel disobeys the laws of God, then diseases will flourish in the land and enemies will invade and rule them. If they still refuse to obey God, then in successive stages more and more misfortunes will befall them. Under siege in their cities they will starve to death. Their cities and altars will be destroyed. Worse yet they will be taken into captivity in exile, where they will live a life of constant fear and anxiety.

It is a chilling warning of a situation of insecurity and terror. It is a situation that has been experienced all too often by Jewish communities in exile.

This detailed spelling out of punishment seems to reinforce the image of the God of the Hebrew Bible as a vengeful, angry God, always ready to punish the Israelites.

But on the other hand, a contract is a contract. Much of our life is about negotiations, compromises and agreements we make with others. The moment there are two people in the world, they have to examine their relationship with each other: how to share resources; how to respect each other's needs, property and personal space; how to define their mutual responsibilities to each other.

We build our relationships on the basis of trust, and much of the time we hardly even think about this. But when things go wrong, when a crisis occurs, then we realize how fragile many relationships actually are, and how many unspoken problems exist between us. Groups of people who have coexisted for long periods can suddenly find themselves in violent disagreement with each other, and then discover that there is no proper framework for resolving their difficulties. Then emotions take over, demands are made for loyalty to one's own group and confrontation and conflict with the 'other' becomes almost inevitable. That is why it is so important that at the time when people do make an agreement with each other, when there is good will on both sides, that provisions for the future be made.

This applies not only to business agreements. Whenever there is a deep emotional commitment as well, such as when two people marry each other, then the terms and conditions need to be spelled out even more carefully. But a couple deeply in love may well resent this. They may not be able to imagine, or want to imagine, that they might one day change their minds and wish to separate. To talk about the practicalities of settling some possible future disagreement seems to undermine the very basis of their new relationship. Yet, traditional wisdom has always led societies to make such provisions, especially where something so central to the community as marriage is concerned.

If all this seems to be a very negative way of looking at relationships between people, there is also a positive side, especially when it involves two people in love. Precisely because we know that there is a contract, and that contracts contain the possibility of being dissolved, both partners can recognize and accept the freedom that they have within the contract. In theory, at least, there should be no dependency or manipulation here when both are free to walk away. Their individuality and sense of responsibility are recognized and validated. They can build something together, but know that it will only work if they actually choose to stay together. It is not external pressures, not even religious pressures, that hold them together in the end, but such mutual respect and loyalty as they can create between themselves. The contract also means that there is a structure and framework to use for dealing with problems that arise and one which can be turned to in times of tension or difficulty.

The sanctions in the contract, sanctions that they have both understood and accepted, are a kind of warning. But they are also a reminder of the value of what they have built together, the care with which they created their partnership and what they risk losing by dissolving the relationship.

Something of these ideas exists in our *parashah* as well. These 'blessings and curses' are expressions of love and of anger, so they remind us of the deep emotional bonds between God and Israel and the paradox of the God of the entire cosmos entering into a covenant with a human society. If God's love was given full reign, it would be all-devouring; if God's anger was set free, it would be utterly destructive. Instead these emotions are contained within a ritualized language of warnings and graded sanctions. They are shocking threats because they are so graphic and real; but they establish boundaries and limits, and contain the promise of reconciliation and restoration.

In the end, we also know that God cannot be contained within the pages of a contract. Israel too, in all its diversity and complexity, can no longer be defined by the language and metaphors of Leviticus. But the emotional ties remain, the love and the anger. In Jewish history, pain and suffering, the lure of idols and the challenge of new loves have time and again threatened to pull Israel and God apart. But in bad times and in good ones the formal ties and sanctions and promises of the covenant have helped us freely and consciously to choose to remain bound to one another.

26

Holy Places

Numbers 4.21—7.89

This reading from the Book of Numbers describes a moment of change in the life of the children of Israel on their journey through the wilderness. They have built the sanctuary that is to be at the centre of their encampment. While that sanctuary exists, God will be present among the people. But certain precautions have to be taken so that the sanctuary does not become ritually impure. If that should happen, the anger of God would be aroused, and plague would break out in the camp. Holy places need to be handled with respect and care.

The passages in this section detail the precautions that had to be taken. In theory when the people finally set out on their march, everything would be perfectly in place and nothing could go wrong.

Of course a few chapters later, when the theory gets tested, things do go wrong. Mistakes happen; the people disobey God; and on one occasion a plague does indeed break out. All religious systems have to find a balance between an ideal way in which things are to happen and human reality. Chance and change affect us all. Often the best we can hope for, especially in religious matters, is some kind of holy compromise.

I became acutely aware of the need to cope with change because of a particular experience. For over 30 years I had helped to organize an annual conference in Germany. It brings together Jewish, Christian and Muslim students, future leaders of the three faiths. The aim is to give them a greater understanding of each other's beliefs and practices.

Above all the hope is that this will create relationships and a network of contacts that will continue into their lives and professional work.

For most of the 30 years the conference had been held at the same place, the Hedwig Dransfeld Haus in Bendorf (HDH). But when the HDH had to be closed for financial reasons we had to transfer at short notice to a new location. Though we had to make adjustments to the programme, we were able to retain all the basic elements, and the conference was successful. But there was one unexpected problem we had to address.

One of the highlights of the conference each year is the opportunity to attend each other's religious services. In the HDH there was a large room set aside to be used as a non-denominational room of prayer. During the conference, on Friday it could serve as a Mosque, on Saturday as a Synagogue and on Sunday as a Church. During the rest of the year the local Catholic community used it for their regular daily worship. During the week of the conference all the Christian symbols were either removed or covered so as to create a neutral space in which all the participants of different religions could feel comfortable as they conducted their services. It showed a great sensitivity on the part of those who directed the HDH and the great generosity of spirit on the part of those who prayed there regularly, to allow the room to be used in this way. As hosts they wanted to be sure that their guests felt at home. But they also recognized the power of religious symbols both to their own religious community and to others. Somehow the right balance had to be reached between their own needs and those of their guests.

It is a mark of our own religious security and trust that we are willing to sacrifice something of our own sacred space to make room for others. During the 30 years of the conference we felt the presence of God in that room on many occasions – but despite making changes to our shared sanctuary, no biblical plague ever broke out!

When we moved to our new temporary home we found a very different situation. The place we were using was a Catholic house with a conservative tradition. In virtually every room there was a large crucifix as well as religious pictures and symbols. Some members of the organizing team experienced quite a strong reaction to them. Instead of the neutral territory we were used to, we were in a place with a powerful religious identity of a particular type. We felt that this was potentially disturbing for the participants at the conference, especially those coming for the first time.

When the organizing team met for the final planning session we recognized the relevance of this issue for the topic of the conference itself. Our theme was the contribution of our different religious traditions to current socio-political issues. We had encountered one of today's major questions. How do we deal with the public display of the religious symbols of another community? How are we to react to Muslim headscarves, Jewish skullcaps, Christian crosses or Sikh turbans in a multicultural society? Do we allow all such symbols to be displayed? Do we allow none of them? Do we assume that there is a majority culture that is allowed free expression of its religious symbols but deny the right to others?

We became very aware of our own particular situation as a conference. After so many years in the same place where we had felt at home and could control our environment, we were now in exile. We were dependent upon the generosity and openness of our new host. Like others in exile we carried with us memories of the place we had left behind and the freedom of worship that we had known. We were grateful to our new host, and wished to respect their culture and religious expressions. But how could we find space for our own needs?

We discussed a number of possible strategies. We could request that all religious symbols in the building be removed, and if our hosts were unwilling, look for another place. We could try to ignore them, as if they were simply part of the decorations and wallpaper and of no significance. But that would mean showing little respect for the religious life and the traditions of our host. We began to appreciate the difficulties faced by those forced to start a new life in a strange place. How far do you try to preserve your own traditions and identity? How far do you assimilate to the traditions of the new place? Or do you find a way of balancing the two by creating a private space within which you can preserve your own ways while fitting into the outside world as far as possible?

Of course the choice may not be yours to make. The host may insist that you conform to their ways and practices. How far they will allow you to preserve your identity is probably a measure of their sense of security in their own identity. If those in the host culture are also insecure they will be less tolerant of the presence and the needs of others. When two sets of insecure people confront each other in this way then the situation is potentially explosive.

In the event we spoke to the director of the house and he was very sympathetic to our needs. We had decided for ourselves the compromise we wanted that would respect both parties. We requested that the crucifixes be removed from the public rooms for the duration of the conference. However, they would remain in the bedrooms and people would be free to leave them on the wall or remove them as they wished. But we also proposed that the other religious pictures and symbols should remain so that the identity of the house would be preserved. The director agreed at once. He felt it important that as the host he should do everything in his power to make his guests feel at home. And that is how it was resolved. We explained what had been decided to the participants of the conference and it never became an issue. As soon as the conference was over the crucifixes were replaced in time for the next group of visitors who would expect to see them there.

Of course this was a limited situation in which it was relatively easy to negotiate a solution. But it allowed the generosity and openness that is at the heart of our religious traditions to find their expression. We had learnt to share our sanctuary. We could celebrate a successful holy compromise.

27

Spying out the Land

Numbers 13–15

This reading comes from the Book of Numbers and tells the story about the men sent by Moses to spy out the promised land of Canaan. The effect of the mission was disastrous. All of the spies agreed that the land was indeed fruitful. But they also reported that the people were strong, the cities were well fortified and there were even giants there. Ten of the twelve spies were convinced that they would never be able to conquer the land. But two of them, Caleb and Joshua, argued that they would be able to do so. This triggered a crisis that nearly destroyed the entire project. Some people even suggested that they should appoint a new leader, turn round and go back to Egypt.

When we look at the story in more detail we find that there were actually two stages in the report of the spies. They were given to different audiences, and, in each case, there was a different emphasis. This seeming repetition has led scholars to suggest that there were two different accounts of what happened, and they have been edited together. But whenever there are such seeming repetitions in the Hebrew Bible, it is worth looking more closely at the differences between them.

The sequence is quite clear. The returning spies brought their report to Moses, Aaron and a selected group of the leaders of the people. They showed the fruit, praised the quality of the land, but then emphasized the military difficulties involved in conquering it. It is at this point that Caleb intervened. He silenced the people and said: 'Let us go up and we shall inherit the land. We can do it!'

But the ten spies contradicted him: 'We cannot go up against the people, for they are stronger than we are.'

The discussion appears to have been conducted in purely military terms. Were the Israelites powerful enough to undertake the conquest of the land? Clearly the ten spies had a legitimate argument. The Israelites had only recently been freed from centuries of slavery in Egypt. They probably lacked the necessary military skills. But above all they did not have the self-confidence to take this kind of risk. Certainly this group of leaders of the people lacked the willpower to undertake such an adventure.

As so often in the Hebrew Bible, between this discussion and what follows something seems to have happened that has not been recorded. For in the next sentence we are told, even though no reason is given, that the spies leaked their negative report to the people. Since they were trying to convince the people of their views, the land itself became a problem in their description. Now it is a land that 'devours its inhabitants'. Moreover, all of the inhabitants are now giants and the spies felt themselves to be insignificant in their eyes. It may be that they simply told these stories to their families, when they got home, and that is how the word got round. However, it is more likely that they spread these tales deliberately. Despite their misgivings and warnings, Moses must have said that they were going to go ahead with the conquest. In order to stop Moses, they leaked the negative report, so as to stir up public opinion against him.

The next chapter describes what happened that night. The community leaders met together and shouted and argued about what to do. In contrast, the people in the camp wept the whole night long. In the morning, they all turned against Moses and the talk began about appointing a new leader to take them back to Egypt.

In response, Moses and Aaron fell on their faces before the full assembly of the people. There are various explanations for this action. Perhaps they were praying to God. But the act of falling on their face may have been a formal matter in the language of the Bible. It meant that Moses and Aaron showed that they were willing to accept the authority and decisions of this full assembly of the people. There would be a public debate and referendum to decide what was to happen next, and Moses was signalling that he would accept the will of the people.

It is in this context that we hear a second report about the land. But this time it is Joshua who is mentioned before Caleb, and we must assume that he is taking the lead in the argument. They begin by asserting that the land is very good. But now bring in a different factor. If God favours them, then it is God who will give them the land not their own military power. Their refusal to undertake the conquest is a rebellion against God. The people of the land should not be feared, because their protecting spirits had departed.

But despite all they had experienced of God's power in rescuing them from Egypt and bringing them safely through the Sea of Reeds, the people were unconvinced by these arguments. They even threatened to stone Joshua and Caleb to death. It was only God's intervention that saved the day.

It is noteworthy that throughout the public debate about the report of the spies Moses is silent. Caleb suggests his military option. Joshua relies on God's intervention on their behalf. The spies themselves are torn by doubts and fears. The people experience confusion and anger. But Moses is silent.

All of these are recognizable reactions to a crisis in the life of the nation. The Bible offers its own view of who turned out to be right in the end and who had understood the will of God. Joshua will eventually become Moses' successor as leader of the people. But at the time when such life or death decisions had to be made about what to do, no one could have known which option to take or who to believe. So the biblical record is painfully accurate in describing all the different voices and opinions at such a time, and the difficulty of making a choice. The will of God is not so easy to recognize.

This story of the spies inevitably takes on special dimensions today. The land of Canaan, after 2,000 years, is once again in the hands of the Jewish people. As before, there are other people who live there who are perceived as a threat. There are leaders like Caleb, who would offer a military solution to the problems they pose. There are others who believe that God will fight their battles for them and remove all obstacles. But these apparent certainties of a few people mask the deep uncertainty of the mass of the nation.

Today a new kind of territory has to be entered. This territory is not simply a geographical area but an inner landscape, inhabited by two peoples reluctantly struggling to find a way of living together. There is still a vision, of a fruitful land, flowing with milk and honey, but now it has to be a land shared by both peoples. What stands in the way of that vision are the same elements that the biblical spies encountered. Both peoples who inhabit this inner landscape have a history and experience that make it almost impossible for them to imagine a way of living together in peace. There are fortified cities to be overthrown, places and attitudes where defensiveness and aggression have become ingrained responses to any change. And there are giants to be defeated as well, monstrous images of each other, based on past horrors and rumours that haunt the imagination of both peoples. Such images make it almost impossible to see the humanity and vulnerability of those on the other side. Any report about this new territory brought by spies is likely, once again, to lead to disaster.

So we are left with conflicting opinions about what to do. Political leaders meet in all night sessions and shout and argue with each other. And in their respective encampments both peoples weep in despair and hopelessness.

In the biblical story, as a result of this crisis, the Israelites had to wander for 40 years in the wilderness. They had to wait for another generation, born in freedom, to have the courage and inner security, to take the risk of entering the Promised Land. But today neither side can afford to wait another 40 years. Together they are fated to stand on the border and together endure the bitterness, insecurity and self-destruction of exile. Or else together, without spies, without a Moses, and without any divine guarantee, they have to take the risk and enter this new land together.

28

Rebelling against Moses

Numbers 16–18

This Torah reading tells the dramatic story of the rebellion in the wilderness against the leadership of Moses by Korach and various other Israelites. The reading from the prophets that accompanies it, the Haftarah, is taken from the First Book of Samuel 11 and 12. It tells of the anointing of King Saul and the warning by the prophet Samuel that Israel has to remain obedient to God, even though they now have a king as leader. Israel's covenant with God requires the creation of a society based on justice for everyone. Samuel is concerned that with the appointment of their first king he might abuse his power and undermine the values of the covenant. In both of the passages, a leader of the nation, whether Moses or Samuel, invites a public scrutiny of his activities for any evidence that he has acted in a corrupt way or abused his power.

In the rebellion against Moses, he is accused of failing as a political leader to bring the children of Israel into a land flowing with milk and honey, as he had promised. The Bible records for the first time that Moses loses his temper!

And Moses was greatly angry and said to the Eternal: 'Do not turn to their offering! Not one donkey of theirs did I take, nor did I harm any single one of them.' (Num. 16.15)

Moses was making a public oath before God so as to demonstrate that he had been totally honest in his dealings. But why illustrate his honesty by referring to never having taken a donkey? The rabbis suggested a solution. Moses had used his own donkey, when he travelled from Midian back to Egypt to confront Pharaoh. He was so scrupulous in his behaviour that, even though he was entitled to ask the Israelites to refund him for the food the donkey had eaten on the way and any other legitimate expenses, he refused to ask for payment! He refused to charge mileage.

When Samuel handed over authority to King Saul he also made a declaration before the people that he had never taken advantage of his leadership position for his own private purposes. So this is one of the themes linking the two passages. Samuel says:

> Here I am, testify against me before the Eternal and before his anointed: Whose ox have I taken? Or whose donkey have I taken? Whom have I defrauded? Whom have I oppressed? From whose hand have I taken a bribe to blind my eyes with it, so that I may restore it to you? (1 Sam. 12.3)

The people confirm that Samuel is indeed guiltless of any such crimes. When Samuel asserts that he has always acted with integrity, he is also giving another hint to the people about the risks of appointing a king. He had already warned them that a king would confiscate their land and give it to his friends. He would also take their young men and women, and even take their donkeys to work for him (1 Sam. 8.16). Samuel is stepping down, but he is demonstrating to the people and, indeed, to his successor King Saul, that a true leader in Israel must act within the law and behave with integrity.

Both of our passages show that leaders must be publicly accountable, and that their activities, in particular their financial transactions, must be utterly transparent and open to inspection.

Moses only referred to one specific wrongdoing, taking a donkey, whereas Samuel speaks of five separate situations that a leader might exploit for his own advantage. For Moses leading the Israelites through the wilderness, the opportunities for abusing his power were relatively few so one example was enough. For Samuel, living among a settled community on the verge of becoming a nation, the temptations of office were far greater. How might we understand Samuel's list today?

An ox in biblical times was an expensive animal to own, so to steal someone's ox would have been a serious crime. But the rabbis understood the verse in another way. They pointed out that Samuel used to offer sacrifices of oxen to God and use the occasion to plead to God to show mercy on the people. So the rabbis suggested that whenever Samuel made such a sacrifice he did so using one of his own oxen and never asked the people to pay for it. That suggests that a leader should not be motivated primarily by the desire for personal gain, whether that meant financial reward or greater prestige, but should put the needs of the people he leads first. Leadership in this sense is a kind of personal sacrifice for the good of others.

The rabbis thought that Samuel, like Moses, used his own donkey, when he travelled round the country on behalf of the people and never received payment, even though he was entitled to it. So this example would relate to all the perks of office that become available to political leaders. Using government transport for private travel, or making expense account purchases for what are really personal items, or hiring family or friends for special tasks, all such things are an abuse of the privileges of office. Samuel insists that his record in this area should also be properly examined.

The rabbis understood the third wrongdoing that Samuel mentions to mean 'defrauding' people. They meant when people take unfair advantage of a trust that has been given to them. A modern illustration would be the promises that politicians make before an election which they do not always fulfil once they are in power. Government is always more complicated than it might seem to those outside, so it is understandable, if election promises have to be adjusted and compromises made. But promises that are given cynically just for the sake of being elected, with no intention of honouring them, are a breach of trust. Moreover, they bring the whole process of politics and government into disrepute. The rabbis call that kind of unacceptable behaviour, 'stealing the heart'.

Samuel's fourth question 'Whom have I oppressed?' is potentially even more serious. Leadership is often a delicate attempt to balance the needs and interests of a wide variety of groups within society. As one rabbi expressed it:

Pray for the welfare of the government, for but for the fear it inspires, we would swallow each other alive! (Sayings of the Fathers 3.2)

But the temptation to any leader is to favour those who are most likely to re-elect him or her, to the neglect of others. In its mildest, form this can lead to unfair treatment and discrimination. At its worst, it can mean the deliberate isolation and even persecution of a particular minority. All too often, leaders have stirred up the emotions of one sector of a society against another so as to further their own political ends or simply hold onto power. Samuel warns us that we must be aware of the particular biases or even prejudices of those we elect to positions of authority and put in place the mechanisms which can monitor and correct any abuse of power.

The last element Samuel mentions, bribery, the selling of favours by those in power, is the most subversive and corrosive of crimes. For bribery destroys the judgement, and ultimately the reputation, of the one who accepts it, and corrupts the integrity of the one who gives it. Bribery undermines the basis of trust in the rule of law without which society cannot hold together.

If Moses and Samuel, among the greatest leaders of the biblical period, felt the need to place their record before the public for scrutiny, how much more so should anyone entrusted with a leadership role. No one is above the temptations of power. It is our responsibility to ensure that safeguards are in place to prevent the kinds of abuse by leaders that Samuel describes and to encourage honest behaviour, for the sake of those in power as much as for ourselves. Unless we do so, we should not be surprised if our leaders fail us. For ultimately we have failed them.

29

The Loss of Miriam

Numbers 20

This reading includes Numbers 20, which records two deaths. At the beginning comes the brief announcement of the death of Miriam, the sister of Moses. She has featured in a number of dramatic episodes in the Hebrew Bible. When Moses was born, and it was no longer possible to conceal him from the Egyptians, his mother placed him in a basket on the Nile. Miriam, his sister, followed its course until eventually it was found by Pharaoh's daughter. Miriam's initiative enabled Moses' true mother to wet-nurse him and watch over his earliest years.

Miriam next appears leading the women in song and dance after the Israelites have successfully crossed the Sea of Reeds. Here she is called a prophetess (Exod. 15.20), though nothing more is said about this title. In a later episode (Num. 12), she and Moses' brother Aaron complain about Moses' leadership. Surely God has also spoken to them as well! As a punishment, Miriam is struck with a disease that makes here skin turn white. Moses prays to God on her behalf and she is cured. Now, in our chapter, without warning, we are told simply that she died.

At the end of the same chapter, we learn about the death of Aaron, Moses' brother. He has been a more prominent figure than Miriam, the first High Priest and the founder of a dynasty of priests. At the court of Pharaoh, he was Moses' spokesman. He shares some of the responsibilities of leadership, but seems to have been a less decisive figure than his brother. When Moses was delayed by God on Mount Sinai and the people feared that he would not return, it was Aaron who created the golden calf to give them a tangible god to worship. At a later time, in a tragic moment, Aaron witnessed the death of two of his sons, struck down by a fire from heaven when they tried to come into the presence of God in the wrong way. Now when he dies, there is public mourning for 30 days, a sign of his importance and popularity.

The rabbis said that three good leaders arose for Israel: Moses, Aaron and Miriam. And three great gifts were given through them: the well of water, the cloud and the manna (Babylonian Talmud Ta'anit 9a). The cloud led them through the wilderness and the manna was their food. But the first thing listed, the well of water, is related by the rabbis specifically to Miriam. Our chapter simply records that she died and was buried. But the sentence that follows starts a new subject entirely. It tells us that there was no water and the people held a public protest against Moses and Aaron.

One of the methods used by the rabbis when they interpreted the Bible was to try to understand why two seemingly unrelated passages are placed next to one another. In this case, they tried to understand the connection between the death of Miriam and the absence of water. This led to the idea that during her lifetime a well of water accompanied the Israelites on their journeys through the wilderness, appearing every time that they encamped. So when she died, the well disappeared.

Our chapter contains one other major dramatic event. When faced with this latest protest of the people about the lack of water, Moses turns to God for support. He is told to take his staff, with which he has previously worked miracles. He is then to speak to a prominent rock in the wilderness, and God promises that water will flow from it. Moses takes his staff, but instead of simply speaking to the rock, he vents his anger and frustration on the people. 'Listen, you rebels,' he says, 'shall we bring water out of this rock?!' Then he strikes the rock with his staff just, as he had done once before (Exod. 17.6). As promised by God, abundant water flows from it. But God is angry at his behaviour. As a result, both Moses and Aaron, like the whole of that generation, are condemned to die in the wilderness and not enter the Promised Land.

A great deal has been written about the severity of this judgement on Moses by God. Also many theories exist as to exactly what it was that Moses had done wrong. But since we are discussing the sequence of events in this chapter, perhaps there is another question to be asked. Why is it that despite all his leadership experience and all the crises Moses had successfully faced in the past, he made such an elementary mistake this time? Why not just speak to the rock as he was told? And why lose his temper with the people? Could it also have something to do with the death of Miriam?

Of the three leaders, Aaron dealt with ritual matters and the cult. Moses spoke directly with God and defined the general purpose and direction of the journey of the Israelites to the Promised Land. However, someone else had to deal with the practical day-to-day issues raised by the people. Perhaps that was the particular role played by Miriam. After all, she had shown her practical skills when she saved Moses. That she and Aaron shared some kinds of responsibility is clear from the time when they complained about Moses' leadership. Why was he the prominent one, when they were also special? This typical argument among siblings becomes much more serious when the brothers and sisters are also the leaders of the nation.

In our chapter, people complain about the absence of water, as they have done in the past. Perhaps until now, Miriam had been the person who dealt with these day-to-day concerns of the people. She was the one who encouraged them, offered practical solutions for their problems, or simply acknowledged the legitimacy of their fears and concerns. She was the one of the three leaders to whom the people could turn, the one who listened to them. She in turn would be the intermediary, who would bring these issues to the attention of Moses. But in doing, so she could present them in such a way that Moses did not feel personally attacked and could understand what was needed. He could then deal with the problem with the right degree of detachment and effectiveness. Without Miriam, Moses was now directly confronted with the anger and fear of the people, and his judgement was affected. Without her calming presence as a buffer, he felt threatened and over-reacted.

Is there any evidence for this suggestion? Possibly in the title 'prophet' that Miriam has been given. One task of the prophets was to be intermediaries, standing between the people and God. To the people they convey God's will, often criticizing their behaviour, but also consoling them in times of trouble. The great prophets, like Moses himself and Jeremiah, stood before God and tried to represent the needs and weakness of the people. They pleaded for mercy on their behalf. Miriam may have played such a role in the life of Moses. She helped him cope with the challenges and demands of leadership by protecting him from the direct attack of the people. With her death, a key figure in the governance of the people was lost. And an essential support for Moses was taken away. At the first new challenge to his leadership, Moses, without Miriam, failed. The well of water that had sustained him for so long was no more.

30

Listen to your Donkey

Numbers 22

If we first learn about the Bible as children, we often do so using books especially designed to entertain us. The stories we read are simplified, and they are picked for their obvious appeal. They are often beautifully illustrated so that certain pictures become imprinted on our minds: little David defeats the giant Goliath with his slingshot; Noah supervises the pairs of animals entering the ark.

Bible stories become part of our lives in much the same way as fairy stories or the legends of ancient Greece and Rome.

For children, a heroic animal and a really villainous bad man are especially appealing. This Torah reading, from the Book of Numbers, has both: a faithful donkey and a wicked sorcerer called Balaam. Our children's picture would show us Balaam on his way to curse the people of Israel. He is snarling in anger and holds a big stick in his hand, raised as if to strike his donkey. But he cannot see that there is an angel with a drawn sword standing in the way, even though it has golden wings and shimmers with light. So Balaam seems extremely stupid and cruel, completely unaware of what is going on around him. But the donkey on which he is riding is clearly the real hero of the story and of the picture. Loyal to his master the faithful animal has stopped in its tracks to protect him when it sees the angel ahead.

Such a children's picture suggests that animals have not only a language of their own, but are also perfectly capable of human speech. Most of the time, they just let human beings get on with

their lives, however silly they may seem to a wise animal. But sometimes even human beings need to be warned, and that is when an
animal is forced to break its customary silence and speak. That, at
least, is how we might understand the story of Balaam's donkey, if
we only read about it as children and only have that picture in our
memory.

But what if we read the biblical story itself as adults? Clearly, we
have to cope with our own scepticism about talking animals. If we
are told we have to take everything in the Bible as being literally
true, then we may find ourselves in trouble at this point. Neither
talking animals nor golden-winged angels are part of our normal
everyday experience today. In the Middle Ages, Moses Maimonides, the great Jewish philosopher, faced the same problem. As a
rationalist, he solved the difficulty by assuming that everything
that happened to Balaam occurred in a prophetic vision. If the
donkey actually talked, it only did so in Balaam's imagination. But
is that really what the Bible intended?

If we look more carefully at the way the story develops, we find
an even more serious difficulty. There is a major internal contradiction within it about the way that God behaves towards Balaam.

King Balak of Moab is worried about the dangers posed by the
arrival of the Israelites in his territory. So he sends a delegation
to Balaam, famed as a sorcerer who has the power of the word.
Whoever Balaam blesses is blessed, and whoever he curses is truly
cursed. Balak asks him to curse the Israelites and destroy them.
Balaam seems perfectly willing to do so, but needs to consult first
with God. But God tells him in no uncertain terms: 'Don't go
with these people, and don't curse Israel, for they are blessed.'
(Num. 22.12). Balaam is now in trouble. His reputation as a reliable professional sorcerer is at stake. So when he speaks to Balak's
envoys, he quotes only the first part of God's words and simply
says: 'God does not give me permission to go with you!' (v. 13).

The envoys return to King Balak. Having failed in a royal mission,
they have to protect themselves and so they too are careful about

what they tell the king. So they give a slightly different version of Balaam's answer. They say nothing about God but simply explain: 'Balaam refused to come with us!' (v. 14). King Balak is obviously a practical man and rather cynical about business affairs. This is surely only a negotiating ploy by Balaam to get a better deal! So he sends a second delegation, more honourable than the first, and with a better offer.

This must have been Balaam's worst nightmare. He is caught between an important commission from a major client and a God who is spoiling his chances. So he tells the envoys he will consult with God again, even though he knows, as he will later say, that God is not someone who changes his mind. But when he speaks to God again that night, God says: 'If the men have come to fetch you, get up and go with them, but only say the words that I tell you!' (v. 20). It is an astonishing change of mind by God, but Balaam takes the opportunity, and off he goes with the delegation on his trusty donkey. At which point, God gets angry and sends the angel with the sword. When the donkey sees it and turns aside, Balaam strikes it. The second time it does so, Balaam bangs his leg against the wall and strikes again. The third time the donkey has nowhere to go, stops and speaks.

How do we explain the fact that God, who 'never changes his mind', seems to change it twice in this story: telling Balaam not to go, then letting him go, then trying to kill him because he has gone?! A possible answer was given by Martin Buber and Franz Rosenzweig, when they were working on their monumental German translation of the Hebrew Bible. They discovered that in biblical stories, certain significant words tended to be repeated. This pointed to a theme under the surface of the story, linked by these words, which helped explain what was really happening. They noticed one such word in the Balaam story, the Hebrew word '*yosef*', meaning 'to add' or 'to do something again'. It first appears when the second delegation visits Balaam and he says he will 'again' ask God's opinion. From then on the word 'again' reappears as the angel 'again' and 'again' moves to intercept Balaam, and Balaam 'again' strikes his donkey.

For Buber and Rosenzweig, this repetition suggests that from the moment Balaam went 'again' to God, even though he knew God would not change his mind, he lost touch with reality. His desire to work for King Balak and to curse Israel led him to convince himself that he had God's permission. Since the Bible almost never describes things in a psychological way, but only refers to outer events, this is the nearest it comes to depicting an inner state of mind.

Whether we understand the story literally or as a vision, Balaam's story raises an interesting question. How do we know when our journey is going wrong, when our desires or ambitions have led us on a path that might prove to be self-destructive? Balaam should have seen the signs, when the donkey he trusted all his life started behaving in an unusual way. Even more so, from the moment he began to hit it, he should have noticed that his own behaviour was wrong. Finally, when he damaged his leg, he should have realized how self-destructive his journey was becoming. These were the warning signs of a collision up ahead.

Sadly, it is often only when it is too late, when we have already hurt other people or damaged ourselves or crashed into the angel with the sword, that our eyes are opened and we see what it is we have been doing. So whether Balaam's donkey belongs to a prophetic vision, or is our own subconscious warning us, or is even an actual talking donkey, we need to pay attention to its voice.

31

Coping with Fanatics

Numbers 25.10—30.1

This reading from the Torah is named after someone who is mentioned in the opening verses, Pinchas son of Eliezer son of Aaron. He is singled out for special attention because of an event described at the end of the previous chapter.

The Israelites had settled in a place called Shittim on their journey towards the land of Canaan. There the Israelite men were seduced by the local women and began to worship their god, Baal Peor. In anger, God commanded Moses to hang all the tribal leaders. Presumably, this is meant to emphasize their responsibility for the behaviour of the people. But the next verse informs us that Moses commands the judges to condemn to death those who had linked themselves to Baal Peor. It is not clear whether this was as well as hanging the leaders of the tribes or instead of doing so. Was Moses being more zealous than God, or instead was he insisting on the rule of law? Even God could not behave in this arbitrary way. People were responsible for their actions under the covenant, and only the guilty should be punished.

In defiance of Moses, one man, later named as Zimri son of Salu, a prince of the tribe of Simeon, publicly took to his bed one of the Midianite women. This symbolic act would have created a permanent link between the two peoples and their gods. Moses and the leaders of the people stood by helpless. Perhaps this is already a sign that Moses' days as leader are coming to an end. He is unable to take decisive action in this crisis.

When there is a power vacuum, other forces, often more violent, break through. In this case, it is Pinchas, the priest who acted. He took a spear and ran the couple through as they lay together. This action stopped a plague from God that had broken out. At the beginning of the reading God says that by his passion for God, Pinchas has removed God's anger. Moreover, because of his concern for God's honour, he is to be rewarded. He and his descendants will be priests forever. In addition God makes with Pinchas a *brit shalom*, a 'covenant of peace'.

There are any number of problems with this story. From the point of view of the Bible, it seems that Pinchas' action is justified. The couple who were killed were deliberately and publicly denying the authority of Israel's God. This was something that the new Israelite society in the making could not tolerate. The helplessness of Moses and the leadership is clearly disastrous when so much is at stake. But Pinchas' action of murdering the couple in public is just as problematic. He is portrayed as a fanatic, acting alone. But if such behaviour is shown to be acceptable to God, it opens the door to other such violent actions in the future. To murder people in the name of God is an ever-recurring event in the history of religions, down to our own day. Such a text gives biblical justification for it.

Is there any other way to understand what is happening? One recent explanation brings an ironic twist to the story. It recognizes that fanatics are always likely to appear and some strategy needs to be devised to control them. God's answer is to put Pinchas as a priest in charge of the sacrificial cult for all eternity. His fanaticism is to be dedicated to all the details of animal sacrifice. He must oversee the inspection of every single animal that was slaughtered, looking for faults or physical blemishes that would mean it could not be used. He would have to ensure that the slaughter was done properly, the appropriate parts of the animal were offered, or discarded. Then he would have to be certain that all the accompanying rituals were performed with meticulous care and attention to every detail. How better channel such energy and zeal into a relatively harmless activity. Someone with exactly the right qualities would now be in charge of the cult. God's anger need never again break out because of mistakes made during sacrifices. For Pinchas it must have seemed like a divine gift for himself and his descendants. Others may have been relieved that he was effectively prevented from mixing in more sensitive matters.

Yet perhaps there is another dimension to this story. God makes with Pinchas a 'covenant of peace'. It is not at all clear what this means, but perhaps he has been given a special responsibility for the creation and maintenance of peace. All his energy, his passion, his fanaticism, should be turned away from violence, and instead be directed to the quest for peace and harmony.

Nice though such explanations may be, the core problem of Pinchas' action remains, with its potential for justifying such violent behaviour in the future. But it is not only our modern sensitivities that see a problem here. The rabbinic tradition was also concerned about the behaviour of Pinchas, and we can see this directly in two ways. Since the story of Pinchas is part of Holy Scripture, the rabbis could not simply remove it from the Bible. But they could indicate how it should be read. First, as we have already noted, they split the story into two parts. The tale of Pinchas' actions is told in the first nine verses of Chapter 25 of the Book of Numbers. But the rabbis ensured that the section we read begins with verse 10 of that chapter. The emphasis in this section that bears his name is not on what Pinchas' actually did but on God's response. So we simply read that God makes with him a 'covenant of peace' and that Pinchas and his family are to be priests forever. We are encouraged to focus on the positive aspects and not on the violence.

Of equal significance is the choice of the Haftarah, the prophetic reading. The rabbis chose Chapter 19 of the First Book of Kings, which tells of a crisis in the life of the prophet Elijah. The rabbis often identified Pinchas with Elijah, as both were passionate in their service of God and both likely to take sudden dramatic actions and use violence in the name of God. But in this chapter, when Elijah complains that he alone is zealous for God, God tells him to stand upon a mountain. A great wind comes, one that can break mountains and shatter rocks, but God was not in the wind. Then came an earthquake, but God was not in the earthquake. Then came a fire, but God was not in the fire. But after the fire came 'a still small voice'. God was not to be identified with these violent elements, but with the quiet, questioning voice.

The passage in the Book of Kings criticizes Elijah for thinking that he alone is passionate for God, and that he alone knows how to act. The violence of the wind, earthquake and fire are not what God wishes to see acted out by human beings. In this way, the rabbis challenge the story of Pinchas, not by removing it, but by giving it a critical interpretation.

But what about the previous section that ends with Pinchas' actions? Here too the rabbis chose a Haftarah that would force us to question what Pinchas did. It is a text from the prophet Micah, Chapter 6, which ends with the words: 'It has been told to you, O man, and what God wants from you, only to do justice, to love mercy and walk humbly with your God.'

32

Letting Go of Power

Numbers 25.10—30.1

The major part of this Torah reading is taken up by two long descriptions. At the beginning is a census of the new generation of Israelites taken in the wilderness at the end of the 40 years of wandering. At the end of our section is an equally long description of the sacrifices to be given at each of the annual festivals. Yet sandwiched between them is a powerful narrative about the approaching end of Moses' leadership. At a moment of crisis in the encampment, Moses and the elders seemed incapable of acting and stood weeping before the Tent of Meeting. Instead a zealous priest called Pinchas intervened, killed the offending people and his action seems to have averted the crisis.

But something is clearly wrong for Moses to have had so little control over events. So it is no surprise that within this section God reminds Moses that though he can see the land promised to his people, he will not live to enter it. Either because of his own recent weakness as a leader or his awareness of his approaching death, Moses realizes that it is time to hand over leadership to someone else. He prays to God for help.

Let the Eternal, the God of the spirits of all flesh, appoint a man over the congregation, who shall go out before them and come in before them, who shall lead them out and bring them in; so that the community of the Eternal may not be as sheep which have no shepherd. (Num. 27.16–17)

In response, God instructs Moses to appoint Joshua bin Nun as his successor in a public ceremony.

In Moses' prayer to God are a number of interesting phrases. He appeals to God as 'the God of the spirits of all flesh'. This is a phrase that Moses has used only once before but in very different circumstances. During the most serious rebellion against Moses' leadership, led by his cousin Korach, God has threatened to destroy the entire community. Moses and Aaron pray to God with the same words:

> O God, the God of the spirits of all flesh, shall one man sin, and will You be angry with all the community? (Num. 16.22)

God accepts Moses' words and allows the people to stand back from Korach and his rebels so that the people are not destroyed with them. In both these situations, Moses appeals to God's unique knowledge of each individual person, though with a different emphasis in each situation. In the case of the rebellion, God is asked to act against one person alone and not harm the rest of the community. It is a powerful plea for recognizing individual responsibility. In the passage, Moses asks God to find the one person who has the inner qualities to take on the leadership at this crucial stage in the life of the people. Only 'the God of the spirits of all flesh' can see into the heart of each individual and make such a choice. Whoever succeeds Moses, whatever his qualities, will not be Moses, and only God can judge what he will need to bring to this task.

When nominating Joshua as the person, God speaks of him as 'a man who has the spirit in him'. This leads the rabbis to suggest that a true leader is also someone who is able to understand the individual needs of all the very different kinds of people that he has to lead.

But our passage also describes what the task of this leader is to be: he is to 'go out before the people and come in before them'. Most commentators assume that this phrase is a military one. A good military leader will lead his troops from the front and not simply sit comfortably at the rear and watch his men do the fighting. For most of his life King David was just such a leader. It was only when he stayed at home and did not join his troops that he got into trouble, taking the married women Bathsheba to his bed! But there are other passages in the Bible that distinguish between the purely military role of the leader and the broader tasks he has to undertake, as judge and in public affairs (compare 1 Kings 3.7, 9 and Josh. 14.11).

A politician who was active in Jewish affairs once said: 'The role of the leader is to lead the Jewish people from the front – in the direction in which *they* wish to go.' He meant this as a positive quality but sometimes a leader has to take his or her people in the direction in which they *need* to go, whether they wish it or not! But perhaps that simply reflects two different types of leader – the one who works by consensus, compromise and agreement, and the one who is prepared to risk exploring new directions and bring others along afterwards. But the second part of the phrase, 'to come in before them', is a reminder that no leader will be effective if he goes so far in front of his people that he leaves them behind and cannot find his way back! Ultimately, leadership does mean bringing people along to follow a particular direction or vision, however difficult it may be. It is no easy task that Moses bequeaths to his successor.

As well as going out before the people, Moses asks that this new leader should 'lead the people out and lead them in'. One rabbinic explanation picks up on the image of the leader as a shepherd with responsibility to ensure the safety of his flock. They said, let him not be like a military commander who leads his soldiers out to war in their thousands, but brings the survivors back only in their hundreds!

Was Moses happy with the choice of Joshua? Possibly, but like so many leaders Moses found it hard to let go of his role, despite knowing how essential it was to do so. There are many rabbinic stories about Moses' unwillingness to die and how he struggled against it.

In one of them, he asks God a favour, to let Joshua take his place but to allow Moses to carry on living and become Joshua's disciple, just as Joshua had been Moses' disciple. God agrees, and Moses went to listen while Joshua taught the Torah to the people. When the people saw Moses standing there, they said to him: 'Moses, our teacher, teach us Torah.' He replied: 'I no longer have the authority.' They said: 'We will not leave you.' But a voice came from heaven saying: 'Be willing to learn from Joshua', and the people agreed and sat at the feet of Joshua. At that moment the tradition of wisdom was taken from Moses and given to Joshua. When the people left, Moses walked with Joshua to the Tent of Meeting where Moses used to hear the word of God. But when they entered, a pillar of cloud came down and made a partition between them. Afterwards, Moses asked Joshua what God had said to him, and Joshua answered: 'When God used to reveal the word to you, did I know what was said to you?' That was too much for Moses and he cried out in anguish: 'I'd rather die a hundred times than put up with this awful feeling of envy! Master of the universe, until now I wanted to stay alive – but now I surrender my soul to you' (based on *The Book of Legends*, Sefer Ha-Aggadah).[1]

That suggests yet another explanation of the phrase we have been considering. A true leader knows when to accept his leadership role and 'go out before the people', but also knows when it is time to relinquish the task and to come back in.

The beginning of this reading tells of the census that was to determine the size of the tribes of this new generation, born in freedom during 40 years wandering in the wilderness. The end of it looks towards the sacrifices that will one day be made in the land once they have entered it. Both of them look towards the future, and Moses has to recognize that it will be a future without him. There is great dignity in the way he accepts this new reality. God commands him to take Joshua and lay his hand upon him and make him stand before Elazar the priest and the entire community and commission him in their sight. The Bible records:

And Moses did as the Eternal commanded him; he took Joshua and made him stand before Elazar the priest and the entire community and he laid his hands upon him and commissioned him as the Eternal spoke through Moses. (Num. 27.22–23)

But there was one slight change in the way Moses carried out God's instructions. Perhaps out of respect for Moses' feelings God told him to lay only one of his hands on Joshua's head, as if to say that only part of Moses' authority was to be passed over to his successor. But Moses realized the need both to hand over power and to give Joshua his complete support in the difficult task ahead. Instead of laying one hand on him as God had commanded, Moses laid both hands on the head of the one who was soon to take his place.

33

The Daughters of Zelophehad

Numbers 30–36

At the end of this reading from the Torah, we complete the Book of Numbers. We also complete a sequence of biblical books that explore the journeys of the Children of Israel. In the Book of Exodus, they escape from Egypt and journey to Mount Sinai for their meeting with God. In Numbers, they journey from Sinai on their 40 years of wandering through the wilderness on their way to the Promised Land. Between these two books about journeying, stands Leviticus which focuses on the religious centre of the community, the sanctuary. It explores what it means that this people is to become a holy nation. It is the still centre around which unfold the social and political dramas of the formation of a distinctive people.

At the end of the Book of Numbers, we are poised to enter the Promised Land. So how does the Book end? What is the final message we must contemplate before the new phase begins?

At first glance, it is a rather disappointing message. It is a ruling about a legal problem. It poses a question that has arisen before in the same Book and which seemed at the time to have been satisfactorily resolved. According to the laws of the Ancient Near East, when a man died, his property was inherited by his oldest son. But what if the man had no sons, or indeed, only daughters? This was the question posed to Moses in Chapter 27 by the daughters of a man called Zelophehad. So important and so well argued is their question that the five women are named: Machlah, Noah, Hoglah, Milkah and Tirzah. Not only are they named in full here, but in three other places in the Bible as well, an exceptional mark of respect.

They point out to Moses that their father died during the 40 years in the wilderness. Because of this, his name was not included when the land was divided up according to the various families of his tribe. Moreover, he had not joined the rebellion against Moses led by Korach, so there should be no impediment to his receiving his portion. The problem was that he had no son to inherit, but only daughters, so his name and his portion of land had been left out. Why could the daughters not inherit the land instead and so preserve the name of their father? Moses had to consult God before he could bring an answer – a positive one in their favour. These five daughters were right to argue as they did. They could inherit the portion of land that would have gone to their father had he lived. Moses then makes a general law out of this particular instance, granting daughters the right to inherit in the absence of a son.

Given the male-dominated nature of the cultural background to the Bible, this is a major contribution to women's rights and the five daughters are rightly honoured.

But in Chapter 36, the last in the Book, someone spots a snag! If the daughters marry men from another tribe, the inheritance of land would be passed on to a son who would belong to that other tribe. This is the problem raised by members of Zelophehad's tribe who could see some of their tribal land being lost because of this. This time, Moses does not even have to consult with God, but himself comes up with a solution. The daughters of Zelophehad can indeed marry the person of their choice, but they have to choose someone from within their own tribe. It is an elegant solution, though it could all fall apart if the daughters were not prepared to abide by it. Fortunately, all five of them do. They marry within their own tribe, and their father's portion of the land, and his name, are preserved.

We may not be so comfortable today with Moses' solution. And the daughters of Zelophehad, if they lived today, might also find it problematic. In the biblical period and until quite recently in the West, people felt themselves bound by their responsibility to their family or community. If there was a conflict between someone's individual desires and his or her duty to the community, duty would come first whatever the price in personal happiness. But that has changed today, and the balance is overwhelmingly on the side of personal choice, certainly in matters like whom you marry. Yet, life throws up any number of situations where communities have to make decisions about some aspect of their nature and not all members may find themselves in agreement. The Jewish community is almost proud of the number of issues on which we have disagreed in the past and continue to disagree today! So it is very encouraging to read in the Bible of at least one potentially divisive problem that was solved.

When we complete the reading of a biblical book in synagogue, the community calls out in Hebrew: 'Chazak chazak v'nitchazek.' It means: 'Be strong! Be strong! And let us strengthen one another!' This call has a special meaning at the end of this Book. Life in community is always a delicate balance between individual interests and the needs of the community as a whole. For the community to survive, all parties have to accept a certain limitation on their wishes and come to some sort of compromise. In the heat of the argument, this can be very difficult and people may take extreme positions. We have seen throughout the Book of Numbers examples of this kind of extremism which leads to conflict and destructiveness. So it is encouraging to find at the very end of the Book a serious dispute that is resolved by a legal process and a compromise that works for all parties. However, in order to make a compromise we need an inner strength and security that allows us to yield our position just enough for a solution to be found. And there are any number of internal Jewish conflicts today, where just this kind of courage is needed.

That is one way to understand the strength we ask for each other at the end of our Torah reading, 'chazak chazak'. We wish each side of any dispute the inner strength to find an acceptable middle ground or compromise. For only then can we say, 'v'nitchazek', we are all of us strengthened!

34

New Rituals for Women

Deuteronomy 7.12—11.25

I attended recently an interfaith conference and met again a woman pastor, someone I have known for many years. We had a few minutes free from the busy conference programme, and she said that she wanted to tell me something.

She reminded me of a conversation we had had a couple of years before. At that time, she was recovering from a recent miscarriage, late in her pregnancy. It was particularly disappointing, as she and her husband had been trying for a long time to have a child. She had still been recovering from the shock and the sense of loss, when we had talked. At the time, I had asked her a question based on my experience in Britain. There are now a growing number of women rabbis, graduates of the Leo Baeck College, who have raised our awareness about many issues that particularly affect women. Sometimes, women members of their congregations bring to them problems that they would never have brought to a man, problems that have not been properly addressed in Jewish tradition. When talking to the pastor about her situation, I remembered one such problem. So the question I asked was: had she found any kind of religious ritual or worship service to help her come to terms with the loss of the unborn child?

It is a question I might never have asked, or even dared to ask, had it not been something discussed by my women colleagues. They have encouraged all of us, men and women alike, to broaden our awareness of, and sensitivity to, such important events in our personal lives. I had learnt from them that in this particular situation, Jewish tradition was not very helpful.

Jewish law has a very detailed system of mourning after the death of someone in our family. For the first seven days after the funeral, the mourner remains at home, is visited by family and friends, who take care of all practical needs, and special prayers are recited daily. The second period extends to 30 days, during which the mourner is gradually brought back into daily life. For the next eleven months, the mourner recites daily a special prayer, the *Kaddish*. After that period, the formal mourning time is ended, but the *Kaddish* continues to be recited on the anniversary of the death. This is a complex but powerful process in which the loss suffered by the mourner is recognized by the community, support is offered and the transition is gradually made back to normal life. But the end of that first year, when the daily recital of the *Kaddish* comes to an end is also very important. It provides a formal closure to that first intense period. It helps the mourner make the adjustment to the tasks and responsibilities of a life that now has to be lived without the one who has died. The process, when it works, shows a deep respect both for the one who has died and for those who survive and must carry on with their life.

But there is one exception to this practice. According to Jewish tradition, when a child dies within 30 days of its birth, there is no formal period of mourning or any of the rituals that accompany death. Presumably, this ruling arose in a world where child mortality was high. The underlying philosophy would seem to be that it was best to forget as soon as possible what had happened, to carry on with life and try again to become pregnant. Fertility and a large number of children were seen in the time of the Bible and the later rabbinic tradition as evidence of God's blessing.

However, it must be pointed out that this approach, that ignores the need to mourn, comes out of a tradition largely created by men. However well intentioned they may have been, theirs was not the experience of pregnancy, of feeling the child grow and move within them. Men and women led very separate lives in the past, especially in such intimate areas. If the baby miscarried, was still-born or died shortly after birth, the rabbis might simply not have understood the depth of the suffering involved. For many women, such a loss could not simply be forgotten. It could affect her as much as the loss of any older child or adult who was an intimate part of her life. As I learnt from my women rabbi colleagues, this loss also needs to be acknowledged, both personally and publicly, and the emotional impact worked through.

Out of an awareness of this lack of support in Jewish tradition, women rabbis have begun to devise religious rituals to enable women to come to terms with their experience of loss and begin the process of mourning that was so essential. When one of my women colleagues in Britain advertised for the first time that her synagogue was going to hold a religious service for women who had suffered such a loss, she was surprised by the number of women who came to participate. Some of them had experienced a miscarriage or the loss of a newborn baby many years previously. For them, the absence of a formal process of mourning within the tradition at the time when they needed it made them feel particularly unsupported and iso-lated. Since no one seemed able to understand what that loss meant for them, they still carried the burden of their pain and anger and other unresolved feelings years later.

Apparently I had mentioned all of this to the pastor after she had told me about her miscarriage. That was when I asked her the ques-tion about what religious support and comfort she had received. Now that we had met again, she told me that my words had been very important to her. Not only had she taken my suggestion seri-ously for herself, but she had organized a religious service for women in her parish who had also suffered the experience of losing a child before or immediately after birth. She had worked with another woman pastor and two therapists as advisers in preparing an appro-priate form of service. They soon learnt that all four of them had themselves experienced miscarriages at some time in their married life and had similar feelings about the lack of acknowledgement of what that loss had meant to them. During this preparatory work, they discovered that miscarriages were very common. But women were often unaware of this fact and felt isolated in their situation, because they thought that their feelings and suffering were unique. Those preparing the service realized how important it had been for them to have shared their experience and decided to include such an opportunity within the service itself.

Just as it had been for the woman rabbi, but this time in a Christian community, the invitation to such a service produced a large response. The women who took part found it to be very important, and some of them continued to meet regularly afterwards.

I was very moved by what she told me. It is always nice when some help one has offered bears fruit. But it was also a classical example of mutual support across religious boundaries. In this case, the work of women rabbis had found an echo with a Christian pastor, because certain shared problems led to similar responses. This is also a good example of how a modern religious initiative can fill a gap in traditional religious life.

This brings me finally to the Torah reading, which addresses this issue but in a very problematic way. The passage from Deuteronomy speaks of God's promise. If the Israelites obey God's laws, God would love, bless and multiply them. In particular God would 'bless the fruit of your body' (Deut. 7.13). Later, the text reinforces this idea with the claim that no woman among the Israelites would be barren (Deut. 7.14).

Such verses must be deeply troubling for women in this situation. They suggest that things like fertility depend on good behaviour, and so a miscarriage would have to be seen as a punishment from God for something they had done wrong. Such situations need a very different kind of religious message, one that supports people in their loss and gives them the strength to carry on with their lives. Sometimes we have to look hard to find the blessing hidden in a passage from the Hebrew Bible. And sometimes we have to turn the biblical text inside out and create a very different kind of blessing for ourselves despite what has happened. That is when we need the support we can give each other. That is when we need the kind of worship service where we are free to give our pain, and sorrow and our anger back into the hands of God.

35

Cause and Effect

Deuteronomy 7.12—11.25

Towards the end of this Torah reading (Deut. 11.13–21) comes a passage that is very familiar to anyone who prays in a Jewish service on a regular basis. It is known in the Jewish liturgy as the 'second paragraph of the *Shema*' and is usually read silently by the community. The '*Shema*' is the affirmation of the unity of God, 'Hear, O Israel, the Eternal our God, the Eternal is One', which is found in Deuteronomy 6.4, and, together with the following biblical verses, plays an essential role in Jewish liturgy and life.

The reason why Deuteronomy 11.13–21 is included in the service is because of some of the words that it contains which are identical with those in the *Shema* itself. Both passages say that we should talk about the teachings of God, 'when you lie down and when you rise up'. This is understood to mean that we should recite in the morning and evening services the *Shema* itself.

But this particular paragraph has another dimension as well. Jewish tradition teaches us that when we recite the first paragraph of the *Shema*, we take upon ourselves the '*ol malkhut shamayim*', the 'yoke of the kingdom of heaven'. That is to say, we accept that our lives are given over to the service of God. By reciting the second paragraph, we are said to submit ourselves to the '*ol ha-mitzvot*', the 'yoke of the commandments', we accept the commandments of God as binding upon ourselves.

Nevertheless, there are problems with the paragraph itself. It says, in effect, if you obey my commandments, I will bring the rain to the land, and everything will go well. But if you do not obey, then I will withhold the rain, the land will not give up its produce, and you will perish swiftly from off the good land I have given you.

It is a very tidy theology. Obedience to God brings reward, disobedience brings punishment. It assumes a system that works mechanically and efficiently. But the reality of human experience is nothing like this. In fact, much of the Hebrew Bible is asking questions about this very problem: why is it that good people are not always rewarded? In fact they may suffer tragically in their lives. Conversely, there are many bad people walking about on the earth who seem to live charmed lives; certainly no divine punishment falls upon them. The prophet Jeremiah challenges God on this score. Some of the Psalms ask pointed questions about the same problem. The entire Book of Job is a challenge to this kind of simple reward and punishment view of the universe. None of them come to a fully satisfactory solution. Job concludes that the workings of God are greater and more mysterious than we can fathom. God can be challenged, must be challenged, but our final response can only be resignation and humility. This may be the answer for some but when faced with events of the magnitude of the *Shoah* (the Holocaust), even such deeply felt answers feel inadequate.

But is our text in Deuteronomy really as simplistic as it appears at first glance? There is one oddity about the text that needs to be looked at. Most of the passage is expressed in the plural form – Israel as a whole is addressed. However, from time to time the verbs change into the singular form. The individual is addressed.

Our section begins in the plural, for the whole of Israel is being spoken to.

If you will surely listen to My commandments which I command you this day, to love the Eternal your God and to serve God with all your heart and with all your soul, then I shall give the rain of your land in its season, the former and the latter rain . . . (Deut. 11.13–14a)

At this point the person being addressed becomes the single individual.

> And thou shalt gather thy grain and thy wine and thy oil. And I will give grass in thy fields for thy cattle, and thou shalt eat and be full. (Deut. 11.14b–15)

If all of Israel is obedient to the will of God then blessings will be given to every single household. But immediately after this, the text switches back to the plural form again. This is the part which includes the warnings that disobedience to God will lead to the rain being withheld and the land not yielding its fruit, so that the people is destroyed. It should be pointed out that the commands we are to obey include those about caring for the land itself, for example, letting it lie fallow every seven years and not destroying trees. So there is also an ecological basis to this warning.

Our text now returns to the positive command to make God's words a central part of our lives. We are still in the plural, at least for the opening words:

> You shall put these words upon your heart and upon your soul and you shall bind them as a sign upon your hands and they shall be as frontlets between your eyes, and you shall teach them to your children to speak of them . . . (Deut. 11.18–19a)

At this point once again the text returns to the singular form, and in fact picks up the exact version that is so familiar from the first paragraph of the *Shema*.

> when thou sittest in thine house and when thou walkest by the way and when thou liest down and when thou risest up, and thou shalt write them as a sign upon the doorposts of thy house and at thy gates. (Deut. 11.19b–20)

What is the purpose of this change of language? It may simply be a wish to repeat the exact same words in the same form as appeared earlier in the *Shema* paragraph so that they become more deeply embedded in our hearts and minds. Perhaps it is also to reinforce the idea that these general principles are to apply to each and every individual. It is you who is meant, you who are to teach your own children, to speak of these things in your own personal home and to keep a tangible sign of them on your own personal doorpost.

But perhaps it is also a way of acknowledging that our individual fate is not so easily described or explained. If all of Israel does wrong or right, then maybe we can literally affect the climate, change the seasons to bring rain or prevent it. But even if it were possible to measure the good or bad of a society in such terms, our own individual story cannot simply be fitted into some such general pattern. We can be the victims of the failings of our society – but we each contribute to the forces that make that society what it is. Our passage does make a general statement about reward and punishment, but recognizes the reality of our individual fate and our individual choice.

The story is told of a young man who went away from his home to undertake Jewish studies for seven years. When he returned his father asked him what he had learned? He answered, 'I learned that you should love your neighbour as yourself.' 'You needed seven years to learn that?' exclaimed his father. 'Everyone knows that. You even knew it before you went away!' 'Yes,' said his son, 'but now I know that it means that *I* should love my neighbour as myself.'

36

Officers

This Torah reading begins with Moses' instruction to the people to appoint '*shofetimv'shoterim*'. It is clear that *shofetim* are judges, and their task is immediately spelled out, as well as warnings against misusing their power. This echoes similar material in Deuteronomy 1, where again the two groups, *shofetim* and *shoterim*, are associated:

> So I took your tribal leaders, wise and experienced men, and appointed them heads over you: chiefs of thousands, chiefs of hundreds, chiefs of fifties, and chiefs of tens and *shoterim*, 'officials', for your tribes. And I commanded your *shofetim*, judges . . . (Deut. 1.15–16)

Who are the *shoterim* and what is their task?

On this passage, Rashi quotes a disturbing explanation from the *midrash* collection, *Sifre*: 'these are they who bind and flog with the lash at the bidding of the judges'. Presumably in the absence of custodial sentences, fines and lashes would have been standard punishments available for crimes. Even if this is only a later interpretation it reflects their biblical role as adjuncts to the legal system.

Nevertheless, the association with violence actually goes back to a much earlier reference to this term, for the *shoterim* were the Hebrew overseers or foremen of the work gangs of Hebrew slaves, appointed by the Egyptian taskmasters (Exod. 5.6, 10, 14). The term '*kapo*' conjures up the ambiguity of such a role: Hebrews appointed to supervise other Hebrews and ensure the completion of the work.

The position would probably have entailed certain privileges, but at the price of potentially oppressing their fellow Hebrews, and hence estranging them from their own people. On one level, this would have worked as a system of divide and conquer (a technique of which Pharaoh was a master) but also effectively placed a buffer between the slaves and their real masters, the Egyptians. The *shoterim* were the visible representatives of the power of the state that the slaves might attack, if the system broke down. From the Egyptian perspective, they were disposable and replaceable if they gave the Egyptians any trouble. Pharaoh exploited precisely this system in response to Moses' initial challenge when he forced the Hebrews to forage for straw while still keeping up the same quota of bricks. When they failed to do so, the *shoterim* were blamed and physically beaten (Exod. 5.14). The *shoterim* then blamed the Hebrew slaves who in turn blamed Moses. Nevertheless, the Bible records no actual abuse of their power in this circumstance, and Rashi quotes the midrash (Exodus Rabba 5), which regards the *shoterim* as selflessly accepting the beating and not passing it on. Rashi concludes that for this reason they were listed among the 70 elders upon whom God promised to place some of Moses' 'spirit' (Num. 11.16–17). However, in the event Moses gathers the elders, but the *shoterim* are not mentioned (Num. 11.24). Why the omission? Perhaps Moses was less convinced than God about the wisdom of giving that particular group special powers.

Given this background of violence, it is no surprise that when they next appear it is in the context of war. In Joshua (1.10; 3.1–4), they will marshal the people for the crossing of the Jordan river. But before that, in Deuteronomy (20.5–7), they will work with the priest appointed for warfare, in informing the people about who may be exempt from the fighting: those who have built a house and not dedicated it, planted a vineyard and have not yet been able to enjoy the fruit, become engaged but not yet married. These examples emphasize the importance of giving simple human values and tasks greater priority than warfare. But the *shoterim,* seemingly at their own initiative, add a fourth separate category (20.8): exempting anyone whose fearfulness might affect the resolve of his comrades in arms. Here the *shoterim* are not acting out of compassion for such a person but are simply aware of the military need to maintain morale. Who better than those who understand something of violence to ensure that people who cannot cope with it are not allowed to endanger others.

Their final appearance is in the service of the judges and the king in First and Second Chronicles (1 Chr. 27.1; 2 Chr. 19.11, 34.12).

The questions remain about who they were; how they were appointed; were they salaried employees of the state; did they belong to a specific class or was the term simply used for any kind of middle ranking official with specific functions in particular contexts. Certainly, on the basis of the texts we have seen, they would have ensured that the priests and judges could remain physically distanced from direct engagement with the more unpleasant aspects of their roles. So it is tempting to recognize in them people charged professionally with getting things done, and tackling the difficult and sometimes even brutal tasks needed to ensure the effective working of a complex society: sometimes policemen, sometimes enforcers, sometimes 'sergeant majors'.

These references serve as a reminder of a strand of toughness and practical competence within the Israelite and Jewish people, which should not be overlooked or denied. Maybe it was part of Moses' wisdom to find a responsible, contained and supervised role for those in Israelite society whose aptitude for violence might otherwise have found more destructive outlets.

37

When Tradition is Wrong

Deuteronomy 21.18–21

This reading from the Torah presents us with a challenging law that seems to be completely out of place in the Hebrew Bible. It is found amidst a number of miscellaneous laws in the Book of Deuteronomy. It is known in Jewish tradition as the law about the 'stubborn and rebellious son'.

The text reads:

> If a man has a stubborn and rebellious son, who will not obey the voice of his father or the voice of his mother, and though they chastise him, he will not give heed to them, then his father and his mother shall take hold of him and bring him out to the elders of his city at the gate of the place where he lives, and they shall say to the elders of his city, 'This our son is stubborn and rebellious, he will not obey our voice; he is a glutton and a drunkard.' Then all the men of the city shall stone him to death with stones; so you shall purge the evil from your midst; and all Israel shall hear, and fear. (Deut. 21.18–21)

This hardly accords with current views on child-rearing. Moreover, it provides plenty of ammunition for those who think of the Old Testament God as cruel or of the biblical world as primitive and uncivilized. The fact that there is no recorded incident in the Bible of such an event ever happening does not really help. The argument from silence is never very persuasive. Moreover, the law is there as part of Holy Scripture and cannot simply be ignored.

There is one redeeming feature in the law itself. In the biblical period, it would seem that the father did have the power of life and death over his children. The Bible records the ongoing struggle against the prevailing custom of child sacrifice. But in this case the power of the parents is actually severely limited. They have to bring the matter before the elders, and it is the elders who are the ones to sit in judgement, not the parents themselves. In this way, the potential arbitrariness and the possible abuse of power by the parents are controlled.

In the Ancient Near East, disobedience to the father was a very serious offence, as it undermined the entire authority structure of the tribal society. But if we are to judge the law by modern standards, we can only condemn it. So how was it seen in earlier periods? This is an important question, because the way that the early rabbis treated it helps us understand their values. It also offers an insight into the way they managed to deal with difficult laws that they themselves found unacceptable. Such laws were given by God, so they could not simply be ignored or set aside. But precisely because they were the word of God every detail had to be scrutinized to see what God was trying to teach us through them. And here was the paradox. However problematic the law might appear to be, in their understanding God could only be acting according to the highest moral values. So if this was not obvious at first glance, then it was up to the rabbis to dig deeper into the text and interpret it in line with such moral values. Indeed, this law became a classic example of how the art of interpretation could radically change something that the rabbis found to be morally unacceptable. Their way of dealing with it can be found in the earliest strand of rabbinic writings, in the Mishnah (Sanhedrin 8.1–5), the collection of oral traditions edited by the rabbis in the second century CE.

The biblical text refers to a 'stubborn and rebellious son', so, the rabbis taught, this clearly excludes a daughter. Moreover, since it refers to a son, the rabbis try to define this term. It cannot refer to a minor, someone under the age of 13, since he cannot be held responsible under the law. Moreover, once the boy has shown signs of puberty, he is no longer considered a boy, so the law could not apply to him either. This dramatically reduces the number of people who could be affected by the law.

The son is accused of being a glutton and drunkard, so the rabbis set about defining how much food or drink he must have consumed so as to qualify as a glutton or drunkard. Moreover, they set limits on the kinds of food that he might have eaten and the circumstances in which he might have eaten them. In addition, the law only comes into effect if he eats the food in his parents' home.

Since both parents are mentioned in the law, both have to be alive at the time, and if only one of them is prepared to accuse him, then the law cannot apply. Since it also says that his mother and father shall 'lay hold of him', then neither of them should be physically handicapped. They are to speak to the elders, so if either has a speech defect, once again the law does not apply. In the same way, the rabbis found other elements in the text that would disqualify the parents.

If these limitations were not enough to make the law impossible to apply, the rabbis also established the series of courts that would have to decide on such a case. It had to be tried the first time in a court of three judges, and 23 judges had to preside at the court that finally condemned him! In short, the rabbis did absolutely everything to make sure that the death penalty could never be invoked. In fact, they seem to have treated this law as a textbook example of how to exercise their ingenuity for finding ways of abolishing an impossible law. Nevertheless, all of this was achieved by strictly adhering to the methods of legal interpretation they had developed as part of their religious tradition.

However odd this example may be, it points to a deeper issue that faces all religious communities that have to live with a revealed scripture. For whatever the commandment may be that comes from God, it can only be applied in the way that those who have authority to interpret it wish it to be applied. Whatever the scripture may say, it is still human interpreters who have the responsibility of understanding it and applying it. They may feel themselves partly bound by the decisions of previous generations, but ultimately real power lies in their hands.

There are any number of biblical laws that have been amended or made to disappear because rabbinic authorities of a later period felt them to be too problematic. For example, the Bible forbids adultery in no uncertain terms and provides a penalty of death by stoning for both the man and woman. Though the rabbis condemned adultery, nevertheless they hedged this law in with so many conditions that the death penalty could never be applied. (For example, the adulterous act has to take place in the presence of two witnesses who have formally warned the man in advance of the penalty he will incur. This is guaranteed to prevent an effective performance.)

This kind of human flexibility is in stark contrast to another kind of attitude that is so often sold in the name of religion. Religious fanaticism, often in the service of political goals, has become one of the scourges of our time. Once again, we are in a period when people are appealing to 'the word of God' to justify actions that by any humane or moral standard are totally unacceptable. Yet, there is always a scriptural verse available to justify such actions. This narrow approach has been labelled by Father Gordian Marshall as 'selective literalism'. It focuses on one idea or text and ignores the enormous diversity of teachings to be found in the same religious tradition. This deliberately limited view may be used to justify a kind of wilful insensitivity that makes human life secondary to the particular ideology or cause. Whenever people assert that only one meaning of scripture is possible, that which happens to fit their own religious or political agenda, then it is important to remember the law of 'the stubborn and rebellious son'. We should consider how the rabbis in the name of God struggled with the word of God so as to save a human life. They had the courage to insist that scripture can yield many meanings and not only one. They saw it as our responsibility to seek out and apply those interpretations that do not harm life or diminish life, but rather those that enhance life and celebrate life.

38

Judges

Deuteronomy 26.1—29.8

This reading offers a good example of how a few extra words in a biblical sentence have opened the way to some important ideas. At the beginning of our reading from Deuteronomy 26, the Israelites are instructed to take some of the first fruit of the harvest and bring it to a central place of worship in the land of Israel and give it to the priest. But the sentence adds to the priest the phrase: 'who shall be in those days'. The common sense meaning of these extra words is quite simple. The speaker is Moses and he is looking forward to a future time when the Israelites will have entered the Promised Land. The Israelites are to bring the fruit to the priest, who will be there at that time in the future.

But since it is common sense that you can only bring the fruit to the priest who is there at the time, the phrase 'who shall be in those days' seems to be superfluous. Since the rabbis assumed that no word of Torah could be without particular meaning, the door is now open to looking for a deeper interpretation of these extra words. The same extra phrase has already appeared in an earlier verse in the Book of Deuteronomy. This passage concerns a legal procedure and the text says:

You shall come to the levitical priests and to the judge who shall be in those days and ask, and they shall tell you the words of judgement. (Deut. 17.9)

Again the question arises – to what judge can you go except to the one who will be there 'in those days'?

The rabbinic explanation is powerful and has considerable consequences. They understood it as follows: even though the judge in your own days is not like the judges that have been there in previous times, you have to accept the judgement he gives, because he is the competent person in your time and place (Rosh Hashanah 25b). To illustrate their point, the Rabbis compare the judge Jephthah, whose story is told in the Book of Judges, with the great judge and prophet Samuel. Jephthah was a successful military leader. but he so wanted to win a particular battle that he vowed to sacrifice to God the first creature to come and greet him on his successful return. It happened to be his daughter who came out, and Jephthah kept his vow. Clearly, Jephthah is not the best example of how a judge should behave! Nevertheless, the rabbis made the point that 'Jephthah in his generation was equivalent to Samuel in his generation'. In one sense it may mean that each generation gets the leadership it deserves! But it points to the need to accept and respect the authority of those you place in leadership positions in your own time.

The problem is that this attitude is contradicted by an equally strong tendency in Judaism to assert that the leaders of previous generations were far greater than we could ever be in our generation. So how could we presume to offer our own opinions, if they differ from those of the past. Who are we to dare to change what they have decided in their greater wisdom?! Such respect for the past must have its proper place, but it may also paralyse our own creativity and our ability to address new situations.

The passage we just read referred to judges, the legal and political authorities of the time. But our passage speaks about the priest who shall be 'in those days', the spiritual leader of the Israelite community. So in matters of contemporary religious issues we also have to recognize the authority of the spiritual leaders we appoint in our own times. New times, new circumstances may need new religious answers, even if they contradict those that we venerate from the past.

So should we simply preserve the traditions inherited from past leaders or should we follow instead the innovations of the leaders of today? The answer, of course, is that either option can be followed depending on the circumstances. But who is to decide which line to follow at any given time?

The answer to this question also lies in the texts we have read, for there is a third party present in both of them – the people to whom Moses is speaking. We are the ones who are spoken to; we are the ones who are to go to the judge or priest of our own days, because we are the ones who give them authority to decide on our behalf. So these texts contain another kind of challenge. We also have to take full responsibility for the election of our leadership, political and religious. But our responsibility does not stop there. We have to ensure that they are publicly accountable for their actions. Everything we give into the hands of our leadership must be open to inspection and made transparent – from financial matters to decisions of religious practice. A community that does not take such responsibility for its appointed representatives and functionaries invites corruption. If we do not monitor their actions and question their decisions, we are unfair to them as well, because we open the door to temptation, whether it be financial misuse or the abuse of the power they have over others. We are held responsible for the things that they do in our name. We too have to face a judgement.

39

Promised Lands

Deuteronomy 26.1—29.8

This reading from the Torah looks forward to the arrival of the Israelites in the land of Canaan and the celebration of the first harvest. It begins: 'When you come into the land which the Eternal your God gives you as an inheritance.' For almost two millennia, Jews have dreamed of returning to that 'inheritance', to that 'promised land'. Instead we lived in other lands where we or our ancestors had been allowed to settle.

I began to think about which land one considers home during my three months living in Würzburg in Southern Germany as the Schalom ben Chorin Professor of Jewish Studies. While wandering through the town, I became increasingly aware of the small brass plaques inserted into the pavement giving the names of Jewish families who had lived in the nearby house and who had been deported to their deaths in one of the concentration camps. I always find these *stolpersteine*, 'stones you stumble over', deeply moving. They give a personal human face to the tragic history of so many millions of Jews who were killed. But seeing them alerted me also to the history of the Jews in Würzburg and to look for other public witnesses to that former Jewish life.

One afternoon, I went to hear an outdoor music concert and found that it was located in a community centre named after Felix Fechenbach. I had known nothing about him and was fascinated to learn his history. He was a journalist, poet, writer of children's stories and above all a political activist. He was so influential that he was arrested in March 1933 for his anti-fascist activities and was shot in

August that year, while on his way to Dachau Concentration Camp. This community centre and a professional school in Detmold with his name bear witness to someone who fought and died to preserve the political integrity of the land of his 'inheritance'.

On a wall in another part of town I noticed a plaque with the name of Norbert Glanzberg. Born in Galicia, his family moved to Würzburg. A composer of film music, he was identified by Goebbels as a 'degenerate Jewish artist', and in 1933 went into exile in Paris. He fought in the French resistance and survived the war thanks to the intervention of friends in the music profession. He composed songs for artists like Edith Piaf (including Padam Padam Padam) and for Yves Montand, as well as film music, a song cycle based on Yiddish poems and classical pieces. In the years before his death in 2001, he performed concerts in Würzburg. He had lost the land of his 'inheritance', but found in France a land of refuge and a home.

But the greatest surprise occurred one day on leaving my apartment in the university guest house. The street in front of the building is divided by a wide strip of trees and parkland. A small road cuts through the park and I suddenly noticed that it was named after Yehudah Amichai, the most celebrated Israeli poet of modern times. Born in 1924 in Würzburg, he emigrated to Palestine with his family in 1934. He fought as a soldier in many of Israel's wars and became an advocate for peace and reconciliation in the region. Here was another Würzburger, who had been forced to leave the land of his birth, but unlike the others he was able to settle in the 'promised land' of the Bible. He gave to the Hebrew language a new richness, and personally found in the land of Israel the 'inheritance' of which our Torah reading speaks.

40

From Holy to Profane

Deuteronomy 26.1–11

At the beginning of this Torah reading, Moses gives instructions about a ritual the children of Israel are to perform when they are settled in the Promised Land. They are to dedicate the first fruits of the harvest to God by bringing them to the priest at the central sanctuary. They are also to recite a formula thanking God for rescuing them from slavery in Egypt and bringing them to the land (Deut. 26.1–11).

This is to happen each year at the beginning of the harvest. But there are also regulations in the Bible about what to do when they first plant fruit trees. According to the Book of Leviticus, for the first three years after the planting they are not to take any of the fruit that grows. In the fourth year, they are to consider it as holy and dedicated to God, so it is still not available to them. Only in the fifth year and afterwards may they begin to eat it as part of their regular supply of food (Lev. 19.23–5).

Behind this law may be some agricultural knowledge about how to ensure the best growth of newly planted fruit trees. But for the Bible, the law seems to be based on a principle that is mentioned elsewhere in the Book of Leviticus. In Chapter 25 there are a number of laws about obligations to the land itself. For six years, the Israelites are allowed to sow and harvest the land, but in the seventh year, it is not to be worked at all. Instead it is to lie fallow. Just like the rest that is to take place on the seventh day of the week, the Shabbat, the land too is to have a rest on every seventh year. Again, this may have its origins in agricultural knowledge about the best

152

way to ensure that the land is not overworked. But the reason given for this and for other laws in the chapter is to remind us that the land belongs not to us but to God. As the text expresses it, we are just temporary residents on the land; we are God's tenants (Lev. 25.23). If the land belongs to God, then so does everything that grows on it. We should not take for granted either the fertility of the land, our ownership of its produce or our right to exploit the land in any way that we wish.

As tenants, we may eat the fruit, but only if we acknowledge the source from which that fruit and all other nourishment comes. How is this acknowledgement to be made? The restrictions on the use of the produce in the first years after planting and the annual dedication of the first fruits are ways of reminding us that what we have comes from God. These dedication rituals are a kind of symbolic transfer of ownership of the produce of the land from God to us so that we may have the benefit.

This principle became expressed in a tradition developed by the rabbis after the biblical period. Before a meal, when we are about to eat bread, we recite a blessing: 'Blessed are You, our Living God, Sovereign of the universe, who brings forth bread from the earth.' Similarly before we drink wine, especially on Shabbat and Festivals, we recite: 'Blessed are You, our Living God, Sovereign of the universe, who creates the fruit of the vine.' It may seem at first glance that reciting the blessing over bread and wine makes them holy and special. But within the rabbinic understanding it is actually the opposite that is intended. By reciting the blessing, by acknowledging that what we are about to eat or drink is a gift from God, we are taking it out of the divine domain and making it available for human use. The change in the status of the food brought about by the blessing is not from the ordinary to the holy, but from the holy to the ordinary.

In the biblical world, it was easy for people to recognize and understand the direct relationship between the land, its produce and God. In an agrarian society, most people would have been involved at some stage in the growing and gathering of food. They would have been acutely aware of how dependent they were on the rainfall to ensure the success of their harvests. In the Book of Deuteronomy, God makes the arrival of the rain each year dependent on the behaviour of the people and their obedience to God's laws. Some of these laws do indeed deal directly with agriculture. But intended here are all the laws that have been given to the people. These are to ensure that food is made available to everyone, including the poorest and weakest in society, so that no one goes hungry. We are to be God's agents to ensure that food is available for all. At the heart of such laws are the ethical values and the moral behaviour of the society as a whole.

These connections between the land and the food we eat are not so obvious to us today if we live in urban societies. We are personally several stages removed from the production to food itself. We have lost our sense of the change of seasons because we are able to enjoy seasonal fruits all the year round simply by importing them from elsewhere. Indeed, what was once a special treat or surprise, like having fresh strawberries available in the winter, is now something we take for granted. What we eat often comes to us standardized, preselected and pre-packaged, so that we have even less sense of the earth out of which it came or the tree from which it was plucked. Moreover, we are largely protected from the direct experience of drought and famine that devastate large parts of the world.

In Deuteronomy, when God says to the Israelites that 'all the land is mine', the word for land 'eretz' refers to the land of Canaan. Yet, eretz can equally mean 'the earth' itself. On this basis, God is saying 'all the earth is mine' so that everywhere that we live upon the earth we are God's tenants. The produce of the earth is available to us, but only on condition that we guard and protect the earth and acknowledge the laws that are needed to ensure that it continues to provide for us and for all people.

In our largely secular age, the recital of a blessing before eating may feel uncomfortable or anachronistic. We do not experience a direct relationship between God and the earth and the production of food. Moreover, science can explain many of the connections much better than our religious traditions and can advise us on what we need to do to preserve the earth as a habitable place. Nevertheless, we have increasingly come to recognize the biblical view that our behaviour has consequences for the natural world around us. We need to find ways of reinforcing our understanding of this and of accepting our individual and collective responsibilities to the earth as tenants. Perhaps, the reciting of a blessing before eating, like the elaborate rituals of the biblical period, can serve as a reminder of that wider task.

As the rabbis expressed it, if we derive benefit from this world without reciting a blessing, it is as if we had stolen it from God.

41

In a Culture of Fear

Deuteronomy 28

Some of the most disturbing passages in the Hebrew Bible occur in the verses that we read from the end of the Book of Deuteronomy. The basis of the relationship between the Israelites and their God is the covenant, the Hebrew term '*brit*'. A covenant is at one level a legal contract between two partners. So the obligations of the two partners have to be detailed, but also the penalties that will apply if these obligations are not met. In two places in the Torah, a series of increasingly more severe penalties are spelled out if Israel fails to live up to its obligations. We find them at the end of the Book of Leviticus and also here at the end of the Book of Deuteronomy. All that the Israelites own, their homes, their crops, their families, will be damaged or destroyed or taken from them with violence. As the final blow they will be sent into exile from their land. What happens to them in exile is described in Leviticus 26.36–37:

> As for those of you who are left, I will send faintness into their heart in the lands of their enemies; and the sound of a driven leaf shall chase them; and they shall flee, as one flees from the sword; and they shall fall when no one is pursuing them. And they shall stumble, each person over his brother, as if before the sword, when there is no one pursuing; and you shall have no power to stand before your enemies.

In Deuteronomy 28.66 a further dimension is added:

> And your life will hang there before you, and you will fear night and day, and have no trust in your life. In the morning you will say, if only it were evening, and in the evening you will say, if only it were morning, because of the fear in your heart that you fear, and because of the vision before your eyes that you see.

This picture of a debilitating fear that makes life unbearable and positive action impossible has been at times the fate of the Jewish people in their experience of exile among the nations of the world. But it has also universal resonance. Throughout history and throughout the world today, because of government suppression or civil war, political extremism or urban brutality, private vendettas or family violence, people know only too well the terrors described in these verses: the fear of the threat of violence even when it is not actually present; the dread of the horrors that the next day may bring. To those kinds of fear we now witness, on a growing scale, a new element: the random murders and maiming of innocent people by terrorists. At one time, this seemed remote from Western Europe, but now it is also a feature of our reality, in part imported, but increasingly likely to be home-grown.

The threat of terror works on many levels beginning with the fear of sudden death or injury with which we are confronted. But there are also effects produced by fighting against terrorists, the danger that the legislation that is brought in may curtail our hard-won freedoms and target innocent people. Worse still, politicians play on this fear, and even exaggerate it, so as to ensure that legislation is passed; the media feed on it because sensationalism sells their product. Deuteronomy speaks of the 'fear of the fear in your heart'. This seems to be the same warning that President Roosevelt gave in his inaugural address in 1933 during the depths of the Depression in America: 'the only thing we have to fear is fear itself.' Beyond the rational level of concern that terrorist actions cause, terrorism feeds on deeper levels of irrational anxiety within our society.

But there is a further effect of terrorism that is potentially even worse in the long run. It insinuates into our daily lives suspicion and fear of 'the other'. Anyone who is different, not 'one of us', seems to present us with a potential threat. As Leviticus expressed it, because of this kind of fear, 'they shall stumble, each person, over his brother'. Fear itself will undermine the normal relationship of trust and mutual respect that exists, or should exist, between people who know each other. If that is the case among those whom the Bible calls 'brothers', those who are close to us, how much more problematic must the effect of this fear be as regards strangers.

We saw in Britain the results of this phenomenon following the bombings in London in July 2005. Despite the condemnation of the bombings by leading members of the Muslim community, the numbers of assaults on individual Muslims and attacks on Muslim property increased alarmingly. Such events add to the feelings of isolation, insecurity and even alienation, felt by some within the Muslim community. The effect can only be to provide a potential breeding ground for future candidates for radical movements. But this climate of fear also serves to reinforce the prejudices against minorities within society, and encourage further acts of violence or vandalism against them.

How do we break out of this cycle of fear and over-reaction? There are no simple solutions. Clearly all kinds of appropriate steps have to be taken to protect the public and relevant legal safeguards put in place. But these do not address the fear that comes from ignorance of the others who share our society with us. What is needed is a consistent attempt to build bridges between the different communities within our society.

One approach is through interfaith dialogue. This activity developed considerably in Europe after the Second World War, especially between Christians and Jews. It was once seen as an interesting but peripheral activity for a few interested people, often on the margins of their own religious tradition. Today, as a growing movement, it has to be recognized as an essential tool in the safeguarding of civil society. It works alongside other activities that encourage people to meet across boundaries at a deeper level of understanding and respect.

Such activities will not remove the threat of terrorism. But by promoting and extending this kind of dialogue we prevent ourselves becoming the psychological victims of terror, too paralysed to do anything at all. Moreover, through the activities and encounters themselves, we broaden our horizons. We come to see who are our true 'brothers' and 'sisters' in the pluralist societies that are emerging in Europe. The warnings in Leviticus and Deuteronomy of a society disintegrating out of anxiety then cease to be just a threat to be feared. Instead they become a challenge to be overcome.

42

Facing Jerusalem

Deuteronomy 29.9—30.20

This Torah reading from Deuteronomy 29–30 is the last before the end of the Jewish year. So we approach the passage from the Torah and also the traditional reading from the prophets, the Haftarah, with certain hopes and expectations. Can they help us make sense of the year that has passed – and give us some guidance for the one that lies ahead?

As so often the case at this time, Jewish life tends to be overshadowed by events in the Middle East. It seems that we are doomed always to be looking back on a year of pain and suffering for Israelis and Palestinians alike, a year of shattered hopes and bitter, personal tragedies. People on both sides of the conflict have strong opinions about why this continues and allot responsibility, usually blaming the other side. Not surprisingly any such one-sided convictions, accusations and retaliations do not stop the bloodshed, change attitudes or offer hope.

With feelings of helplessness in the face of such violence and political complexity we turn to our texts. The Torah reading from Deuteronomy 29 is a passage that moves me every year. Moses calls the entire people together for a final message. He begins: '*Attem nitzavim ha-yom*', 'You are standing here today.' But the Hebrew word for 'standing', '*nitzavim*', has many dimensions. It means standing for a purpose, taking a position, somehow committed and ready for whatever lies ahead.

Moses specifies who is present: men, women and children, leaders of the people but also outsiders, members of other nations

who have aligned themselves with the fate of the children of Israel
and share their journey. Moses draws on an even wider circle of
people. At this moment, they are entering a covenant with their
God that is binding not only on those who are present but also
those who are not physically present. Perhaps the text itself simply means people who were unwell or otherwise prevented from
attending on that day. But Jewish tradition looks into the distant
future and binds the souls of all those destined to be born into this
covenant, a people united with their God across time and space.
It is an awesome commitment that is demanded here. And it is
somehow realized at this season, the one time of the year when
Jews of whatever personal belief or tradition, or of none at all, are
drawn to the synagogue.

When we turn to the prophetic reading from the latter part of
the Book of Isaiah, the tragedy of our current situation becomes
overwhelming. It is the last of a series of prophetic readings, all
from this part of the Book of Isaiah, leading up to the New Year.
Each of them offers hope and consolation, promising an end to
exile and the return to the land of Israel. In this one, the climax of
the series, the speaker calls urgently for Zion and Jerusalem to be
restored.

> For Zion's sake I will not keep silent
> and for Jerusalem's sake I will not rest,
> until her righteousness goes forth as brightness
> and her salvation as a burning torch.
> The nations shall see your righteousness
> and all the kings your glory,
> and you shall be called by a new name
> which the mouth of the Eternal will give. (Isa. 62.1–2)

One key term is at the heart of this passage, '*tzedakah*', 'righteousness'. It was the absence of righteousness that led to Jerusalem's
destruction, according to the earlier writings in this same Book

of Isaiah. When righteousness is restored it will shine out from Jerusalem like a lamp, and nations will see and recognize it.

But what does this restoration of Jerusalem mean? For the prophet's audience two and a half thousand years ago, and for generations of Jews since then, it can only have meant the return of the Jewish people to their homeland and their capital city. Whether Isaiah speaks of Zion, the religious centre of the society, or Jerusalem, the political capital of the nation, his audience is his own people. But is that the whole of the matter? For in the closing chapters of the same book of Isaiah, the prophet speaks of a new heaven and a new earth. In this changed world, the nations will themselves bring the Jews back to the land, and some from these nations will be called upon to act as priests in this new religious centre, where 'all humanity shall come to worship before God'.

But that has always been the paradox of Jerusalem. When Solomon dedicated the Temple he welcomed the nations of the world to come and worship there and called on God to answer their prayers. Isaiah himself had a vision of the nations streaming to Jerusalem so as to learn the Torah from God. But other passages in the Hebrew Bible attest to another political reality, that of nations surrounding Jerusalem and waging war against it, fighting and killing so as to own and control it. That same city has been ruled at different times from Babylon, Susa, Thebes, Alexandria, Antioch, Rome, Byzantium, Damascus, Baghdad, Cairo, Aleppo, Constantinople, London and Amman. At the heart of today's struggle lies the same issue, who owns Jerusalem. What greater irony, what greater tragedy, than to shed blood over a city called '*Yerushalayim*', the city of '*shalom*', of peace.

Our Torah reading speaks of the unity of the Jewish people over time and space. Yet Moses, at this most intimate moment, could include in his vision other peoples who shared a life with Israel. The different voices that make up the Book of Isaiah, from their different historical periods, could likewise see a Jerusalem intimately part of the Israelite nation, yet also open to the nations of the world. But the problem, one that has never been resolved, is how to make such a vision possible, a unity and a sharing, at one and the same time. One clue to the solution must lie in the word 'tzedakah', the 'righteousness' that is to be the basis of such a society, a respect for the rights of all who wish to live there. That is the righteousness that is to shine out of Zion and Jerusalem. Justice and generosity of spirit have to be at the heart of Jerusalem, if it is to deserve the title 'holy'. How that is to come about is the challenge for all directly engaged in conflict over Jerusalem and for all who care about it. But the quest for righteousness does at least offer a higher aim than national aspirations alone and a greater hope.

The Isaiah of our Haftarah in his own time was also deeply troubled. He offered a challenge to his contemporaries, to Israel and the other nations, but also to God. His was a call not only to prayer and hope, but also to action, to help bring about this vision of what Jerusalem could and should be:

Upon your walls, O Jerusalem, I have set watchmen;
all the day and all the night they shall never be silent.
You who keep the Eternal in remembrance, take no rest.
And give God no rest until He establishes,
until He makes Jerusalem a praise throughout the earth.
(Isa. 62.6–7)

43

Anticipating Purim

This readingis for the first of four special Sabbaths that remind us that two Jewish religious festivals are rapidly approaching: Purim and Pesach (Passover). These special Sabbaths help us to prepare for the festivals and reflect on their meaning. This is particularly important in the case of Purim, because during the festival itself, there is almost no opportunity to think too deeply about it. On the contrary, all the normal rules are turned on their head. It is a time for pageants and fancy dress parties, for giving and receiving gifts, and for extraordinary behaviour in the synagogue, when we read Megillat Esther, the Scroll of the Book of Esther. It records an event in the Persian Empire when the king's vizier Haman sought to destroy the Jewish people in an act of genocide, only to be prevented by the actions of Queen Esther and her guardian Mordechai. During the reading, whenever we mention the name of 'wicked Haman', out come the noise makers and chaos erupts, as we try to drown out his name. At Purim, we are traditionally encouraged to drink alcohol without restraint. Indeed we should become so confused that we cannot distinguish between saying, 'Blessed be Mordechai and cursed be Haman'!

So when we read the Book of Esther at Purim, we do everything in our power to make sure that we do not pay close attention to its message. This is understandable, because the Book of Esther is very disturbing. It speaks directly to the reality of Jewish life in exile, in the Diaspora. The story tells of the Jewish community comfortably settled and assimilated in the land of Persia. Even the names of Mordechai and Esther are probably popular local names related to the god Marduk and the goddess Astarte. But in this world of exile, their fate is in the hands of forces over which they have no control. King Ahasuerus can appoint as a minister, a man like Haman. It just takes the refusal of Mordechai to bow down to Haman, to honour him in public, for Haman to unleash a murderous attack on the entire Jewish population. In charge of 'homeland security', Haman reports to the king that there is a people scattered throughout his empire who are a threat to the king, and so they must be destroyed. He even offers to pay a large sum of money to offset any budget deficit caused by the potential loss of revenue from the Jews. Seemingly without a second thought the king agrees. In this world of exile, life or death, success or catastrophe, are dependent on the arbitrary moods of those in power.

Even more disturbing is the complete absence of God from the Book of Esther. There is a suggestion that when Mordechai tells Esther that perhaps help will come from 'another place', this refers to God. But even this only reinforces the divine silence. Instead, that same random chance that puts Haman in power, puts Esther on the throne, with enough beauty and cunning to counteract the threat to her people. At the end of the book, she has won her victory, Mordechai is promoted to the place of Haman, and the danger is past. But we know that this is only a temporary reprieve. For like other 'Court Jews', Mordechai's position is only as secure as the next change of policy or struggle for power in the Court. We laugh at the 'thousand and one nights' quality of the writing of the Book of Esther, we marvel at the exciting twists and turns of the plot, but our laughter is hollow at this gallows humour.

Perhaps it is precisely for this reason that we go to such lengths at Purim to drown out this reality. For just one day, we escape into a kind of forgetfulness, to celebrate a fantasy of triumph. Perhaps that is why the Shabbat immediately before Purim, the second of our special Sabbaths, is called Shabbat Zachor, the Shabbat of remembrance. There we read of Amalek, the arch enemy of Israel from the time of the wandering in the wilderness, the figure of evil, with whom we are destined to struggle till the end of time. Now at least, in these special Sabbaths, is the time to be serious. So that when Purim comes, we can briefly forget, and lose ourselves in a joyous release.

44

Passover Past

We are in the middle of the Festival of Pesach, Passover, the one time in the year when Jewish families come together to share a religious home celebration, the *Seder*. So it is also a time for memories of past years, of family events and stories linked to that evening. Yet, when I look back, I remember little of the *Seder* celebrations of my childhood. There is a memory of my father conducting the prayers in Hebrew, which no one understood, and seemingly at great speed. Indeed, the speed increased as the evening wore on and people grew more and more impatient to finish. Nor do I recall the faces of those who sat around the table, and that is a source of great sadness. Was I less curious as a child or too withdrawn to pay much attention? What does remain is the taste of the chicken soup that we ate, and not even the soup itself, but the taste and texture of the *kneidlach*, the doughy balls made of *matzah* meal, the unleavened bread that is central to the festival. It was only later that I discovered that this seemingly unique Jewish contribution to cooking was well known in Germany as a *knödel*, dumpling, though the German variety never has quite the same taste or texture as the ones that I remember. Perhaps it was the chicken soup that made the difference.

If the *Seders* of my childhood have not stayed with me, then those I learnt to conduct myself as an adult remain. It is only when you have your own home celebration that you begin to realize what an enormous amount of work goes into the preparation. In traditional households, it amounts to a major exercise in spring cleaning as every last bit of bread or related products has to be discovered and removed. But even beyond this extraordinary household upheaval, the preparation of the meal for the *Seder* is a major undertaking that has traditionally fallen on the women of the house. Since dozens of family members or friends may participate, the sheer volume of cooking and preparation is enormous. An essential part of the teaching of Pesach is freedom, so all who are seated around the table are supposed to lean comfortably on cushions throughout to symbolize this privilege. If anything shows the patriarchal nature of Judaism at its most traditional, it is the picture of the women slaving away in the kitchen long before and during the *Seder* evening, while the 'master of the house' and the guests can relax. There is always a hidden cost that someone has to pay for freedom. Today, of course, more egalitarian arrangements are made in many households.

But reminiscing about the *Seder* reminds me of two extraordinary ones that I conducted far away from home. I had the unusual opportunity to be the technical adviser on a biblical movie about the life of King David. Much of the filming was done in Matera, in southern Italy, where they had built a replica of biblical Jerusalem. The real Jerusalem had too many television aerials and other modern aspects to be available. We were filming in the spring, and it turned out to be the coldest and wettest spring for decades, which played havoc with the schedule. But Pesach fell in the middle of the filming, and the producer generously invited my wife and children to fly over and join us on the set. We arranged a *Seder* for the Jewish members of the cast and crew. My wife spent hours with the Italian chef hired to feed the leading actors, and we sat down to a magnificent *Seder* meal on the film set in pseudo-Jerusalem. Though the Jewish members of the crew were invited to attend, none of them actually came. Instead we celebrated with the producer and director and the leading actor in the movie, Richard Gere, who used the ceremonial to feel his way emotionally into the part of King David. Alas my son, then aged five, had a tummy bug and was violently sick. This is a not unknown happening at a

Seder, when children get over excited. It added a touch of authenticity to the occasion.

At the end of the *Seder*, the closing words express the hope that the exile of the Jewish people will end soon, and we will return to the 'promised land'. Reciting '*l'shanah ha-ba'ah birushalayim*', 'next year in Jerusalem', in a fibre-glass reproduction of Jerusalem on the top of an Italian mountain was an appropriately bizarre conclusion to a bizarre evening.

Far more authentic was a secret *Seder* I conducted in Moscow a few years before the fall of the Soviet Union. During those years, it was possible for Jews to apply to leave Russia for Israel. But the price for doing so was to lose their citizenship and to live out their lives in a kind of limbo, until given the opportunity to leave. They were called refuseniks, and there was a major campaign by Jewish communities in the West to support them. So my wife and I, with our baby son, found ourselves one cold March morning in Moscow. We had been given a telephone number to call at exactly 8.45 am with instructions to use a call-box and not the hotel. We rang and rang for 15 minutes only to get an engaged tone. One minute after 9.00 we got through and a voice said: 'This number is no longer in operation!', and put down the receiver. It was a chilling moment. Between fears of being followed by the KGB and of having our hotel room bugged, we felt that we had wandered into a spy movie. In fact nothing serious happened to us. We were contacted and taken to a small apartment where the *Seder* was to take place.

Many of those present were relatives of well-known refuseniks. The only people in the room who had ever experienced a *Seder* before were the elderly ones, who had known it as a child. For 70 years, in the Soviet Union all Jewish religious activities had been controlled or prohibited so celebrations like the *Seder* were completely unknown for many who were present. My explanations were translated and well received. We read in turn around the table from the *Haggadah*, the order of service, either in Hebrew or

Russian. Then came the meal. Afterwards, there is a major con-
cluding part of the service that has to be read – the part my father
used to go through at breakneck speed. But when we sat down to
complete this part of the evening, most of the participants had
disappeared into another room. There was nothing mysterious
about this. It was clearly time for a cigarette, and as far as they were
concerned with the completion of the meal, the important part of
the ceremony was over. Only the older people, remembering the
Seders of their childhood, stayed on to sing the songs that come at
the end. I couldn't help teasing the people who had disappeared
into the other room, since this is often what happens in family
gatherings in the West as well. We joked about it. How did they
know that Jews often skip the last part of the service? Was it built
into their genes? Was it a secret tradition passed down in their family for the past 70 years? Just as some are casual about such things,
there are always those willing to stay on to make sure the service
is completed properly. That both skipping and staying happen is
what makes the *Seder* a true family event. That both things happen
is what makes Judaism a very human religious tradition.

45

The Wilderness Journey

Leviticus 23

A special period in the Jewish year is the seven weeks between the festival of Pesach, Passover, which commemorates the exodus from Egypt, and Shavuot, Pentecost, which commemorates the giving of the Ten Commandments at Mount Sinai, when the children of Israel entered a covenant with God. This period is known as the Counting of the Omer and the roots of it can be traced back to the time when the Temple stood in Jerusalem. Passover coincided with the barley harvest and as part of the ceremony to mark this occasion, a measure of barley, an omer, was waved at the altar by the priest. This law is mentioned in the Torah reading (Lev. 23.10–11):

> When you come into the land which I give you and reap its harvest, you shall bring the sheaf of the first fruits of your harvest to the priest; and he shall wave the sheaf before the Lord, that you may find acceptance; on the morrow after the Sabbath the priest shall wave it.

When the Temple was destroyed, this ceremony stopped, but the tradition arose of counting the 49 days of the grain harvest, ending with the festival of Shavuot, which marked the beginning of the wheat harvest.

Though the harvest theme lies behind the tradition, other ideas have been read into it as well. For example, the great medieval philosopher Maimonides, offers a nice analogy. When you are looking forward to meeting a special friend, you count the days and hours until you meet. In the same way, Israel looks forward to the encounter with God on Shavuot and counts the days. Another suggestion points out that at this period of the year, we have not yet received the Torah, the teaching, from God, so we are somehow incomplete as a people, waiting eagerly for the word of God to come into our lives.

Since the second century, the Omer period has been observed as a period of semi-mourning. It became associated with the tragic history of the Bar Kochba rebellion against Rome which led to a disastrous loss of life. So the traditional practice has been to avoid any kind of celebration during this period, including weddings. The one exception is the thirty-third day of the counting, *lag ba'omer*, when all such restrictions are removed. The reason is again tied to a legend that on this day a plague that had affected the students of Rabbi Akiva stopped. So this day has also become known as the 'scholar's festival'.

Such a period of time, that is counted daily, lends itself to any number of special interpretations. Since we are approaching the giving of the Torah, mystical traditions associate each day with the raising of our spiritual consciousness by contemplating aspects of the divine – such as love, power, pride, beauty, authority. In another tradition, some Jews link each week with particular biblical figures and try to imitate the special characteristics associated with them. So the first week would be devoted to Abraham, famed for his hospitality. The second week is linked with Isaac, remembered for his trust in God. Jacob is the subject of the third week, known for his simplicity. In the fourth week, Moses would be the figure, and this would focus on the study of Torah. His brother Aaron, the priest, is the subject of the fifth week, famed as someone who tried to make peace between people. The sixth week would focus on Joseph, someone who resisted worldly temptations. In the seventh week, the figure would be King David, who brings with him the thought of the kingdom of God on earth.

Yet another way is to recognize that the period also commemorates a physical journey – from Egypt through the desert to Mount Sinai. This journey is also an exploration of the experience of freedom from slavery and the testing out of what that freedom might mean. If that is the case, can we imagine what the stages of such a journey might have been? In the first week, there would have been the simple euphoria and excitement of freedom, of release from the fear and destructiveness of slavery. In the biblical story, it included the crossing of the Sea of Reeds, and the parting of the waters is a kind of symbolic birth of the people. A new life has begun.

But by the second week, the first realization must come that freedom has a price. Slavery offered a certain kind of security. However bad it was, one did at least know what to expect, and life was organized around certain routines and rituals. Here in the desert, nothing could be taken for granted, from the finding of food to the relationship with other former slaves. Who had authority in this new situation? Who could be trusted? How do we relate to people who had taken advantage of the former situation for their own good and even done harm to their own people? Creating a new society is no easy matter when past experiences and old abuses can haunt the attempt to create something new.

Perhaps that is why in the third week we may lose our way. The desert has no signposts, or rather we have to learn how to read and understand a new landscape. Conflicts will arise over leadership and the direction to take. Roads that seem to lead in the right direction may turn out to be dead ends. We may even have to retrace our steps and start again in what we hope will be the right direction. Some will become nostalgic for the good old days of slavery. Some may even propose that we give up the entire enterprise and return to Egypt. At least as slaves we knew who we were and what was our place. This is a difficult period of doubt and anger. It is the time when the whole enterprise could fail and the people break apart. The children of Israel spent 40 years in the wilderness, and it was only when a new generation arose, one born in freedom, that they were ready to leave it.

By the fourth week, the journey itself has become the whole of reality. The practicalities of the march, of supplies and water, of life on the move will have become routine. Questions of a final destination will have slipped into the background, for what matters now is simply the fact of moving on. Each new obstacle must simply be faced and overcome. Perhaps someone knows where we are going. We must simply take it on trust and continue.

The fifth week brings a new kind of energy and strength. Perhaps it is a 'second wind', the emergence of a kind of resistance to despair. We are too far from Egypt to wish to turn back any more. We have learnt how to survive in this unknown territory. We recognize our achievements and the skills we have acquired. Something like anticipation arises, and hopes for a different kind of future.

In the sixth week, we may even come to realize that the wilderness has become a kind of home. Its landscapes are familiar, and more than that, we begin to see their beauty and purity. Their emptiness had once been too much to bear, and we had to fill the space somehow. So we projected upon it our fears. The emptiness outside mirrored the emptiness within us. The slavery that defined us in the past was gone. Would there be anything to replace it? Who were we? But now we could understand what it meant simply to be open, to welcome into ourselves whatever it was that came to us. The wilderness became our teacher and its emptiness a challenge to our imagination and creativity.

So by the seventh week, we are ready to come to Sinai. This was not to be the end of our journey. Rather it would be a moment of self-definition and of acceptance of who we had become. We were a people with a purpose and a destiny. Our journey out of slavery had taught us what a society should be that was the opposite of slavery. Mutual respect among us, shared responsibility for the people as a whole, caring for one another and especially for those in need – all these were waiting to be formulated and clarified when we met with our God on the slopes of the mountain. We could accept the covenant that was handed down to us, because in the course of our journey through the wilderness, we had come to understand it from our own experience. We were no longer slaves, now we had to take upon ourselves the responsibilities of freedom.

And every year we will have to undergo the same journey once again. In case we should forget the slavery from which we have come. In case we should forget the place to which we journey.

46

The Black Fast (*Tisha b'Av*)

Some years ago I spent a summer in Jerusalem. On *Tisha b'Av*, the ninth day of the month of Av, in the middle of the summer, a group of us went to the Western Wall to commemorate in the traditional way the tragic destructions associated with this day. The fast of *Tisha b'Av* recalls some of the darkest moments in Jewish history, especially the destruction of the First and Second Temples, both of which signalled the beginning of exile from the land of Israel. Throughout Jewish history, other tragic events have become associated with the day, such as the slaughter of Jews during the Crusades and the expulsion from Spain. But the rabbis located the first tragic *Tisha b'Av* even earlier in Jewish history. While in the wilderness, shortly after the Exodus from Egypt, the Israelites sent spies into the land to learn about it. But they brought back such a negative report about the power of the inhabitants of the land and the impossibility of conquering it that the people rebelled against Moses and even wanted to return to Egypt. This so angered God that the Israelites were forced to wander for 40 years in the wilderness, till a new generation was born. The day on which this catastrophe occurred, so the rabbis taught, was also *Tisha b'Av*! So the exile from the land even preceded their first entry into it. *Tisha b'Av* and the experience of exile are bound to one another.

On this occasion in Jerusalem when we reached the *Kotel*, the Western Wall, we found a scene of utter chaos. Some people were following the traditional practice: sitting on the ground in mourning and reading or chanting *Eicha*, the Book of Lamentations, and *kinot*, dirges. But around them were others who were very deliberately partying and celebrating. Their argument was that *Tisha b'Av* belonged to the time of exile only. Today, the Jews were back in their land, Jerusalem was now reunited and unified, there was a new reality and this ancient fast day should be abolished.

It was a dramatic example of Jewish tradition clashing with changed circumstances. But even the question of whether or not to fast at such a time of return and restoration is not altogether new. It was asked already in the biblical period by those who came back after the 70 years of exile in Babylon. Some elders approached the prophet Zechariah with the question: 'Shall we weep and practice abstinence during the fifth month (the month of Av), as we have been doing all these years?' (Zech. 7.3). The answer of the prophet is somewhat enigmatic. He asks the counter question in God's name: 'When you fasted all these 70 years, did you fast for my benefit? And when you eat and drink, who but you does the eating and drinking?' (Zech. 7.5–6).

What the prophet seems to be saying in the name of God is: if you were fasting, because you were unhappy about the experience of exile; if your fasting, like your eating and drinking, was purely for your own sake, then it makes sense to stop the fasting now that you are back. But if you have been fasting out of regret that your previous behaviour was offensive to God, so that you were punished by being sent into exile, then your fasting is really about re-establishing that broken relationship with God and ensuring that such a failure never happens again. Your fasting is then not just for your own sake but is truly 'for God's sake', and you should continue to do it.

The prophet then goes on to list their previous failings: defrauding the widow, the orphan, the stranger and the poor; plotting against one another. It was these actions that had led to God punishing them. So the message was: if you understand the true nature of the fast, it will remind you each year of your responsibilities to the underprivileged in society who come under God's special protection. If that is the goal of the fasting, then it should be continued as it enhances the quality of the life of your society today.

The prophet will later offer the hope that the time will come, when all the mourning of those fast days that commemorate the destruction of Jerusalem and the Temple will be turned into days of celebration and joy. But until that time comes, our Jewish liturgy offers us some consolation for the present. The Shabbat after *Tisha b'Av* is called *Shabbat nachamu*, the Shabbat of consolation and comfort, when we read Isaiah 40, beginning: 'Comfort, comfort my people.' It is followed by six Shabbats, when the prophetic readings promise restoration, leading up to Rosh Hashanah, the New Year, and a new beginning to our spiritual life. In order to appreciate the consolation that comes to us, we have to have first experienced the depths of sorrow and trouble that the Jewish people have known. So our tradition, by emphasizing both the sadness of *Tisha b'Av* and the consolation that follows it, takes us on a spiritual journey in our imagination on the roller-coaster ride that is Jewish history and destiny.

47

Names of the New Year

The beginning of the most serious season of the Jewish spiritual calendar is the eve of Rosh Hashanah, the New Year. In the following ten days we are called upon to consider all our activities of the past year, to examine them in the light of the highest values of our tradition and form a judgement on our behaviour. Where we can recognize things that we have done, which are wrong in any way, we must seek to correct them. Where we have hurt another human being, we must seek to make amends and become reconciled. We are called upon to repair whatever we can, so as to make this New Year a fresh beginning to our lives. At the end of these ten days, on Yom Kippur, the Day of Atonement, we ask God to accept the work of repentance we have done, to 'cover over' the sins of the past, and support us in this new year before us.

That at least is the theory behind this period. It is not an easy task. A recent American book indicates how unprepared we often are to undertake it. It is called: *This is Reality, and you are not ready for it! A Guide to the High Holydays.*

Many Jews have little experience of Jewish religious life today. Often, they lack a basic Jewish education that helps them to understand the significance and potential value of our festivals. The New Year simply arrives as a date in a calendar. It may be ignored, or remembered as some kind of family event or obligation. Indeed the New Year is often a time when families come together. However, it is not like the Passover, which we celebrate around the family table in the home and focus on the history of our people. The New Year rituals are based on the synagogue and are more focused on the individual, so there is not the same intensity of meeting together.

The themes of the New Year period are bound up with religious language and for many this is not familiar or comfortable in our secular society. We may accept that we do wrong things from time to time or even hurt other people. However, words like 'sin', 'repentance' and 'atonement' belong to a very special kind of understanding of a life lived in relation to God. If God is not present in our lives, at least not the God of our religious tradition, then much of the meaning of this language simply disappears or even alienates us. Nevertheless, the underlying ideas and teachings of the New Year period can offer us something, if we examine them more closely.

Rosh Hashanah itself has a number of different titles that reflect the different ideas within it. It is first Yom Ha-zikaron, the Day of Remembrance. We are to remember the year that is past and reflect upon all that has happened, and how we have responded to the challenges it has brought. We are called upon to be serious and consistent in our remembering because the things we forget, or do not wish to remember, God certainly remembers. So this encourages a kind of honesty and integrity that helps us recognize and accept both the good and the bad things of the past year. We recall the faces of those who have been significant in our lives, and especially those who have died in the past year and the empty space they leave. We begin to see how we are bound up with one another and the importance of these relationships. Certainly we can see where we have lost friendships or missed opportunities. We cannot know what the future will bring and how long we have to enjoy the company of those who have a place in our lives. Remembering in this way is an impetus to make the fullest use of the precious time we have together with friends and those we love.

But Rosh Hashanah is also Yom Ha-din, the Day of Judgement, when God examines all of humanity and all of creation. This theme challenges us to look beyond ourselves at the world around us and our wider responsibilities. It is very easy to feel powerless in the face of the great movements and issues in the world. We are daily reminded of the injustices, the wars, the hunger and poverty that are everywhere around us. Yet, a day of self-judgement forces us to ask the question: What difference will my own life have made to the world? If I cannot affect things on a global scale, at least in my own immediate society I have a role to play and a responsibility. The gifts that I have been given by God, whether material or spiritual, are really only on loan. They become mine to the extent that I use them wisely and share them with others.

We have moved from looking inward through the act of remembering, to looking outward through the theme of judgement. The third idea associated with the New Year takes us a stage further. For in the Jewish view, this day is also the anniversary of and a celebration of the creation of the world. One of the poems recited on this day begins: '*Ha-yomharatolam*', 'This day is the birthday of the world'. So Rosh Hashanah and the following period offer the possibility for rebirth and renewal. They remind us that the universe is larger than our own limited view of it and that humanity as a whole, is only a small part of the extraordinary beauty and complexity of life. The cycle of our individual lives, birth, growth, maturity and death, are only a tiny part of a process of continual change that affects everything about us. So how do we find the right perspective on our life?

An old rabbinic teaching suggests that we should carry two pieces of paper with us. Whenever we feel ourselves to be too important and self-satisfied, we should take out the paper on which is written the words: 'I am but dust and ashes.' But when we feel ourselves to be insignificant or unworthy, we should take out the paper on which is written the words: 'For my sake the world was created.'

Rosh Hashanah, the Ten Days of Penitence that follow it and Yom Kippur, offer an extraordinary opportunity to stand back from the pressures and demands of our everyday lives. We can look with a different kind of objectivity at all that we do, our hopes and the reality of what our life is about. Yom Kippur itself is a day of fasting. It is as if we cut ourselves off from the familiar routines of daily life and can devote time to ourselves alone. The tradition is to wear a white garment, the kittel, which will one day serve as the shroud in which we are buried. So we are freed on this day to look upon our life as if from the grave, summing up its achievements and failures. We write our own obituary. But we also know that there will be a day after Yom Kippur, so that we can act on what we have discovered about ourselves, recast our lives, begin again as a new creation.

48

The Sin of Scapegoating

Approaching the Jewish New Year is a time for sustained reflection on our lives, as individuals, as part of the Jewish community and as members of the wider society. We use this time to look back on the past year. But we do so with a critical view of our behaviour: the things that we did that were wrong and those that we failed to do which we should have done. This serious attempt at self-criticism is the legacy of the biblical prophets. Their primary task was not to look into the future. Instead they looked into the present, trying to see it through God's eyes. Only then could the behaviour of the nation change, and this would itself change the future. That activity and hope remain part of the task of the High Holydays that are before us.

When I began to look back on this past year, I found myself remembering a particular incident. I had the privilege of attending the Evangelische Kirchentag in Cologne and giving lectures on Judaism and the Hebrew Bible at the Jüdische Lehrhaus. But I also took part in a couple of interfaith panels which focused on Jewish–Christian–Muslim dialogue.

During my time in Cologne I had been impressed by a number of initiatives that have been undertaken there to promote greater understanding between the three faiths. Opposite the Cathedral is a centre where people can drop in, meet one another and learn about the three religious communities.

A programme under the umbrella of the Mayor, and sponsored by representative bodies of the three faiths, is called '*Weißt Du, werich bin?*', 'Do you know who I am?' It invites communities to meet one another and provides a well-documented set of materials of information about the three faiths, but also of methods for ensuring the best results from the encounter.

Another new initiative is called 'Make your picture of Abraham'. It encourages people to find and photograph evidence of the influence of Abraham around the city itself, because he is seen as the common ancestor of all three faiths. These and other local initiatives are important small steps towards creating mutual understanding and respect.

But the incident that concerned me showed just how difficult this important work is within our society at this time. Following the presentations of the three panellists, the session was opened up for discussion. Almost all the questions were addressed to the Muslim speaker. This is understandable on one level, as Islam is the least familiar of the religions represented, despite the extraordinary contribution of Islam to our European society. But what was worrying was the tone of the questions. There was about them an aggressiveness that was painful to hear. Effectively, the Muslim speaker was being put on trial on the assumption that all Muslims were to be held responsible for the actions of a few. Moreover Islam itself was being labelled as a religion of violence – which was in complete contrast to the tone and actions and indeed the record of the speaker himself. He was simply dismissed as the exception that proves the rule. It reminded me of the old line about how stubborn people can sometimes be: 'I've made up my mind, don't confuse me with facts!'

It made me remember something very similar I experienced on a lecture tour of America a few years ago. I have been helping to organize an annual Jewish–Christian–Muslim student conference for more than 30 years in Germany. All the student rabbis at Leo Baeck College attend as part of their training. The intention is that the future spiritual leaders of the three faiths will come to know each other in their student days and bring this experience into their later work.

Because of this, I am often invited to speak about my experience in this area. In America after 9/11 the fears, suspicions and opinions about Islam and Muslims accompanied me throughout my visit. The commonest attack was from people who asked where was the Muslim condemnation of 9/11, where were the Muslim voices in protest? I had my answer in the book I was carrying with me published in England by the Muslim community. It documented the condemnations of the atrocity by important Muslim spiritual leaders and organizations from all over the world. But it was clear that not only were these voices not heard, it was almost as if there was a desire not to hear them or believe them. It was as if we preferred to see the Muslim world in plain black and white terms. We did not want to hear voices of moderation because they complicated the single message we were feeding ourselves through the media. I even know of an occasion where a Muslim speaker due to appear on a television discussion was cancelled, because it was felt he was not extreme enough in his views to make good drama.

Of course, we all know this. We know that our popular media will always present extreme dramatic stories. Good news is boring. Bad news sells papers. But despite knowing this, we constantly allow it to colour our judgement.

Clearly we have to be on guard against the threat of terrorist activity.

Moreover it is also clear that much of that activity is carried out by groups acting under what they consider to be an Islamic justification, even if the vast majority of Muslims are horrified by their violence.

But as great as the danger posed by terrorist incidents is the danger of the damage done to our society and its values by our responses. For we are constantly demonizing one particular minority group within our society. The potential sequence is all too familiar and disturbing. By labelling an entire group of people as different, and then as threatening, it is only a short step to scape-goating them collectively which justifies mistreating them, either individually or collectively.

It is a process that Jews experienced in the last century, and we know the ultimate consequences. Any person with authority within society who speaks in generalities about 'the Muslims', has fallen into that trap, and needs to be challenged. The issue is not simply about demanding a response from Muslims, but of ensuring that their voices are heard because we in the wider society support them.

What is the alternative to the climate of fear that we are helping to cultivate by our own silence? It can only be a commitment to building a climate of understanding and respect across our different communities.

And such a climate only comes from active engagement with one another, from building relationships with people across and beyond our comfortable borders. Some within the faith communities are already involved in such activities with meetings among churches, mosques and synagogues, like the examples in Cologne. Schools are beginning to invite speakers, sometimes with representative of all three communities together, to demonstrate the reality of cooperation and mutual respect. But there remains much more to do, including taking individual responsibility for questioning and challenging the simplistic message we feed ourselves every day through the media.

If we have a new sin to confess when the Jewish New Year comes, it will be that we allowed ourselves to go along with the popular demonization of Islam and of Muslims; that we contributed to the climate of mistrust and fear instead of helping build the personal relationships of mutual respect and trust that offer an alternative vision and hope for the future.

49

The Day of Atonement and Sacrifice

Each Yom Kippur during the Musaf Service, we remember the traditions that belonged to this day at the time when the Temple stood. Particularly striking is the ritual involving two goats whose fate is decided by lot. One is selected to be a sin-offering to God, the other is led into the wilderness and there set free.

The biblical description of this ceremony appears in Leviticus Chapter 16. However, it is preceded at the beginning of the chapter by a sentence that gives the section its name as one of the weekly Torah portions, '*acharei mot*', 'after the death': 'God spoke to Moses after the death of the two sons of Aaron who died when they drew near to the presence of God' (Lev. 16.1).

What is the link between this story and the information about the Yom Kippur ritual that follows?

The Torah provides it by explaining that Aaron must take certain precautions when he enters the presence of God lest he also die. This then leads into the detailed description of the Yom Kippur ceremony.

The story about Aaron's sons, Nadav and Avihu, is first told in Leviticus 10. They took their censers, put fire in them and incense, 'and brought before God strange fire that God had not commanded them'. Fire came down from heaven and consumed them. In Chapter 16, no mention is made of this 'strange' fire, just that they drew near to God.

It is a curious story, and even stranger to be reminded of it as an introduction to the ceremony of Yom Kippur. Yet, perhaps there is a deeper connection to be discerned.

Nadav and Avihu have already appeared in the Bible in a particular context. When the Israelites stood at Mount Sinai and entered into the covenant with God, the ceremony was formally completed with a ritual sacrifice. But when this was over, in one of the most mysterious passages in the Torah, Moses and Aaron, Nadav and Avihu, and 70 elders of Israel, climbed the mountain 'and they saw the God of Israel. Under God's feet, there was the likeness of a pavement of sapphire, like the very sky for purity. But God did nothing to them. They saw God and ate and drank' (Exod. 24.9–11).

It is not hard to imagine the effect of this extraordinary experience on those who were there. Elsewhere we are told that none may see God's face and live, yet these were privileged to do so and survived this deepest of mystical experiences, unique in the Torah. Perhaps for Nadav and Avihu this transformed their role as priests and potential successors to their father Aaron into something much more deeply intense, spiritual and ultimately all-consuming. To serve God with their whole heart ceased to be simply an intellectual or emotional commitment and became the burning desire that was central to their very existence. It was religious zeal to serve God with their whole being that led them into the sanctuary without permission or the proper precautions.

Their story is narrated immediately after the account of the setting up of the sanctuary itself and the first sacrifices made upon the altar. These were consumed by a fire that descended from heaven, to show God's acceptance of the sacrificial system. So it seems that Nadav and Avihu were consumed at that very moment by that same heavenly fire that took the first sacrifice on the newly dedicated altar. Because of the inner fire of their mystical devotion to God, they were consumed by that same flame. They became themselves, what they actually wished to be, sacrifices to God out of their overwhelming love of God.

So why are we reminded of that tragic event at the beginning of the account of the Yom Kippur ceremony?

Two very different types of religious piety meet at this moment: the deeply mystical, that is ecstatic, passionate, individualistic, but may become fanatical and self-destructive; and the disciplined, collective, ritualized and formalized religion associated with Aaron and the priesthood, a religion designed to regulate the normal everyday collective life of a society.

The experience of the two sons of Aaron represents the former. The symbolic ritual of Yom Kippur represents the latter.

The drawing of lots that determines the fate of the two goats speaks to a particular human reality: that we cannot ever know what awaits us from moment to moment in our lives. We may understand what we encounter as mere chance or, instead, as our own special destiny; as purely random or as part of a pattern of divine care and purpose. Yom Kippur reminds us that what we encounter in life may seem to be a kind of lottery, but what we do with it is our particular responsibility and opportunity.

Like the sons of Aaron, one of the goats will become a sacrifice, consumed in an instant. But the other one is not killed but goes into the wilderness, its natural habitat, and must fend for itself in a place of unknown dangers and possibilities.

All the preparatory work on ourselves that we do for Yom Kippur, in attempting to correct things that we have done wrong and mend broken relationships, gives us the inner resources to survive and flourish in the unknown world that awaits us at every moment. On this the most deeply religious day of the Jewish year we remember briefly the mystical dimension, but focus instead on the solid basis of a life lived in community that Judaism offers us.

50

The Day of Atonement and Fasting

If you ask the average Jew, or even a well-informed non-Jew, what they know about Yom Kippur, the first thing that is likely to come to mind is the fasting. The unofficial greeting among friends in the time leading up to Yom Kippur, is 'well over the fast'. The centrality of this theme is obvious. That is why it is rather shocking to look at the texts selected by the rabbinic tradition to read on this day.

For the morning service, we read from Isaiah 57.14—58.14. Scholars debate the background to this part of the Book of Isaiah. It is clearly later than the first 39 chapters that are set in Jerusalem a century before its fall to the Babylonians. From Chapter 40, the author addresses those in exile in Babylon, but Chapter 56 onward seems to relate to an even later period, when the author feels able to criticize his re-established society. But in doing so he obviously takes a certain pleasure in playing with the Hebrew language itself.

From the beginning of Chapter 58, he attacks what he calls the rebellious sins of his people, and his first target is their hypocrisy.

Indeed they seek Me day after day, and yearn to know My ways, like a nation that does what is right and never abandoned the Law of its God. They ask Me for righteous laws and yearn to be close to God.

One of my teachers suggested that this desire to be 'close to God' really meant that they wanted a seat of honour near the front of the Synagogue!

When Isaiah says, 'they yearn', the verb is *chafatz*, and he will play with this shortly.

But they in turn have a complaint to God:

'Why have we fasted if You do not see? Why afflict our souls if You pay no heed?'

'To afflict our souls' is the very language of the Torah about what we are expected to do on Yom Kippur, with fasting being a significant element. But Isaiah now hits them with his message, in a series of word-plays on the Hebrew term for fasting, '*tzom*'. He challenges them: '*b'yom tzom'chem timtz'u cheifetz*', 'on the day of your fasting you find business'. He takes the word '*tzom*', fast, and turns it around to make '*matza*', to find. Their very fasting is 'inside out'. And their 'yearning', '*chafatz*', to be near God is revealed instead as their true 'yearning', to carry on with their 'business', '*cheifetz*'. It reminds me of the old rabbinic complaint: 'I don't mind if they talk about their business in synagogue, if only they would talk about God in their business!'

But Isaiah has not finished with his word play. In verse three he complains that they only fast for quarrel and strife, and 'strife', here '*matzah*', is yet another play on '*tzom*'. He goes on to condemn fasting that is just an outer show, what God wants is that they 'let the oppressed go free, share their food with the hungry, bring the homeless into their homes, clothe the naked'. It is a 'fasting' from self-indulgence and from ignoring their responsibilities to others in their society. That is the kind of sacrifice God expects by their fast.

It is a very powerful attack, and surely those he was targeting knew exactly whom he had in mind. It is this kind of risky activity that led the rabbis to suggest that in order to survive the prophets had to be independently wealthy!

The point of choosing precisely this Haftarah for Yom Kippur is now obvious. It totally subverts our understanding of the day. It is not the fact of fasting that is important, but the renewal of our commitment to the needs of others that is at stake.

The Haftarah for the afternoon service is the Book of Jonah, which contains a myriad of lessons for this day, delivered to us with great irony. But a central idea comes in the third chapter. When the people of Nineveh realize that destruction is coming, they put on sackcloth and ashes, the conventional signs of mourning that are meant to appease the angry god. The king of Nineveh does the same, but then adds a dimension that explodes out of the text. It is part of the irony of the book that his words are actually taken from the Book of Jeremiah and placed in the mouth of this pagan king.

'And let every man turn from his evil way and from the violence in his hands.' As the rabbis noted, God responds positively to the words of the king, but totally ignores the fasting and mourning: 'And God saw their actions, how they turned from their evil ways, and God relented of the evil He had said He would do to them, and did not do it.' Once again it is actions that count, a change in behaviour, not simply the mechanical act of fasting.

By choosing these two Haftarot, the rabbis are in fact following exactly in the footsteps of Isaiah and Jonah, subverting the obvious symbol of repentance, fasting, and saying it is not enough. Yom Kippur is a call to change, to acknowledge the things we do that damage others and stop, and to take greater responsibility for the world around us. 'This is the fast I have chosen.'

51

Lessons of Sukkot (Tabernacles)

We begin to celebrate the festival of Sukkot, Tabernacles. Like all Jewish festivals it contains many layers of ideas, ideas which are reinforced by the different symbols and activities of the festival. At one level, Sukkot celebrates the autumn harvest, the time of year when fruits are ripe and gathered in. In the biblical period it meant that there was a brief moment when it was possible to relax and celebrate the successful close of the agricultural year. But like the other agricultural festivals in the Jewish calendar, Pesach (Passover) and Shavuot (Pentecost), additional historical ideas were grafted onto this agricultural basis. So Pesach celebrates the exodus from Egypt, Shavuot the encounter with God at Sinai, and Sukkot the wandering in the wilderness for 40 years on the way to the Promised Land.

Whether Jews actually work the land or live in cities, at Sukkot we construct outside our house or synagogue a *sukkah*, a temporary structure covered with branches, decorated with fruit and vegetables, open to the sky. This frail shelter represents those that the Israelites lived in on their 40-year journey through the wilderness. But there is something puzzling about this particular structure. Because, according to the biblical account, the Israelites on their wanderings actually lived in tents. The frail lean-to huts with open roofs, the 'booths' of Sukkot, seem to be modelled instead on the temporary shelters built in the fields during harvest time to provide shade from the heat of the sun. They belong to people living and working in the fields of their own land, not people travelling for 40 years through a desert.

So is the *sukkah* a symbol to help us re-enact the experience of the Exodus from Egypt and the wilderness period? Or, instead, does it reflect a later period when the people of Israel felt at home and rooted in their own land? This twofold nature of the symbol itself is echoed in the teachings and tensions within the festival. For the *sukkah* reminds us of the repeated situation of the Jewish people throughout most of our history. We have lived in many places as a tolerated minority for a while, only to be expelled when political or religious circumstances changed, and forced to wander the world in search of yet another new home. Ours has been a nomadic history lived in a private 'No-man's land' on the margins of other societies and civilizations.

By living for a week in the *sukkah* we symbolically re-enact that history. We leave the safety and security of our physical homes to expose ourselves to the vagaries of the weather. Through that physical act we acknowledge that security does not come only from buildings of brick and mortar. We identify with the often tragic experience of the victims of floods, fires or the disruption of war. Instead of trusting in the world of outer things we try to understand what it means to find an inner security, one that comes through the support offered to us throughout our life by our trust in God.

It is painful and disturbing to remember the wilderness stories in the Bible because of the images they evoke. They tell of the constant search for food and water and the fear of death for us and our children if sustenance cannot be found. They speak of the frightened and hostile reactions of neighbouring peoples, the Moabites and Edomites, when the Israelites came near. Some refused the Israelites access to their territory, even simply to pass through, even if they paid a heavy toll for the privilege. Some peoples even sent their army to the borders to keep the Israelites out. Sukkot takes us into the heart of the experience of refugees of all times and places and calls us to identify with and help those who come to us today seeking refuge.

Perhaps the people of Moab or Edom in the biblical period had the same discussions about the Israelites that have become all too familiar to us today in Europe. Their leaders would have asked the question: did the Israelites really need to leave Egypt and come here to us? The debate would have run as follows: On the one hand the Israelites clearly faced the threat of genocide at the hands of Pharaoh who was killing all the male children. That would make the Israelites genuine political refugees, eligible for asylum on humanitarian grounds and under international law. But perhaps many of the Israelites left Egypt because they were simply tired of being slaves and wanted to improve their financial and social circumstances by moving to Moab or Edom or the land of Canaan. That would make them economic refugees, and therefore not really in need of asylum. At the end of the discussion, the decisive argument for keeping the Israelites out would probably be of a very different order. There were bound to be Moabite politicians who said that the Israelites would need welfare and become a drain on the economy, while others feared that they might pose a threat to the local job market by providing cheap labour and putting their own people out of work. On the whole it would be better simply to keep them all out.

We have made a large jump from a religious festival celebrated in a little lean-to hut in a suburban garden to the global problem of refugees in our world. But Sukkot belongs to a great annual meditation on the nature of human society and our mutual responsibility to one another that lie at the heart of our Jewish festivals. It begins at Pesach with the celebration of the exodus from Egypt, and the question of the nature of human freedom. At Shavuot, we look at our mutual responsibility to one another as we formally create a human community through our covenant with God. At Sukkot, we visit our *sukkah*, often beautifully decorated with fruit and enjoy the gifts of nature, but at the same time feel on our bodies the cooler wind of autumn warning of a winter to come and we recognize the fragility of all human striving and success.

Of course, it is no great hardship for a week to visit our *sukkah* for meals, going indoors as soon as it rains. But it is very different to be a refugee who may have lost home, language, a sense of self-worth and even the bare elements essential for physical survival.

Sukkot calls us to exercise our imagination and extend our compassion. It sends a shiver of discomfort through our complacency and reminds us in a gentle way of our own mortality.

But Sukkot also asserts that we can find the inner resources and mutual support from each other to face the challenges that life brings. That hope is expressed in the words of the novelist Natalia Ginzburg, writing as a survivor putting her life together again after the Second World War. She wrote: 'we are forced to go on discovering an inner calm that is not born of carpets and vases of flowers . . .'[1] The search for that 'inner calm' also belongs to the message of Sukkot, for it tells us in its symbolic way that all of our life is actually spent in a frail shelter open to the sky.

52

Prophet and Profit

We tend to have rather stereotyped images of the biblical prophets. One is certainly that of hairy men dressed in loincloths standing in the market place shouting words of condemnation at their fellow citizens. There is a further assumption that the word 'prophet' itself implies the ability to foretell events that will come about and that this is the basis of their activities. Among the many figures described as 'prophets' in the Hebrew Bible there are certainly some who would conform to these images, but the title and the role contains many other dimensions and subtleties.

A number of Hebrew terms are used to describe the same phenomenon; of people who felt that they had received a direct word from God and who sought to convey it to their contemporaries. They may be described as a 'seer' or a 'visionary', possibly reflecting how they attained the divine message, but others are simply called 'a man of God' or most commonly a *navee*, perhaps meaning 'messenger'. Some, like Elijah and Elisha had supernatural powers; others seem to be better understood as social critics who saw in their society the violation of the 'covenant', the religious constitution that bound the people of Israel to their God. They set about warning of the potential consequences of the way that society was operating. Their vision of the future was based upon a critical reading of the present and painting possible future scenarios, using powerful poetic or rhetorical language. Some of them paid with their lives for the message they felt forced to deliver to authorities that did not wish to hear them or allow them to be heard by the populace.

Perhaps the first thing to recognize is that the biblical prophets whose records have come down to us were to a large extent 'professionals'. They underwent some kind of apprenticeship or training with other prophets that gave them a title and a role as interpreters of the will of God to their society. They were employed, for example, by the court to predict the outcome of policy decisions, often simply saying 'yes' to whatever was the wish of the powers of the day. Others might be asked by individuals seeking divine guidance for personal needs. It is out of the ranks of these professionals that there emerged the particular prophets whose stories or words were recorded by the biblical tradition, largely because their commitment to truth, preserved by their own disciples, was vindicated by history. Yet, one of them, Amos, even insisted that he was not a professional (neither a prophet nor the 'son'), but probably apprentice of a prophet. God had called him and who could not but answer. They utilized a particular vocabulary ('Thus says the Lord', 'an oracle of the Lord', the 'burden of the Lord' – this latter referring to prophecies against other nations) as a mark of their status and the authority of their words.

Nevertheless, the Hebrew Bible, in its customary self-critical mode, records the problem that even a prophet could not always distinguish between the word of God he was to transmit and his own personal opinion. Thus Samuel is reprimanded for choosing the wrong son of Jesse to be king, before choosing David, because he was over-impressed with the appearance of the first one he saw. The struggle between the 'true' prophets and the 'false' prophets is frequently addressed, the latter often implying those who simply blessed the status quo and never looked more deeply into the ills and injustices of society. The narrative about Micaiah ben Imlah (1 Kings 22) illustrates the conflict between one individual and 400 court prophets. It has been suggested that one prophet may or may not have the correct opinion – but when 400 prophets say the same thing, this is not prophecy but hysteria! Ultimately the question of determining the truth or otherwise of a prophet's words remains the responsibility of his audience, particularly when prophets of seemingly equal authority simply disagree (see, for example the public debate between 'Jeremiah the prophet' and 'Hananiah the prophet' (Jer. 28)).

There is another way of looking at the biblical prophets, or rather at their role in the economy of power within biblical society. The prophet Samuel, the last of the 'judges', political leaders, before the institution of the monarchy under King Saul, had three roles: political leader, prophet and priest. Saul, the first king, attempted to fulfil the same three roles, and effectively failed in each – he 'prophesied' but no message came, he failed in an attempt to offer sacrifices, and his leadership was flawed. His successor King David clearly undertook the role of political leadership alone, but was always accompanied by a priest and a court prophet, one who was prepared to criticize his actions. Here in embryo is a tripartite division of authority that in different ways characterized a biblical and later rabbinic theory of governance. The three domains, each accorded equal power, were designated in rabbinic parlance as the 'crown of kingship', the political leadership; the 'crown of priesthood', responsible for the maintenance of the regular worship and service of God through the cult and prayer; and the 'crown of Torah', the conveying of the will of God, earlier the prophetic role, casting an eye on society from the divine perspective.

When the Jerusalem Temple was destroyed by the Romans, and what we know today as rabbinic Judaism emerged, the rabbis taught that prophecy ceased at that moment, and was handed over to children and to fools! The word of God was to be found from then on through interpreting the texts in the Hebrew Bible, in line with the best of contemporary knowledge and values. For this newly emerging society, the anarchic power of individual prophets, claiming to speak directly in the name of God, needed to be contained at a time of crisis when the essential landmarks of previous Jewish existence, the Temple, the land of Israel and the monarchy, had all been destroyed. The self-critical role of the prophets, whose words the rabbis preserved and studied, was undertaken by the rabbis themselves through their internal debates and the democracy of learning and study that characterized their leadership of the people.

Given this, albeit brief, overview of a Jewish understanding of prophecy, the question inevitably arises as to who fulfils such a role today, and indeed whether such a role could ever again be institutionalized. Politically, the 'loyal opposition' of democratic institutions and societies may play such a critical role in secular terms. But the relegation of religion to the private sphere has limited its prophetic role, with a few notable exceptions. Today's re-emergence of politically engaged religious movements, often with a conservative or 'fundamentalist' agenda, may appear at first glance to herald a return of the prophetic voice; at least that may be the rhetoric that accompanies such movements. But their role is often more akin to that of the priesthood, seeking to preserve real or imagined past norms and values, rather than opening people to broader concerns and needs of society as a whole. Time alone will tell how to recognize and assess the true prophetic voices of our time.

Notes and References

Introduction

1 Jonathan Magonet, *From Autumn to Summer*, SCM Press, 2000.

19 The Absent Congregation

1 In Jewish tradition each weekly reading from the Torah is known by one of its opening words rather than by the chapter and verse reference. So the reading beginning with Genesis 25.19 is called '*Toledot*', 'the history of the generations' – see p. 16 above. When two sections are read together on the same Shabbat, they are known by their combined name, hence '*vahakhel-pekudey*' combines '*vayakhel*', 'he gathered' (Exod. 35.1) and '*pekudey*', 'this is the sum . . .' (Exod. 38.21).

32 Letting Go of Power

1 Hayim Nahman Bialik and Yehoshua Hana Ravnitzky, eds, *The Book of Legends (Sefer Ha-Aggadah) Legends from the Talmud and Midrash*, (trans. William G. Braude), Schocken Books, New York, 1992, p. 103.

51 Lessons of Sukkot (Tabernacles)

1 Natalia Ginzburg, 'The Son of Man' (trans. Richard Burns), in *European Judaism*, Vol. 6, No. 2, Summer, 1972, pp. 7–9, p. 8.

Index of Torah Passages

Contents

About the authors

Joy Chang

Joy Chang is a core medical trainee in the London Deanery. She completed her medical degree at the University of Manchester. She has a keen interest in medical education and hopes to undertake further postgraduate training in this in the future.

Chirag Mehta

Chirag Mehta is a GP trainee in the West Midland Deanery who qualified from Manchester University in 2006. He has an interest in medical education and is currently doing his postgraduate certificate in Medical Education at Keele University. He has also written a question revision book for the nMRCGP AKT exam.

Foreword by Mr Julian Wong

This book is a comprehensive aid written with medical students and junior doctors in mind, to address the ever-growing medical knowledge they require. In each system of the body, the authors have selected common clinical cases which a final year medical student may encounter in their final examinations. The book can also act as a quick reference guide for Foundation Year trainees in relevant specialties. Relevant references including recent guidelines from NICE and SIGN, which are based on the best available evidence, are referred to within the book for relevant topics.

As an undergraduate examiner, I find this book very helpful, with its useful tips which will allow students to impress senior clinicians on the ward or in exams. The book is written in a pragmatic way to help medical students grasp common medical situations. I wish the readers the best of luck in their final exams and success in their foundation training.

Mr Julian Wong
MBChB FRCS (General surgery)
Consultant General and Vascular Surgeon
University Hospital of North Staffordshire

Undergraduate Examiner for Manchester and Keele Medical School
Court of Examiners, Royal College of Surgeons, London
Foundation Education Coordinator for Keele Foundation School

Foreword by Dr Fiona Leslie

I'm delighted to be asked to write a foreword for what I believe is an excellent resource for medical students and junior doctors, most specifically those in Foundation training, written by recent graduates, who have first-hand knowledge of what is needed at this stage of training.

There is a move both in the UK and internationally for students to learn by problem- or case-based learning, but few comprehensive books like this that use clinical cases as the framework and provide such evidence-based and well referenced answers.

The 124 realistic scenarios from the whole breadth of the medical specialties, including medicine, surgery, psychiatry and paediatrics, will help prepare students for a variety of assessments from OSCEs to multiple choice papers; but more importantly it will prepare them for seeing real patients once qualified and support them during their Foundation training. I wish there had been a resource like this available while I was training.

Dr Fiona Leslie
Consultant Physician & Gastroenterologist
Senior Lecturer in Medical Education
University of Keele

Preface

An important aspect of being a doctor is learning and teaching. This is a continuous process and as our learning needs differ greatly amongst ourselves we, as adults, need to develop our own style so we are able to get the most out of this process. Problem-based learning is one strategy which facilitates this, and many medical schools have adopted this as a teaching/learning method for their medical students. The cases contained within this book cover key relevant topics which are likely to occur in medical finals. Every effort has been made to make them as realistic as possible, using a problem-based approach, prompting the reader to consider differentials, relevant investigations and management of the patient. The process in which the reader is made to think with these cases relates to the way in which doctors approach patients and will help the reader's progression from a medical student to a junior doctor. Up-to-date information has been added in each case and relates to current guidelines; and there are helpful references for further information and reading.

We hope that you use this book effectively and wish you every success with your finals.

Joy Chang MBChB BSc(Hons)
Chirag Mehta MBChB DRCOG, DFSRH

Contributors

Dr Melinda L. Munang, B.Med.Sci, BMBS, MRCP, ST3 Infectious Diseases, University Hospital of North Staffordshire.

Mrs Hannah Sharma, MBChB MRCOphth, Ophthalmology Registrar, Birmingham and Midland Eye Centre.

Dr Caitlyn Dowson, Consultant Rheumatologist, University Hospital of North Staffordshire.

Dr Andrew Stewart, BA, MD, FRCP, FRCPath, Consultant Haematologist, University Hospital of North Staffordshire.

Mr Julian Wong, MBChB FRCS (General surgery), Consultant General and Vascular Surgeon, University Hospital of North Staffordshire; Undergraduate Examiner for Manchester and Keele Medical School; Court of Examiners, Royal College of Surgeons, London; Foundation Education Coordinator for Keele Foundation School.

Mr Robert M Kirby, MA, FRCS, Consultant and Hospital Dean for Keele University Medical School, University Hospital of North Staffordshire.

Mr Mark Saxby, BSc, MD, FRCS (Urol), Consultant Urologist, University Hospital of North Staffordshire.

Dr Julie Wessels, FRACP, Consultant Nephrologist, University Hospital of North Staffordshire.

Dr D de Takats, MA FRCP, Consultant Nephrologist, University Hospital of North Staffordshire.

Dr Neil Sharma, Specialty Registrar Otolaryngology, North Western Deanery, MBChB MRCS DOHNS.

Dr Colin A.S. Melville, Senior Lecturer in Paediatrics, Keele Medical School, MBChB (Aberdeen), FRCPCH, MMedEd (Dundee).

Dr Mark Griffiths, BSc (Hons), MBChB, MRCP, SpR Dermatology, Selly Oak Hospital, Birmingham.

Dr Fiona Leslie, Consultant Gastroenterologist, University Hospital of North Staffordshire.

Dr Joseph Anderson, MBBS, MRCP, Neurology Registrar, University Hospital of North Staffordshire.

Acknowledgements

,

We would like to thank the following individuals for their generous assistance.

Mr Julian Wong and Dr Fiona Leslie for writing forewords to this book.

Dr Mark Gunning MBChB MD FRCP, Consultant Cardiologist, University Hospital of North Staffordshire, for reviewing the Cardiovascular chapter.

Dr Charles Pantin, Consultant Respiratory Physician at the University Hospital of North Staffordshire, for reviewing the Respiratory chapter.

Dr Arjun Mukherjee MBBS MD (Tropical Medicine) MRCP, Consultant in Acute Medicine and Diabetes and Endocrinology, University Hospital of North Staffordshire, for reviewing the Endocrinology chapter.

Dr Milind Pant MBBS MRCPsych, ST4 in General Adult Psychiatry, Peninsula Deanery, Cornwall, for reviewing the Psychiatry chapter.

Mr Khaled MK Ismail MSc MD PhD FRCOG, Consultant Obstetrician and Gynaecologist, University Hospital of North Staffordshire, Senior Lecturer Keele University Medical School, for being an independent reviewer of the cases for the Obstetrics and Gynaecology chapter.

Mr Vinay Jasani, Consultant Orthopaedics Surgeon at the University Hospital of North Staffordshire, for reviewing the chapter on Orthopaedics.

Mr Paul S. Wilson, ENT Consultant, University Hospital of North Staffordshire, Year 5 Leader at Keele University Medical School, for reviewing the ENT chapter.

Dr Kay Mohanna, Director of Postgraduate Programmes at Keele University Medical School, Chair of the Midland Faculty RCGP, for reviewing the chapter on Communication and Ethics.

We also gratefully acknowledge the following organisations and individuals who have allowed us to use images, as follows:

The Heart Attack Centre at the University Hospital of North Staffordshire for Figures 1.1, 1.2, 2.1, 20.1.

Dr John Asquith, Consultant Radiologist at the University Hospital of North Staffordshire, for Figures 2.2, 2.3, 2.6, 13.1, 13.2, 20.10, 20.17, and 20.18.

Dr Grant Stewart, for the image of a Pancoast tumour in Figure 2.4.

Dr Mark Griffiths for Figures 10.1, 10.2, 10.3, 10.4, 10.5, 10.6.

Dr Colin Melville and Stafford Hospital for Figures 11.1, 11.2, 20.14, 20.15 and 20.16.

Mrs Hannah Sharma for Figures 18.1 and 20.20.

Mr Tim Jackson PhD FRCOphth, Consultant Ophthalmic Surgeon, Honorary Senior Lecturer, King's College Hospital London, for Figure 18.2.

The National Institute for Health and Clinical Excellence for allowing us to use and adapt the following figures in the Answers chapter for Cardiology:

Figure 20.3 Diagnosis of heart failure

Figure 20.5 Pharmacological treatment for symptomatic heart failure
Figure 20.6 Treatment of newly diagnosed hypertension
Figure 20.7 Diagnosis of AF
Figure 20.8 When to anticoagulate

The Faculty of Sexual and Reproductive Healthcare for Figure 20.19, which is taken from Figure1: *Advice for women missing combined oral contraceptive pills,* in the *Faculty of Family Planning and Reproductive Health Care Clinical Guidance 'First Prescription of Combined Oral Contraception July 2006 (updated January 2007).'*

The Arthritis Research Campaign for permission to use their images of osteoarthritis of the knee and rheumatoid arthritis in our Musculoskeletal answers section:

Figure 20.12: Normal and rheumatoid joint. Taken from the ARC information booklet on rheumatoid arthritis, June 2006. *www.arc.org.uk*

Figure 20.13: Normal joint, mild OA and severe OA joint. Taken from the ARC information booklet on osteoarthritis, April 2005. www.arc.org.uk.

Abbreviations

A&E	Accident and Emergency	DEXA	Dual Energy X-ray Absorptiometry
AAA	Abdominal Aortic Aneurysm	DHS	Dynamic Hip Screw
ABG	Arterial Blood Gas	DIC	Disseminated Intravascular Coagulation
ACEI	Angiotensin Converting Enzyme Inhibitor	DKA	Diabetic Ketoacidosis
		DM	Diabetes Mellitus
ACTH	Adrenocorticotrophic hormone	DMARD	Disease Modifying Antirheumatic Drug
ADH	Antidiuretic Hormone	DRE	Digital Rectal Examination
AED	Antiepileptic Drug	DVLA	Driver and Vehicle Licensing Association
AFP	α fetoprotein		
AIDS	Acquired Immune Deficiency Syndrome	DVT	Deep Vein Thrombosis
AKI	Acute Kidney Injury	EBV	Epstein-Barr Virus
ALP	Alkaline Phosphatase	ECG	Electrocardiogram
ALT	Alanine Aminotransferase	ECT	Electroconvulsive Therapy
ANA	Antinuclear Antibody	EEG	Electroencephalogram
AST	Aspartate Aminotransferase	EMG	Electromyography
AXR	Abdominal X-Ray	ENT	Ear Nose and Throat
BAL	Bronchoalveolar Lavage	ERCP	Endoscopic Retrograde Cholangiopancreatography
BD	Twice Daily		
BMI	Body Mass Index	ESR	Erythrocyte Sedimentation Rate
BNP	Brain Natriuretic Peptide	FBC	Full Blood Count
BP	Blood Pressure	FEV1	Forced Expiratory Volume in 1 second
BPH	Benign Prostatic Hyperplasia	FSH	Follicle Stimulating Hormone
BPPV	Benign Paroxysmal Positional Vertigo	FVC	Forced Vital Capacity
CCU	Coronary Care Unit	GCS	Glasgow Coma Scale
CHD	Coronary Heart Disease	GFR	Glomerular Filtration Rate
CKD	Chronic Kidney Disease	GH	Growth Hormone
CMV	Cytomegalovirus	GI	Gastrointestinal
CN	Cranial Nerve	GMC	General Medical Council
CNS	Central Nervous system	GN	Glomerulonephritis
COPD	Chronic Obstructive Pulmonary Disease	GORD	Gastro-Oesophageal Reflux Disease
		GP	General Practitioner
CPR	Cardiopulmonary Rescuscitation	GTN	Glyceryl Trinitrate
CRP	C Reactive Protein	HAV	Hepatitis A (HBV, HCV – hepatitis B, C respectively)
CSF	Cerebrospinal Fluid		
CT scan	Computerised Tomography	HbA1c	Glycated haemoglobin
CVA	Cardiovascular Accident	HIV	Human Immunodeficiency Virus

HONK	Hyperosmolar, non ketotic	PE	Pulmonary Embolism
HR	Heart rate	PEFR	Peak Expiratory Flow Rate
HRT	Hormone Replacement Therapy	pO_2	Partial pressure of oxygen
HSV	Herpes Simplex Virus	PPI	Proton Pump Inhibitor
IBD	Inflammatory Bowel Disease	PRN	As required (Pro Re Nata)
ICP	Intracranial pressure	PTH	Parathyroid Hormone
IHD	Ischaemic Heart Disease	PVD	Peripheral Vascular Disease
IM	Intramuscular	QDS	Four Times Daily
INR	International Normalised Ratio	RA	Rheumatoid Arthritis
ITU	Intensive Therapy Unit	RBBB	Right Bundle Branch Block
IUGR	Intrauterine Growth Retardation	RR	Respiratory Rate
IV	Intravenous	RTC	Road Traffic Collision
IVIg	Intravenous immunoglobulin	SAH	Subarachnoid haemorrhage
JVP	Jugular Venous Pressure	saO_2	Oxygen saturation
LAD	Left Anterior Descending	SIADH	Syndrome of Inappropriate Antidiuretic Hormone Secretion
LBBB	Left Bundle Branch Block		
LDH	Lactate Dehydrogenase	SIGN	Scottish Intercollegiate Guideline Network
LFTs	Liver Function Tests		
LMN	Lower Motor Neuron	SLE	Systemic Lupus Erythematosus
LP	Lumbar Puncture	SSRI	Selective Serotonin Reuptake Inhibitor
LVF	Left Ventricular Failure	STI	Sexually Transmitted Infection
LVH	Left Ventricular Hypertrophy	SVCO	Superior Vena Caval Obstruction
MAU	Medical Assessment Unit	TB	Tuberculosis
MCV	Mean Cell Volume	TCA	Tricyclic Antidepressant
MI	Myocardial Infarction	TDS	Three Times Daily
MMSE	Mini Mental State Examination	TFTs	Thyroid Function Tests
MND	Motor Neurone Disease	TIA	Transient Ischaemic Attack
MRA	Magnetic Resonance Angiogram	TSH	Thyroid Stimulating Hormone
MRI	Magnetic Resonance Imaging	TURBT	Transurethral Resection of Bladder Tumour
MRSA	Methicillin-Resistant Staphylococcus Aureus		
		TURP	Transurethral Resection of the Prostate
MS	Multiple Sclerosis	U&Es	Urea and Electrolytes
NICE	National Institute for Health and Clinical Excellence	UC	Ulcerative Colitis
		UMN	Upper Motor Neuron
NSAIDs	Non-Steroidal Anti-Inflammatory Drugs	USS	Ultrasound Scan
OA	Osteoarthritis	UTI	Urinary Tract Infection
OCP	Oral Contraceptive Pill	VF	Ventricular Fibrillation
OD	Once Daily	VT	Ventricular Tachycardia
OGD	Oesophago-gastro-duodenoscopy	VZV	Varicella Zoster Virus
OGTT	Oral Glucose Tolerance Test	WBC	White Blood Cell
pCO_2	Partial pressure of carbon dioxide	WCC	White Cell Count

Chapter 1   Cardiovascular

Case 1

A 62-year-old obese lawyer presents to the emergency department with crushing, central chest pain associated with dyspnoea which began three hours ago at rest. He does not complain of nausea or vomiting. On examination he is tachycardic, hypertensive, his JVP is not elevated and xanthelasmata are present. His chest is clear and his heart sounds are normal. There is no evidence of any leg swelling. He also mentions that he has had minor chest pain in the past, but never thought much of it as the pain was short-lived.

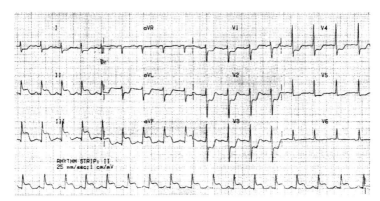

Figure 1.1   The patient's ECG (courtesy of the Heart Attack Centre, University Hospital of North Staffordshire)

1.1   What are the differential diagnoses?

1.2   The patient's ECG is shown above. What is the diagnosis?

1.3   What is the term given to the disease spectrum to which this belongs?

1.4   Which coronary vessel is likely to be affected in this patient?

1.5   What is the immediate management of this patient?

1.6   What other questions would be important to ask in the history?

1.7   What investigations would you perform and why?

1.8   What are the complications of this condition?

1.9   What are the indications for thrombolysis?

1.10 List the contraindications for thrombolysis.

The patient is thrombolysed and transferred to the Cardiology ward. Two weeks later, when he is about to be discharged, he complains of chest pain which is sharp in nature and worse on inspiration. When his observations are taken he is found have a high temperature.

1.11   What pathological process has occurred?

The patient makes a good recovery and is ready to be discharged home. You remember that the patient admitted to being a heavy smoker (smoking on average 50 cigarettes a day) and also drinking one to two glasses of wine every day. He tells you that his job has been very stressful lately. You give him some advice and arrange a follow-up appointment for him.

1.12   How would you further manage this patient and what advice would you give?

Case 2

A 70-year-old woman is admitted as an emergency to MAU with increasing dyspnoea and she has told the doctor that she has put on weight rapidly over the last week or so. She has recently been using four pillows at night as she has been coughing and wheezing when lying flat. Her past medical history includes a previous myocardial infarction, angina and hypertension. On examination her blood pressure is 140/80 mmHg, pulse rate is 80 per minute and JVP was raised at 3 cm. On auscultation there were bibasal crepitatations and a third heart sound could be heard. She has severe bilateral pitting oedema up to her sacrum.

1.13   What is the likely diagnosis?

1.14   Patients with this condition can present with various symptoms. How would you define her condition and what other symptoms, excluding those mentioned in the case, would you expect?

1.15   What are the causes of this condition?

1.16   What investigations would you perform?

1.17   What features would you expect to see on a chest X-ray?

1.18   What classification is used to assess the severity of the condition?

1.19   How would you manage this patient?

The patient is found to have atrial fibrillation and is commenced on digoxin.

1.20   What are the features of digoxin toxicity?

Case 3

A 55-year-old man has come to see his GP. The GP discovers that he has a family history of hypertension (father and brother who are currently on treatment). His clinical examination revealed that he is overweight and had an elevated blood pressure at 165/95 mmHg.

1.21   Does this mean that the patient has hypertension?

1.22   How do you measure blood pressure?

1.23   How is hypertension classified?

1.24   What are the causes of hypertension?

The patient is surprised to hear that he has high blood pressure. When delving more into his history the GP discovers that the patient's diet consists of takeaways as he has a busy job and also does not have the time to exercise. He also reports drinking on average 26 units of alcohol a week.

1.25   What further management should the GP undertake?

1.26   What investigations should be performed?

The patient's blood results come back and show an elevated fasting blood sugar and a mixed dyslipidaemia. His Framingham risk score is 4%.

1.27   What does this mean?

Two years later the patient is followed up by his GP complaining of poor eyesight and reports that he had already been to the opticians who advised him to see his own GP.

1.28   What is the likely diagnosis and what are the different stages of this condition?

The patient's blood pressure was 170/96 mmHg and also mentioned that his urine had been frothy recently but thought it would improve.

1.29   When should you refer the patient to a specialist?

1.30   List risk factors which predispose an individual to hypertension.

1.31   What complications are associated with hypertension if left untreated?

1.32   What medications would you commence for the patient?

1.33   Can you think of any contraindications to any of the medications used in the treatment of hypertension?

Case 4

An 82-year-old woman has presented with collapse. A friend who has accompanied her tells the doctor that the patient had been complaining of palpitations for a couple of weeks and just before she collapsed she had complained of breathlessness. On examination her pulse is found to be irregularly irregular. Her ECG is shown below.

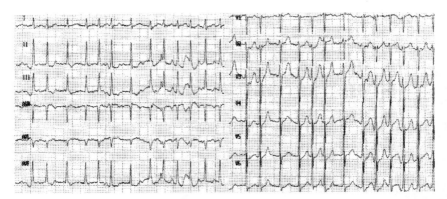

Figure 1.2   The Patient's ECG (courtesy of the Heart Attack Centre, University Hospital of North Staffordshire)

1.34   What is the likely diagnosis?

1.35   What are the different subtypes of this condition?

1.36   What are the causes of this condition?

1.37   What investigations should be performed to rule out other causes of this condition?

1.38   How is this condition managed?

1.39   What should you use to anticoagulate?

Case 5

A 66-year-old man comes to see his GP presenting with recent history of shortness of breath and collapse. On examination an ejection systolic murmur is heard which radiates to the carotids.

1.40   What is the likely diagnosis?

1.41   What are the causes of this condition?

1.42   What other features would you see with this condition?

1.43   What investigations would you perform?

1.44   What further management options are there?

Case 6

A 58-year-old man self-presented to A&E. He is a smoker of 40 cigarettes a day. Whilst walking back from the post office he started to experience central chest pain radiating down his left arm. He has had previous episodes but these were not as severe as this most recent one. There were no other symptoms associated with his pain.

1.45   What is the likely diagnosis?

1.46   How can you classify this condition?

1.47   Are there different types of this condition? If so what are they?

1.48   What investigations would you do?

1.49   How would you treat this condition?

Case 7

A 42-year-old woman presents to A&E with flu-like symptoms and a fever. She has a history of rheumatic fever as a child. On examination she is tachycardic and has aortic regurgitation.

1.50   What is the most likely diagnosis?

1.51   What organisms can cause this condition?

1.52   What are the other features of this condition?

1.53   What might you see on fundoscopy and what is the mechanism involved?

1.54   What investigation will help to reach a diagnosis?

1.55   What are the diagnostic criteria?

1.56   What treatment would you give?

1.57   Are there any associated complications?

1.58   Which patients require prophylaxis?

Case 8

A 25-year-old woman presented to A&E with a 2-day history of left calf swelling and pain. She denied any breathlessness. Her family history was unable to be ascertained as she was adopted.

1.59   What is the most likely diagnosis?

The patient is on the oral contraceptive pill and also is a smoker of 20 cigarettes a day. Incidentally she mentions that she has had two miscarriages.

1.60   List other risk factors for this condition.

1.61   What investigations would you order?

1.62   What treatment should be given?

Chapter 2   Respiratory

Case 1

A 73-year-old man was walking to his hotel room when he suddenly felt breathless and collapsed in front of his wife. The patient's wife called for help and an ambulance arrived promptly to take him to the nearest A&E department. On examination breath sounds were heard bilaterally and there was a weakly palpable radial pulse.

2.1   What is the most likely diagnosis?

IV access is gained along with an ECG which shows the following:

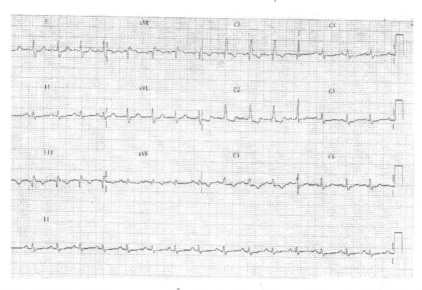

Figure 2.1   Patient's ECG (courtesy of the Heart Attack Centre, University Hospital of North Staffordshire)

2.2   Interpret the above ECG.

2.3   What urgent investigation would confirm your most likely diagnosis?

2.4   What other investigations would you perform to aid you towards the most likely diagnosis?

2.5   What risk factors will predispose to this condition?

Here is the patient's CTPA:

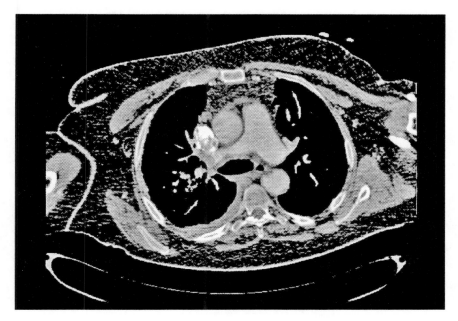

Figure 2.2   CTPA (courtesy of Dr John Asquith)

This shows a filling defect in the right upper lobe.

2.6   How would you treat this patient?

Case 2

A 76-year-old woman is admitted from home by her GP with a chest infection that she has had for the last 2 weeks. She reports that her cough is now productive with thick green sputum. On examination she had decreased air entry on the right side with transmitted upper airway noise. She was pyrexial at 38.6°C.

2.7   What is the most likely diagnosis?

2.8   What are the differential diagnoses?

2.9   For your most likely diagnosis what other symptoms and signs may be present?

2.10   List risk factors that contribute to the development of your most likely diagnosis.

2.11   How would you assess the severity of the patient's condition?

A chest X-ray is requested.

2.12   What does the chest X-ray show?

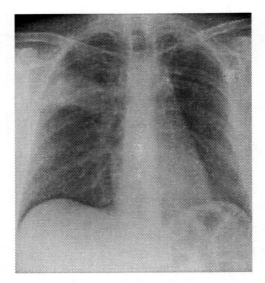

Figure 2.3   Chest X-ray of 76-year-old woman (courtesy of Dr John Asquith)

2.13   Which organisms are implicated in this condition?

2.14   Her ABG result is shown below. Interpret the ABG results.

pH	7.33
$paCO_2$	5.8
PaO_2	7.8
HCO_3	19

2.15   What other investigations would you perform?

2.16   How would you manage this patient?

2.17   Are there any complications that may develop with this condition?

Case 3

A 75-year-old retired painter/decorator who smokes on average 40 cigarettes a day, presented to A&E with general deterioration and lethargy. He was accompanied by his wife who reports a recent productive cough and breathlessness. Also today he had brought up a few drops of bright red blood whilst coughing.

On examination chest expansion was decreased on the right side and the right apex was dull to percussion with increased breath sounds over this area. He had a right droopy eyelid and a small pupil.

2.18   What preliminary investigations would you request given the above clinical features?

The patient's chest X-ray is shown below.

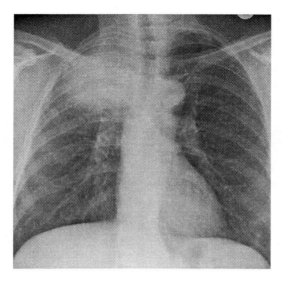

Figure 2.4   Chest X-ray (courtesy of Dr Grant Stewart)

2.19   What further imaging investigations may be required in the management of this condition?

2.20   What is the most likely diagnosis?

2.21   Can you explain the droopy right eyelid and small pupil that the patient presented with?

2.22   What are the main histological types of this condition?

2.23   There are a number of paraneoplastic syndromes associated with this condition. What are they, and what type of the condition are they related to?

2.24   What are the management options for this condition?

A few months later he is admitted again via A&E with increasing shortness of breath and cough. On examination he was tachypnoeic and had facial and neck swelling with venous distension.

2.25   What could be causing the symptoms with which the patient is now presenting?

Case 4

A 21-year-old woman presents to A&E with a 2-day history of worsening shortness of breath and wheezing which is not relieved with her salbutamol inhaler. She is concerned as she is working as a university student and her symptoms are disturbing her sleep and has found difficulty in concentrating during classes. She has a background of asthma since childhood. Medications she is currently taking include an inhaled corticosteroid and salbutamol inhaler when required.

On examination she is speaking in broken sentences. On auscultation she has widespread wheeze.

2.26   What is the most likely diagnosis?

2.27   What features indicate the severity of her condition?

2.28   How will you manage this patient in the acute stages?

2.29   What preliminary investigations will you organise?

She suddenly collapses. On examination she has reduced air entry on the left side and it is also hyper-resonant with her trachea deviated to the right. A chest X-ray is done and is shown below.

2.30   What does the X-ray show?

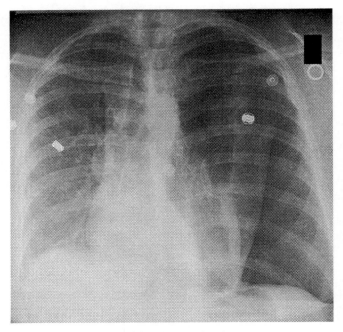

Figure 2.5   X-ray of patient

2.31   How would you manage this?

2.32   What are the risk factors that predispose to the condition shown in the X-ray?

She has come round a little bit and seems better. An hour later you check up on her and she has an audible wheeze and a high respiratory rate. She seems unusually drowsy and she is difficult to rouse. An ABG is done and shows the results below:

pH	7.2
PCO_2	6.9
PO_2	8.2

2.33   Why is the patient getting increasingly drowsy?

Following admission and treatment, the patient recovers and is discharged home. She is followed up in the outpatient clinic.

2.34   How would you manage a patient with this condition in an outpatient setting?

Case 5

A 67-year-old man presented to A&E with increasing shortness of breath and decreased exercise tolerance as well as a two-year history of chronic cough with yellowish expectorate.

He lives alone at home and has a 50 pack year smoking history. On examination he is cachectic and has pursed-lip breathing. His neck veins are distended and he has a barrel chest. There is poor air entry bilaterally with widespread wheeze and asterixis is present.

2.35   From the history, what is the most likely diagnosis?

2.36   How would you define this condition?

2.37   What initial investigations would you perform in this patient?

He has just come back from the X-ray department and the nurse who is looking after him asks you to review his CXR.

2.38   Interpret his chest X-ray.

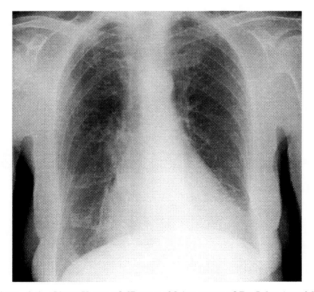

Figure 2.6   Chest X-ray of 67-year-old (courtesy of Dr John Asquith)

2.39   How will you manage the patient in the acute phase?

2.40   What further investigations will help you to confirm the diagnosis?

2.41   Are there any staging criteria for this condition?

2.42   How would you manage this patient, once he is stable, in an outpatient setting?

Chapter 3   Gastroenterology

Case 1

A 32-year-old obese man, Gordon, visits his GP complaining of a 3-week history of occasional epigastric pain which is associated with heartburn. He smokes 20 cigarettes a day and drinks half a bottle of wine most nights.

3.1   What is the most likely diagnosis?

3.2   His GP suggests some lifestyle changes. What advice may the GP suggest?

Gordon asks whether there are any medications available which may help.

3.3   What will you initially advise or prescribe for him?

A few months later Gordon returns with worsening of symptoms which are affecting his sleep. He is complaining of persistent symptoms and difficulty swallowing.

3.4   Do any of his symptoms warrant any further investigation? If so what signs or symptoms would concern you?

3.5   What are the causes of dysphagia?

Gordon has some worrying symptoms which you want to investigate further.

3.6   Which investigation should Gordon have?

3.7   Can you list any complications of Gordon's condition?

His OGD shows that he has oesophagitis.

3.8   How would you manage his symptoms initially?

A CLO test was taken during the OGD.

3.9   What is a CLO test and what is it testing for?

Gordon's CLO test comes back positive and this requires treatment.

3.10   What treatment would you give for this positive result?

A number of years later Gordon represents with difficulty in swallowing and persistent vomiting. You decide to send him for another OGD. When you receive the report you discover that he has Barrett's oesophagus.

3.11   What pathological change would you see in this condition?

A few years later he returns to his GP with further difficulty in swallowing, weight loss and retrosternal pain. He has a recent surveillance endoscopy done together with a biopsy.

3.12   What is the likely diagnosis?

3.13   What other investigations would you perform?

3.14   What further management would you consider once the diagnosis is confirmed?

Case 2

A 42-year-old man is admitted to A&E with haematemesis and smells strongly of alcohol. His observations are as follows: HR 115/min, BP 78/58 mmHg, sats 98% on air, RR 16/minute and his peripheries are cold.

3.15   What is your immediate management of this patient?

3.16   How would you assess the severity of his haematemesis?

3.17   What are the possible causes of his haematemesis?

3.18   What is your provisional diagnosis and what are the risk factors which predispose to this condition?

He has no further haematemesis. He receives 4 units of crossmatched blood.

3.19   What medication/s should be administered?

His condition is stabilised and you are now able to obtain a reliable history off him.

3.20   What questions would you like to ask?

He admits to drinking heavily – equivalent of 46 units a week. His LFTs are also deranged.

He is transferred, in his stable state, to the gastro ward to await further investigations.

3.21   The patient has had an OGD which shows oesophageal varices. What is the most likely cause of this?

3.22   How is this condition treated?

3.23   What other medications can be prescribed to help treat this condition?

3.24   What signs or symptoms would alert you to a re-bleed?

On further physical examination he has signs of alcoholic liver disease.

3.25   Can you list any signs seen in alcoholic liver disease?

On abdominal examination the patient has a large amount of fluid in his abdomen, there is a definite shifting dullness with a fluid thrill. He tells you that his abdomen has been progressively getting large over the last few weeks.

3.26   List causes of this clinical sign.

Whilst on the ward he deteriorates and complains of his abdomen feeling more swollen and is spiking temperatures.

3.27   Which diagnosis needs to be considered here?

3.28   How will you test for this?

Whilst on the ward the patient complains of feeling generally unwell and is in a lot of discomfort with his abdomen. His temperature is 37.5°C.

On advice from microbiology the patient has been commenced on the appropriate antibiotics and his condition improves and he is discharged home.

A few months later the patient's wife brings him to A&E and gives a history of increasing confusion. He has a flapping tremor and has constructional apraxia.

3.29   What is your diagnosis?

You are concerned about the patient's alcohol intake and you take a collateral history from his wife who mentions that he is drinking more and that she wishes someone could help her. She wants to know what other harm alcohol could cause to the body and wishes for you to have a chat with her husband.

3.30   You go to speak with the patient. What screening tool can you use to assess alcohol abuse in this patient?

3.31   List any complications associated with alcohol abuse.

Case 3

A 45-year-old woman presents to her GP with a three-week history of lower abdominal discomfort and bloating which is relieved when she opens her bowels. She denies any presence of mucus or blood in her stools, weight loss or anorexia. She also complains of alternating diarrhoea and constipation. Her diarrhoeal symptoms are aggravated by the consumption of dairy products.

3.32   What is the likely diagnosis?

3.33   What symptoms would be classed as red flag symptoms which warrant further investigation?

3.34   What investigations will you do to aid you with the diagnosis?

3.35   What is your initial management of this condition?

Case 4

A 26-year-old man presents to A&E with malaise, anorexia, vomiting and abdominal pain. On examination he looks unwell and has a high temperature of 38.7°C. He is jaundiced and is tender in his RUQ of the abdomen and has tattoos on his arms.

3.36   What questions do you specifically want to ask about in the history?

3.37   What may be the cause of his jaundice?

He tells you that he has never used any IV drugs but that he is keen on muscle building and has taken a course of steroids two months ago. He smokes 20 cigarettes a day and binge drinks.

3.38   What blood tests will you do and which of these are useful in assessing liver synthetic function?

3.39   What other investigations would you consider performing?

3.40   His LFTs are shown below. What is your likely diagnosis?

>ALP 372
>
>ALT 660
>
>AST 627
>
>Albumin 34

His USS abdomen shows hepatomegaly with changes consistent with cirrhosis.

3.41   What are the causes of cirrhosis?

3.42   What are the complications of cirrhosis?

3.43   What is the scoring system used to determine the prognosis in patients with cirrhosis?

The patient becomes acutely confused.

3.44   What is your likely diagnosis?

Case 5

A 25-year-old man is admitted to A&E with a one-week history of bloody diarrhoea and severe abdominal cramps. On examination he is clinically dehydrated and is pyrexial at 38.7°C.

3.45   What are the differential diagnosis?

His diarrhoea settled down whilst in hospital and he was discharged home. A few days later he was readmitted to A&E with severe abdominal pain, associated abdominal distension and further bloody diarrhoea. He was tachycardic and had a high fever.

3.46   What is the most likely diagnosis?

3.47   What is the difference between ulcerative colitis and Crohn's disease macroscopically and microscopically?

3.48   What are the extra intestinal manifestations of inflammatory bowel disease?

3.49   What are the complications of ulcerative colitis and Crohn's disease?

3.50   What investigations would you request?

3.51   What are the dangers of leaving this condition untreated?

3.52   How would you manage this patient?

3.53   What are the main treatment options?

Case 6

A 64-year-old man comes to see his GP with a six-week history of weight loss (unintentional), loss of appetite and epigastric pain radiating to his back. On examination he had a palpable epigastric mass with an enlarged left supraclavicular lymph node.

3.54   What is the most likely diagnosis?

3.55   What signs and symptoms would you expect in this condition?

3.56   What are the risk factors associated with this condition?

3.57   What investigations would confirm your diagnosis?

3.58   What further investigations would you do once the diagnosis is confirmed?

3.59   What management options are available for this condition?

Chapter 4   Neurology

Case 1

A 22-year-old student is admitted to A&E with a one-day history of flu-like symptoms with photophobia, neck stiffness and a severe generalised headache. She has vomited a few times and she has not taken any analgesia. On examination she looks unwell with a temperature of 39.1°C, and is tachycardic at 125 bpm. On further examination Kernig's sign is positive but there are no other focal neurological signs. Both pupils are equal and reactive to light. The patient is able to tell you where she is but is unable to tell you what day it is.

4.1   What are the differential diagnoses?

4.2   What investigations would you perform?

Her CT brain is done and is reported as normal.

4.3   What would you like to do next and how would you do this?

Her results from this are shown below.

4.4   Interpret the results below:

The fluid when obtained is turbid.

CSF protein	1.4 g/L (normal ranges 0.20–0.45 g/L)
CSF glucose	2.0 mmol/L
Serum glucose	5.2 mmol/L
White cell count	95% neutrophils, 5% lymphocytes

The CSF culture results are not available.

4.5   What is the most likely diagnosis?

4.6   What are the signs and symptoms of this condition?

4.7   How would you manage this patient?

Case 2

A 24-year-old male is brought into A&E after collapsing with a seizure in the local shopping centre. Witnesses say he has been fitting for the last half an hour. On examination he is deeply cyanosed.

4.8   What is your immediate management?

4.9   What immediate investigations would you request?

4.10   Which anti-epileptic drug (AED) would you commence?

Case 3

A 78-year-old man is referred to the Neurology clinic by his GP for a further opinion. He has progressive worsening of his mobility over a one-year period. On further questioning he describes himself as getting increasingly slow, putting it down to age, and finds it difficult to get his balance. He also says that his writing has decreased in size and he has developed a tremor in his right hand.

4.11   What is the likely diagnosis?

4.12   What are the classical triad of motor symptoms or signs seen in this condition?

4.13   What other signs or symptoms might you see?

4.14   How would you treat the patient?

Case 4

A 23-year-old female presents to her GP with a two-week history of bilateral leg weakness having started with pins and needles and numbness in her hands and feet. She has had a few days of urinary incontinence which has resolved. Two years ago she had an episode of blurred vision and pain in the right eye which lasted a month and fully recovered.

4.15   What is the most likely diagnosis?

4.16   What other signs or symptoms might you see in this condition?

4.17   What is the pathological basis of this disorder?

4.18   What further investigations would you do?

4.19   How would you manage this patient?

Case 5

A 61-year-old retired barmaid is brought into A&E by ambulance after becoming increasingly weak on her right side over a one-week period. She is unable to walk, has slurred speech and her right face is drooping. Her husband mentions that she does not seem to be able to see him when he speaks to her from her right side. She has previously had a breast cancer removed but has been given the all clear after repeated follow-up for this.

On examination she has a right facial weakness, grade 4/5 weakness of the right arm and leg, a right homonymous hemianopia and some difficulties naming objects. Her reflexes are brisk on the right side and her right plantar response is upgoing.

4.20   What is the likely diagnosis?

A CT head was done and shows extensive oedema surrounding the subtle impression of a ring enhanced lesion in the left frontal lobe, extending into the left parietal lobe. There is associated mass effect displacing the lateral ventricle to the right.

She is admitted to hospital to await further imaging. During this time she develops a headache, nausea and vomiting.

4.21   What is the likely cause?

4.22   What management options are available for this patient?

Case 6

A 70-year-old man presents to the emergency eye clinic with a one-week history of a drooping left eyelid and increasing pain and double vision in the left eye. On examination he has a complete left ptosis and his left eye is in a 'down and out' position. His pupils were equal and reactive. MRI brain and cerebral angiography were normal.

4.23   Which eye movements will be impaired/absent in the left eye?

4.24   What do these findings imply and how would you manage this patient?

Case 7

A 42-year-old woman presents to her local A&E department with a three-day history of left-sided facial weakness. On examination she is unable to lift her left eyebrow and has obvious weakness of the left side of her mouth. She has no other neurological deficit. She has no significant past medical history.

4.25   What is the likely diagnosis?

4.26   Where is the lesion?

4.27   What are the main causes of an isolated LMN facial palsy?

4.28   How would you manage this patient?

Case 8

A 76-year-old man with a background of atrial fibrillation (on warfarin therapy) is sent to A&E by his GP with a two-hour history of severe global right-sided weakness. He is eye-opening to painful stimuli and is moving his left side spontaneously. When questioned he seems confused.

4.29   What is his Glasgow Coma Scale score?

4.30   What is the diagnosis?

4.31   What investigations would you do?

4.32   What are the important risk factors for stroke?

4.33   How would you manage this patient?

Case 9

An 80-year-old man is referred by his GP to a memory clinic. He attends with his wife who reports a one-year history of progressive deterioration in his memory and mood, associated with confusion and urinary incontinence. He has been admitted to hospital three times having become worse with confusion and disorientation, and had been treated for a UTI but not really recovered well. He has been hypertensive for many years and sustained a stroke three years ago. On examination he walks with a slow gait with lots of small steps.

4.34   What is the likely diagnosis?

4.35   How would you assess cognitive function?

4.36   How would you manage this patient?

Case 10

A 56-year-old man is referred to the Neurology outpatient clinic by his GP with a six-month history of progressive weakness of his right hand. He also reports that recently he has had problems with swallowing and has choked whilst eating on several occasions. On examination he had wasting of his upper and lower limbs and some fasciculations were noted. His right plantar was upgoing and his reflexes were generally brisk.

4.37   What diagnosis do his symptoms suggest?

4.38   What investigations would you perform?

4.39   How would you manage this patient?

Case 11

A 24-year-old girl attends neurology out-patients with a two-year history of headaches. They were each lasting a day and occurring only once a month initially but now she is having them every week. The pain is always over her left eye and forehead and is severe and throbbing. When it is at its worst she feels sick and on a few occasions she has had an enlarging black shape in her vision for a few minutes prior to her headache. She has no other medical history and is on the combined oral contraceptive pill. Examination is normal.

4.40   What is the diagnosis?

4.41   How would you manage this patient?

Case 12

A 34-year-old man is brought to A&E by a concerned bystander after collapsing in a supermarket. He is alert and tells of an eight-year history of recurrent blackouts. Each blackout has been similar and starts with a feeling of nausea and his vision becoming blurred. He feels unwell before developing ringing in his ears and collapsing after a few seconds. This has occurred in numerous public places but never in bed and is worse during hot weather. The witness who is with him says he appeared pale and had jerking movements of his arms when he collapsed. He has no medical or family history and takes no medication. His ECG is normal.

4.42   What is the diagnosis?

4.43   What features suggest this is a faint rather than a seizure?

4.44   How would you manage this patient?

Chapter 5 Infectious diseases

Case 1

A 34-year-old businessman presents to his GP with a four-day history of fever, muscle aches, tiredness and loss of appetite. His wife was concerned that over the last 24 hours he had become confused, forgetful and had started vomiting. He also began passing dark urine. They had recently returned from a charity climb of Mount Kenya when his symptoms began. They had spent a few days in Mombasa at the start of their holidays three weeks earlier.

On examination the man has a temperature of 38.7 and is mildly jaundiced. He is mumbling incoherently. He appears to have some neck stiffness and mild photophobia.

5.1   What additional information would you ask for in the history?

They had taken all recommended immunisations before their trip and had taken malarone as malaria prophylaxis. While in Kenya they had eaten local food including some wild fruit. The patient did have an episode of diarrhoea and vomiting during their trip which resolved after a few days. He had struggled to take his malaria tablets then. They had no close contact with animals and cannot recall any insect bites. They had swum in the sea but not in any lakes.

5.2   What is the differential diagnosis?

5.3   What should your immediate management be?

The patient goes to hospital where he becomes increasingly drowsy.

5.4   What initial investigations would you perform?

5.5   While waiting for the results of the investigations what treatment should be commenced?

A CT head scan is done and shows no abnormality.

5.6   What investigation is it now safe to perform?

The cerebrospinal fluid (CSF) shows 54 red blood cells, 0 white blood cells, protein of 0.4 g/L and glucose 3.2 mmol/L (serum glucose 5.4 mmol/L). The blood film comes back as positive for *P. falciparum* with a parasitaemia level of 2%.

5.7   What further treatment and management should this patient have?

Case 2

A 30-year-old woman comes to see you with a generalised rash mainly affecting her chest wall and face. The rash was not particularly itchy, but she was concerned about its sudden appearance. Before the onset of the rash she had felt unwell for a week with fevers, malaise, headache, myalgia and sore throat. On examination her tonsils are not enlarged or exudative but there are some ulcers on her oral mucosa. Her pharynx looks oedematous and red. There are palpable cervical and occipital lymph nodes, which are non-tender.

5.8   What are the possible diagnoses?

5.9   What other questions would you like to ask in the history?

On further questioning, the patient tells you that she takes no medication regularly and has no allergies. She has had treatment for genital ulceration a few years ago but no other past medical history of note. She works in an office and travels regularly to the Mediterranean for holidays. She is single and has had three male sexual partners in the last six months.

5.10   What is the likely diagnosis?

5.11   What investigations would you request?

You explain the possible diagnoses to her and discuss the likely investigations required. She is surprised at the mention of HIV as she does not think she is at risk.

5.12   How would you counsel her for an HIV test?

The HIV test comes back as positive.

5.13   What should be the management now?

Case 3

A 43-year-old builder developed sudden pain and tingling sensations around his left eye some days ago. Prior to that he was feeling slightly off colour with a fever, malaise and headache. The area of skin around his left eye has now become red and spots have started appearing around that eye and left forehead. On examination you can see a vesicular eruption which does not cross the midline. On closer inspection he appears to also have vesicles on the tip of his nose and he has moderate conjunctivitis.

5.14   What other questions would you ask in the history?

He says the rash started some 36 hours ago. The patient has had chickenpox aged 10. He is normally fit and well and takes no regular medication. However about several weeks ago he was troubled by an ear infection on the left. He received antibiotics at one of the NHS walk-in centres.

5.15   What is the likely diagnosis?

5.16   What is the significance of the vesicles on his nose and what is this sign known as?

5.17   How would you manage the patient?

The patient is concerned regarding his sight, he asks whether there is a risk that his face will droop and he will contract encephalitis as well, as his uncle had shingles and developed similar problems.

5.18   What is the clinical syndrome he describes called? Is encephalitis a concern?

As the patient is leaving he mentions that he is in a rush to pick up his wife, who is 30 weeks pregnant, from the train station.

5.19   What should you say to the patient?

Case 4

A 68-year-old retired publican is referred to the hospital by his GP for increasing shortness of breath and worsening cough for 3 weeks. Over the last few months he has been feeling tired and although he is eating as much as he can he thinks he has lost about 10lb in weight. He tends to have a dry cough in the mornings but recently started bringing up small amounts of sputum. Previously he could walk a few miles without difficulty but now he is breathless on walking 200 yards to his local pub.

5.20   What other questions should you ask?

He tells you that he has not coughed up any blood. He has noticed some ankle swelling but he thinks this is because he is not as active as he used to be. He feels cold most of the time but has not had fevers. He has never been to the hospital until now, but last year he had three courses of antibiotics from his GP for chest infections with a further course of antibiotics two weeks ago. He takes the occasional painkiller only. He has smoked 25 cigarettes per day for the last 30 years. He recalls his uncle dying of tuberculosis when he was growing up, but his uncle had lived about 10 miles away.

On examination his temperature is 37.8°C and his respiratory rate is 18. He has nicotine-stained fingernails but they are not clubbed. He is saturating 95% on room air and his lungs sound clear.

5.21   What are the differential diagnoses?

5.22   What investigations would you do?

The chest X-ray shows cavitation in the left upper lobe and background emphysematous changes. He produces small amounts of watery sputum which grows mixed upper respiratory tract flora only. No acid-fast bacilli are seen on staining. He is empirically started on augmentin.

5.23   What should the management be?

He undergoes a bronchoscopy and his bronchoalveolar lavage (BAL) shows acid-fast bacilli on staining. He is started on rifampicin, isoniazid, pyrazinamide and ethambutol.

5.24   What should be done prior to starting treatment?

5.25   What else should be done?

Chapter 6   Endocrinology

Case 1

An 18-year-old boy presents to A&E with symptoms of abdominal pain, vomiting, increased thirst and polyuria. He also says he has been losing weight recently. On urine dipstick he has +++ ketones and +++ glucose and his fingerprick glucose is 35 mmol/L.

6.1   What is the likely diagnosis?

6.2   What investigations would you do?

On his blood gas he is found to be acidotic with a pH <7.2 and his blood glucose is 27 mmol/L.

6.3   How should you manage this patient?

6.4   What are the complications of this?

Once the patient is stable, he asks what has been happening and what the diagnosis is.

6.5   What should you tell him?

6.6   What will he need to do from now on?

6.7   What are the complications of this condition?

Case 2

A 55-year-old man comes to see his GP. He has requested a general well-man check and as part of this you have requested bloods for a fasting glucose. The blood glucose result was 6.5 mmol/L.

6.8   What does this result mean?

You send the patient for an oral glucose tolerance test which comes back with a result of 9.8 mmol/L.

6.9   What does this result mean?

6.10   What is the management of this?

Case 3

An elderly woman is found to be diabetic after some routine annual blood tests she had for her hypertension.

6.11   What is the initial management of type 2 diabetes?

6.12   What causes type 2 diabetes?

This woman is obese. Despite diet and exercise after several months her blood glucose is still high and so you decide to start her on medication.

6.13   What medication would you start for her?

After titrating the dose of metformin, the woman is still not well controlled even on 500 mg tds. You decide to start her on gliclazide also.

6.14   What are the side effects of this?

Her blood glucose is 1.8 mmol/L.

6.15   What should the management be?

The patient gets on better with the two medications. However she is found unconscious one day by her daughter.

6.16   What are the symptoms of a hypoglycaemic attack?

Case 4

A 52-year-old woman comes to see her GP with a year's history of cold intolerance, lethargy, constipation and weight gain.

6.17   What other questions would you ask her?

She tells you that she has not been trying to gain weight. She does not suffer with any medical problems but her mother had some problems with her thyroid gland. She also reports that her skin has been dry recently and her hair has become very coarse and brittle.

On examination her skin is dry, her face is puffy around her eyes and her pulse is regular at 60 bpm. There is no goitre in the neck and she has slow, relaxing reflexes.

6.18   What is the likely diagnosis?

6.19   What investigations would you do?

Her results show a serum-free thyroxine which is low, a free triiodothyronine level which is low and a serum TSH which is grossly elevated. She is positive for anti-thyroid peroxidise antibodies.

6.20   What are the causes of this condition?

6.21   What other symptoms and signs can occur with this condition?

6.22   How would you manage this patient?

Case 5

A 28-year-old woman presents to the MAU with a history of fatigue, palpitations and weight loss despite a good appetite.

6.23   What other questions would you ask her?

She is fit and well apart from this. She also says she has been having heat intolerance and slight tremor of her hands. Her sister has got type 1 diabetes.

On examination she has lid lag and lid retraction and proptosis. She has bilateral hand tremors and her palms are sweaty. She is tachycardic at 120 bpm. She has a smooth, symmetrical goitre.

6.24   What is the likely diagnosis?

6.25   What are the causes of this condition?

6.26   What other clinical findings might you see?

6.27   What investigations would you request?

She has a raised T4 and T3 and low TSH. TSH receptor antibodies are positive.

6.28   What treatment options are there for this patient and what are the side effects of these?

Case 6

A 54-year-old woman presents to MAU with a six-month history of weight loss, malaise, weakness and skin hyperpigmentation.

6.29   What is the likely diagnosis?

6.30   What are the other causes of this condition?

6.31   What other clinical features would you expect to see associated with this condition?

6.32   What investigations would you do and what would you expect to see from the results?

6.33   Which tests will confirm the diagnosis?

The patient has a high plasma ACTH and has a suboptimal response to the synachten test. His renin is high and his aldosterone is low. He has positive adrenal autoantibodies.

6.34   How will you manage this patient in an acute presentation?

Case 7

A 48-year-old man is referred by his GP to the endocrinology outpatient clinic with a 12-month history of joint pains and recent new onset type II diabetes mellitus. The patient also complained that he is no longer able to fit into his shoes and seems that both his feet and his hands have grown bigger. His wife who has accompanied him has noticed coarsening of his facial features.

6.35   What is the likely diagnosis?

6.36   What are the causes of this condition?

6.37   What investigations would you do?

The man fails to suppress plasma growth hormone after the oral glucose tolerance test. His MRI shows a pituitary tumour measuring 2 cm.

6.38   List other signs or symptoms that you would expect to see in this condition?

6.39   How would you manage this patient?

6.40   What are the complications of this condition?

Case 8

A 38-year-old woman presents to A&E with increased swelling over her face, easy bruising and increased weight.

6.41   What other questions would you ask her?

6.42   What is the likely diagnosis?

6.43   What other features are there in this condition?

6.44   What investigations would you do and what would you expect these to show?

The patient has a high cortisol, high ACTH and the high dose dexamethasone suppression test suppresses the cortisol to <50%. A MRI of the pituitary gland confirms a pituitary tumour.

6.45   How would you manage this patient?

Chapter 7   Renal

Case 1

A 32-year-old man presents to his GP with colicky pain which radiates from his back to his groin on the left. He has also been feeling nauseated and has vomited several times.

7.1   What is the differential diagnosis?

7.2   What other questions would you ask about?

The patient relates that he has never had this kind of problem before and that nobody else in his family has either. He is a fit and well man with no medical problems and does not take any medications. He has not had any urinary symptoms or fever. He does eat a lot of chocolate and drinks a lot of tea. He works outdoors as a gardener and so often gets very hot and does not always have time for a drink. The pain comes in waves and can last about 30 minutes.

On examination he is very tender in the left loin. The pain radiates into his left groin. The rest of his abdomen is soft and non-tender. His urine dipstick shows non-visible haematuria and is negative for nitrites and leucocytes. His temperature is 38.2. He is clinically dehydrated and is still vomiting.

7.3   What is the most likely diagnosis?

7.4   What other investigations would you request?

7.5   How should this patient be managed?

When in hospital the patient had his IV urogram which showed no evidence of obstruction. His renal ultrasound showed a 4 mm stone. The patient passed the stone and when analysed it was found to be a calcium oxalate stone. The patient was fit for discharge.

7.6   What advice should you give this patient?

Case 2

A 67-year-old man has come to see his GP. His wife has recently been ill and admitted to hospital with a stroke and pneumonia. He has been very upset and worried by this and so has not been eating and drinking. He presents looking very tired, with a reduced urine output, and is clinically dehydrated.

The GP admits the patient for further assessment and for IV fluids. As part of the investigations requested he has his urea and creatinine checked. His blood tests come back showing a urea of 42.6 mmol/L and creatinine of 355 mmol/L.

7.7   What questions would you ask in the history?

He is not on any medications at present and he does not report any other symptoms. He has no previous medical problems.

On examination the patient is clinically hypovolaemic and his bladder is not palpable, his abdominal examination is normal and he has a reduced urine output of 20 ml/hour.

7.8   What are significant features of hypovolaemia?

7.9   What is the diagnosis and what caused it?

7.10   What other investigations should you do?

The patient does have a high potassium of 6.0 mmol/L but the rest of the electrolytes are normal. His ECG does not show any signs of hyperkalaemia.

7.11   How should this patient be managed?

The patient responds well to the fluids and his renal function improves and so does his urine output. He starts to feel well again.

7.12   What are the indications for dialysis?

Case 3

A 54-year-old man with type 2 diabetes mellitus and hypertension has had his bloods done for his routine review. His eGFR is 65. His previous eGFR last year was 78. His albumin:creatinine ratio is 5 mg/mmol. This has increased from last year also when it was 3.5 mg/mmol. His full blood count and other electrolytes were normal.

He is still a smoker (about 10/day) and drinks about 10 units of alcohol a week. He says that his diet is not as good as it should be.

7.13   What other things would you want to know?

He is currently on ramipril 10 mg and simvastatin.

7.14   What is the likely diagnosis?

7.15   How would you investigate the cause of this?

7.16   How can you manage this?

Chapter 8   Haematology

Case 1

A 55-year-old man presents to his GP with increasing lower back pain and tiredness. This started three months earlier. There was no history of trauma and he had been referred for physiotherapy. Despite the physiotherapy, the pain has increased in severity. It now occasionally wakes him during the night and he finds it difficult to get comfortable in bed. He also describes a two-week history of constipation.

On examination, he looks pale. Examination of his cardiovascular and respiratory systems and abdomen is normal. No neurological abnormalities are present in his lower limbs.

8.1   What other symptoms would you enquire about?

He has a 30 pack/year history of smoking and drinks 3-4 units of alcohol per week. He has noticed no change in his bowel habit apart from the constipation, and no difficulty in passing urine. There is no history of night sweats, weight loss or fever. The pain does not radiate.

8.2   What is the differential diagnosis?

8.3   What investigations would you request?

The results show:

      Hb   8.9 g/dL

      MCV   86 fL

      Creatinine 200 micromol/L

      Calcium 3.3 mmol/L

      Albumin 25 g/L

      Total protein 100 g/L

Lumbar spine X-rays show generalised osteoporosis with partial collapse of several vertebral bodies

8.4   What action would you take now?

8.5   How should his hypercalcaemia be treated?

8.6   What is the most likely diagnosis?

8.7   What further investigations should be performed after admission to hospital?

Immunoglobulin levels show a raised IgG, and reduced levels of IgA and IgM. Electrophoresis reveals the presence of an IgG kappa paraprotein. Kappa free light chains (Bence Jones protein) are present in the urine. Renal ultrasound is normal and there is no evidence of a UTI.

8.8   What action should you take now?

8.9   What additional tests is the haematologist likely to request to confirm the diagnosis?

You explain the results and diagnosis to the patient.

8.10   What is the management of this?

8.11   What are common complications that can occur?

Case 2

A 46-year-old woman presents to her GP with a few months' history of breathlessness and fatigue. She says she could previously walk with no limitation but now is getting breathless on exertion and finding it harder to do activities. She is a business woman and has two children with whom she has been busy recently as they are on their school holidays.

8.12   What are possible differential diagnoses?

8.13   What other questions would you ask about in the history?

8.14   What other symptoms and signs would you look for?

She suffers with no medical problems and says she has regular periods which are not very heavy. She does not drink alcohol or smoke and is not on any medications. She says her sister has some problem with her thyroid.

On examination she has conjunctival pallor and glossitis. Her pulse is 88 and blood pressure 130/84 mmHg. Her cardiovascular, respiratory and abdominal examinations are all normal. Her neurological examination reveals absent deep tendon reflexes in both her knees and ankles and she had a positive Babinski's sign bilaterally.

8.15   What investigations would you do?

The results come back showing her Hb of 9.4 g/dL and MCV of 115 fL with hypersegmented neutrophils . Her thyroid function is normal. Her renal function and bone profile are normal. Her lactate dehydrogenase is elevated at 2000 IU/L. Her reticulocyte count is low at 30×10^9 L.

8.16   What is the diagnosis?

8.17   What tests would you request now and what should you do whilst awaiting the results?

The results come back showing low B12 and normal folate.

8.18   What should you do now?

The patient had positive antibodies for parietal cells and intrinsic factor and a positive Schilling test.

8.19   What is the diagnosis?

8.20   What is the management of this?

Case 3

A 45-year-old woman presents to her GP with a two-month history of painless, spontaneous bruising on her limbs and torso. She has not injured herself or been unwell but is worried about the increasing frequency of bruising.

8.21   What are possible differential diagnoses?

8.22   What other questions would you ask in the history?

She suffers with no medical problems and is not on any medications. She reports no history of any bleeding problems in the family. She has not had any nose bleeds but says her periods have been heavier in the last 2 months. She is a non-smoker and only drinks socially at weekends.

On examination she has purpura over both her legs and also her arms, back and abdomen. Her blood pressure is 126/78 mmHg and her cardiovascular, respiratory and abdominal examination is normal.

8.23   What other investigations would be useful to do?

Her bloods show a Hb of 11.9 g/dL, platelet count of 9×10^9/L, the white cell count is normal, her clotting is normal and her blood film confirms a reduced number of platelets.

8.24   What is the most likely diagnosis?

8.25   What should you do with this patient?

The ultrasound scan showed a normal size spleen, no masses and no lymphadenopathy.

8.26   What does this suggest?

8.27   What is the further management of the patient?

The patient's bleeding persisted despite steroids and immuno-suppression. She had a splenectomy.

8.28   What should be given along with this to the patient?

Case 4

A 57-year-old woman with leukaemia presents to A&E having just finished her course of chemotherapy seven days ago. She has developed a fever and feels unwell. Apart from the leukaemia she has no other medical problems and is not on any other medications.

On examination she has a temperature of 39.5 degrees Celcius, she is tachycardic with pulse of 120 and has a respiratory rate of 36 and she is hypotensive.

8.29   What questions would you ask?

8.30   What investigations would you request?

Her blood tests confirm a pancytopenia with a Hb of 8.7 g/dL, white cell count of 0.9×10^9/L, neutrophils of 0.4×10^9/L, platelets of 45×10^9/L.

8.31   What is the diagnosis?

8.32   How would you manage this patient?

The patient is started on tazocin.

8.33   What should you do after the patient is stable?

After 48 hours the patient showed no improvement.

8.34   What can be changed in the treatment?

The patient subsequently improved and the blood cultures confirmed a Gram positive infection. Her bloods improved and she was discharged.

Chapter 9   Musculoskeletal

Case 1

A 46-year-old woman presents with pain and swelling in the joints of both her hands. She says she has had this for the last eight weeks. The pain is worse at rest and she has early morning stiffness lasting about an hour every day.

9.1   What are the differential diagnoses?

9.2   What other questions would you ask?

She says it affects her hands almost identically in the same joints. No other joints are affected and she has no other symptoms. On examination there is swelling of the small joints of both hands. The patient is unable to make a fist with either hand. There is tenderness on squeezing the metacarpophalangeal joints.

9.3   What is the likely diagnosis?

9.4   What joint deformities can you get in rheumatoid arthritis?

9.5   What investigations are indicated?

9.6   What findings can you see on an X-ray of a badly affected joint in rheumatoid arthritis?

9.7   What is the urgent management needed?

When she sees the rheumatologist she is diagnosed with rheumatoid arthritis.

9.8   What medication would be started for a newly diagnosed person with rheumatoid arthritis?

Case 2

A 60-year-old man presents with a progressive pain and stiffness of his left shoulder. He says he has been doing some painting at his home recently. He is left-handed. He has diabetes mellitus. He says he can't sleep on his left side because of the pain.

9.9   What are the differential diagnoses?

9.10   What other questions would you ask?

9.11   What are red flag symptoms to be worried about?

On examination he has global restriction of all movements of the shoulder, especially external rotation and he has pain with it. He is tender along his shoulder joint and there is some muscle wasting. There are no red flag indicators.

9.12   What muscle externally rotates the shoulder?

9.13   What is the likely diagnosis?

9.14   What investigations should you request?

9.15   How should this patient be managed?

Case 3

A 22-year-old man presents to A&E with a spontaneous, acutely swollen, hot, red, tender left knee joint. He reports no injury to his knee. He has also had a fever.

9.16   What is the differential of an acute monoarthritis?

9.17   What other questions would you ask?

The patient does not suffer with any medical problems and is not on any medications. On examination he has a red, hot, tender knee. He is unable to move the knee joint much because of pain and is unable to weight-bear on this leg.

9.18   What is the likely diagnosis?

9.19   What investigations should you request?

The patient has his bloods and cultures taken and a knee joint aspiration done. The results of the synovial fluid show:

- Appearance: turbid

- WCC: $100,000 \times 10^6$/L Neutrophils

- Crystals: NONE

- Gram stain – gram positive cocci seen? Staphylococci

- Culture: positive

9.20   How should you manage this patient?

Case 4

A 57-year-old woman presents with pain, stiffness and swelling of her left knee. She says it is worse when moving and eases when she is sitting and resting. She also says sometimes she hears it cracking. There is no locking but her leg has given way on several occasions. She has been having worsening symptoms over the last few months.

9.21   What other questions would you ask?

The woman is a housewife and does not do a lot of exercise. The pain is starting to get her down but has not limited her day-to-day activities that much. The fact that her knee has given way now a few times has made her more concerned. Her mother suffered with OA of the knee.

9.22   What is the likely diagnosis?

On examination the left knee is more swollen than the right. There is no joint line tenderness and there is a full range of motion of the knee joint. The ligaments are all stable. There is crepitus felt on movement of the left knee. The left hip joint is also normal.

9.23   What investigations should you do?

9.24   What features on a knee X-ray characterise osteoarthritis?

The patient's X-ray comes back showing mild OA changes.

9.25   What advice and treatment can you offer the patient?

9.26   When should you refer for surgery?

Case 5

An elderly 72-year-old woman trips and injures her left wrist. X-rays show a Colles fracture. This is immobilised in plaster. She has been advised by A&E to see her doctor about measures to reduce her risk of further fractures.

9.27   What other questions would you want to ask her?

She tells you that her mother did have a hip fracture when she was in her 60s. She has not had any previous falls and she is not on any medications at present and does not suffer with any other medical problems.

9.28   What things should you test when examining her for her falls risk?

She does not have postural hypotension and she did not have any problems with her gait and balance.

9.29   What should you do at this stage?

9.30   What are the indications for a DEXA scan?

The patient goes for her DEXA scan and the result comes back showing a bone mineral density T-score of −2.9.

9.31   What does this mean?

9.32   What treatment should this lady be started on?

Case 6

A 42-year-old man presents with an acute swollen, painful left big toe. He is a known alcoholic and smoker.

9.33   What are the differential diagnoses?

9.34   What other questions would you ask in the history?

The patient suffers with heart failure and is on diuretics for this.

On examination the big toe is red, hot and tender.

9.35   What is the most likely diagnosis?

9.36   What investigations would you do to confirm this?

You send off synovial fluid for microscopy and results come back showing negatively birefringent, needle-shaped crystals.

9.37   What is the acute management of this?

9.38   What other lifestyle changes would you advise this patient about?

The patient's gout settles down. Three months later he returns with another episode of gout and then again two months after this.

9.39   What medication would you consider now and how would you tell the patient to take it?

Case 7

A 25-year-old male presents to his GP with lower back pain and stiffness which is worst on waking up in the mornings. He also says he has had a painful left heel for the last few weeks.

9.40   What are the causes of low back pain?

9.41   What other questions would you ask?

9.42   What are the red flag signs of low back pain?

He says that doing exercise makes the pain better and eases the stiffness in his spine. On examination he has tender plantar fascia of his left heel and slightly reduced chest expansion. He had limited flexion of his lumbar spine.

9.43   What is the test that assesses lumbar flexion?

9.44   What is the likely diagnosis?

9.45   What other features are typical of ankylosing spondylitis?

9.46   What extra-articular manifestations are associated with ankylosing spondylitis?

9.47   What investigations would you request?

An X-ray of the lower spine is done.

9.48   What might you see on this?

9.49   How would you manage this patient?

Case 8

A 65-year-old woman presents to her GP with a four-week history of pain and stiffness in both her upper arms and thighs. This has got progressively worse over time. The last few days she has had tenderness when combing her hair and a right sided headache. Today she has noticed reduced vision in her right eye.

9.50   What is the likely diagnosis?

9.51   What investigations would you do?

9.52   How would you confirm the diagnosis?

The patient's biopsy confirmed temporal arteritis

9.53   What should the treatment be?

The patient's vision improved however she struggled to come off the steroids due to recurrence of her shoulder pain and headache.

9.54   What can be done?

Case 9

A 35-year-old woman presents to her GP with multiple joint pains and swelling in her hands, shoulders and knees over the last four months. She has been feeling very tired. Yesterday she developed a rash over her cheeks and forehead.

9.55   What are the differential diagnoses?

9.56   What other questions would you ask?

On further questioning she reports no other medical problems and she is not on any medications. On examination there is a photosensitive rash on her face and she has synovitis in the small joints of her hands.

9.57   What is the likely diagnosis?

9.58   What investigations would you do?

The patient is found to have positive ANA and anti-Ro and La.

You refer the patient to the rheumatologist. They tell her that she has SLE and that it is a mild form in her case.

9.59   How should she be managed?

Chapter 10 Dermatology

Case 1

A 17-year-old girl comes to see you in the surgery complaining of spots over her face, neck and back. She is clearly embarrassed and very distressed and is frustrated, having tried various treatments from her local chemist with no improvement.

10.1   What questions should you ask?

She tells you that she has had them for several months now and they are getting worse. She has used a number of creams from the chemist and can not remember the name of the current one. She does not have any other medical problems and is not taking any other medications. The spots are getting her very down and she is very embarrassed about them.

On examination there are open and closed comedones (blackheads and whiteheads), and inflammatory papules and pustules on the face and back.

10.2   What are the differential diagnoses?

10.3   What is the likely diagnosis?

10.4   How do you classify this condition?

10.5   What should you tell the patient and how should you manage her condition?

She asks if it is related to her eating lots of chocolate.

10.6   What advice do you give?

10.7   She asks how to care for her skin. What do you advise?

10.8   What treatments are available and what would you offer this woman?

10.9   What else should you tell her about treatment?

She is started on oxytetracycline and benzoyl peroxide gel. You review her after six months and her acne has not improved. She is understandably frustrated.

10.10 At what stage would you consider referral to a dermatologist?

Case 2

A 65-year-old man attends the surgery with a persistent facial rash affecting the cheeks, nose and forehead. Recently he has developed a number of spots and is concerned because he thought that only people in their teens and twenties had spots.

10.11 What is the differential diagnosis?

On examination there is erythema affecting the checks, nose and forehead. A number of telangiectasia can be seen and there are a number of papules and pustules (not shown). There are no comedones.

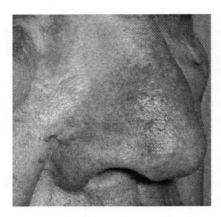

Figure 10.1   Facial erythema (courtesy of Dr Mark Griffiths)

10.12 What is the diagnosis?

10.13 What are the subtypes of this condition?

He has noticed that it is more obvious when he is stressed at work.

10.14 He asks you what makes this condition worse?

He asks what treatments are available.

10.15 What do you tell him?

After educating the patient about this condition and avoiding the aggravating factors you prescribe metronidazole gel to be applied twice daily. You ask him to come back in two months; he has noticed only a slight improvement but does not feel that the condition is adequately controlled.

10.16 What treatment do you offer next?

10.17 When should you refer?

Case 3

A 4-year-old boy attends the surgery with an itchy rash on the forearms, behind the knees and forehead. His mum explains that he has had it for a few years but seems to be getting worse. Lately he has been scratching in the evenings and he has not been settling well overnight because of the itching.

10.18 What is the differential diagnosis?

10.19 What else should you ask?

His mother says that she does have asthma and also suffered with eczema as a child. Her eldest son who is 15 also had eczema.

On examination there is poorly defined erythema with dry scale and multiple excoriations in the antecubital and popliteal fossae. On the wrists there is lichenification (thickening of the skin with accentuation of markings).

10.20 What is the most likely diagnosis?

10.21 How should this condition be managed?

His mother asks you how to recognise infection.

10.22 What do you tell her?

His mother asks if certain food can make atopic eczema worse.

10.23 What is the role of diet in atopic eczema?

He is prescribed an emollient to use as a moisturiser, soap substitute and bath additive. Hydrocortisone 1% ointment is given for facial eczema and clobetasone butyrate for eczema on the body. Despite following your instructions carefully his eczema continues to get worse. There is no evidence of infection and you consider increasing the potency of the topical steroid.

10.24 What are the indications for referral?

Case 4

A 54-year-old man attends the surgery with a scaly rash in the scalp, back, elbows and knees. He has no history of previous skin problems.

10.25 What is the differential diagnosis?

10.26 What specific questions should you include in the history?

10.27 What is the most likely diagnosis?

On examination there are multiple discrete well defined plaques with silvery scale in the scalp and on the back, elbows and knees.

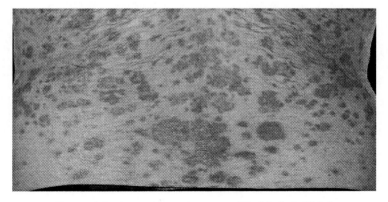

Figure 10.2   Scaly plaques (courtesy of Dr Mark Griffiths)

10.28 What types of this condition are there?

10.29 What do you tell him about his condition?

10.30 What treatments are available and how would you treat this man?

You prescribe topical therapies, initially emollients with vitamin D analogues. He uses these for a couple of months but his condition deteriorates. He attends the surgery and you prescribe a tar preparation. One month later he returns again and states that his skin is getting worse despite the treatments you have offered.

10.31 He has not had a satisfactory response to treatment. What do you do next?

Case 5

An 86-year-old man attends the surgery with a rash. He has been troubled for some time with generalised pruritis. He has been using a moisturizer which has helped with the itching. He is now worried as he has noticed some blisters on his hands and feet.

10.32 What is the differential diagnosis?

On examination there are urticated plaques and a number of intact bullae on the limbs and trunk. There is no conjunctival infection and there are no mucous membrane lesions.

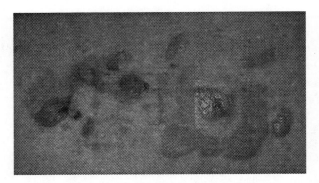

Figure 10.3   Blisters (courtesy of Dr Mark Griffiths)

10.33 What is the most likely diagnosis?

He asks you what causes it and if it is contagious.

10.34 What do you tell him?

10.35 How will the diagnosis be confirmed?

10.36 Can the condition be cured?

10.37 What treatments are available?

10.38 How should this patient be managed?

Case 6

A 26-year-old man presents with an eight-week history of intense itching which is keeping him awake at night. He has noticed a rash on the hands, in the axillae and groin and some spots on his penis, scrotum and buttocks. He tells you that he has no previous skin problems.

10.39 What is the differential diagnosis?

10.40 What questions would you ask him?

On examination there are multiple excoriations. There is scaling and erythema in the web spaces and burrows. There are excoriated papules on the penis and erythematosus nodules are seen on the scrotum and buttocks.

10.41 What is the likely diagnosis?

10.42 What should you tell the patient and how should you manage him?

10.43 How should the cream/lotion be applied?

10.44 Is there any follow up needed?

Case 7

A 38-year-old man attends the surgery with back pain. It is localised to his left mid-back. He had been working in the garden over the weekend and thought it might be a sprain. Yesterday his wife noticed a faint rash with spots within the painful area and today a number of blisters have appeared.

10.45 What is the differential diagnosis?

On examination there are numerous vesicles on an erythematous base on the back, confined to one area on the left side.

10.46 What is the most likely diagnosis?

He asks if it is infectious.

10.47 What do you tell him?

10.48 What treatment would you offer, if any?

10.49 What is the feared long-term complication of this condition?

10.50 What are the complications of ophthalmic zoster (herpes zoster in the ophthalmic division of trigeminal nerve)?

Case 8

A 21-year-old woman comes to see you because she is worried about a mole she has on her anterior thigh. She has noticed it getting darker, increasing in size and changing shape over the past two months.

10.51 What else would you ask about the mole?

On examination there is an irregularly shaped non-palpable pigmented lesion on her anterior thigh. It is mid-brown and has areas of darker pigmentation. It measures 8 mm in diameter.

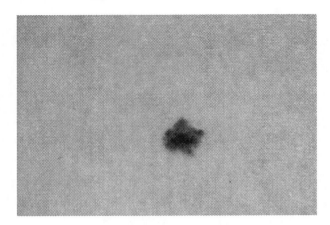

Figure 10.4   Irregularly pigmented lesion on the anterior thigh (courtesy of Dr Mark Griffiths)

10.52 What is the differential diagnosis?

10.53 What is the likely diagnosis?

10.54 What are the risk factors for this condition?

10.55 What is the ABCD checklist?

10.56 What is the weighted seven-point checklist for the clinical diagnosis of melanoma? Should you refer this patient urgently?

10.57 What are the different types of this condition?

10.58 What advice should you give patients to reduce the risk of getting skin cancer?

Case 9

A 78-year-old woman comes to see you in clinic with a persistent red scaly area on the right of her forehead. She has tried various moisturising creams with no significant improvement.

10.59 What questions do you want to ask her?

On examination there is a poorly defined erythematous plaque with surface scale. There is no ulceration. On palpation the surface is rough like sandpaper. There is no induration or tenderness.

10.60 What is the diagnosis?

10.61 What treatments are available?

10.62 What treatment would you recommend to this patient?

10.63 What do you advise on leaving the consultation?

Case 10

A 78-year-old man attends the surgery with a lesion on his hand. It developed around two months ago and has increased in size. Recently it has bled and tends to ooze.

10.64 What is the differential diagnosis?

On examination there is an indurated erythematous nodule with surface scale.

Figure 10.5   Lesion on hand (courtesy of Dr Mark Griffiths)

10.65 What is the most likely diagnosis?

10.66 What are the risk factors for this condition?

The patient asks you about treatment.

10.67 What treatments options are available?

He asks you if this condition can be cured.

10.68 What do you tell him?

10.69 What factors are associated with a higher risk of recurrence and metastasis?

10.70 Does he require urgent referral?

The patient then asks you if there are any precautions to help prevent this condition.

10.71 What do you tell him?

Case 11

A 64-year-old woman attends the surgery with a non-healing lesion on her nose. She tells you that she thought it was just a spot but it has persisted for three months.

On examination there is a pearly nodule with a well-defined rolled edge. There are overlying telangiectasia and central ulceration.

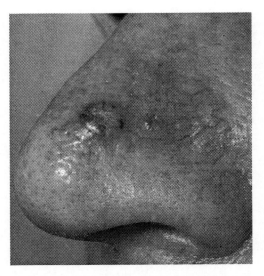

Figure 10.6   Non-healing lesion with a rolled edge and telangiectasia (courtesy of Dr Mark Griffiths)

10.72 What is the differential diagnosis?

10.73 What is the most likely diagnosis?

10.74 What are the sub-types of this condition?

10.75 What do you tell the patient?

10.76 What are the treatment options for BCC?

10.77 What factors are associated with a higher risk of recurrence?

10.78 Does this patient require an urgent referral?

10.79 What are the risk factors for this condition?

10.80 What advice do you give this patient on leaving the clinic?

Chapter 11 Paediatrics

Case 1

A 5-week-old boy has started to vomit after his feeds. He is an only child and his mother says that the vomit has become progressively more forceful. She says it is just the feed she can see in the vomit and she has not seen any blood or bile. She says he is still hungry though, and continues to feed after vomiting.

11.1   What are the main differential diagnoses?

11.2   What else would you want to know in the history?

There are no other symptoms apart from the vomiting. The baby is being breast fed. On examination he is clinically dehydrated but his heart rate and blood pressure are fine. There is visible peristalsis in the abdomen, and you witness the boy vomiting forcefully.

11.3   What is the most likely diagnosis?

11.4   What would you see during a test feed?

11.5   The baby has an ultrasound of the abdomen which is shown below. What other investigation might assist in making the diagnosis?

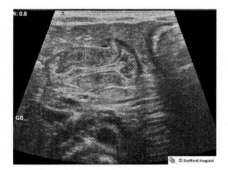

Figure 11.1   Ultrasound scan of abdomen: longitudinal view of the pylorus. The length and width of the pylorus are both excessive in this condition, causing gastric outlet obstruction. (courtesy of Dr Colin Melville and Stafford Hospital)

11.6   Outline the management.

Case 2

A 4-year-old girl has had an episode of generalised shaking earlier this morning and so her parents have brought her in to see you very concerned. She has had a cold for the past few days, and had felt hot just prior to the episode. The episode lasted for 3 minutes and during it she was shaking all over and was staring unresponsively. She has never had any previous similar episodes and there are no known medical problems.

11.7   What are the differential diagnoses?

11.8   What specific questions would you ask in the history?

11.9   What should your immediate management be?

The girl has recently had a sore throat. The child's mother says the girl went stiff and then she had generalised shaking of all limbs. After the episode the girl was drowsy, and took 15 minutes to recover back to full consciousness. She had no problems during pregnancy or birth and has had no developmental delay.

On examination her airway is patent, she is breathing normally and her pulse and blood pressure are normal. Her temperature is 38.2. She is alert and her blood sugar is 4.7 mmol/l.

11.10 What is the most likely diagnosis?

The child's temperature has now settled, and she is back to her normal self.

11.11 What further investigations are required?

11.12 Outline your management and the advice you would give to the parents.

Case 3

A 13-year-old boy's parents come to see you in the surgery. They are concerned that he has not been growing at the same rate as his other classmates and he is now the shortest boy in the class.

11.13 What are differential diagnoses for short stature?

11.14 What further questions would you ask?

There appears to be no psychological problems and there are no other medical concerns. His parents are also both short. His dad is 155 cm and his mother is 145 cm. They have no other children and they are both fit and well. He is 150 cm.

11.15 What clinical examination would you focus on?

11.16 What is his mid-parental height?

When his growth is plotted on the chart it shows that he is on the 4th centile, he has been growing steadily and that there has been no fall across centiles. On examination you find that he has no signs of anaemia nor weight loss, and his cardiovascular, respiratory and abdominal examinations are all normal. He has no pubic nor axillary hair, his penis is small and his testes bilaterally 4 cm^3.

11.17 What is the likely diagnosis?

11.18 What investigations would you do?

His blood tests are all normal.

11.19 What are the management options?

Case 4

A 9-month-old boy has fallen more than two standard deviations on his weight chart. The health visitor has weighed him weekly, and has become concerned.

11.20 What is failure to thrive and what are the main causes?

11.21 What other history would you make specific enquiry about?

On further questioning the mother says he eats well and has been having offensive loose pale stools but no vomiting. She is a housewife and her husband is very supportive. They have no other children. He had no problems during pregnancy or birth and has no other symptoms. He is being breastfed at present. He was weaned at four months on to stage 1 (pureed) foods, and at seven months on to stage 2 (lumpy) foods. On examination he is pale and has a protuberant abdomen and wasted buttocks and legs.

11.22 What investigations would you request?

The results come back showing the boy has a haemoglobin of 9 g/dl and positive coeliac antibodies.

11.23 What is the diagnosis and how can this be confirmed?

11.24 What is the treatment?

Case 5

A concerned mother brings her 7-year-old son with her to see you in the surgery. He has had a cold last week but this has now resolved. Yesterday his mum noticed he had a rash on his buttocks and back of his legs. She is has checked this using a tumbler test and says it is non-blanching. He has a swollen left ankle.

11.25 What are the differential diagnoses?

11.26 What other questions would you ask?

His mother says he is a healthy child and the boy says he has not got any headache but has had some pains in his tummy.

11.27 What is the likely diagnosis?

11.28 What examination would you do?

On examination he is systemically well. The rash is a palpable, purpuric rash on his buttocks and over the extensor surfaces of his legs. The rest of the examination is unremarkable.

His full blood count shows a platelet count of 237×10^9/l, a total white cell count of 7.2×10^9/l and a haemoglobin of 12.3 g/dl. INR is 1.0 and APTT ratio 1.1.

11.29 What is the treatment?

Case 6

An 8-year-old boy is wetting his bed at night. He has been dry by day since three years of age, but his parents are concerned as they thought his nightime wetting would have stopped by his age. He has no other medical problems and his urine test is normal.

11.30 What is the likely diagnosis?

His father says he used to wet the bed until he was 7 also.

11.31 What advice can you give them?

11.32 What is the management?

Case 7

A six-month-old Caucasian baby presents with a history of recurrent chest infections over the last few months. Her mother says she has not put on weight over the last month and she is very concerned by this.

11.33 What other questions would you ask about in the history?

The mother tells you that her daughter is the only child and that she had a normal delivery weighing 3.2 kg, had no complications after birth and has had no other medical problems of note. She says that the GP has ordered a chest x-ray which showed the lungs to be hyperinflated but nothing else abnormal.

On examination she is apyrexial, she looks pale and thin. She has an audible wheeze and her abdomen is soft and she is hypotonic.

11.34 What are your differentials?

11.35 What investigations would you request?

Blood tests show that a haemoglobin of 8.1 g/dl and her sweat test shows a sodium > 70 mmol and sweat chloride > 70 mmol.

11.36 What is the diagnosis?

11.37 Outline your further management.

Case 8

A 4-year-old boy presents to his GP with a right-sided painful limp. He says he was playing football and fell but did not have any cuts or bruising. Initially his leg was ok but then as the game went on he started to get worse pain and had to stop playing. There are no other symptoms.

11.38 What other questions would you ask?

11.39 What are the differential diagnoses?

On examination he is apyrexial and he cannot weight-bear on his right leg. The hip is held in flexion and internal rotation. He has restricted movements on the right side especially with hip flexion and external rotation. The hip does not feel warm. There are no problems with movement on the left side hip, and other joints are normal.

11.40 Why is the hip held in this position?

11.41 What investigations would you request?

Bloods show a normal white cell count and CRP and ESR. Hip X-ray shows a loss of the normal hemispherical contour of the femoral head.

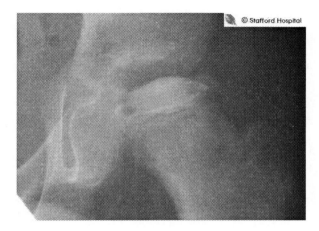

Figure 11.2   X-ray of hip (courtesy of Dr Colin Melville and Stafford Hospital)

11.42 What is the most likely diagnosis?

11.43 What is the management of this condition?

Chapter 12 Psychiatry

Case 1

A 42-year-old woman has recently split up from her husband after finding out he was having an affair. She comes to see you and tells you that she has been feeling low for the last four weeks and has not been sleeping well. She normally enjoys going shopping and seeing her friends but has no interest in doing anything at the moment and has been crying a lot. She has not been eating properly either, she is feeling very pessimistic about the future and wants some help.

12.1   What is the likely diagnosis?

12.2   What are the symptoms you should ask about in this condition?

12.3   What signs might you pick up from this patient in the consultation?

12.4   What are the risk factors in the history you should ask about?

12.5   What are other causes of low mood?

12.6   What investigations may be needed to exclude other differential diagnoses?

12.7   What is the management of her depression and does she need urgent referral?

You start the patient on citalopram.

12.8   What should you tell the patient about the medication?

The patient is not deemed to be at risk of suicide.

12.9   When do you need to review her again?

The patient had been on citalopram at the optimal dose for a month but is still not getting better.

12.10 What can be done now?

Three months later she comes to see you for one of her reviews and she is feeling a lot better. She asks if she can stop taking the medications.

12.11 What should you do?

Case 2

A 20-year-old man has recently been behaving very oddly. His parents come to see you saying that he has become more withdrawn and his personal hygiene has deteriorated. He has been saying people are coming to get him and that he can hear people talking about him. The patient himself is not aware he has a problem.

12.12 What is the likely diagnosis?

12.13 What are the differential diagnoses?

12.14 What are Schneider's first rank symptoms?

This patient is male and has some negative symptoms.

12.15 What are other poor prognostic factors?

12.16 What should this man's management be?

After discussion with the patient you decide to start him on medication.

12.17 What kind of medication is first line treatment?

You explain that he will need to be reviewed regularly now.

12.18 What things will you need to check regularly in patients with schizophrenia?

The patient was started on olanzapine. After several months he is starting to show symptoms of relapse. You arrange for him to be seen urgently in clinic.

12.19 When should you also consider referral?

Case 3

A mother comes to see you with her 17-year-old girl. She says that her daughter has started to eat alone and has become very interested in what calories there are in meals. She is concerned that her daughter has been losing weight and is obsessed with being thin despite already being slim and lower in mood. She knows that her daughter has been going to the gym a lot and is concerned she may be making herself sick. She wants some help.

12.20 What is the differential diagnosis?

12.21 What questions should you ask the patient?

12.22 Who should GPs screen for eating disorders?

You think that this is anorexia nervosa.

12.23 What is the diagnostic criteria for this?

12.24 What kind of physical problems and findings may be present?

On examination you notice she has dental erosion and also callouses on the back of her hand.

12.25 What are these caused by?

12.26 What electrolyte disturbance may you find?

12.27 How should this girl be managed?

Case 4

A 26-year-old man has come in intoxicated with alcohol and having taken an overdose of paracetamol. He tells you that he has recently split from his girlfriend and since then has been depressed. He has never taken an overdose before. He says he wanted to kill himself and if it had not been for a friend of his who found him he would have succeeded. On questioning he says he can't remember how many tablets he took. A note was found on the floor in his house saying that he had planned to do this.

12.28 What questions should you ask someone who has tried to commit suicide?

12.29 What are the risk factors for suicide?

His paracetamol level comes back above the normal treatment line.

12.30 What factors can cause you to be on the higher treatment line?

12.31 What should the management of this patient be?

The patient has had his U&Es, FBC, PT, LFTs, INR, glucose and arterial blood gases checked daily. After 24 hours his pH on the ABG is 7.25.

12.32 What should be done?

Chapter 13 General surgery

Case 1

A 35-year-old woman presents to her GP having noticed a lump on her left breast while she was showering. She says she routinely checks for lumps and has found this only in the last few days. She says it is under the skin and it moves around. She is very anxious about this.

13.1   What are the differential diagnoses?

13.2   What other questions should you ask her?

She is a fit and well woman with no medical problems and is not on any medications. She has not noticed any change with her menstrual cycle and says the lump is small and non-tender. She has not had any nipple discharge or noticed any skin changes. She has no family history of breast cancer.

On examination you find a small, mobile non-tender lump within the left breast in the upper, outer quadrant. There is no skin tethering. There are no other lumps felt in either breast or axillae and there are no other sinister findings.

13.3   What is the likely diagnosis?

13.4   What investigations should you do?

The woman is found to have a fibroadenoma confirmed from these investigations which is 2.5 cm.

13.5   What should the management be?

Case 2

A 67-year-old man presents to his GP with a two-month history of worsening dysphagia. He says this is with both solids and fluids. He also says he has lost weight in the last few months.

13.6   What other questions would you ask him?

He reports no other symptoms apart from those he has mentioned. Initially the difficulty swallowing was with solids only but then progressed to liquids. He is a smoker (25/day) and has been so for the last 45 years. He is a farmer.

On examination he is a thin man with signs of weight loss. His abdominal examination is unremarkable and there were no lymph nodes palpable.

13.7   What is the likely diagnosis?

13.8   What investigations would you do?

The barium swallow is shown below.

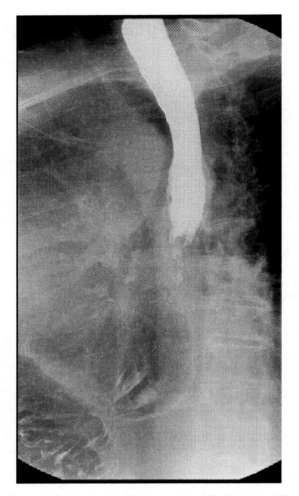

Figure 13.1   Barium swallow (courtesy of Dr John Asquith)

The barium swallow has demonstrated a stricture and the endoscopy confirms a tumour in the upper third of the oesophagus.

13.9   What should the management be?

Case 3

A 45-year-old woman presents to A&E with right upper quadrant pains that have been coming and going over the last week with increasing severity. She has also vomited. She says the pain is the worst today after she had eaten some fried chicken.

13.10   What other questions would you ask?

13.11   What are the differential diagnoses?

On examination she is an obese woman. She is tender in the right upper quadrant and she has a positive Murphy's sign. She is not jaundiced or anaemic. Her temperature is 38°C.

13.12 What is Murphy's sign?

13.13 What is the diagnosis?

13.14 What investigations would you do?

The patient's blood tests were all normal. However, the patient is found to have multiple gallstones on the ultrasound but the common bile duct is not dilated.

13.15 What is the management?

13.16 Why do patients with acute cholecystitis have an elective cholecystectomy when symptoms have settled down, whilst patients with appendicitis need an urgent appendicectomy?

13.17 What are the complications of cholecystitis?

Case 4

A 37-year-old man who was doing some heavy lifting suddenly developed a painful lump in his right groin. He works as a builder but has not had this happen before. He says the lump goes back in when he is lying down but comes back when he is standing.

13.18 What are the differential diagnoses?

13.19 What other things would you ask about?

On examination he is found to have a lump in the right groin in the region of the inguinal canal. It has a cough impulse. The rest of the abdominal examination is normal. It is reducible. There are no signs of any previous surgery.

13.20 What is the diagnosis?

13.21 How can you distinguish a direct inguinal hernia from an indirect one?

13.22 What is the management of this?

13.23 The patient had an open mesh repair carried out. What advice should be given to the patient post-op?

Case 5

A 17-year-old girl presents to A&E with nausea and abdominal pain in her right lower abdomen. She is in a lot of pain and this is worse if she moves.

13.24 What are the differential diagnoses?

13.25 What other questions would you ask?

She says that the pain initially was in the centre of her abdomen and felt dull, and then shifted to the right lower side. It is now very severe and continuous.

13.26 What is the likely diagnosis?

On examination she is tachycardic at 110 beats per minute, pyrexial with a temperature of 37.8°C, has guarding, rebound tenderness and a positive Rovsing's sign. She is tender on percussion and also when asked to cough. Rectal examination revealed an empty rectum with some tenderness to the right. (PV examination is not usually carried out in this situation, but would be normal).

13.27 What is Rovsing's sign?

13.28 What investigations would you do?

She has a raised white cell count of 15×10^9/L with a high neutrophil count. The pregnancy test is negative. The urine was negative for infection. She has had a laparoscopy which shows appendicitis.

13.29 What is the management of this?

Case 6

A 46-year-old man presents to his GP with a two-month history of looser and more frequent stools and also some red blood mixed with his stools.

13.30 What is the differential diagnosis?

13.31 What other questions would you ask?

He has no family history of bowel cancer and does not suffer with any other medical problems. He eats a healthy diet.

13.32 What is the likely diagnosis?

On examination his abdomen is soft and non-tender and no masses are palpable. On PR examination there are no masses palpable and no blood seen.

13.33 What investigations should you request?

The patient's blood tests were all normal. On flexible sigmoidoscopy the patient is found to have a mass on the sigmoid colon.

13.34 What is the management of this?

Case 7

A 65-year-old man presents with a three-day history of vomiting, abdominal pain and distension and constipation.

13.35 What are the differential diagnoses?

13.36 What questions would you ask?

The patient says that the vomiting started first and the abdominal pain is higher up in his abdomen. He has not opened his bowels at all the last 3 days or passed any gas. He does not suffer with any medical problems currently but has had his gallbladder removed previously. On examination the patient's abdomen was distended, there was guarding, he was tender all over and there were increased bowel sounds. You note the scar from his cholecystectomy and there are no hernias present. PR exam was normal. His pulse was 98 bpm and his blood pressure was 128/78 mmHg.

13.37 What is the diagnosis?

13.38 What investigations would you do?

Here is the patient's abdominal X-ray:

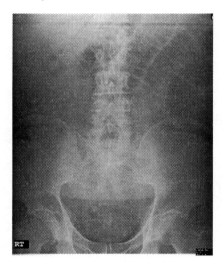

Figure 13.2   Patient's abdominal X-ray (courtesy of Dr John Asquith)

The patient's supine abdominal X-ray showed dilated loops of bowel and the valvulae conniventes were seen to cross the entire lumen.

13.39 What is the management?

13.40 When would you consider surgery?

Case 8

A 58-year-old man presents to A&E with severe epigastric pain radiating into his back. He says the pain started several days ago and has got worse and it was so bad today that he collapsed.

13.41 What are the differential diagnoses?

13.42 What other questions would you ask?

The patient is a known hypertensive but this is controlled with his anti-hypertensives. He has never had angina or a MI and there is no family history of AAA. He is a smoker about 10/day.

13.43 What is the likely diagnosis?

On examination he has a tender abdomen and signs of hypovolaemia. You can feel an expansile abdominal mass.

13.44 What is the management?

Case 9

A 72-year-old man presents to his GP with a three-month history of pain in both calves after walking. It is worse when walking uphill and is relieved by resting. He is a known diabetic and hypertensive. He is on aspirin, furosemide and metformin.

13.45 What other questions would you ask?

13.46 What are the differential diagnoses?

The patient smokes 20 cigarettes a day and has done so for the last 50 years. He is overweight. On examination he has cold feet and weak pulses in both feet but has popliteal and femoral pulses bilaterally. There are no ulcers seen or discolouration.

Buerger's angle test does not indicate severe ischaemia.

13.47 What is Buerger's angle test?

13.48 What are the signs/symptoms of acute ischaemia?

13.49 What is the diagnosis in this patient?

13.50 What investigations would you do?

His ABPI was 0.7

13.51 How would you manage this patient?

13.52 What options are available if these measures do not work?

13.53 What is critical ischaemia?

Chapter 14 Obstetrics and gynaecology

Case 1

A 31-year-old woman has had a routine cervical smear done which was abnormal. The letter she was sent said she will need to have a colposcopy for further investigation. Her smear showed that she had moderate dyskaryosis. Her previous smear when she was 28 was normal.

14.1 How often should women have their smears?

She says she has been very anxious about the result and she is worried that this means she has cancer.

14.2 What is dyskaryosis?

You explain the results of the smear test to her and that this does not mean cancer but that the cells are pre-cancerous and if left untreated may go on to develop into cancer.

14.3 What should the management be now?

14.4 What questions would you ask the patient to elicit any risk factors for cervical cancer?

The patient attended her colposcopy appointment. At the colposcopy clinic she is found to have a white area once acetic acid is applied and the same area stains pale with Lugol's iodine.

14.5 What do these findings mean?

14.6 The biopsy taken shows CIN2. What does this mean?

The patient had a large loop excision of the transformation zone.

14.7 When should she have a follow up smear?

Case 2

A 29-year-old Afro-Caribbean woman presents with pelvic pain, dyspareunia and dysmenorrhoea. Her periods are regular and there is no postcoital or intermenstrual bleeding.

14.8 What are the differential diagnoses?

On examination she is apyrexial, she has lower abdominal pain but no palpable masses. The cervix looks healthy on speculum examination. There is cervical excitation.

14.9 What is the likely diagnosis?

14.10 What investigations would you order to confirm the diagnosis?

The patient had her transvaginal ultrasound which was normal. Her laparoscopy showed some blue-black lesions and biopsy confirmed endometriosis.

14.11 What is the management?

Case 3

A 44-year-old woman has been complaining of leaking urine. She says it started when she had her second child 15 years ago. She says this tends to happen on coughing and laughing.

14.12 What other questions would you ask in the history?

14.13 What is the likely diagnosis?

There is nothing abnormal to find on abdominal or vaginal examination.

14.14 What investigations would you do to confirm this?

The woman has a normal urine dipstick.

14.15 What is the management at this stage?

Four months later the woman returns to see you saying that the exercises have not helped her and she is suffering more than ever with her symptoms.

14.16 What would you do now?

The woman goes on to have her urodynamic studies. The report from this shows loss of urine with coughing and there is no detrusor activity.

14.17 What does this mean and what is the importance of confirming the diagnosis?

The woman went on to have a tension-free vaginal tape procedure which alleviated her symptoms.

Case 4

A 24-year-old woman presents to A&E with abdominal pain and vaginal bleeding.

14.18 What are the differential diagnoses?

14.19 What other questions would you ask in the history?

On further questioning she reveals the pain is more on the right side and she has some right-sided shoulder tip pain. She says her last period was six weeks ago and she uses condoms most of the time and has had a regular partner for the last three years. She has no other medical problems and is not on any medications.

14.20 What is the likely diagnosis?

14.21 What investigations would you want to do?

You do a pregnancy test which is positive.

14.22 What do you do now?

The ultrasound confirms an ectopic pregnancy.

14.23 What are the options?

The mass on ultrasound is 3 cm and the patient is haemodynamically stable.

14.24 What is the best option for her then?

Case 5

A 32-year-old woman is ten weeks five days' gestation and she has come to see you as she has had some vaginal spotting and some lower abdominal pain. The dates of her gestation have been confirmed by an ultrasound scan.

14.25 What are the causes of this?

On examination her cervical os is closed and there is no blood or vaginal discharge seen. She is apyrexial and her abdominal examination is normal. Her uterus is small for her gestation.

14.26 What is the likely diagnosis?

14.27 What investigations should you do?

The report shows a gestational sac with a fetal pole but fetal heart not seen. Crown-rump length is 35 mm.

14.28 What does this mean?

14.29 What are the management options?

14.30 What things are important to explain to the woman?

Case 6

A woman at 35 weeks' gestation presents with vaginal bleeding and abdominal pain. She describes the pain as constant with heavier pains coming and going. She has no urinary or bowel symptoms. She is not sure about the fetal movements but thinks they may be reduced.

14.31 What are the differential diagnoses?

On examination she is apyrexial, her blood pressure is 152/86 mmHg and her pulse is regular at 80 beats per minute. The uterus feels hard and tender. No fetal heart is heard on auscultation. On speculum examination blood can be seen. Her CTG is normal.

14.32 What is the likely diagnosis?

14.33 What are risk factors for it?

You admit the patient to the hospital for investigations.

14.34 What investigations should she have?

14.35 What are the features of a normal CTG?

The CTG is abnormal showing a high heart rate, reduced variability and decelerations.

14.36 How should this woman be managed?

14.37 How does placental abruption differ from placenta praevia?

Case 7

A 23-year-old woman in her first pregnancy is admitted to hospital with severe headache and reduced fetal movements. Her booking blood pressure was 120/80 and today it is measured at 158/102 mmHg. She is 27 weeks gestation and she is also complaining of blurred vision and some epigastric discomfort.

14.38 What is the likely diagnosis?

On examination she is apyrexial. Fundoscopy is normal and on abdominal examination she has a tender epigastrium. She has swelling of her hands and feet and a urine dipstick is strongly positive for protein.

14.39 What other investigation would you do?

Her CTG shows decelerations and reduced variability. Her bloods show abnormal LFTs, low platelets and raised urate and creatinine.

14.40 What syndrome does this constitute?

14.41 How should this patient be managed?

Case 8

A 22-year-old woman comes to see her GP. She tells you that she has taken a pregnancy test at home twice and that it is positive. She does not have any children and she has been in a relationship with her boyfriend for the last 3 years.

14.42 What kind of questions would you ask?

14.43 What would you check whilst she is in the surgery?

You calculate her gestation to be at 8 weeks 5 days.

14.44 What advice should you give to the woman now?

She asks you about testing for Down's Syndrome.

14.45 What information should you tell her?

14.46 How many appointments should a nulliparous woman have in an uncomplicated pregnancy?

Case 9

A 17-year-old girl comes to see you wanting to start contraception. She has not been on anything before and is with a regular partner and has been using condoms. She has never forgotten to use them, so knows she cannot be pregnant.

14.47 What questions would you ask in the history?

She is fit and well and has no medical problems and no family history and is not on any medications.

14.48 What are the recommended options from NICE?

After a discussion of these options the patient is not keen on having anything inserted anywhere and she has a needle phobia. She mentions her friend is on something called Microgynon. She asks about this.

14.49 What should you tell her about this?

She says her period started four days ago and so you advise her to start taking the pill today.

14.50 What other important points should you discuss with her?

14.51 What should you check while she is with you in the surgery?

Case 10

A 19-year-old girl comes to see you with a history of two days of vaginal discharge.

14.52 What are the possible causes?

She describes the discharge as non-itchy and having a fishy odour to it. She is with a regular partner at present.

14.53 What else should you ask about?

14.54 What is the likely diagnosis?

14.55 What are risk factors for this?

She is worried about this and asks if it is a sexually transmitted disease.

14.56 What should you tell her?

14.57 How do you treat it and what advice should you give?

Chapter 15 Orthopaedics

Case 1

A 13-year-old girl with known sickle cell anaemia presents to A&E with pain in her left leg. The pain has become worse and she is unable to weight bear on it. She says she has been feeling hot and tired.

15.1   What other questions would you ask in the history?

She says the pain has got worse over the last four days. She had fallen off her bike and injured her leg with a cut. The pain is worst around her knee and thigh and she is very tender over this area. She does not suffer with any other medical problems and the only medication she takes is penicillin.

On examination she is pyrexial with a temperature of 38.2. Her pulse is 112 bpm. Her cardiovascular, respiratory, abdominal and neurological examinations are normal. There is no deformity of the leg and she is unable to move her left leg because of pain. There is redness and warmth over her thigh.

15.2   What are the potential differential diagnoses?

Bloods tests are done for a full blood count, urea and electrolytes, inflammatory markers and blood cultures. They show a raised white cell count of 18, raised CRP (100) and ESR (56 mm/hr).

15.3   What is the likely diagnosis?

Antibiotics are given once the blood cultures have reached the laboratory.

15.4   What antibiotics should be started?

15.5   What other investigations would you do to confirm this?

The X-ray does not show anything. The technetium bone scan confirms osteomyelitis and the fluid aspirated from the knee shows staphylococcus aureus.

15.6   How should this patient be managed?

Case 2

A 23-year-old man who is a keen sportsman presents to A&E with left knee pain and swelling. He was playing football and was tackled, and felt his knee pop. He has been unable to move it properly since then.

15.7   What other questions would you ask in the history?

The patient is fit and well and is not on any medications. He plays a lot of football and rugby and fortunately has never had any injuries until today. He says he was running with the ball and then another player tackled him from behind. He says he felt something 'pop' in the knee and that is when the pain started and also the swelling. He has not been able to weight bear on it since then.

15.8   What are the potential differential diagnoses?

On examination the patient has a painful, swollen left knee and there is a haemarthrosis. He is unable to move the knee due to the pain. Lachman test is positive.

15.9   What is the likely diagnosis?

15.10   What investigations would you do?

The X-ray of the knee confirms soft tissue swelling and no fractures. A MRI scan of the confirms that there is an anterior cruciate ligament rupture.

15.11   How should this patient be managed?

Case 3

A 30-year-old man presents to the GP with sudden onset low back pain radiating down both his legs. He says he was doing a lot of gardening and this may have caused it. He is finding it difficult to bend his back and also says it is very tender. The pain started 10 hours ago.

15.12   What other questions would you want to ask him?

He says he has never had back trouble before and is not on any medications. He says he has not passed urine since the back pain started which is not normal for him.

15.13   What are the potential differential diagnoses?

On examination he is tender over his lumbar spine and he has bilateral straight leg raise of only 10 degrees and saddle and genital anaesthesia. He has a palpable bladder. He has down going plantars on both legs and also absent ankle reflexes.

15.14   What is the likely diagnosis?

15.15   How should this patient be managed?

The patient has a MRI scan once in hospital and is found to have a large central L5/S1 disc prolapse which is compressing the cauda equina.

15.16   What should happen next?

Case 4

An 84-year-old woman was out walking and had a fall as she slipped on some ice. She tried to stop herself by putting her hand out and fell onto her outstretched left hand. She is brought into the A&E department by her son. She is complaining of pain in her left hand.

15.17   What other questions would you ask in the history?

The woman is a recent widow and has two children that live close by and help her a lot but she lives alone independently. She suffers with hypertension and is on bendroflumethiazide 2.5 mg for this. She has not had any previous falls and there are no medical problems that run in her family. She did not injure anything else when she fell except for her hand.

15.18 What are the potential differential diagnoses?

On examination her vitals are stable. There is an obvious dinner fork wrist deformity. No distal neurovascular deficit is found.

15.19 What is the likely diagnosis?

15.20 How should this patient be managed?

The patient comes back to the fracture clinic ten days later, and the fracture is healing nicely.

15.21 The patient asks what other complications she may get and when she should expect the fracture to have healed fully?

Case 5

An 80-year-old woman had a fall whilst out shopping. She says she simply lost her balance. She is now suffering with pain in her left hip and says she is unable to weight bear properly on her left leg.

15.22 What other questions would you ask her?

She says she does not suffer with any other medical problems and is not on any medications. She is a very fit and active person. She says it was just a fall.

On examination her left leg is shorter than the right leg and also externally rotated. She can not actively lift her left leg and on passive movement of the left leg she is in pain.

15.23 What is the diagnosis?

15.24 What investigations would you do?

She is found to have a displaced intracapsular fracture.

15.25 How should she be managed?

Case 6

A 35-year-old man was admitted to hospital following a motor cycle accident. He sustained a closed fracture of his right tibia and fibula. His leg was immobilised in a plaster of Paris backslab and he was admitted to an orthopaedic ward to await surgery the next day. The patient was in a lot of pain and had been asking for a lot of morphine overnight.

15.26 What is the diagnosis?

On examination the patient is in a lot of discomfort. He is haemodynamically stable. His foot pulses are palpable on the right side. He has pain in his calf on passive extension of his toes on the right foot. He also has a loss of sensation in his first two toes.

The consultant reviews the patient and decides that there are no late features yet and the patient should be treated urgently.

15.27   What are late features of compartment syndrome?

15.28   How should this patient be managed?

The patient had an urgent fasciotomy. Following this his wound was left open.

15.29   How long should the wound be left open?

Case 7

A 30-year-old woman comes to see her GP complaining of pain and a tingling sensation in her right hand. The pain started three weeks ago and has been getting worse, and it is worst at night.

15.30   What other questions would you ask in the history?

The patient suffers with hypothyroidism. The pain is just in her hand and she says that the tingling is mainly in her index and middle fingers. She says that it is worst at night and she finds relief with shaking her hand. She reports no injury to her neck or arm.

15.31   What are the possible differential diagnoses?

On examination there is no obvious deformity of the hand or elbow or shoulder. There is a marked sensory disturbance on the lateral three and half fingers. There is weakness of thumb abduction. Tapping over her wrist causes the patient to experience the tingling in those fingers. Hyperflexion of her wrist for 60 seconds causes tingling also.

15.32   What is the diagnosis?

15.33   What further tests can be done to confirm the diagnosis?

The EMG and NCS confirms the diagnosis of carpal tunnel syndrome.

15.34   How should you manage this patient?

Case 8

A 38-year-old male is brought into A&E via ambulance. He has been involved in a motorcycle accident with a stationary car. He was travelling at a speed of about 40 mph. The paramedics have put the patient in a stable position, safely immobilising his C spine. The patient's GCS is 15/15 (E4V5M6), pupils both equal and reactive.

15.35   What should the doctor do?

The patient is able to hold a conversation with the doctor although he seems to be struggling. The doctor asks the paramedics to administer 100% oxygen via a re-breathe mask and attach the patient to a monitor so his observations can be monitored.

15.36   What should happen now?

The patient is tachypnoeic. On examination, the chest sounds clear and there is equal air entry bilaterally.

15.37 What should the doctor do now?

The patient is tachycardic at 105 bpm, BP is 135/85, capillary refill is about 2 seconds and his peripheries feel warm.

15.38 What should be done now?

The patient has a GCS of 15/15 and says he has been conscious since the accident.

15.39 What should be done now?

Chest, c-spine and pelvic x-rays are all normal.

15.40 What should be done next?

The patient has a right leg deformity with an open shin fracture with a 2 cm wound. The bone is visible protruding through the skin. His distal foot pulses and sensation are intact.

15.41 What should be done next?

15.42 How should this be managed?

Chapter 16 ENT

Case 1

4-year-old, Peter, comes to see you with his mum. He has been irritable and crying for the past 48 hours and has been tugging at his right ear, saying that it is hurting him. He had a cough and runny nose for the few days prior to the onset of earache. His mum tells you he had a fever yesterday.

16.1   What are the differential diagnoses?

Otoscopy demonstrates a normal left tympanic membrane but his right tympanic membrane is red and bulging.

16.2   What is the likely diagnosis?

Peter's mother is quite anxious about this condition and is asking what you can do. She also wants to know if you will prescribe him antibiotics.

16.3   What would your management plan be?

You begin treatment for Peter and send him home with his mother. Before she leaves she asks what sort of things could happen to Peter if this problem does not get better.

16.4   What are the potential complications of AOM?

Peter's mum also asks you if there are any operations Peter could have to stop this happening again. She specifically mentions that her neighbour's child had 'grommets' put in.

16.5   Should Peter be referred for ventilation tube insertion?

16.5   Is there any other treatment that Peter may benefit from?

Case 2

A 21-year-old woman presents to you complaining of a sore throat, odynophagia, headache and flushing. She is normally fit and well and is not on any medications.

16.7   What are the differential diagnoses?

On examination, she has a temperature of 38°C, bilaterally enlarged tonsils with white spots and halitosis. She has enlarged, tender cervical lymph nodes bilaterally.

16.8   What is the likely diagnosis and how would you manage it?

She is treated with paracetamol, ibuprofen and phenoxymethylpenicillin (500 mg qds). She returns three days later as she is struggling to eat and drink due to the pain and cannot open her mouth fully. On your limited view, it appears the left tonsil is pushed towards the midline.

16.9   What has happened and what is the management of this?

The patient comes back three months later with a similar presentation, and then two months after this once again. She asks you if she would benefit from a tonsillectomy.

16.10   What advice should you give her?

She is a little concerned about the thought of surgery as one of her friends had problems following an operation to remove her tonsils.

16.11   What are the main complications of tonsillectomy?

Case 3

A 53-year-old woman comes to see you complaining of an intermittent spinning sensation that occurs when she turns her head to the right. Each episode lasts a few seconds only. Although short-lived, the episodes are quite distressing to her.

16.12   What otological symptoms would you ask about?

Detailed questioning does not reveal anything else significant in her history. You decide to move on to examining her.

16.13   What examinations would you perform?

Your examinations do not elicit any positive findings. She is understandably concerned that you will not be able to help her problem.

16.14   What could the diagnosis be and what specific test could be done to diagnose it?

The test is positive and you reassure your patient that you should be able to help her symptoms.

16.15   How can this condition be treated?

Case 4

Mrs Jones, a 65-year-old woman, attends the A&E department with a severe nose bleed. She says it started 30 minutes ago and has not settled; she has become very distressed. She says she has never had this before.

16.16   What specific questions would you ask her?

Mrs Jones is a known hypertensive with no prior history of trauma or epistaxis. She does not drink alcohol or smoke and has no allergies. She takes simvastatin, aspirin and bendroflumethiazide.

On examination there is blood seen coming from the right nostril. Her blood pressure is 180/105 mmHg and her pulse is 95 beats per minute. There is no other significant abnormality on examination.

16.17   What is the site of the majority of epistaxes?

16.18   What are the causes of epistaxis?

While taking your history, Mrs Jones is continuing to bleed from the right nostril. You are the first doctor to see her.

16.19   How should this patient be managed?

Chapter 17 Urology

Case 1

A 70-year-old man presents to his GP having noticed blood in his urine for the last few days. He says there is no pain passing urine and no other urinary symptoms. He has never had this before and so is very concerned.

17.1   What are the differential diagnoses?

17.2   What other questions would you ask the patient?

On further questioning the patient says he has noticed some weight loss over the last few months and does smoke 30 cigarettes a day, and has done so for the last 50 years. He says he used to work in a chemical factory for over 30 years. On examination he is found to be pale but abdominal examination is unremarkable as is his rectal examination.

17.3   What is the likely diagnosis?

17.4   What investigations would you request?

17.5   What should your management be?

The patient was referred to the urologist and the investigations confirmed a low grade non-muscle invasive (superficial) bladder cancer.

17.6   What is the management of this?

Case 2

A 39-year-old woman comes to see her GP saying that she gets burning when passing water and she has been having discomfort in her abdomen for the last few days. She also says she has been going to the toilet to pass urine more often. She says she has felt generally unwell.

17.7   What are the differential diagnoses?

17.8   What other questions would you ask her in the history?

She suffers with no medical problems and is not on any medications. She does not have any children and has been married to her husband for 20 years.

17.9   What is the likely diagnosis?

17.10   What investigations would you request?

The woman has a positive dipstick for nitrites and leucocytes and along with her symptoms you decide to start her on treatment.

17.11 What medication would you give?

You prescribe co-amoxiclav for her. The patient finishes her course of antibiotics and her symptoms resolve. The urine MC&S confirmed an E.coli infection sensitive to co-amoxiclav.

The woman asks you how she can try to prevent getting infections in the future.

17.12 What advice can you give her to reduce UTIs in the future?

Case 3

A 24-year-old man presents with pain and swelling in his scrotum and burning when passing urine which has developed over the preceding three days.

17.13 What are the differential diagnoses?

17.14 What other questions would you ask in the history?

On examination his left scrotum is swollen, the scrotal skin is red and warm and he is very tender. His temperature is 38. There is no penile discharge. He says that he has had STIs in the past but did not want to talk about this in much detail.

17.15 What test can be used to help differentiate between torsion of testis and epididymo-orchitis?

17.16 What investigations should you do if infection is suspected?

The man is found to have Chlamydia.

17.17 What is the management?

Case 4

A 65-year-old man presents to his GP with hesitancy and nocturia. He also says that he has been losing weight over the last few months and started to get lower back pain despite no injury to his back.

17.18 What are the differential diagnoses?

17.19 What other questions would you ask in the history?

On examination he is found to have an enlarged prostate gland which is hard and irregular with obliteration of the median sulcus.

17.20 What is the likely diagnosis and what investigations would you do to confirm it?

His PSA comes back as 35.

17.21 What does this mean?

17.22 What else can cause elevated PSA values?

17.23 What is the management of this?

17.24 How are prostate cancers graded?

His Gleason score is 8.

17.25 What would the management of this be?

Chapter 18 Ophthalmology

Case 1

A 33-year-old woman presents with redness of her left eye associated with gritty irritation and stinging. She says that her eyelashes are stuck together on waking and that her eye is sticky throughout the day.

18.1   What are the differential diagnoses of red eye?

18.2   What further questions would you ask her?

18.3   What is the likely diagnosis in this case?

18.4   How would you treat this patient?

18.5   What features would make allergic conjunctivitis more likely?

18.6   Describe the main features of other causes of red eye.

18.7   What examinations should you do for all patients presenting with a red eye?

Case 2

An elderly man comes to see you with a sudden, painless loss of vision in his left eye.

18.8   What are the differential diagnoses?

18.9   What other things would you check in the history?

On examination you see this:

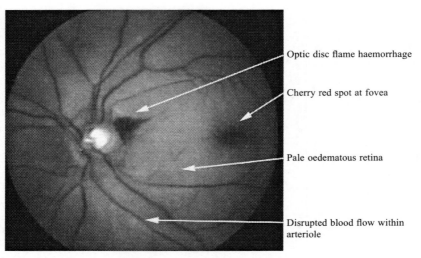

Figure 18.1   Picture of eye (courtesy of Mrs Hannah Sharma)

18.10 What is the diagnosis in this case?

18.11 What is the management?

Case 3

A 50-year-old woman presents to her GP with a history of flashing lights and floaters in her right eye. There is no pain and no other symptoms and she is otherwise fit and well. She wears glasses for short-sightedness.

18.12 What is the differential diagnosis?

18.13 What else would you ask in the history?

On examination you see this:

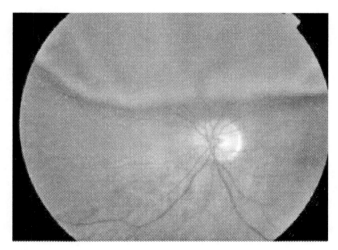

Figure 18.2   Fundus photograph of the right eye showing a superior retinal detachment (courtesy of Mr Tim Jackson)

18.14 What factors predispose to an increased risk of retinal detachment?

18.15 How does a retinal detachment develop?

18.16 What is the management?

Chapter 19 Communication and ethics

Case 1

A 64-year-old man has been getting progressively short of breath over the last few months and also losing weight. He is an ex-smoker and used to work in the pits. The GP had requested a chest X-ray which has shown a mass in the left lung suspicious of cancer.

He comes to see you for the result and so you need to tell him what the X-ray showed and also what the management will be now.

19.1   What are the key points when breaking bad news?

Case 2

A 15-year-old comes to see you alone and requests to be put on the pill. She says that her friends are on it and so she wants to be on it also, and that if you will not give it to her she will get it from someone else.

19.2   What questions would you ask her?

She tells you that she has a boyfriend who is also 15 and that they have not had sexual intercourse yet but she is planning on it soon. She has not told her parents about this as she thinks they will get angry and stop her seeing her boyfriend.

19.3   What things do you need to check to deem her Gillick competent?

After your assessment you deem her to meet the criteria and so start her on Microgynon 30.

A few days later her mother comes to see you as she has found the prescription for the pill when she was cleaning her daughter's room, and demands to know who prescribed this, whether her daughter is having sex and why she was not informed.

19.4   How should you handle this situation?

Case 3

A colleague of yours has recently been turning up to work late, and usually quite dishevelled. On a few occasions you have smelt alcohol on him. You are aware that he has had some personal issues recently but you do not know much more about it.

19.5   What concerns does this raise and how should you best address them?

The colleague denies everything when you ask him about his drinking and if he is all right. He asks you to leave him alone and says that it is none of your business. Patients have started to notice his manner has been aggressive and nurses have noticed some mistakes in prescribing doses and order requests.

19.6   What should you do now?

Case 4

An elderly woman who is recently widowed comes to see her GP with a chest infection. She lives alone and has been finding it difficult to cope since her husband died from cancer. Over the last few months you have been seeing her and helping her cope with the bereavement. The GP assessed her and felt that she had a chest infection for which he gave her antibiotics. In appreciation for looking after her and for your support over the last few months she comes to see you with a bottle of wine to say thank you.

19.7   What would you do in this situation?

19.8   What is the guidance that governs accepting gifts from patients?

19.9   What kind of reasons would make it inappropriate to accept gifts?

Chapter 20 Answers to chapters 1–19

Cardiovascular answers

Case 1 Answers

1.1   What are the differential diagnoses?

- Acute coronary syndrome

- Pericarditis

- Pulmonary embolism

- Aortic dissection (also back pain)

- Gastro-oesophageal reflux disorder

- Musculoskeletal chest pain (costochondritis)

- Pneumothorax

1.2   The patient's ECG is shown (Fig 1.1). What is the diagnosis?

The ECG shows an acute inferior myocardial infarction – ST elevation in inferior leads II, III and aVF.

The diagnosis of an acute myocardial infarction is based on the clinical history, evidence of ischaemic changes on the ECG and cardiac enzymes.

Below is an ECG example of an anterior MI.

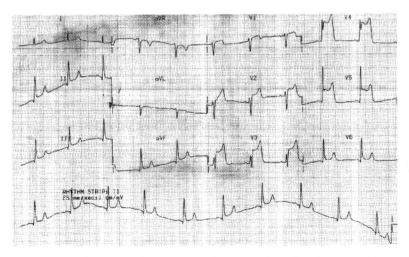

Figure 20.1   Acute anterior myocardial infarction (courtesy of the Heart Attack Centre, University Hospital of North Staffordshire)

1.3   What is the term given to the disease spectrum to which this belongs?

Acute coronary syndrome (ACS) refers to a spectrum of the same disease process including unstable angina, non -ST elevation myocardial infarction (NSTEMI) and ST elevation myocardial infarction (STEMI). To make the diagnosis of acute coronary syndrome a good history is needed as well as the presence of ECG changes and biochemical markers.

1.4   Which coronary vessel is likely to be affected in this patient?

Occlusion of right coronary artery.

Below is a diagram of the heart, and a table showing which coronary vessels correlate to which type of MI.

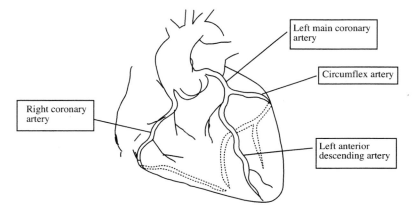

Figure 20.2   Arterial supply of the heart

Myocardial infarction	Correlating vessel occlusion	Changes on ECG
Posterior MI	Left circumflex artery (usually)/ right coronary artery*	Tall R waves V1 and V2, ST segment depression, upright T waves
Inferior MI	Right coronary artery	Leads II, III and aVF
Anterior MI	Left coronary artery	Precordial leads affected
Anteroseptal MI	Left anterior descending	Leads V1-3 affected
Lateral	Left circumflex	Leads I, aVL and V4-6 affected

*Depends on dominance

Table 20.1   Types of MI with their correlating vessel occlusion and ECG changes

1.5   What is the immediate management of this patient?

- High flow oxygen
- Cardiac monitoring
- Sublingual GTN 2 sprays/tablets sublingual
- Aspirin 300 mg

- Clopidogrel 300 mg
- Morphine for pain relief intravenously with antiemetic
- Low molecular weight heparin (dalteparin)
- Consider reperfusion:
  - Primary Percutaneous Coronary Intervention (PCI) for ST elevation MIs (STEMI). During this procedure patient may require stent. When PCI is not available within 90 minutes of diagnosis the patient will need thrombolysis if within the time limit of 4 hours with Reteplase.
  - Anterior MI is more commonly thrombolysed with Tissue Plasminogen Activator (TPA) or Tenecteplase.
- IV Glycoprotein IIb/IIIa receptor antagonist for high risk patients with non ST elevation, particularly if they are to undergo percutaneous coronary intervention (PCI)
- IV or oral beta blocker to be given in the absence of bradycardia or hypotension

The **TIMI risk score** is one method that can be used to assess risk in patients with ACS. The TIMI risk score gives a score of 1 for each of the following:

- Age older than 65 years
- More than three coronary artery disease risk factors (hypertension, hyperlipidaemia, family history, diabetes, smoking)
- Known coronary artery disease
- Use of aspirin within the last 7 days
- Severe angina (more than 2 episodes of rest pain in 24 hours)
- ST deviation on ECG > 1 mm
- Elevated cardiac markers (CK-MB) or troponin

The risk of myocardial infarction or death within 14 days increases with increased total score and the higher the risk, the more urgent it is for the patient to have a coronary angiogram as soon as possible.

1.6   What other questions would be important to ask in the history?

- Is there any history of ischaemic heart disease?
- Is there any family history of ischaemic heart disease?
- Are there any other risk factors such as smoking, hypertension, hypercholesterolaemia, diabetes?
- Medication history

1.7   What investigations would you perform and why?

- Blood tests:
  - U&Es
  - Lipids – to look for hyperlipidaemia/hypercholestero-laemia
  - Glucose – tight glycaemic control is required in a diabetic patient
  - Troponin T – should be taken 12 hours after the onset of chest pain

In the event of myocardial injury cardiac enzymes are released into the bloodstream.

- Myoglobin is released first but is non-specific for cardiac injury.

- Creatine kinase peaks within 24 hours. CK-MB (myocardial bound isoenzyme fraction of CK) is specific for cardiac muscle damage. CK is helpful in ascertaining a re-infarction.

- Aspartate aminotransferase (AST) and lactate dehydrogenase (LDH) were used to assess MI as they remain elevated for several days after the CK has settled but the use of these is now obsolete.

- Elevated troponin I or T concentrations in the blood are reliable markers and most reliable 8–12 hours post-MI. They remain elevated for several weeks.

- ECG – to look for any ischaemic changes, serial ECGs should be done to see if there are any new ischaemic changes developing

- CXR – to exclude any other causes of chest pain

1.8   What are the complications of this condition?

Early Complications	Late Complications
Arrhythmia	Heart failure
Heart failure	Ventricular aneurysm
Pericarditis	Dressler's syndrome (~7% of cases)
Angina	
Recurrent infarction	
Thromboembolism	
Mitral regurgitation	
Ventricular septal rupture	
Death	

Table 20.2   Complications of acute coronary syndrome

1.9   What are the indications for thrombolysis?

- ST segment elevation > 2 mm in 2 contiguous chest leads
- ST segment elevation >1 mm in 2 limb leads
- New onset left bundle branch block (indicative of large anterior infarct)

1.10   List the contraindications for thrombolysis?

Absolute contraindications	Relative contraindications
Active bleeding	Anticoagulant treatment
Known bleeding disorder	Peptic ulcer disease
Previous haemorrhagic stroke	Pregnancy or less than 1 week postpartum
Ischaemic stroke during last 6 months	TIA in preceding 6 months
Recent major surgery, head injury or major trauma	Recent trauma/surgery in last 2 months
Known or suspected aortic dissection	Infective endocarditis
CNS neoplasm or trauma	

Table 20.3   Contraindications to thrombolysis

1.11   What pathological process has occurred?

Dressler's Syndrome is thought to be a result of an autoimmune inflammatory reaction and typically occurs 1–4 weeks post MI and consists of a low grade fever (elevated ESR), pleuritic sounding chest pain, pericardial rub, pericardial effusion. It is treated with NSAIDs or steroids.

1.12   How would you further manage the patient and what advice would you give?

- Post MI advice to give includes avoiding strenuous exercise and avoiding sexual intercourse for one month
- Lifestyle modifications including smoking cessation, regular exercise, diet if overweight
- DVLA: if successfully treated by coronary angioplasty, driving may recommence after 1 week, if not then refrain from driving for four weeks (DVLA need not be notified)
- Acute coronary syndrome will disqualify the patient for at least six weeks if HGV or public vehicle driver
- Regular aspirin 75 mg per day
- Clopidogrel 75 mg for twelve months in patients with NSTEMI and four weeks in patients with STEMI
- Long term statin
- Beta blocker
- ACE inhibitor

Further investigations to identify the risk of having another episode:

- Echocardiogram, exercise ECG, angiogram
- Cardiac rehabilitation

Case 2 Answers

1.13   What is the likely diagnosis?

Congestive cardiac failure (CCF).

1.14   Patients with this condition can present with various symptoms. How would you define her condition and what other symptoms, excluding those mentioned in the case, would you expect?

CCF is a syndrome which results from functional or structural disease that impairs the ability of the heart to adequately perfuse and oxygenate the body. Left Ventricular Failure and Right Ventricular Failure may occur independently of each other, or together as CCF.

LVF leads to pulmonary oedema.

Symptoms	Signs
Dyspnoea	Tachycardia
Paroxysmal nocturnal dyspnoea (PND)	Pulsus alternans
Orthopnoea	Cyanosis
Wheeze (cardiac 'asthma')	Tachypnoea
Nocturnal cough (=/− pink froth)	3rd heart sound (gallop rhythm)
Haemoptysis	Inspiratory basal crackles
Fatigue, lethargy	Pleural effusion
Poor exercise tolerance	Cardiomegaly

Table 20.4   LVF symptoms and signs

RVF

Symptoms	Signs
Fatigue, lethargy	Tachycardia
Nausea	Elevated JVP
Peripheral oedema	Right ventricular heave
Abdominal discomfort (hepatomegaly)	Hepatomegaly
	Ascites
	Pitting oedema
	Cardiomegaly
	Cachexia

Table 20.5   RVF symptoms and signs

1.15   What are the causes of this condition?

Conditions causing a high output failure or abnormality of the heart can lead to heart failure.

High output failure causes		Causes of abnormality of the heart	
•	Anaemia	•	Ischaemic heart disease
•	Thyrotoxicosis	•	Hypertension
•	Pregnancy	•	Myocardial infarction
•	Fever	•	Valvular disease
•	Atrioventricular (AV) shunts	•	Cardiomyopathy
•	Paget's disease	•	Arrhythmias
•	Beri-Beri	•	Infection (e.g. viral)
		•	HOCM*
		•	Toxins (e.g. alcohol)

*HOCM (hypertrophic obstructive cardiomyopathy) is a genetic condition and is a cause of sudden death.

Table 20.6   High output failure and abnormality of the heart

1.16   What investigations would you perform?

- Blood tests:
    - o   FBC looking for any anaemia
    - o   U&Es looking for evidence of hypoalbuminaemia, renal failure, electrolyte disturbance
    - o   LFTs looking for evidence of liver congestion
    - o   TFTs
- ECG looking for arrhythmias, left ventricular hypertrophy and ischaemic changes
- CXR
- Urinalysis, peak flow or spirometry

- Echocardiogram to look for any structural abnormality and to assess the valvular and ventricular function of the heart.

- Coronary angiography to identify any evidence of coronary heart disease

- 24-hour tape to look for arrhythmias

- Brain (B type) Natriuretic Peptide (BNP) is a peptide hormone produced by the ventricular myocardium in response to distension and is a marker of ventricular dysfunction. BNP causes natriuresis, diuresis, vasodilation and muscle relaxation. The concentration of BNP is raised in heart failure.

Below is an algorithm from the NICE guidelines on heart failure summarising the recommendations for diagnosis:

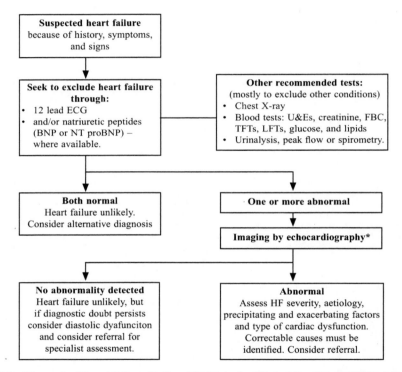

Figure 20.3   Diagnosis of heart failure. National Institute for Clinical Excellence (2003). Adapted from CG5 chronic heart failure: management of chronic heart failure in primary and secondary care. London: NICE. Available from www.nice.org.uk/CG5. Reproduced with permission.

* Alternative methods of imaging the heart should be considered when a poor image is produced by transthoracic Doppler 2D echocardiography. Alternatives include transoesophageal Doppler 2D echocardiography, radionuclide imaging or cardiac magnetic resonance imaging.

1.17   What features would you expect to see on the chest X-ray?

Below is a picture illustrating the classic findings on a chest X-ray in heart failure:

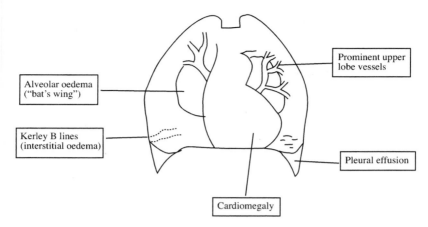

Figure 20.4   Heart Failure

1.18   What classification is used to assess the severity of the condition?

The classification system used is the New York Heart Association Classification (NYHA)

Class	Features
I	No limitations. Ordinary physical activity does not cause fatigue, breathlessness or palpitations.
II	Slight limitation of physical activity. Such patients are comfortable at rest. Ordinary activity results in fatigue, breathlessness, palpitations or angina pectoris
III	Marked limitation of physical activity. Less than ordinary activity will lead to symptoms
IV	Inability to carry on any physical activity without discomfort. Symptoms of congestive cardiac failure are present even at rest.

Table 20.7   New York Heart Association Classification

1.19   How would you manage this patient?

Acute management

- Sit the patient up

- High flow oxygen

- IV access + bloods

- 12 lead ECG

- ABG

- CXR

- Nitrates (sublingual or buccal) e.g. GTN spray or tablets. It is important to ensure that the patient's blood pressure is > 90 mmHg if this is to be administered.

- Diamorphine 2.5–5 mg. This helps with anxiety and pain as well as producing venodilatation (reduces myocardial oxygen demand).

- IV furosemide (40–80 mg). This also helps to produce venodilatation and causes diuresis.

- Digoxin can be given if the patient is in AF.

- Catheterisation for accurate measurement of fluid balance.

- Echocardiography

If there is respiratory failure despite initial treatment it would be wise to involve an anaesthetist early and consider continuous positive airway pressure (CPAP) or non invasive ventilation (NIV). If the above therapy fails to improve the condition of the patient then they will require further support in a HDU or ITU setting (possibly for inotropic support or haemofiltration).

Further management

Consider adding beta blocker, ACE inhibitor, and spironolactone to control the heart failure. It is important to remember other factors which could help improve their condition, bar medical therapy, such as lifestyle changes including exercise, rehabilitation, smoking cessation, and abstaining from alcohol.

Below is an algorithm taken from the NICE guidelines on pharmacological treatment for symptomatic heart failure due to LV systolic dysfunction.

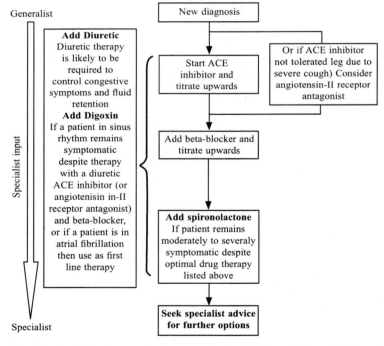

Figure 20.5   Pharmacological treatment for symptomatic heart failure. National Institute for Clinical Excellence (2003). Adapted from CG5 chronic heart failure: management of chronic heart failure in primary and secondary case. London: NICE. Available from www.nice.org.uk/CG5. Reproduced with permission.

1.20   What are the features of digoxin toxicity?

- Arrhythmia

- Nausea
- Vomiting
- Confusion
- Yellow vision (xanthopsia)
- Blurred vision
- Photophobia

Digoxin has a weak positive inotropic effect. Digoxin inhibits the Na/K pump causing an increase in intracellular calcium increasing the force of myocardial contraction and has a low therapeutic index. Digoxin toxicity may cause hyperkalaemia and hyponatraemia – this is the result of inhibition of the Na/K pump at the cellular level, preventing cellular uptake of K in exchange for sodium. Digibind is an antidote given in digoxin toxicity.

ECG changes in digoxin toxicity – down sloping ST depression, T wave inversion in V 5–6 in a reversed tick pattern and shortened QT interval

Case 3 Answers

1.21   Does this mean that the patient has hypertension?

Current guidelines say hypertension is defined as a sustained systolic blood pressure above 140 mmHg and/or diastolic blood pressure above 90 mmHg confirmed on three consecutive occasions approximately one month apart.

1.22   How do you measure blood pressure?

- Standardise the environment i.e. relaxed, patient seated, arm outstretched in line with mid sternum, supported.
- Measure blood pressure on both of the patient's arms and use the arm with higher blood pressure as reference arm for future measurements.
- Wrap a cuff, appropriate sized bladder, around the upper arm and connect to a manometer.
- Palpate the brachial pulse in the antecubital fossa of that arm.
- Rapidly inflate the cuff to 20 mmHg above the point where the brachial pulse disappears.
- Deflate the cuff and note the pressure at which the pulse reappears (approximate systolic pressure).
- Re-inflate the cuff to 20 mmHg above the point at which the brachial pulse disappears.
- Using one hand, place the stethoscope over the brachial artery ensuring complete skin contact with no clothing in between.
- Slowly deflate the cuff at 2–3 mmHg per second listening for Korotkoff sounds.
- Phase I: The first appearance of faint repetitive clear tapping sounds gradually increasing in intensity and lasting for at least two consecutive beats (note systolic pressure).
- Phase II: a brief period may follow when the sounds soften.
- Auscultatory gap – in some patients the sounds may disappear altogether.
- Phase III: the return of sharper sounds becoming crisper for a short time.

- Phase IV: the distinct, abrupt muffling of sounds, becoming soft and blowing in quality.

- Phase V: the point at which all sounds disappear completely: note diastolic pressure.

- When the sounds have disappeared, quickly deflate the cuff completely if repeating the measurement.

- When possible, take readings at the beginning and end of consultations.

1.23   How is hypertension classified?

Blood pressure can be classified in grades as mild, moderate and severe.

Category	Systolic	Diastolic
Normal	< 120	< 80
High normal	120–139	80–89
Grade 1 mild	140–159	90–99
Grade 2 moderate	160–179	100–109
Grade 3 severe	≥ 180	≥ 110
Isolated systolic hypertension	> 140	< 90

Table 20.8   British Heart Foundation guide on grading of blood pressure

1.24   What are the causes of hypertension?

Essential hypertension (95% of cases).

Secondary causes:

- Renal disease – renal artery stenosis, glomerulonephritis, polycystic kidneys

- Endocrine – Cushing's, Conn's syndrome, acromegaly, phaeochromocytoma, hyperparathyroidism

- Other – coarctation of the aorta, pregnancy, steroids, OCP (oral contraceptive pill)

1.25   What further management should the GP undertake?

Advice on lifestyle modifications: diet, regular exercise, reduced alcohol consumption, decreased caffeine consumption, reduced salt intake and smoking cessation.

1.26   What investigations should be performed?

- FBC: normocytic anaemia may be associated with CRF

- U&Es: exclude impaired renal function, hypokalaemia (Conn's)

- Fasting lipids: hypercholesterolaemia

- Fasting glucose: diabetes

- Urine dipstick – for any protein and blood and may indicate renal disease

- ECG
- CXR

1.27   What does this mean?

The Framingham risk score is used to estimate an individual's absolute ten-year risk of developing CVD based on their gender, smoking status, age, diabetes status, systolic blood pressure and the ratio of total cholesterol to high-density lipoprotein (HDL) cholesterol meet. If the risk is > 20% then the patient should be treated for primary prevention. In this case as his score came back as 4% there is no need to start any other treatment for primary prevention.

1.28   What is the likely diagnosis and what are the different stages of this condition?

I   Mild generalised arteriolar narrowing

II   Definite focal arteriolar narrowing

III   Grade II plus retinal haemorrhages, exudates, cotton wool spots

IV   Severe grade III and papilloedema

This is hypertensive retinopathy.

1.29   When should you refer the patient to a specialist?

- Suspicion of secondary hypertension
- Young age
- Impaired renal function
- Proteinuria/haematuria
- Hypokalaemia
- Refractory hypertension in multiple combined antihypertensive medications
- Accelerated malignant hypertension + bilateral retinal haemorrhages, cotton wool spots

1.30   List risk factors which predispose an individual to hypertension.

- Family history
- Race – African Americans more at risk
- Gender – men are at greater risk than women
- Increasing age
- Obesity

1.31   What complications are associated with hypertension if left untreated?

- Stroke (risk increased × 6)
- Cerebrovascular disease
- Heart failure
- Peripheral vascular disease
- Chronic renal failure, impaired vision

1.32   What medications would you commence for this patient?

ACE inhibitor

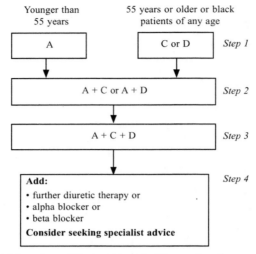

Younger than 55 years		55 years or older or black patients of any age	

A = ACE inhibitor; C = calcium channel blocker; D = thiazide type diuretic

Black patients are those of African or Caribbean descent, and not mixed-race, Asian or Chinese patients.

Beta blockers are not a preferred initial therapy for hypertension but are an alternative to A in patients < 55 years in whom A is not tolerated, or contraindicated (includes women of child bearing potential).

Figure 20.6   Treatment of newly diagnosed hypertension algorithm from NICE guidelines. National Institute for Health and Clinical Excellence (2006). CG34 Hypertension: management of hypertension in adults in primary case. London: NICE. Available from www.nice.org.uk/CG34. Reproduced with permission.

- First line therapy for hypertensive patients ≥ 55 years of age or Afro-Caribbean should be either calcium channel blocker or thiazide type diuretic.
- Second line therapy includes adding an ACE inhibitor.
- First line therapy for hypertensive patients < 55 years of age should be an ACE inhibitor (or angiotensin II antagonist if ACE inhibitor not tolerated).
- Second line therapy includes adding a calcium channel blocker or thiazide type diuretic.
- If a third drug is required a combination of ACE inhibitors, calcium channel blocker and thiazide diuretic should be used.
- If blood pressure remains uncontrolled seek a specialist opinion before adding fourth drug.
- If a fourth drug is required a higher dose of thiazide diuretic or addition of another diuretic, beta blockers, or selective alpha blockers may be used.
- Beta blockers may be considered in younger patients especially, those with an intolerance or contraindication to ACE inhibitors and angiotensin II receptor antagonists; or women of child bearing potential; or people with evidence of increased sympathetic drive.

1.33   Can you think of any contraindications to any of the medications used in the treatment of hypertension?

- Beta blockers should be avoided in asthmatics
- ACE inhibitors should not be prescribed in a patient with renal artery stenosis, aortic stenosis

Case 4 Answers

1.34   What is the likely diagnosis?

Atrial fibrillation is the commonest arrhythmia and occurs when there is disordered electrical activity in the atria.

1.35   What are the different subtypes of this condition?

- Primary (lone) atrial fibrillation – cause unknown.

- Chronic atrial fibrillation, usually found in older adults and frequently associated with an existing heart problem.

- Paroxysmal atrial fibrillation, in which the irregular rhythm occurs periodically, i.e. the rhythm will revert to a regular rhythm, the timing of this may vary from minutes, hours or days and can be unpredictable. Spontaneous termination < 7 days and most often < 48 hours. Pattern may be recurrent.

- Persistent atrial fibrillation, which is characterised by an irregular rhythm that lasts longer than seven days and will not self terminate, but will respond to treatment. Likely to be recurrent.

- Permanent atrial fibrillation occurs when the irregular rhythm continues indefinitely and can no longer be corrected with treatment. If treated may relapse. This is established atrial fibrillation.

- Atrial fibrillation is considered to be recurrent when a patient experiences two or more episodes.

1.36   What are the causes of this condition?

Cardiac causes	Non cardiac causes
Ischaemic heart disease	Acute infections eg, pneumonia
Hypertension	Electrolyte abnormalities
Rheumatic heart disease	Pulmonary embolism
Sick sinus syndrome	Thyrotoxicosis
Pre excitation syndromes (eg, Wolff Parkinson White)	Intrathoracic pathology (eg lung carcinoma, pleural effusion)
Cardiomyopathy	
Pericardial disease	
Atrial septal defect	
Atrial myxoma	

Table 20.9   Causes of atrial fibrillation

1.37   What investigations should be performed to rule out other causes of this condition?

- FBC – to look for any signs of infection
- U&Es – to look for any electrolyte imbalance
- TFTs – could suggest hyperthyroidism
- CXR – to look for any signs of heart failure or pneumonia

- Cardiac enzymes – to exclude MI
- ECHO – to assess the valves and structure of the heart

1.38   How is this condition managed?

- For patients with occasional symptoms it would be appropriate to advise them to avoid things such as caffeine, alcohol and stress.
- Management generally includes medication, electrical cardioversion, changes to diet and lifestyle and surgical procedures.
- If fast AF – use digoxin, beta blocker, calcium channel blocker, if resistant consider amiodarone.

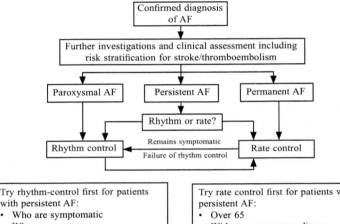

*Patients unsuitable for cardioversion include those with: contraindications to anticoagulation; structural heart disease (e.g. large left atrium > 5.5 cm, mitral stenosis) that precludes long-term maintenance of sinus rhythm; a long duration of AF (usually > 12 months); a history of multiple failed attempts at cardioversion and/or relapses, even with concomitant use of antiarrhythmic drugs or non-pharmacological approaches; an ongoing but reversible cause of AF (e.g. thyrotoxicosis).

Figure 20.7   Diagnosis of AF (from NICE guidelines). National Institute for Health and Clinical Excellence (2006) CG36 Atrial fibrillation: the management of atrial fibrillation. London: NICE. Available from www. nice.org.uk/CG. http://www.nice.org.uk/CG36. Reproduced with permission.

Cardioversion

- Pharmacological: in absence of structural heart disease, a class 1c drug (such as flecainide) should be the drug of choice, in the presence of structural heart disease, amiodarone should be the drug of choice. Side effects include hyper or hypothyroidism, deranged LFTs and pulmonary fibrosis.
- Electrical: DC cardioversion may be performed as an emergency if patient is haemodynamically compromised. If AF is of recent onset (< 48 hrs) and heart is normal on echo, there is no need to anticoagulate before cardioversion. Otherwise anticoagulate for four weeks before and four to six weeks post cardioversion.

1.39   What should you use to anticoagulate?

A patient should be anticoagulated with warfarin for a minimum of three weeks before cardioversion. Following cardioversion, patients should remain on therapeutic anticoagulation with warfarin (Target INR 2.5) for a minimum of four weeks. In those patients with persistent AF where cardioversion cannot be postponed for three weeks, heparin should be given and then warfarin for a minimum of four weeks post cardioversion.

Anticoagulation should be continued long term in patients with AF who have undergone cardioversion where the risk of recurrence is high.

In patients with AF of confirmed duration of < 48 hours undergoing cardioversion, anticoagulation is not required following restoration of sinus rhythm.

Below is a diagram from NICE guidelines showing when to anticoagulate with aspirin/warfarin.

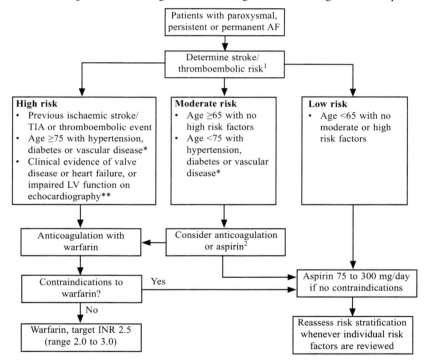

1   Note that risk factors are not mutually exclusive, and are additive to each other in producing a composite risk. Since the incidence of stroke and thromboembolic events in patients with thyrotoxicosis appears similar to that in patients with other aetiologies of AF, antithrombotic treatment should be chosen based on the presence of validated stroke risk factors.

2   Owing to lack of sufficient clear-cut evidence, treatment may be decided on an individual basis, and the physician must balance the risks and benefits of warfarin versus aspirin. As stroke risk factors are cumulative, warfarin may, for example, be used in the presence of two or more moderate stroke risk factors. Referral and echocardiography may help in cases of uncertainty.

*   Coronary artery disease or peripheral artery disease.

**   An echocardiogram is not needed for routine assessment, but refines clinical risk stratification in the case of moderate or severe LV dysfunction and valve disease.

Figure 20.8   When to anticoagulate. National Institute for Health and Clinical Excellence (2006) CG36 Atrial fibrillation: the management of atrial fibrillation. London: NICE. Available from www.nice.org. uk/CG. http://www.nice.org.uk/CG36. Reproduced with permission.

Case 5 Answers

1.40   What is the likely diagnosis?

Aortic stenosis.

1.41   What are the causes of this condition?

- Congenital
- Rheumatic fever
- Biscuspid valve
- Hypertrophic cardiomyopathy
- Degenerative calcification

1.42   What other features would you see with this condition?

- Angina, syncope, breathlessness, dizziness, sudden death
- Small volume pulse, narrow pulse pressure

1.43   What investigations would you perform?

ECHO to investigate severity of condition.

1.44   What further management options are there?

If needed, surgery is an option. If not fit for surgery then a percutaneous valvuloplasty may be attempted.

Below is a table showing other heart murmurs with correlating symptoms, signs and causes.

Murmur	Signs	Findings	Causes	Management
Aortic stenosis	Ejection systolic murmur Radiates to carotids	Slow rising pulse Undisplaced heaving apex Low systolic BP LVH on ECG & CXR Narrow pulse pressure	Congenital Bicuspid valve and degeneration Rheumatic	
Aortic regurgitation	Blowing early diastolic murmur Aortic area or LSE with patient sitting up in expiration	Water hammer pulse Wide pulse pressure Corrigan's sign De Musset's sign Quincke's sign Displaced thrusting apex LVH on ECG & CXR	Rheumatic Dissecting aortic aneurysm Ankylosing spondylitis Marfan's syndrome Congenital Syphilis Infective endocarditis	
Mitral stenosis	Rumbling mid diastolic murmur at apex	Palpable first heart sound Presystolic accentuation if patient in sinus rhythm AF, opening snap JVP may be raised, giant V waves Malar flush	Usually rheumatic	Digoxin for associated AF Anticoagulants for prevention of systemic embolisation from left atrial thrombi Diuretics for any associated right heart failure Mitral valvotomy/Mitral valve replacement

Mitral regurgitation	Pansystolic murmur at apex	Radiates to axilla, best heard at left lateral position Displaced/thrusting apex beat Parasternal heave Soft first heart sound Third heart sound	Rheumatic LV dilatation (any cause) Ruptured chordae Mitral valve prolapsed Infective endocarditis Connective tissue disorders SLE, RA, ankylosing spondylitis, marfan's, hypertrophic obstructive cardiomyopathy	
Mixed aortic valve disease		Slow rising pulse, heaving apex, low systolic BP, narrow pulse pressure → predominant aortic stenosis Collapsing pulse, displaced/ thrusting apex, high BP, wide pulse pressure → predominant aortic regurgitation	Rheumatic heart disease Infective endocarditis on previously stenotic valve	
Mixed mitral valve disease		Tapping apex, loud first heart sound, absent third heart sound, AF → predominant mitral stenosis Displaced/thrusting apex, soft first heart sound, third heart sound → predominant mitral regurgitation	Excessive valvular damage Previous mitral valvotomy	

Note: Aortic sclerosis has exactly the same murmur as aortic stenosis, but none of the associated physical findings. It is due to thickening of the aortic valve.

Table 20.10   Heart murmurs

Case 6 Answers

1.45   What is the likely diagnosis?

Angina pectoris.

1.46   How can you classify this condition?

The Canadian Cardiovascular Society Angina classification is as follows:

Class I   Ordinary activity such as walking or climbing stairs does not precipitate angina

Class II   Angina precipitated by emotion, cold weather or meals and by walking up stairs

Class III   Marked limitations of ordinary physical activity

Class IV   Inability to carry out any physical activity without discomfort – angina symptoms may be present at rest

1.47 Are there different types of this condition? If so what are they?

- Crescendo angina (unstable) describes angina that is increasing in severity, frequency or duration. GTN may be ineffective and the pain may appear with minimal exertion.

- Nocturnal (decubitus) angina indicates severe coronary artery disease.

- Second-wind angina occurs on initial exertion but then subsides without the need for rest.

1.48 What investigations would you do?

- BMI
- FBC
- TFTs
- Cholesterol
- Glucose
- Exercise tolerance test

1.49 How would you treat this condition?

- Patients with stable angina should be treated with aspirin 75 mg daily
- If allergic to aspirin, clopidogrel 75 mg daily should be considered
- Patients who require regular symptomatic treatment should be treated initially with a beta blocker unless contraindicated

Case 7 Answers

1.50 What is the most likely diagnosis?

Infective endocarditis.

This is infection of the endocardial surface of the heart which may include the heart valves, septal defect or mural endocardium. It can affect native or prosthetic valves, and can be related to intravenous drug use.

1.51 What organisms can cause this condition?

Streptococcus Viridans is the commonest cause (30–40%). Others include Staphylococcus Aureus, Streptococci and Enterococci.

Rarely, it is caused by the HACEK organisms (**H**aemophilus, **A**ctinobacillus actinomycoses, **C**ardiobacterium hominis, **E**ikenella corrodens, **K**ingella)

Fungi can also cause infective endocarditis.

1.52 What are the other features of this condition?

Pallor, weight loss, petechial haemorrhages, splinter haemorrhages, Osler's nodes, Janeway lesions, Roth's spots (see diagram below).

Fever plus new murmur is endocarditis until proven otherwise.

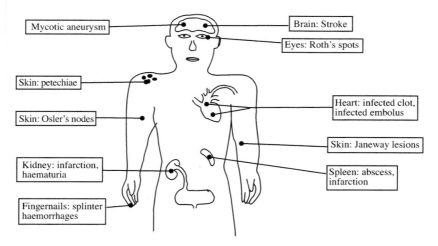

Figure 20.9   **Features of infective endocarditis**

1.53   What might you see on fundoscopy and what is the mechanism involved?

Roth's spots are oval, retinal haemorrhages with a clear, pale centre. Osler's nodes are painful nodes which develop on finger pulps. Janeway lesions are due to septic emboli, painless plaques on palms or soles.

Stimulation of antibodies combined with bacterial antigens form circulating immune complexes that can deposit in kidneys (glomerulonephritis) or other organs (for example, deposits in the choroid plexus can lead to the development of Roth's spots; deposits within the skin can lead to the development of Osler's nodes)

1.54   What investigations will help to reach a diagnosis?

- Blood cultures (see below)
- FBC: normochromic, normocytic anaemia
- ESR elevated
- U&Es
- ECG
- Chest X-ray
- Echo: vegetations/valvular damage
- Urinalysis: haematuria, proteinuria

1.55   What are the diagnostic criteria?

Definitive diagnosis based on Duke's criteria:

- Two major criteria or
- One major and three minor criteria or
- Five minor criteria

Three sets of blood cultures should be taken at different times from different sites.

- Major blood culture criteria:
  - Two positive blood cultures for typical IE organisms
  - Persistently positive cultures for such organisms drawn > 12 hours apart
  - Three or more positive cultures drawn at least one hour apart
- Major echocardiographic criteria:
  - Positive result and no alternative explanation
  - Myocardial abscess
  - Partial dehiscence of prosthetic valve
  - New valvular regurgitation
- Minor criteria:
  - Predisposing cardiac condition
  - Intravenous drug use
  - Fever (38 degrees C or over)
  - Vascular lesions
  - Immunological phenomenon
  - Positive cultures less than 'major'
  - Positive echocardiographic results but insufficient for major criteria

1.56   What treatment would you give?

IV antibiotics. Doses and duration would depend upon causative organisms, severity of infection and response to treatment.

1.57   Are there any associated complications?

- Embolisation, stroke, renal infarction, splenic infarction, Osler's nodes, immune complex formation, glomerulonephritis, Roth's spots, Janeway lesions.
- Endocarditis on prosthetic valves.
- IV drug abusers are at risk of developing right-sided endocarditis, usually of the tricuspid valve.

1.58   Which patients require prophylaxis?

There is little evidence to support use of antibiotics for prevention of endocarditis for people undergoing interventional procedures.

NICE guidelines say:

- Do not offer antibiotic prophylaxis against infective endocarditis to people undergoing dental procedures or to people undergoing non-dental procedures at the following sites: upper and lower GI tract, upper and lower respiratory tract, genitourinary tract.

Case 8 Answers

1.59   What is the most likely diagnosis?

Deep vein thrombosis.

1.60   List other risk factors for this condition.

- Age
- Pregnancy
- Surgery within last four weeks
- Long haul flights or car journeys within the last four weeks
- Immobilisation for more than three days
- Malignancy
- Sepsis
- Previous DVT
- Trauma (including fractures)
- Vasculitic disorders such as SLE, Behcet's
- Haematological disorders such as polycythaemia, Factor V Leiden, thrombocytosis
- Medications such as oral contraceptives, oestrogens, IV drug abuse, heparin-induced thrombocytopaenia

Clinical parameter	Score
Active cancer	+1
Paralysis or recent plaster immobilization of the lower extremities	+1
Recently bedridden for > 3 days or major surgery < 4 weeks ago	+1
Localised tenderness along the distribution line of the deep venous system	+1
Entire leg swollen	+1
Calf swelling > 3 cm compared with the asymptomatic leg	+1
Pitting oedema (greater in the symptomatic leg)	+1
Previous documented DVT	+1
Collateral superficial veins (nonvaricose)	+1
Alternative diagnosis (as likely or greater than that of DVT)	−2

Table 20.11   The Wells Clinical score for venous thromboembolism

Using the scores you can then classify the patient with a probability as low ≤ 0, moderate 1 or 2, or high ≥ 3.

1.61   What investigations would you order?

- Clotting profile (prothrombin time, APTT) before treatment

- Thrombophilia screen (especially in patients with recurrent thromboembolism)
- Doppler ultrasound scan
- D dimer (the presence of a negative D dimer result in a patient with a low Wells score excludes the likelihood of DVT. An elevated D dimer result is not very specific for confirming the presence of a DVT)

1.62   What treatment should be given?

- TED stockings
- Mobilise
- Anticoagulation with LMWH (for a minimum of five days) and then warfarinise
- When the patient is warfarinised they will require regular monitoring and this is done by monitoring INR levels. The therapeutic range is normally between 2 and 3 and this will prevent the development of further clots. For simple calf DVTs warfarin is given for six weeks, or three months for above-knee DVTs.

Other points

- Stop oral contraceptive pill four weeks before any elective surgery
- Immobility associated with more than three hours' continuous travel in the four weeks before and after surgery may increase the risk of VTE

References

Case 1

1. Peters et al. (2007), Acute coronary syndromes without ST segment elevation, *BMJ* 334: 1265–1269
2. Grech and Ramsdale (2003), Acute coronary syndrome: unstable angina and non ST segment elevation myocardial infarction, *BMJ* 326; 1259–1261
3. Goodacre et al. (2003), Clinical predictors of acute coronary syndromes in patients with undifferentiated chest pain. *QJ Med* 96: 893–898
4. Myocardial Infarction – Thrombolysis, NICE Technology Appraisal (2002): http://www.nice.org.uk/nicemedia/pdf/52_Thrombolysis_full_guidance.pdf
5. Myocardial Infarction: secondary prevention, NICE Clinical Guidelines (2007): http://www.nice.org.uk/CG48
6. DVLA Guidance: http://www.dft.gov.uk/dvla/medical/ataglance.aspx

Learning website:

- Test your ECG knowledge: http://library.med.utah.edu/kw/ecg/index.html or with http://www.ecglibrary.com/ecgsbyeg.html

Case 2

1. SIGN guidance on Heart Failure: http://www.sign.ac.uk/pdf/sign95.pdf
2. Clinical knowledge summary on Heart Failure: http://www.cks.library.nhs.uk/heart_failure_chronic
3. NICE guidelines on Heart Failure: http://www.nice.org.uk/nicemedia/pdf/CG5NICEguideline.pdf

Case 3

1. NICE guidelines on Hypertension: www.nice.org.uk/CG034

2. British Hypertension Society guidelines: www.bhsoc.org/Hypertension_management_Guidelines.stm

Case 4

1. NICE guidance on Atrial Fibrillation: http://guidance.nice.org.uk/CG36

2. MB Iqbal et al., (2005), Review of recent developments in Atrial fibrillation, *BMJ* 330: 228–243

Case 6

- SIGN guidelines: http://www.sign.ac.uk/pdf/sign96.pdf

- Chronic stable angina http://clinicalevidence.bmj.com/ceweb/conditions/cvd/0213/0213_guidelines.jsp

Case 7

Prophylaxis against infective endocarditis: www.nice.org.uk/Guidance/CG64

http://www.rcplondon.ac.uk/pubs/books/endocarditis/endocarditis.pdf

Case 8

1. Venous thromboembolism: http://www.nice.org.uk/nicemedia/pdf/CG046NICEguideline.pdf

2. Table 20.11 Wells Clinical Score for thromboembolism. Scarvelis D, Wells P (2006). Diagnosis and treatment of deep-vein thromobosis. *CMAJ* 175 (9): 1087-92.

Recommended further cases:

- Pericarditis

- Cardiac tamponade

- Aortic dissection

- Fallot's Tetralogy

- Coarctation of the aorta

Respiratory answers

Case 1 Answers

2.1   What is the most likely diagnosis?

Pulmonary embolism (PE) is a potentially fatal condition. Thrombus formation in the venous circulation can embolise to the lungs. The most frequent symptom is dyspnoea and tachypnoea in a massive PE. In a smaller PE the patient may complain of pleuritic chest pain, cough, or haemoptysis.

2.2   Interpret the above ECG (Figure 2.1).

An S1 Q3 T3 pattern is seen in the ECG (a prominent S wave in lead I, a Q wave and inverted T wave in lead III), sinus tachycardia, T wave inversion in leads V1-V3 and right bundle branch block. This is consistent with acute pulmonary embolus.

This pattern is uncommon. ECG and chest X-ray are often normal and should not be used to confirm or refute the diagnosis, but are useful for identifying other diseases and explaining symptoms.

2.3   What urgent investigation would confirm your most likely diagnosis?

CTPA (CT pulmonary angiography) is the gold standard used in the diagnosis of PE. This should ideally be performed within 1 hour in a massive PE and ideally within 24 hours in a non massive PE. If CTPA is unavailable a V/Q (perfusion scan) can be performed.

2.4   What other investigations would you perform to aid you towards the most likely diagnosis?

Other investigations that you would perform include:

- ABG: will show that the patient is hypoxic (type I respiratory failure).

- CXR: usually is normal but may show atelectasis.

- ECG: see above.

- D-dimer: remember that a negative D dimer result excludes the diagnosis of thromboemboli, but a positive result does not diagnose a thromboembolus and may be raised in many other conditions.

2.5   What risk factors will predispose to this condition?

Major factors used in clinical scoring for Pulmonary Embolus: see list in the second column of the table below.

Are other diagnoses unlikely?	Is a major risk factor present?

- On clinical grounds
  o After basic investigations:
  o white cell count
  o chest X-ray
  o ECG
  o spirometry or peak flow
  o blood analysis
	- Recent immobilization or major surgery
	- Recent lower limb trauma and/or surgery
	- Clinical deep vein thrombosis
	- Previous proven DVT or PE
	- Pregnancy or postpartum
	- Major medical illness

If YES, score +1	If YES, score +1

Total score	Pre-test probability
0	Low
1	Moderate
2	High

Table 20.12   British Thoracic Society clinical scoring system for PE

Minor risk factors:

- Long haul flights

- Malignancy

- Obesity

- Oral contraceptive pill

(Risk factors are as seen in case 8 of Chapter 1.)

2.6   How would you treat this patient?

- The choice is between breaking the emboli up (thrombolysis), or preventing new clots forming (anti-coagulation) in the legs or pelvis to cause more emboli while the previous emboli break up and is cleared by the body's own thrombolytic mechanisms.

- Thrombolysis is the first line treatment for a massive PE together with life threatening features (i.e. features of right heart failure and/or shock). The same contraindications apply as for thrombolysis in acute MI. The risk of bleeding is high and the British Thoracic Society is emphasising the risks to stop thrombolysis being used in less severe cases. After thrombolysis, patient is anticoagulated, first with unfractionated heparin, and then with warfarin as in non-massive PE.

- If a non-massive PE is diagnosed, patient is anticoagulated with therapeutic low molecular weight heparin (LMWH) immediately and then with warfarin for six months (for idiopathic PEs) or six weeks for temporary risk factors (but the incidence of recurrence is higher with a shorter duration of treatment).

- Long term warfarin is used if the patient has had multiple PEs or a life threatening PE. Whilst on warfarin therapy patients need regular monitoring of their international normalised ratio (INR) and maintain a therapeutic range of 2.0 to 3.0.

- If the patient has a history of recurrent thromboembolic events or a strong positive family history they should be screened for hypercoaguable states.

Case 2 Answers

2.7   What is the most likely diagnosis?

Community acquired pneumonia. This is defined as pneumonia which develops outside hospital or within 48 hours of hospital admission.

2.8   What are the differential diagnoses?

- Pulmonary embolism
- Pulmonary oedema
- Bronchial carcinoma
- Pulmonary haemorrhage

2.9   For your most likely diagnosis what other symptoms and signs may be present?

Symptoms

- Anorexia
- Weakness
- General deterioration
- Confusion
- Cough (may be productive)
- Rigors
- Chest pain (may be pleuritic)

Signs

- Increased temperature

- Tachycardia

- Tachypnoea

- Decreased movement of chest wall on affected side

- Decreased breath sounds, crackles

- If consolidation, breath sounds may be increased with bronchial breathing

2.10   List risk factors that contribute to the development of your most likely diagnosis.

- Smoking

- Increased age

- Immobility

- General anaesthetic

- Alcohol intoxication

- Immunosuppression

2.11   How would you assess the severity of the patient's condition?

The CURB 65 score is commonly used to assess the severity of severe community acquired pneumonia.

Confusion (abbreviated mental test score (AMTS) of 8 or less

Urea > 7 mmol/L

Respiratory rate $\geq$ 30/min

Blood pressure: systolic BP < 90 mmHg or diastolic $\leq$ 60 mmHg

Age $\geq$ 65 years

1 point is given for each positive factor.

A score of 0 indicates a low risk of mortality and it would be appropriate to treat the patient at home.

A score of 1–2 indicates that a hospital referral should be considered.

A score of 3–4 indicates a higher risk of mortality and an urgent hospital admission should be arranged.

Adverse prognostic features include:

- Underlying comorbidity (e.g. lung disease)

- Hypoxaemia (Sats < 92% or PaO_2 < 8KPa on ABG)

- Bilateral or involvement of multiple lobes on chest x-ray

2.12   What does the chest X-ray show?

Right upper lobe consolidation.

2.13   Which organisms are implicated in this condition?

Organism '	Type
Community Acquired	
Streptococcus pneumoniae	Gram positive cocci, typical
Haemophilus influenzae	Gram negative rods,
Legionella	Atypical
Staphylococcus aureus	Gram positive cocci, typical
Escherichia coli	Gram negative bacilli
Hospital Acquired (nosocomial)	
Gram negative bacteria	
Staphylococcus aureus	Gram positive cocci, typical
Immunosuppressed	
Pneumocystis carinii	
Mycobacterium tuberculosis	
Aspergillus	
Other	
Mycoplasma	Atypical
Chlamydia	Atypical

Table 20.13   Organisms implicated in pneumonia

2.14   Interpret the ABG results.

- pH is decreased = acidosis
- pO_2 is decreased
- pCO_2 is high end of normal
- HCO_3 is low
- The patient has a metabolic acidosis and type I respiratory failure.

Other causes of type I respiratory failure include: asthma, PE, pulmonary oedema, pulmonary fibrosis.

Normal values are:

- pH   7.35–7.45
- pO_2 > 11 kPa
- pCO_2 4.7–6.0 kPa
- HCO_3 22–26 mmol/L
- BE   –2 to + 2 mmol/L

	pH	pO_2	Acute response	Compensatory response
Respiratory acidosis	↓	↓	pCO_2↑ .	↑HCO_3
Respiratory alkalosis	↑	N or ↑	pCO_2↓	↓HCO_3
Metabolic acidosis	↓	N or ↑	HCO_3↓	↓pCO_2
Metabolic alkalosis	↑	N or ↑	HCO_3↑	↑pCO_2

Table 20.14   Acid-base balance disorders

2.15   What other investigations would you perform?

- Bloods: WCC > 15×10^9/L or < 4×10^9/L, a raised CRP (is used to monitor therapy response) are consistent with infection

- Chest X-ray: may show consolidation, pulmonary infiltrates, pulmonary cavitation

- Sputum microscopy and culture

- Blood cultures

- Urine can be tested for Legionella or streptococcal antigen

Systemic Response Syndrome (SIRS) includes two or more of the following parameters:

- Temperature: > 38 or < 36

- Heart rate: > 90 bpm

- Respiratory rate: > 30/min

- White cell count: < 4 or > 12×10^6

Sepsis is SIRS with an identified source of infection.

2.16   How would you manage this patient?

If the patient can be treated at home then oral antibiotics can be given depending upon local area sensitivities. If the patient is admitted to hospital then other antibiotics can be used, but this is based upon the hospital guidelines and sensitivities of organisms in the area supplied by the microbiology department.

Other measures:

First aim of treatment is supportive care.

- Oxygen therapy (be wary of administering high flow oxygen in COPD patients)

- Antibiotics (as above)

- Bed rest

- Paracetamol/fan therapy – Antipyretic

- Nebulisers (saline and or salbutamol)

- Mucolytics

- Analgesia

2.17   Are there any complications that may develop with this condition?

- Parapneumonic effusion, can be aspirated and sent for microscopy, culture and sensitivity.
- Lung abscess
- Bronchial obstruction e.g. lung cancer, pulmonary embolus
- Fever from drug therapy
- Pleurisy
- Septicaemia
- Atelectasis
- Chronic heart failure

Case 3 Answers

2.18   What preliminary investigations would you request given the above clinical features?

- Bloods: FBC, U&Es, LFTs, calcium, clotting
- Chest X-ray
- Lung function tests

2.19   What further imaging investigations may be required in the management of this condition?

- Sputum cytology
- Bronchoscopy
- Pleural aspiration if effusion present
- A thoracic CT to assess and stage the full extent of lesion may precede or follow bronchoscopy with biopsies/brushings. CT imaging of chest, abdomen and pelvis (a staging CT) should be done to look for any evidence of metastases.

2.20   What is the most likely diagnosis?

Bronchial carcinoma.

2.21   Can you explain the droopy right eyelid and small pupil that the patient presented with?

Apical bronchial carcinoma associated with ipsilateral Horner's syndrome.

This is characterised by ptosis, miosis, enophthalmos, ipsilateral anhydrosis and occurs due to invasion of cervical sympathetic plexus by the tumour.

2.22   What are the main histological types of this condition?

Bronchial carcinomas are typically divided into small cell carcinoma and non-small cell carcinoma because histology determines the management and prognosis. Non-small cell carcinomas include squamous cell carcinoma, adenocarcinoma and large cell carcinoma, and have similar prognoses.

Sqaumous cell carcinoma (35–45%) grows slowly and metastasises slowly. Associated with Pancoast's syndrome.

Adenocarcinoma (20–30%) are the most common lung cancer in non-smokers, but are still more common in smokers.

Large cell (anaplastic) carcinoma (5–10%)

Small cell (oat cell) carcinoma (15–20%) grows rapidly and metastasises early.

2.23   There are a number of paraneoplastic syndromes associated with this condition. What are they, and what type of the condition are they related to?

The paraneoplastic syndromes associated with lung cancer are:

- Small cell lung carcinoma – syndrome of inappropriate ADH secretion, Eaton Lambert syndrome, Cushing's

- Squamous cell carcinoma – hypercalcaemia, clubbing, hypertrophic pulmonary osteoarthropathy (HPOA)

- Adenocarcinoma – clubbing, HPOA, thrombophlebitis, marantic endocarditis.

2.24   What are the management options for this condition?

- Medical – this is limited but may be used to treat patients with mild symptoms or to achieve short term palliation. E.g. elevation of upper body, administration of supplemental oxygen and/or diuretics, fluid restriction, steroids (although benefits are unknown).

- Radiotherapy/chemotherapy – is made on the basis of the histologic characteristics of the tumour. Chemotherapy for small cell cacrcinoma is less effective.

- Endovascular treatment – angioplasty and stents.

- Surgical treatment – in general, small cell carcinomas have already metastasised at time of presentation and therefore curative surgery would be unsuccessful. They may be treated with chemotherapy +/– radiotherapy. Non-small cell carcinomas present earlier and therefore curative surgery (lobectomy) may be feasible.

2.25   What could be causing the symptoms with which the patient is now presenting?

Superior vena caval obstruction is due to compression of the vessel by the tumour. Dyspnoea is a common symptom. There may be trunk or extremity swelling, facial swelling, cough, orthopnoea, headache and dizziness.

Case 4 Answers

2.26   What is the most likely diagnosis?

Acute asthma is a chronic inflammatory airways disorder. Variable airflow obstruction may be present but this is irreversible either spontaneously or with the use of inhalers.

2.27   What features indicate the severity of her condition?

Moderate exacerbation

- Increasing symptoms

- PEF > 50–75% best or predicted

- No features of severe asthma

- Severe exacerbation
- PEF 33–50% best or predicted
- Respiratory rate ≥ 25/min
- Heart rate ≥ 110/min
- Inability to complete sentences in one breath

Life-threatening

- PEF < 33% best or predicted
- Sats < 92%
- PaO_2 < 8 kPa
- Normal $PaCO_2$ (4.6–6.0 kPa)
- Silent chest
- Cyanosis
- Poor respiratory effort
- Arrhythmia
- Exhaustion, drowsy

2.28   How will you manage this patient in the acute stages?

- Oxygen to maintain saturation levels of 94–98%
- Oxygen driven nebulised β2 agonist bronchodilators (salbutamol)
- Add nebulised ipratropium bromide
- Steroids, e.g. prednisolone 40–50 mg daily or hydrocortisone 100 mg IV (continue for at least five days or until recovery)
- If no recovery consider giving IV magnesium sulphate 2 g
- Also if life-threatening you should make an ITU referral immediately for ventilation, or for those patients who are failing to respond to therapy

2.29   What preliminary investigations will you organise?

- Peak expiratory flow rate
- Pulse oximetry – to monitor oxygen saturations
- ABG – to look for respiratory failure
- CXR
- Bloods – FBC, U&Es, LFTs, CRP
- Blood cultures – to rule out infection
- Urine dip – to rule out infection

2.30   What does the X-ray show?

Large left-sided pneumothorax.

Tension pneumothorax – tracheal deviation, hypotension, unilateral absence of breath sounds, presence of distended neck veins, hyperresonant percussion over affected side.

Pneumothoraces are classified according to size of the visible rim between the lung margin and the chest wall on chest x-ray:

- There are various treatment options for spontaneous pneumothorax. Pneumothoraces are classified according to the size, i.e. 'large' or 'small' depending on the presence of a visible rim of ≥2cm (large) or <2cm (small) between the lung margin and chest wall.

- Observation - This is usually the treatment of choice for small closed pneumothoraces without significant dyspnoea.

- Patients with small (<2cm) primary pneumothoraces not associated with breathlessness should be considered for discharge with an early outpatient review.

- Dyspnoeic patients should not be left without intervention. This is regardless of the size of the pneumothorax.

- Simple aspiration is recommended as first line treatment of primary pneumothoraces requiring intervention. Simple aspiration of secondary pneumothoraces are less likely to be helpful and therefore is only recommended as an initial treatment in small (<2cm) pneumothoraces in minimally breathless patients aged <50 years.

- If simple aspiration of a pneumothorax is unsuccessful in giving symptom control then an inercostal drain should be inserted. Intercostal drainage is recommended in secondary pneumothorax except in patients who are not breathless and have a very small (<1cm or apical) pneumothorax.

2.31   How would you manage this?

Insert a needle into the second intercostal space in the midclavicular line. After this initial management a chest drain should be inserted.

2.32   What are the risk factors that predispose to the condition shown in the X-ray?

- Tall young men

- Marfan's syndrome

- Smoking (increases the risk by 22 fold)

- Asthma

- Pulmonary fibrosis

- Emphysema

- Severe bronchiectasis

- Secondary spontaneous pneumothorax can occur with tuberculosis, cystic fibrosis, sarcoidosis, malignancy

2.33   Why is the patient getting increasingly drowsy?

The patient has a raised CO_2 level, which is a result of muscle fatigue and inability to maintain adequate ventilation. This indicates a near-fatal patient and therefore ITU should be called upon for further management.

2.34 **How would you manage a patient with this condition in an outpatient setting?**

A stepwise approach is used for patients with asthma.

- Step 1: inhaled short acting β2 agonist as required

- Step 2: add inhaled steroid 200–800 micrograms/day (regular preventer therapy)

- Step 3: add inhaled long acting β2 agonist

- Step 4: consider trials of increasing inhaled steroid

- Add a fourth drug e.g. leukotriene receptor antagonist, SR theophylline, β2 agonist inhaler

- Step 5: continuous or frequent use of oral steroids – use daily steroid tablet, maintain high dose inhaled steroid, refer patient for specialist care

Case 5 Answers

2.35 **From the history what is the most likely diagnosis?**

COPD.

2.36 **How would you define this condition?**

COPD is a condition which is characterised by airflow obstruction which is usually progressive, not fully reversible and does not change markedly over several months. It is predominantly caused by smoking and it can have a huge impact on the patient's quality of life.

2.37 **What initial investigations would you perform in this patient?**

- Bloods: FBC looking for raised inflammatory markers, U&Es

- CXR

- ABG

- PEFR

- ECG

- Sputum culture

- Blood cultures if pyrexial

- Theophylline level if the patient is already on this medication

2.38 **Interpret his chest X-ray.**

- Typical findings in a chest X-ray from a patient with COPD include the following:

- Hyperinflated lungs

- Increased pulmonary vasculature

- Flattened diaphragms

- Elongated appearance of heart and mediastinum

- Parenchymal bullae (especially in patients with emphysema)

2.39   How will you manage the patient in the acute phase?

- In the acute episode always take the ABCDE approach.

- For most patients aim for oxygen saturations of 85–92%

- Aim of controlled oxygen therapy is to raise the paO_2 without worsening the acidosis (i.e. to prevent the development of type II respiratory failure). This can be achieved by the use of a Venturi mask.

- Serial ABGs to ensure there is an improvement

- Oxygen therapy to be complemented with bronchodilators, high dose oral steroids and, if need be, antibiotics to treat infection.

- Non-invasive ventilation may be required if medical therapy fails to improve respiratory acidosis.

- If NIV fails then intubation and ventilation should be considered in an ITU/HDU setting.

2.40   What further investigations will help you to confirm the diagnosis?

Pulmonary function testing including spirometry. As well as being diagnostic, this allows monitoring of the condition.

Spirometry results indicate that she has obstructive lung disease. Obstructive lung disease includes asthma, COPD, and upper airway obstruction. It is characterized on spirometry by a decrease in FEV1 which is greater than the decrease measured in FVC, hence an overall decreased FEV1/FVC. The Global Initiative for Chronic Obstructive Lung Disease (GOLD) defines COPD as having a FEV1 of less than 80% predicted normal value and a FEV1:FVC ratio of less than 0.7.

	FEV_1	FVC	FEV_1/FVC
Obstructive Lung Disease	Decreased (<80%)	Decreased	Decreased (<0.7)
Restrictive Lung Disease	Decreased	Decreased (<80%)	Normal (> 0.7) or Increased

Table 20.15   Summary of the typical spirometry result obtained in obstructive and restrictive lung disease.

A post bronchodilator FEV_1/FVC ratio of less than 70% and FEV_1 less than 80% is diagnostic for COPD.

2.41   Are there any staging criteria for this condition?

Stage	Lung Function	Symptoms
0 (at risk)	Normal	Chronic cough and sputum production
I (mild)	$FEV_1 \geq 80\%$ but FEV_1/FVC $\leq 70\%$	Usually chronic cough and sputum production
II (moderate)	$FEV_1 = 50$–79%	Usually progression of chronic cough and sputum production, as well as dyspnea with exertion
III (severe)	$FEV_1 = 30$–49%	Increased dyspnea as well as exacerabations with an overall decrease in quality of life
IV (very severe)	$FEV_1 < 30\%$ OR $FEV_1 < 50\%$ if in chronic respiratory failure	Patient is very impaired by disease with potentially life-threatening exacerbations

Table 20.16   Global Initiative for Chronic Obstructive Lung Disease Staging Criteria

2.42   How would you manage this patient, once he is stable, in an outpatient setting?

- Advice on smoking cessation

- Occupational health – some occupations may predispose to the development of COPD, or aggravate the condition

- Bronchodilators – inhalers, or nebulisers

- Steroids – inhalers, or tablets

- Supplemental oxygen – long term oxygen therapy (LTOT). This is the provision of continual use oxygen therapy in the home for patients with chronic hypoxaemia (PaO_2 below 7.3). Once commenced it is likely to be used lifelong. It is usually administered over a minimum of 15 hours a day (there is no proven benefit to having oxygen therapy for shorter periods) including overnight, when arterial hypoxaemia worsens during sleep.

Indications for LTOT:

- PaO_2 of < 7.3 KPa when stable or PaO_2 of 7.3 to 8.0 KPa when stable but there are additional risks such as polycythaemia, nocturnal hypoxaemia, peripheral oedema, or pulmonary hypertension.

- It should not be prescribed in those chronically hypoxaemia patients with PaO2 of >8 KPa.

References

Case 1

http://www.brit-thoracic.org.uk/clinical-information/Pulmonary-embolism.aspx

BTS Guidelines for the management of suspected acute pulmonary embolism

Thorax 2003; 58: 470–483; doi:10.1136/thorax.58.6.470

Pulmonary embolism – http://www.nice.org.uk/guidance/index.jsp?action=byID&o=11005

·*Case 2*

British Thoracic Guidelines for the Management of Community Acquired Pneumonia in Adults, *Thorax* 2001; 56 (Supplement 4):iv1-iv64; doi:10.1136/thorax.56.suppl_4.iv1

Case 3

British Thoracic Society and Society of Cardiothoracic Surgeons of Great Britain and Ireland Working Party

Guidelines on selection of patients with lung cancer for surgery *Thorax* 2001; 56: 89–108

www.nice.org.uk/nicemedia/pdf/CG024niceguideline.pdf

Case 4

http://www.brit-thoracic.org.uk/clinical-information/asthma.aspx

British thoracic guidelines on management of pneumothoraces

Case 5

Chronic obstructive pulmonary disease, Clinical Knowledge Summaries (2007)

COPD http://www.nice.org.uk/CG12

COPD http://www.goldcopd.com

Gastroenterology answers

Case 1 Answers

3.1   What is the most likely diagnosis?

Reflux oesophagitis.

The main symptoms of this disorder include odynophagia (painful swallowing) dysphagia due to oesophageal dysmotility and chest pain.

There are several factors predisposing to the development of reflux oesophagitis:

- Obesity
- Alcohol intake
- Caffeine intake
- Smoking
- Large meals – especially late at night
- Medications such as nitrates, calcium antagonists, anticholinergics
- Hiatus hernia

3.2   His GP suggests some lifestyle changes. What advice may the GP suggest?

- Weight loss
- Avoid fatty foods
- Avoid large meals before going to sleep
- Smoking cessation
- Reduce alcohol intake
- Avoid foods that may aggravate symptoms such as alcohol, caffeine
- Avoid stress

Also remember to review any medications the patient is on as they may be a cause of dyspepsia for example, NSAIDs, steroids, nitrates and calcium antagonists.

3.3   What will you initially advise or prescribe for him?

- Antacids
- Alginates

3.4   Do any of his symptoms warrant any further investigation? If so what signs or symptoms would concern you?

- No relief with PPIs
- Persistent vomiting
- Dysphagia
- Abdominal swelling
- Persistent symptoms lasting longer than four weeks

- Unintentional weight loss

- Haematemesis/Melaena

3.5   What are the causes of dysphagia?

This can be divided into different categories:

- Extrinsic
  - ○ Lung cancer
  - ○ Goitre
  - ○ Mediastinal lymph nodes
- Intrinsic
  - ○ Foreign body
  - ○ Benign stricture
  - ○ Malignant stricture
  - ○ Pharyngeal pouch
  - ○ Oesophageal web
  - ○ Oesophageal ring
  - ○ Oesophagitis
  - ○ Oesophageal candidiasis
- Motility disorders
  - ○ Achalasia
  - ○ Bulbar palsy
  - ○ Pseudobulbar palsy
  - ○ Myasthenia gravis
  - ○ Systemic sclerosis

3.6   Which investigation should Gordon have?

- OGD

3.7   Can you list any complications of Gordon's condition?

- Strictures

- Haemorrhage

- Barrett's oesophagus

- Carcinoma of the oesophagus (independent of Barrett's)

Complications of Gastro-oesophageal reflux:

- Barrett's oesophagus

- Benign oesophageal stricture

- Oesophagitis/Laryingitis
- Ulcerations

3.8   How would you manage his symptoms initially?

Management options include lifestyle interventions (as mentioned above), antacids, H_2 antagonists or proton pump inhibitors (PPI) in addition to, if necessary, a pro-motility agent (such as metoclopramide or domperidone which also act as anti-emetics) for large volume reflux.

If medical therapy fails a surgical opinion may be sought for a fundoplication. These operations are performed laparoscopically or endoscopically.

3.9   What is a CLO test and what is it testing for?

A CLO (Campylobacter-Like Organism) test detects the presence of helicobacter pylori. One or two samples of gastric mucosa are placed in a well on a slide and the presence of urease causes a colour change from yellow (negative) to red (positive).

There are other methods of detecting the presence of H. pylori which are less invasive, such as the urease breath test, H. pylori serology and stool antigen testing.

3.10   What treatment would you give for this positive result?

- PPI (e.g. lansoprazole or omeprazole)
- Amoxicillin (unless penicillin allergic)
- Clarithromycin/ metronidazole

These are medications which are used for H. pylori eradication and they are normally given for one week.

3.11   What pathological change would you see in this condition?

Gastroesophageal reflux disease damages the squamous oesophageal mucosa and a metaplastic process occurs in which columnar cells replace the squamous cells.

Barrett's oesophagus is found in 10–20% of patients with long-standing history of acid reflux. The above pathological process takes place in this condition and is premalignant (oesophageal carcinoma). It is important that patients who have Barrett's oesophagus undergo regular surveillance.

Barrett's oesophagus can be treated with endoscopic or surgical treatments but the main aim of management is treat the underlying reflux disease.

Hiatus hernia – occurs when the upper stomach herniates through the diaphragm into the chest cavity. This is more common in obese patients and with increasing age. Many patients may be asymptomatic with a hiatus hernia and may be identified incidentally on investigation. A hiatus hernia may be described as either 'sliding' (in 80% of patients) or 'rolling' (in 20% of patients). In the sliding type the patients may suffer from acid reflux and/or aspiration. There is a risk of obstruction/strangulation with a 'rolling' hernia.

3.12   What is the likely diagnosis?

Oesophageal carcinoma – can either be squamous type or adenocarcinoma. The majority of squamous tumours arise in the mid-thoracic part of the oesophagus whereas the majority of adenocarcinomas tend to originate in the lower part of the oesophagus.

Clinically, one would be aware of the diagnosis in a patient who presents with dyspepsia, progressive dysphagia (for liquids first then solids), vomiting, weight loss and pain.

Risk factors include:

- Barrett's oesophagus

- Smoking/alcohol intake

- Obesity

- Achalasia

- Chronic reflux

- Plummer Vinson syndrome (aka Paterson-Brown-Kelly) – a triad of glossitis, dysphagia (due to oesophageal webs) and iron deficiency anaemia.

3.13   What other investigations would you perform?

- Blood tests: FBC looking for anaemia

- CT thorax, abdomen, pelvis – for staging purposes and will reveal any evidence of metastases

- Endoscopic ultrasound – for accuracy of staging

- Barium swallow may show a stricture (irregular).

Staging classification (TNM):

- Tis carcinoma in situ

- T_1 Invasion of lamina propria/sunmucosa

- T_2 Invasion of muscularis propria

- T_3 Invasion of adventitia

- T_4 Invasion of adjacent structures

- NX Nodes cannot be assessed

- N_0 No node spread

- N_1 Regional node metastases

- M_0 No distant spread

- M_1 distant metastases

3.14   What further management would you consider once the diagnosis is confirmed?

Majority of the patients present late in the disease process and have unresectable disease.

- Pharmacological: pain relief.

- Surgical: oesophagectomy, photodynamic therapy, pre-operative/neoadjuvant/adjuvant therapy with medication and radiotherapy may be used. Approximately about a third of lesions are suitable for resection at presentation.

- Palliation: radiotherapy may be used to debulk the tumour. XRT usually for SCC.

The overall 5-year survival rate for resectable tumours ranges from 10–25%.

Case 2 Answers

3.15   What is your immediate management of this patient?

- Use the ABC approach, as for any acute situation.

- Airway – make sure the airway is patent.

- Breathing – administer high flow oxygen, place O_2 sats probe, look for respiratory effort and listen to breath sounds.

- Circulation – attach to cardiac monitor, insert two large bore cannulae into each antecubital fossa and send bloods urgently. In this case a FBC, U&Es, LFTs, Coagulation screen, Group & Save, and crossmatch for 4–6 units.

3.16   How would you assess the severity of his haematemesis

Rockall score:

< 60 years	0
60–79 years	1
> 80 years	2
No evidence of shock	0
Pulse > 100/min, systolic BP > 100 mmHg	1
Systolic BP < 100 mmHg	2
No comorbidity	0
CCF, IHD, or any other major disease	2
Renal/liver failure, disseminated malignancy	3

Low risk 0–1 points; Moderate risk 2–3 points; High risk ≥ 4 points

Table 20.17   Rockall score

3.17   What are the possible causes of his haematemesis?

Causes of upper gastrointestinal haemorrhage:

- Duodenal ulcer 35%

- Gastric ulcer 20%

- Gastric erosions 18%

- Mallory Weiss tear 10%

- Duodenitis

- Oesophageal varices

- Oesophagitis

- Upper GI neoplasia

- Angiodysplasia

- Hereditary haemorrhagic telengiectasia
- Portal hypertensive gastropathy
- Aorto-duodenal fistula

3.18   What is your provisional diagnosis and what are the risk factors which predispose to this condition?

Upper GI haemorrhage secondary to a duodenal ulcer.

Risk factors:

- Helicobacter Pylori infection
- High alcohol intake
- NSAID use
- Severe stress
- High dose steroids
- Male
- Sex
- Smoking
- Zollinger Ellison syndrome is a rare condition. Gastrin secreting adenomas cause severe gastric and/or duodenal ulceration. The tumour is usually pancreatic in origin although it may arise in the stomach, duodenum or adjacent tissues. 50–60% are malignant and it may occur as part of Multiple Endocrine Neoplasia type 1. Clinical signs/symptoms may include: pain, dyspepsia, steatorrhoea, diarrhoea. Treatment with high dose acid suppression, surgical resection of adenoma, chemotherapy, somatostatin analogues to reduce gastric secretion and diarrhoea.

Patients with peptic ulcer disease are treated medically with acid suppression and H. pylori eradication, and surgery is limited to those with complications unresponsive to medical or endoscopic therapy.

All patients with peptic ulceration or gastritis found to be positive for H. pylori should undergo eradication therapy. Effective eradication should be assessed by either repeat biopsies or breath testing in patients with complications (perforation or haemorrhage) and those with persistent symptoms.

Relapse of peptic ulcer disease after H. pylori eradication is < 5% per year. Eradication regimes vary but usually involve triple therapy of a PPI and two antibiotics (eg amoxicillin and clarithromycin).

3.19   What medication/s should be administered?

- Omeprazole infusion (to continue for 72 hrs)– if there is concern regarding alcohol dependency or liver disease, e.g. history or examination findings, consider Terlipressin
- Pabrinex if the patient has a history of alcoholism
- Withdrawal regime (diazepam/chlordiazepoxide – according to local hospital guidelines) if patient has a history of alcoholism

3.20   **What questions would you like to ask?**

Any previous episodes of haematemesis/melaena – cause, severity, management

- Any known causes of upper GI bleeds eg peptic ulcer, liver disease

- Any dyspeptic symptoms

- Alcohol consumption, IV drug use, hep B, hep C

- Medication history

3.21   **The patient has had his OGD which shows oesophageal varices. What is the most likely cause of this?**

Oesophageal varices on OGD. In this patient these are most likely caused by portal hypertension due to cirrhosis secondary to alcohol.

Portal hypertension occurs as a result of increased resistance to portal venous flow. Pressure in the portal vein rises (> 12 mmHg). This causes enlargement of the spleen and anastomoses may develop between the portal and systemic circulation. Collaterals may form at the oesophagogastric junction, umbilicus and rectum. Causes of portal hypertension include: cirrhoses, portal vein thrombosis, Budd Chiari syndrome (thrombosis or obstruction of hepatic vein due to a tumour, haematological disease or oral contraceptive pill), intrahepatic tumours (cholangiocarcinoma, hepatocellular carcinoma), constrictive pericarditis, right heart failure, splenic vein thrombosis.

3.22   **How is this condition treated?**

Variceal banding.

3.23   **What other medications can be prescribed to help treat this condition?**

- Terlipressin (vasoactive drug)

- Beta blockers eg propanolol – aims to reduce portal hypertension

3.24   **What signs or symptoms would alert you to a re-bleed?**

- Tachycardia – but this may be masked by beta blockers

- Hypotension

- Poor urine output

- Haematemesis

- Melaena/fresh PR bleeding

A recurrent haemorrhage may be an indication for TIPPS (Transjugular intrahepatic porto-systemic shunt). This decompresses the portal venous system and is less invasive that surgery. There is a risk of developing hepatic encephalopathy.

3.25   **Can you list any signs seen in alcoholic liver disease?**

- Jaundice

- Clubbing

- Leuconychia

- Dupuytren's contracture

- Palmar erythema

- Asterixis – i.e. liver flap

- Exoriation marks

- Spider naevi

- Gynaecomastia

- Ascites

- Hepato/splenomegaly

- Testicular atrophy

- Peripheral oedema

3.26   List causes of this clinical sign.

- Malignancy

- Liver cirrhosis

- Pancreatitis

- Hypoalbuminaemia

- Heart failure

- Constrictive pericarditis

- Hepatic vein obstruction

- TB infection

3.27   Which diagnosis needs to be considered here?

Spontaneous bacterial peritonitis – patients with alcoholic hepatitis often spike a low grade fever.

3.28   How will you test for this?

Paracentesis (N.B. ensure that a clotting screen has been checked before proceeding). The ascitic fluid should be cultured (both aerobic and anaerobic) and a cell count obtained. Consider sending off for cytology, lactate, pH.

Also think about doing a full septic screen as the abdomen may not be the only source of infection (although in this case this is most likely), blood cultures, urine sample, sputum sample (if chest involvement suspected).

3.29   What is your diagnosis?

Chronic hepatic encephalopathy – may supervene in chronic liver disease and is precipitated by alcohol, drugs, GI haemorrhage, infections and constipation.

Management-wise the patient should be screened for sepsis and be treated appropriately, strict fluid and electrolyte balance, high protein diet, laxatives (lactulose) to clear the gut and reduce toxin absorption.

3.30   **You go to speak with the patient. What screening tool can you use to assess alcohol abuse in this patient?**

CAGE questionnaire:

- Have you ever felt that you should **C**ut down on your drinking?

- Have you ever been **A**nnoyed by people criticising your drinking?

- Have you ever felt **G**uilty about your drinking?

- Do you need an **E**ye opener to start the day?

If ≥ 2 of the above questions are answered as a yes, then a more detailed alcohol history should be taken.

3.31   **List complications associated with alcohol abuse.**

- Hypertension, heart failure, cardiomyopathy, arrhythmias, anaemia

- Hepatitis, cirrhosis

- Oesophageal CA, peptic ulcer disease, pancreatitis

- Myopathy

- Polyneuropathy, subacute combined degeneration, Wernicke Korsakoffs syndrome, epilepsy, cerebellar degeneration head injury

- Foetal alcohol syndrome

- Accidents, violence, relationship, employment problems

Case 3 Answers

3.32   **What is the likely diagnosis?**

Irritable bowel syndrome – this is a chronic relapsing functional gut disorder with no recognisable pathological abnormality. Strict diagnosis is based on Rome criteria

Recurrent abdominal pain or discomfort (uncomfortable sensation not described as pain) at least three days/month in the last three months, associated with ≥ 2 of the following:

1. Improvement with defaecation

2. Onset associated with a change in frequency of stool

3. Onset associated with a change in form (appearance) of stool

3.33   **What symptoms would be classed as red flag symptoms which warrant further investigation?**

- Unintentional weight loss

- Rectal bleeding

- Family history of bowel or ovarian cancer

- On patients aged > 60 years, a change in bowel habit lasting more than six weeks with loose and/or more frequent stools

- Anaemia

- Abdominal mass

- Rectal mass

- Raised inflammatory markers for inflammatory bowel disease

3.34   **What investigations will you do to aid you with the diagnosis?**

The following investigations are for exclusion of other possible diagnoses.

- Full Blood count (FBC)

- Erythrocyte Sedimentation Rate (ESR)

- C-Reactive protein (CRP)

- Coeliac disease antibodies (Endomysial antibodies, tissue transglutaminase)

- Thyroid function tests (TFTs)

- Stool culture

- Sigmoidoscopy

3.35   **What is your initial management of this condition?**

Lifestyle changes will include general dietary advice such as having regular meals, restricting caffeine and alcohol intake, limiting intake of high fibre foods, etc.

Medications are based on symptoms.

Consider the usage of antispasmodics or laxatives but discourage the use of lactulose and loperamide.

Consider tricyclic antidepressants (TCA) for their analgesic effect (begin with low dose).

Consider referring patients who have symptoms which are unresponsive to any of the previous lifestyle modifications and medications, for psychological intervention. Consider referring for cognitive behavioural therapy, hypnotherapy or psychological therapy.

Treatment is usually symptomatic and includes anti-spasmodics, increased dietary fibre, laxatives, constipating agents, antidepressants, hypnotherapy and psychotherapy.

Case 4 Answers

3.36   **What questions do you specifically want to ask about in the history?**

- Recent travel abroad

- IV drug abuse

- Tattoos

- Excess alcohol

- High risk sexual activity

- Healthcare professional

- Farm sewage worker

- Water sports

- Any recent medications e.g. antibiotics (flucloxacillin, co-amoxiclav) excess paracetamol, etc.

3.37   What may be the cause of his jaundice?

This is a common symptom of liver disease and is caused by the accumulation of bilirubin in the tissues. It is clinically detectable when the bilirubin levels are > 40 mmol/L.

Causes of Jaundice	Causes of prehepatic, hepatic and posthepatic jaundice respectively	Biochemistry
Prehepatic causes Excess production of bilirubin or failure of uptake into the liver. Bilirubin is unconjugated and insoluble	Haemolysis Congenital hyperbilirubinaemia	ALT/AST – N ALP – N/↑ GGT – N/↑ Conjugated bilirubin - N Unconjugated bilirubin - ↑↑
Hepatic causes Diminished hepatocyte function Both conjugated and unconjugated bilirubin appear in the urine	Alcoholic hepatitis Viral infection (e.g. hepatitis A, B, Epstein Barr virus) Drugs (e.g. augmentin, phenothiazine) Cirrhosis Hepatic congestion in cardiac failure Hepatic metastases Wilson's disease	ALT/AST - ↑↑ ALP - ↑ GGT - ↑ Conjugated bilirubin - ↑↑ Unconjugated bilirubin - N
Post hepatic Impaired excretion of bile from liver into the gut. Conjugated bilirubin is reabsorbed, which increases serum and urine levels. Therefore producing dark urine. Stools are pale due to the lack of stercobilinogen.	Gallstones Carcinoma of pancreas/bile ducts Lymph nodes at porta hepatis Primary biliary cirrhosis Sclerosing cholangitis Structural abnormality of the biliary tree	ALT/AST - ↑ ALP - ↑↑ GGT - ↑↑ Conjugated bilirubin - ↑↑ Unconjugated bilirubin - N

Table 20.18   Causes of Jaundice

3.38   What blood tests will you do and which of these are useful in assessing liver synthetic function?

- FBC

- U&Es

- LFTs

- Albumin, INR, prothrombin time

3.39   What other investigations would you consider performing?

- USS abdomen

- Liver screen

- Virology – specifically CMV, EBV

- Hepatitis serology – specifically Hepatitis A,B,C

- Iron studies

- Autoantibodies – specifically ANA, SMA, AMA, LKM

3.40   His LFTs are shown below. What is your likely diagnosis?

ALP 372

ALT 1160

AST 1027

Albumin 34

The liver function tests show an increase in the transaminases which indicate a hepatocellular cause for his condition.

The likely diagnosis is acute viral hepatitis.

Hepatitis A

Spread: faecal-oral, RNA virus, supportive treatment, no chronic state.

Hepatitis B

Spread: blood borne (eg sexual, congenital transmission), DNA virus, supportive treatment + antivirals (lamivudine, adefovir), 5% progress to chronic carrier status (risk of cirrhosis and hepatocellular carcinoma).

There are several markers to indicate the progression of hepatitis B infection and can determine whether the patient is a carrier or not. HBsAg (surface antigen) is present from one to six months after exposure. The persistence of HBsAg for > 6 months defines carrier status. This follows 5–10% of infections.

Among those who are HBsAg +ve, those in whom hepatitis B e antigen is also detected in the serum are the most infectious.

Those who are HBsAg positive and HBeAg negative (usually anti HBe positive) are infectious but generally of lower infectivity.

The presence of HBeAg (e antigen) implies high infectivity.

It is usually present for 1 ½ – 3 months after the acute illness.

Antibodies to HBcAg (core antigen, ie anti HBc) imply past infection.

Hepatitis C

Spread blood borne, sexual, RNA virus, treatment with interferon alpha for chronic HCV, 60–80% chronicity, 20% of these develop cirrhosis (a third of whom will develop hepatocellular carcinoma). No vaccine available.

Hepatitis D

Spread blood-borne, dependent on concurrent hep B infection for replication, incomplete virus.

Hepatitis E

Spread faecal-oral, RNA virus, acute self-limiting illness, 25% mortality in pregnancy, supportive treatment, no chronic state.

Hepatitis G

Spread blood-borne, RNA virus. Twenty per cent of patients with chronic HCV are infected with HGV.

3.41   What are the causes of cirrhosis?

- Hepatitis

- Alcohol

- Non-alcoholic fatty liver disease

- Autoimmune hepatitis

- Primary biliary cirrhosis

- Wilson disease

- Alpha 1 antitrypsin deifiency

- Drug induced (eg, methotrexate, amiodarone)

- Haemochromatosis

3.42   What are the complications of cirrhosis?

- Hepatocellular carcinoma

- Hepatorenal syndrome – acute renal failure (ARF) can complicate chronic liver disease, but it can also occur with fulminant hepatic failure. There are two types. Type 1 HRS: occurs as a rapidly progressive renal impairment, with a very high mortality rate, all patients dying within weeks without treatment. Type 2: renal impairment is more stable and some hepatic reserve is preserved. Mortality is high but some patients survive over six months. Treatment is with parenteral fluids. Albumin, terlipressin and dialysis.

- Hepatic encephalopathy

- Portal hypertension

3.43   What is the scoring system used to determine the prognosis in patients with cirrhosis?

The table below shows the Child Pugh scoring which is used to determine the prognosis in patients with cirrhosis (chronic liver disease).

	1 point	2 points	3 points
INR	< 1.7	1.7–2.3	> 2.3
Albumin	> 35 g/L	30–35 g/L	< 30 g/L
Bilirubin*	< 34 μmol/L	34–50 μmol/L	> 50 μmol/L
Ascites	No evidence	Mild-moderate	Severe
Encephalopathy	No evidence	Stages I and II	Stages III and IV

*Note that in primary biliary cirrhosis and primary sclerosing cholangitis will feature higher levels of bilirubin, therefore the limits will be higher (i.e. 1 point 68 μmol/L)

Table 20.19   Child Pugh scoring

- Child Pugh A classification is 5–6 points

- Child Pugh B classification is 7–9 points

- Child Pugh C classification is 10–15 points

3.44   What is the likely diagnosis?

Hepatic encephalopathy.

- Grade 0: normal

- Grade 1: confusion

- Grade 2: drowsiness, lethargy

- Grade 3: incomprehensible speech, marked confusion

- Grade 4: coma

Investigations that you may do include ammonia levels, EEG, MRI/CT, VERs.

Differentials include: intracranial lesions, infection, substance abuse, medications such as sedatives, antidepressants, postictal.

The most common causes of acute hepatic encephalopathy are fulminant viral hepatitis and paracetamol toxicity which are potentially fully reversible. Indicators of a poor prognosis are:

- Acidosis

- Increased prothrombin time

- Decreasing Glasgow Coma Scale (GCS – see Chapter 4 Neurology, case 8.)

These patients should be referred to a specialist centre as they may require a liver transplant.

Chronic hepatic encephalopathy – may supervene in chronic liver disease and is precipitated by alcohol, drugs, GI haemorrhage, infections, constipation.

Case 5 Answers

3.45   What are the differential diagnoses?

- Infective colitis – viral or bacterial.

- Crohn's

- Ulcerative colitis

3.46   What is the most likely diagnosis?

Ulcerative colitis.

	Ulcerative colitis	Crohn's
Symptoms/signs	Diarrhoea + mucus/blood Fever	Diarrhoea +/– blood Oral/perioral/anal ulcers
	Abdominal pain	Strictures – may cause obstruction Fever Severe abdominal pain
	Decreased incidence in smokers	Increased incidence in smokers

Table 20.20   Ulcerative colitis and Crohn's disease

3.47   What is the difference between ulcerative colitis and Crohn's disease macroscopically and microscopically?

Ulcerative colitis extends proximally from the rectum and involves the large colon (may cause backwash ileitis) and is a continuous inflammatory process. Crohns disease affects any part of the gastrointestinal tract (mouth to anus). Skip lesions may be present. The most frequently affected area is the terminal ileum.

- Macroscopically: Crohn's disease – thickened, narrowed bowel with cobblestone appearance of mucosa

- Ulcerative colitis – red, inflamed mucosa, easily friable, psuedopolyps may be present

- Microscopically: Crohn's disease – transmural involvement and granulomas

- Ulcerative colitis – inflammation limited to mucosa and crypt abscesses.

3.48   What are the extra-intestinal manifestations of inflammatory bowel disease?

Uveitis, episcleritis, conjunctivitis, arthropathy, arthralgia, ankylosing spondylitis, back pain, erythema nodosum, pyoderma gangrenosum, sclerosing cholangitis, fatty liver, chronic hepatitis, cirrhosis, gallstones, venous thrombosis.

Ulcerative colitis	Crohn's
Primary biliary cirrhosis (PBC) , Chronic active hepatitis (CAH) Sclerosing cholangitis There are systemic manifestations but to a lesser extent compared to Crohn's	Clubbing Erythema nodosum Pyoderma gangrenosum Uveitis/iritis Arthritis Primary sclerosing cholangitis (PSC)

Table 20.21 Extra-intestinal manifestations of inflammatory bowel disease

3.49   **What are the complications of ulcerative colitis and Crohn's disease?**

Ulcerative colitis	Crohn's
Toxic megacolon Higher risk of development of carcinoma (especially if the patient has had the condition for > 10 yrs) Iron deficiency anaemia Venous thrombo embolism	B12 deficiency (decrased absorption in terminal ileum) Iron deficiency Abscess Venous thromboembolism Fistulae (entero-enteral, entero-vesical, entero-vaginal, perianal)

Table 20.22   Complications of ulcerative colitis and Crohn's disease

Here is an X-ray showing toxic megacolon:

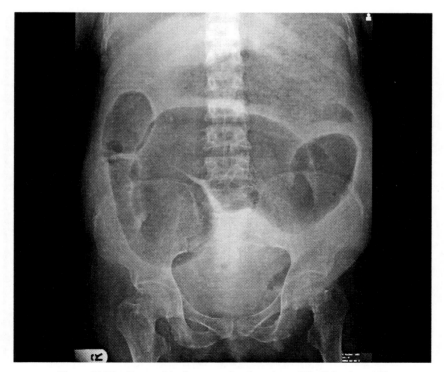

Figure 20.10   X-ray of toxic megacolon (courtesy of Dr John Asquith)

3.50   What investigations would you request?

- FBC to look for anaemia (usually normocytic, normochromic or microcytic), WCC may be elevated in acute episode
- ESR/CRP raised inflammatory markers suggesting acute episode
- Hypoalbuminaemia in severe disease
- LFTs may be abnormal
- Blood cultures if septicaemia suspected
- Stool cultures
- Colonoscopy or flexible sigmoidoscopy (caution is required as there is an increased risk of perforation with severe disease)

Second line investigations include:

- Barium follow through to assess small bowel
- Barium enema
- CT scan
- Radionuclide scans to identify small intestinal and colonic disease and to localise extraintestinal abscesses

3.51   What are the dangers of leaving this condition untreated?

- Toxic megacolon – uncommon but is an indication for urgent colectomy
- Haemorrhage
- Perforation

3.52   How would you manage this patient?

- IV access
- IV fluids
- IV steroids
- Bedrest
- IV antibiotics
- Blood transfusion if necessary
- Surgery if necessary

3.53   What are the main treatment options?

Maintenance:

- Diet (with appropriate fibre intake/elemental diet)
- Vitamins
- Iron
- 5ASA compounds (eg sulfasalazine, mesalazine) – these are used to treat mild-moderate relapses of colitis and are taken long-term to maintain remission. Side-effects include rash, infertility, agranulocytosis, headache, diarrhoea, renal failure.

Relapse:

- Increase 5ASA therapy

- Oral steroids – is the treatment for active disease (topical/oral/IV)

- Retention enemas – 5ASA or steroids

- If condition is severe – require admission to hospital, IV fluids, IV steroids, antibiotics, daily abdominal x-rays, parenteral nutrition

If there are recurrent flare ups, consider immunosuppression therapy e.g. azathioprine (steroid sparing agent). Close monitoring is required whilst taking azathioprine as there is a risk of bone marrow suppression and hepatotoxicity.

Anti-tumour necrosis factor alpha (infliximab), a monoclonal antibody, is effective in the treatment of active Crohn's disease but is expensive therefore the use is restricted to patients who have failed other medical therapies (see above).

Surgical resection is also an option but there is approximately a 50% recurrence rate in Crohn's disease.

Case 6 Answers

3.54   What is the most likely diagnosis?

Gastric carcinoma – majority of lesions occur in the pylorus and are an adenocarcinoma.

Other gastric tumours include lymphoma (~5%), leiomyoscarcomas (<1%), Gastrointestinal Stromal Tumours (GIST) which are submucosal tumours.

3.55   What signs and symptoms would you expect in this condition?

There may be no associated symptoms in patients however they may complain of:

- Dyspepsia

- Dysphagia

- Loss of appetite (anorexia)

- Weight loss

- Postprandial fullness

- Iron deficiency anaemia

- Melaena/haematemesis

Late complications are: peritoneal/pleural effusions; gastric outlet/gastroesophageal junction/small bowel obstruction; oesophageal variceal bleeding; bleeding from anastomotic site from surgery; intrahepatic/extrahepatic jaundice.

3.56   What are the risk factors associated with this condition?

- Japanese

- Male genders

- Diet (low vitamin C intake, high salt)

- Blood Group A

- Pernicious anaemia

- Partial gastrectomy

- Predisposing factors: H pylori infection, atrophic gastritis, intestinal metaplasia, gastric dysplasia, adenomatous polyps – fundic gland polyps are common and not thought to be pre-malignant.

3.57   What investigations would confirm your diagnosis?

OGD + biopsies.

3.58   What further investigations would you do once the diagnosis is confirmed?

- CT thorax, abdomen, pelvis

- PET scan

- Staging laparoscopy

3.59   What management options are available for this condition?

- Surgical resection +/– lymphadenectomy (partial or total gastrectomy)

- Adjuvant/neoadjuvant chemotherapy

- If there is evidence of gastric outlet obstruction an endoscopic stent may be necessary

- Palliative care – multidisciplinary approach and achieving symptom control with e.g. insertion of stent, appropriate analgesia andanti-emetics

References

Case 1

Dyspepsia: www.nice.org.uk/nicemedia/pdf/CG017NICEguideline.pdf

Fox M, Forgacs I (2006) Gastro-oesophageal reflux disease. BMJ 332: 88–93

http://www.cancer.gov/cancertopics/pdq/treatment/esophageal/HealthProfessional

Case 2

Helen J, Dallal K, Palmer R (2001) ABC of the upper gastrointestinal tract. Upper gastrointestinal haemorrhage. *BMJ*; 323(7321) 1115 (10 November).

http://www.bsg.org.uk/clinical-guidelines/endoscopy/guidelines-for-non-variceal-upper-gastrointestinal-haemorrhage.html

Moore KP and Aithal GP (2006) British Society of Gastroenterology: Guidelines on the management of ascites in cirrhosis. *Gut* 55; 1–12

Moss M et al. (2006) Alcohol abuse in the critically ill patient. *Lancet*; 368: 2231, 42.

Case 3

Gitlin N (1997) Hepatitis B: diagnosis, prevention, and treatment. Clin Chem. Aug; 43 (8 Pt 2): 1500–6

Hepatitis B, www.patient.co.uk/doctor/Hepatitis-B.htm

Ryder and Beckingham (2001) ABC of diseases of liver, pancreas, and biliary system: Acute hepatitis, *BMJ*, 322: 151–153

Case 4

Irritable Bowel Syndrome – www.nice.org.uk/CG061

Irritable bowel syndrome (2008) NICE Clinical Guideline *Irritable bowel syndrome in adults: diagnosis and management of irritable bowel syndrome in primary care*

Jones R (2008) Treatment of irritable bowel syndrome in primary care. *BMJ*. Nov 13; 337: a2213. doi: 10.1136/bmj.a2213.

Table 20.19 Child Pugh. – Pugh RN, Murray-Lyon IM, Dawson JL, Pietroni MC, Williams R (1973). Transection of the oesophagus for bleeding oesophageal varices. *The British Journal of Surgery* 60 (8): 646–9.

Case 5

British Society of Gastroenterology (2004) Guidelines for the management of inflammatory bowel disease in adults

Collins P, Rhodes J (2006) Ulcerative colitis: diagnosis and management. *BMJ*. 12; 333(7563): 340–3

Cummings JR, Keshav S, Travis SP (2008) Medical management of Crohn's disease. *BMJ*. May 10; 336(7652): 1062–6

Case 6

W H Allum, S M Griffin, A Watson, D Colin-Jones (2002) Guidelines for the management of oesophageal and gastric cancer. *Gut* 50(Suppl V): v1–v23

NICE guidelines: Referral for suspected cancer: http://www.nice.org.uk/CG027

Recommended further cases:

- Primary biliary cirrhosis
- Autoimmune hepatitis
- Primary sclerosing cholangitis

Neurology answers
Case 1 Answers

4.1   What are the differential diagnoses?

- Meningitis – bacterial, viral, fungal
- Encephalitis – confusion (but no seizures or focal signs)
- Cerebral abscess – unlikely without focal neurology or confusion
- Cerebral neoplasm – very unlikely but possible
- Systemic viral illness (diagnosis of exclusion)

4.2   What investigations would you perform?

- Bloods: FBC, U&Es, LFTs, CRP, serum glucose, coagulation profile

- ABG

- Blood cultures

- Lumbar puncture can be done before CT head if no contraindication exists

- CT brain

- Throat swab

- CXR

4.3   What would you like to do next and how would you do this?

Lumbar puncture.

Ensure that you get written consent from the patient before the procedure, explaining the benefits and possible complications. Position of the patient during a lumbar puncture is critical. The patient is positioned into a left lateral position with their knees bent as close to their chest as possible and ensure that the hips and shoulders are in line.

Draw an imaginary line between the top of the iliac crests. This intersects the spine at approximately the L3-4 space. (The conus medullaris finishes near L1-2 in adults)

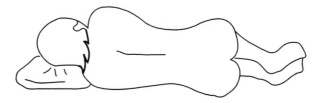

Figure 20.11   Lumbar puncture procedure

Get your equipment ready:

- An assistant

- Sterile drapes

- Sterile gloves

- Sterile pack for minor procedures

- Skin preparation (chlorhexidine)

- Local anaesthetic (lignocaine 1% or 2%), 5 ml syringe, needles ×2 (a green one for drawing up the lignocaine and an orange one for administering it)

- Spinal needle

- CSF bottles ×4 (bottles 1 and 3 for microbiology, bottle 2 for biochemistry and bottle 4 for virology or further testing (i.e. to be stored in the laboratory). If CSF is needed for xanthochromia (to exclude a subarachnoid haemorrhage) this needs to be kept away from light by putting it into a 5th bottle in an envelope.

- Manometer (for measuring the opening pressure)

- A plaster for the patient's back

Contraindications

- Platelet count < 50 (if urgent the case should be discussed with a Haematologist)
- INR > 1.2 (if urgent discuss the case with a Haematologist)
- Known bleeding disorder (eg haemophilia)
- Evidence of increased intracranial pressure (obtunded GCS < 13, convulsions, papilloedema, mass effect from a space-occupying lesion, cerebral oedema and other features on CT scan)
- Meningococcal septicaemia (purpuric rash)
- If in doubt discuss with senior

Complications

- Failure to obtain specimen therefore need to repeat procedure
- Post-dural puncture headache (10–25% depending on the needle/operator)
- Backache
- Traumatic tap
- Bleeding (spinal haematoma – very rare)
- Infection (epidural abscess – very rare)
- Transient/persistent parasthesia/numbness (rare)
- Tonsillar herniation (when LP performed despite contraindications).

4.4   Interpret the results below:

CSF FINDINGS (N = normal, + = mildly raised, ++ = raised, +++ = markedly raised)

Meningitis	Cells	Protein	Glucose
Bacterial	Polymorphonuclear (> 60%)	++	Low (< 50% of serum)
	cells often > 300/mm³		
Viral	Mononuclear < 300 mm³	+/N	N
Tuberculous	Mononuclear < 300 mm³	++/+++	Low/very low
Fungal	Mononuclear < 300 mm³	++/+++	Low
Malignant	Usually mononuclear	++/+++	Low/N

Table 20.23   CSF findings

4.5   What is the most likely diagnosis?

Bacterial meningitis.

Causative organisms will differ with patient's age and co-morbidities:

- Adults – *Streptococcus pneumonia (streptococcal)*
- Young adults – *Neisseria meningitides (meningococcal)*

- Children – *Haemophilus influenza, Neisseria meningitides*

- Neonates – *Escherichia coli, β-haemolytic streptococci, Listeria monocytogenes*

- Elderly, immunocompromised – *Streptococcus pneumoniae, Listeria monocytogenes, Cryptococcus (fungal)*, gram negative organisms, *Mycobacterium tuberculosis ('TB Meningitis')*

- Head trauma, neurosurgical patients – *Staphylococcus aureus*, gram negative organisms

4.6   What are the signs and symptoms of this condition?

- Cerebral dysfunction – confusion, irritability, coma, delirium

- Fever

- Headache

- Photophobia

- Petechial/purpuric rash

- Meningeal irritation

   o   Kernig's sign: in a supine patient, flex hip to 90° while the knee is flexed at 90°. An attempt to further extend the knee produces neck pain.

   o   Brudzinski's sign: passively flex the neck while the patient is supine with the extremities extended. This produces flexion of the hips in patients with meningeal irritation.

   o   Nuchal rigidity (neck stiffness): resistance to passive flexion/extension of the neck

   o   Cranial nerve palsies (may be an indication of increased intracranial pressure or brainstem involvement)

- Papilloedema

- Focal neurological signs

- Seizures

4.7   How would you manage this patient?

Assess airway, breathing and circulation (ABC). Treat any life threatening shock, acidosis, hypoxia etc, before giving specific treatment.

Local guidelines vary, but generally if bacterial meningitis is suspected give IV ceftriaxone empirically. Antibiotics may later change depending on the results of CSF analysis.

Meningitis is a notifiable disease, it needs to be reported to the Consultant in Communicable Disease Control (CDCC) at the nearest Health Protection Unit (HPU). Close contacts of patients with meningococcal meningitis will be traced and treated with prophylactic antibiotics.

If the patient/contact is pregnant this will need discussing with the microbiologist.

Case 2 Answers

4.8   What is your immediate management?

- Airway

- Breathing

- Circulation

- Oxygen

- IV access

- BM (bedside glucose measurement)

- Bloods FBC, U&Es, LFTs, glucose, magnesium, calcium

- ABG

- Blood cultures

- IV lorazepam

If lorazepam fails to stop the seizure, phenytoin should be given (18–20 mg/kg) at a rate of no more than 50 mg/min with cardiac monitoring. If this still does not terminate the seizures then urgent intensive care review is needed.

4.9   What immediate investigations would you request?

- FBC

- U&Es

- Glucose

- LFTs

- Calcium

- Magnesium

- Toxicology (depending on the circumstances)

- Anti-epileptic drug levels (of any already being taken by the patient)

- ABG – looking for any evidence of acidosis

Potential later investigations once patient is stabilised:

- CXR

- CT or MRI brain

- EEG

- LP

Epilepsy is the most common serious neurological disorder, affecting almost 1% of the UK population. There are many different Epilepsy syndromes and many different types and manifestations of seizures. Partial seizures are those that occur only in one part of the brain, with subsequent clinical features that are also localised. Consciousness may be unaltered, as in 'simple' partial seizures, or disturbed, as in 'complex' partial seizures. Generalised seizures occur throughout both cerebral hemispheres and have many different types but most of them are generalised tonic clonic seizures (GTCS). GTCS are what most people understand by an epileptic seizure, where the patient is unconscious and convulses rhythmically in all four limbs. Partial seizures may spread through the brain to become generalised seizures, with a clinical appearance reflecting this, for example, a twitching in the hand that spreads up the arm and becomes a GTCS. Absence seizures are another form of generalised seizure.

4.10   Which anti-epileptic drug (AED) would you commence?

The decision to commence an antiepileptic drug should be made by, or in conjunction with, a person trained in the management of patients with epilepsy, in accordance with NICE guidance. This should be done following a discussion with the patient of the risks and benefits, taking into account their prognosis and lifestyle. Lifestyle issues include employment insurance issues, child care, driving, alcohol, sleep deprivation, family planning and recreational drugs.

Generally anti-epileptic drugs are considered only after a second epileptic seizure or in high risk patients.

Anti-epileptic treatment is considered after a first unprovoked seizure if:

- There is a pre-existing neurological deficit or disease
- There is a structural abnormality on imaging
- An EEG shows possible epileptiform activity
- Patient and or their family consider the risk of having another seizure unacceptable

Generally speaking sodium valproate is used as first line AED in generalised seizures and carbamazepine is fist line choice in partial seizures.

Anti-epileptic	Side-effects
Carbamazepine	Allergic reactions, blurred vision, diplopia, ataxia, nausea
Phenytoin	Hypersensitivity reactions, drowsiness, ataxia, coarsening of facial features, gingival hyperplasia, hirsutism, anaemia, dyskinesias, tremor
Sodium Valproate	Transient hair loss, weight gain, hepatic damage, encephalopathy, pancreatitis, blood dyscrasias, amenorrhoea, teratogenicity

Table 20.24   Side-effects of AEDs

Case 3 Answers

4.11   What is the likely diagnosis?

Parkinson's disease is a progressive neurodegenerative condition characterised by Lewy bodies and loss of dopaminergic neurons in the substantia nigra of the midbrain. Predominantly, Parkinson's disease is a movement disorder but may also cause psychiatric problems (such as depression, dementia, behavioural disorder), autonomic disturbances, sleep disorders and pain; collectively referred to as the 'non-motor' symptoms.

4.12   What are the classical triad of motor symptoms/signs seen in this condition?

Bradykinesia, rigidity and resting tremor, with bradykinesia being the hallmark.

- Resting tremor 4–6 Hz, typically 'pill rolling' between thumb and index finger, often asymmetrical
- 'Lead pipe rigidity' (continuous degree of resistance throughout range of movement, regardless of velocity of movement)
- 'Cogwheel' rigidity (juddering on passive movement of a joint; this is the tremor superimposed on rigidity)

- Bradykinesia (the progressive decrement of repetitive movement in amplitude and speed)

- Postural instability is also a common feature.

A very useful pointer toward Parkinson's disease is that signs are almost always unilateral at first, and remain asymmetrical with the side of onset being worst.

UK Parkinson's Disease Society Brain Bank Criteria

Inclusion criteria:

- Bradykinesia

And at least one of the following:

- Rigidity

- 4–6 Hz rest tremor

- Postural instability

Exclusion criteria:

- History of:

   o   Repeated strokes with stepwise progression of parkinsonism features

   o   Repeated head injury

   o   Definite encephalitis

- Oculogyric crises

- Neuroleptic treatment at onset of symptoms

- More than one affected relative

- Sustained remission

- Strictly unilateral features after 3 yrs

- Supranuclear gaze palsy

- Cerebellar signs

- Early severe autonomic involvement

- Early severe dementia with disturbances of memory, language, and praxis

- Babinski sign

- Presence of cerebral tumour or communicating hydrocephalus on CT scan

- Negative response to large doses of L-dopa

- MPTP exposure

Supportive criteria

- (Three or more required for diagnosis of definite PD)

- Unilateral onset

- Rest tremor present

- Progressive disorder

- Persistent asymmetry affecting side of onset most

- Excellent response (70–100%) to levodopa

- Severe levodopa-induced chorea

- Levodopa response for 5 yrs or more

- Clinical course of 10 yrs or more

4.13   What other signs or symptoms might you see?

- Monotonous and quiet speech (+/– dysarthria)

- Masklike facies

- Dribbling

- Short shuffling steps with flexed trunk (festinant gait), 'freezing' of gait and difficulty turning

- Constipation

- Micrographia (writing decreasing in size with each word)

Parkinson's plus syndromes (or 'Atypical parkinsonism')

These are disorders often confused with Parkinson's disease, having rigidity and bradykinesia (referred to as 'parkinsonism') in common with it, but also with other specific features not seen in Parkinson's disease. They can usually be told apart from Parkinson's disease over time by their poor response to levodopa and their more rapid deterioration.

- 'Drug-induced' parkinsonism: commonly caused by neuroleptics (metoclopramide, prochlorperazine, haloperidol, antipsychotics)

- Vascular parkinsonism: common, often progressing in serial 'step-wise' sudden deteriorations

- Postenecephalic parkinsonism

- Progressive supranuclear palsy (Steele-Richardson-Olszewski syndrome, PSP): uncommon, supra-nuclear gaze palsy (affecting vertical eye movements), dementia, prominent early falls, poor prognosis

- Multisystem atrophy (Shy Drager Syndrome, MSA): uncommon, autonomic failure (orthostatic hypotension, incontinence), ataxia (cerebellar degeneration), poor prognosis

- Cortico-basal degeneration (CBD): rare, asymmetrical signs, dyspraxia, dementia, dystonia, involuntary movements 'alien limb phenomena'

- Carbon monoxide poisoning

- Wilson's disease

- Communication hydrocephalus

- Any basal ganglia lesion

4.14   How would you treat the patient?

Medicines which replace dopamine are the most effective, e.g. co beneldopa, cocareldopa. Side effects include nausea, vomiting, dyskinesias, fluctuating symptoms ('on-off syndrome').

Dopamine agonists can be taken with levodopa. Side effects of dopamine agonists include nausea, postural hypotension, oedema, and sleepiness (e.g. pramipexole, ropinorole, rotigotine) as well as behavioural disturbances such as excessive gambling which patients will not usually mention unless asked specifically.

MAOIs (monoamine oxidase B inhibitors) prevent the breakdown of dopamine and can be used to delay the need for levodopa or, in combination with levodopa, to reduce the on-off syndrome, by promoting its effect. Side effects include hypotension and dry mouth (e.g. selegiline, rasagiline).

COMT (catechol O-Methyl transferase) inhibitors stop the breakdown of dopamine. Side effects include nausea, diarrhoea and abdominal pain (e.g. entacapone, tolcapone).

Amantadine is an anti-viral drug by design that has a mild effect on symptoms and is sometimes used to control dyskinesias.

Anticholinergics block the action of acetylcholine in the brain and help to correct the balance between dopamine and acetylcholine. Side-effects include confusion, dry mouth, constipation and blurred vision. They are only used to help with tremor and are less effective than medications that replace dopamine. They should be avoided in cognitive impairment.

All this being said, the Parkinson's disease patient benefits most by having a good multi disciplinary team (consisting of doctors, nurses, occupational therapy, physiotherapy, dietician, speech therapist, etc) with support and advice readily available.

A surgical option exists in deep brain stimulation for patients who are refractory to medical treatment. Future therapies include gene therapy.

Case 4 Answers

4.15   What is the most likely diagnosis?

Multiple sclerosis.

4.16   What other signs or symptoms might you see in this condition?

- Visual: optic neuritis, diplopia, nystagmus, internuclear ophthalmoplegia
- Uhthoff's phenomenon – the worsening of neurologic symptoms in multiple sclerosis after periods of exercise and increased body heat (eg fever, after a hot bath)
- Lhermitte's sign – an electrical sensation that spreads from the back into the limbs on neck flexion and or extension
- Dysarthria
- Dysphagia
- Weakness
- Muscle spasms ('tonic' spasms)
- Ataxia
- Pain
- Paraesthesias
- Bowel problems – incontinence, diarrhoea, constipation
- Urinary problems – incontinence, frequency, retention

- Fatigue

- Cognitive impairment

- Depression

- Unstable mood

4.17   **What is the pathological basis of this disorder?**

Multiple sclerosis is characterised by plaques of demyelination (loss of myelin from axons) within the central nervous system, caused by an inflammatory process. Different areas of the CNS are involved over time, hence the name of this chronic condition. Loss of axons can also occur, leading to permanent damage.

MS is classified according to its clinical course over time as:

- Relapsing-remitting – most common variant, repeated attacks with recovery

- Primary progressive – continuous progression of symptoms from outset, worst prognosis

- Secondary progressive – continuous progression of symptoms following an initial relapsing-remitting disease course

- Benign – little disease activity for many years, minimal disability

- Progressive relapsing – accumulation of permanent disability over time, with superimposed relapses

4.18   **What further investigations would you do?**

Lumbar puncture – Cell count, protein, glucose and oligoclonal bands. Paired serum samples should be sent for glucose, protein and oligocloncal bands. Generally a white cell count of less than $50/mm^3$ (lymphocytes) is considered compatible with MS. Oligoclonal bands (a few bands of antibodies on electrophoresis) present in the CSF but not in the serum suggest intrathecal (within the CNS) antibody synthesis. This is seen in over 85% of MS patients. Protein and glucose are normally usual.

MRI brain and cervical spine with contrast – characteristic high signal lesions representing inflammation are seen next to the ventricles ('periventricular'), within the corpus callosum, in the brainstem cerebellar connections and in the cervical spine. The McDonald criteria (Ann Neurol 2001; 50: 121–127) are used as a tool in diagnosing MS, and rely strongly on the MRI appearance.

Visual evoked potentials – may show delayed conduction between the retina and the occipital cortex, indicating demyelination somewhere along the visual pathways. This is mainly of use where the MRI is not very supportive of MS, or where dissemination in time, but not space, is evident clinically.

4.19   **How would you manage this patient?**

There is no curative treatment available. Multidisciplinary care is the most important aspect of treatment, however, there are medications available to treat symptoms, as well as 'disease modifying therapies' aimed at reducing relapse rates and progression of disability.

Multidisciplinary Team

- Doctors, MS nurses, physiotherapists, occupational therapists, speech and language therapists, continence service, counselling services, social workers etc.

Symptomatic Treatment

- Spasticity – Baclofen, tizanidine, botulinum toxin

- Pain – Gabapentin, amitriptyline, pregabalin

- Fatigue – Amantadine, modafinil

- Depression – antidepressants

- Continence (bladder and bowel) – oxybutinin, desmopressin, tolterodine, intermitten self-catheterisation, laxatives

Specific Treatment and 'Disease modifying therapies'

- Corticosteroids are used for severe relapses to speed up any recovery that will occur naturally. A severe relapse is usually classed as one that has significantly affected activities of daily living.

- Beta Interferon reduces relapse rates by about 30% and is only used in relapsing-remitting or relapsing progressive disease. The route, dose and frequency of administration vary according to the product used.

- Glatiramer acetate is similarly used to reduce relapse rates.

- Natalizumab is a newer monoclonal antibody treatment used in patients with very active disease that can reduce relapse rates by up to 80% as well as reducing disability progression. Cost, practical considerations and complications limits its use.

Case 5 Answers

4.20   What is the likely diagnosis?

Cerebral metastases from carcinoma of the breast.

4.21   What is the likely cause?

These are features of raised intracranial pressure. It is likely the oedema around the tumour has increased or bleeding has occurred within the tumour.

Other features of raised intracranial pressure include visual loss, seizures and focal neurological deficit such as third and sixth cranial nerve palsies, known as 'false localising signs'. This results where pressure within the skull elsewhere creates traction on these nerves, leading to the false impression that those nerves themselves are where the problem lies.

Other causes of raised intracranial hypertension include infection (meningitis, cerebral abscess), benign tumours (meningioma), malignant tumours (glioblastoma, astrocytoma), malignant hypertension and idiopathic intracranial hypertension.

4.22   What management options are available for this patient?

- Multidisciplinary team meeting, to plan the overall care

- Neurosurgery – biopsy of mass or 'debulking' to reduce the mass effect
- Corticosteroids – high dose dexamethasone is often used, at least initially, to reduce the oedema surrounding cerebral tumours, in order to reduce symptoms
- Radiotherapy – curative, palliative, adjuvant
- Chemotherapy – monotherapy, adjuvant

Case 6 Answers

4.23   Which eye movements will be impaired/absent in the left eye?

All movements medially (adduction) and up (elevation) will be impaired/absent. As a result the eye is deviated inferiorly and laterally ('down and out').

4.24   What do these findings imply and how would you manage this patient?

This patient has a complete third nerve (CN III) palsy with a papillary sparing, in this situation an urgent cerebral angiogram (CTA, MRA, formal angiogram) is indicated to rule out compression from an enlarging posterior communicating artery aneurysm on the third cranial nerve. A complete third nerve palsy implies no movement in the affected muscles, whereas an incomplete palsy implies some residual movement.

CN III (oculomotor nerve) innervates four extraocular muscles (medial rectus superior rectus, inferior rectus and inferior oblique), levator palpebrae superioris (lifting the eyelid) and the iris sphincter (causing pupil constriction.)

Remember: SO_4 = CN **IV** innervates Superior Oblique, LR_6 = CN **VI** innervates Lateral Rectus.

A third nerve palsy with **pupillary sparing** (i.e. pupil is unaffected) is usually caused by microvascular ischaemia and management is usually observation as well as treatment of the underlying cause, usually diabetes or vascular disease. This usually improves over 2–3 months. If there is no further improvement then repeat brain imaging can be considered after this time, as well as clinical re-evaluation.

A third nerve palsy with **pupillary involvement** (dilated pupil) is commonly caused by a posterior communicating artery (PCOM) aneurysm, and so an MRI or CT angiogram should be performed. Formal fluorescence angiography may be required. The PCOM aneurysm compresses the parasympathetic nerve fibres as they travel on the top of the oculomotor nerve, causing the papillary dilatation. In microvascular damage to the oculomotor nerve, as above, these fibres are relatively unaffected. However, this is not a 100% reliable feature and so an angiogram is usually performed in either case and if an aneurysm is found referral to neurosurgery is required.

Central causes of an isolated CN III palsy:

- Tumours of the brainstem
- Vascular lesions (ischaemia or haemorrhage) of the brainstem
- Inflammatory/demyelination brainstem lesions
- Infectious pathology

Peripheral causes of an isolated CN III palsy:

- Compressive lesions
  - Tumour
  - Aneurysm (PCOM)

    o   Basal meningitis

    o   Orbital/cavernous sinus lesions

- Infiltration

    o   Infectious

    o   Neoplastic

- False localising sign (see case 5)

- Infarction (diabetes, hypertension)

Case 7 Answers

4.25   What is the likely diagnosis?

Left Bell's palsy – idiopathic facial nerve (CN VII) palsy.

4.26   Where is the lesion?

There is a lower motor neuron (LMN) lesion of the facial nerve. LMN facial weakness affects all the muscles of facial expression, whereas upper motor neuron (UMN) facial weakness (as in stroke for example) shows relative sparing of the upper facial muscles (forehead and eye closure). This is because the upper facial muscles are represented bilaterally in the brain and so retain some function when their supply from one hemisphere is disrupted.

4.27   What are the main causes of an isolated LMN facial palsy?

- Idiopathic (Bell's palsy)

- Pontine lesions – stroke, inflammation, neoplastic

- Trauma to skull

- Schwannoma of facial nerve

- Parotid infiltration

- Ramsay Hunt syndrome (associated with herpes infection)

- Lymphoma

- Sarcoidosis

- Lyme disease

4.28   How would you manage this patient?

Historically, combinations of corticosteroids and/or acyclovir have been used to treat Bell's palsy but recent evidence suggests that in early presentation (within a few days) corticosteroids are the treatment of choice. However, the majority will resolve spontaneously, but not always completely. Progressive lesions need to be evaluated for the presence of the above conditions.

Case 8 Answers

4.29   What is his Glasgow Coma Scale?

GCS is 12/15 (E2 V4 M6).

Remember that the Glasgow coma scale is composed of three parameters and the best response for each given stimulus is recorded, i.e. the best motor response, the best verbal response and the best eye response. The GCS was originally developed for monitoring the status of head injury patients and so has limitations when applied to medical causes of depressed consciousness such as drug toxicity and stroke.

	1	2	3	4	5	6
Eye opening	None	To pain	To speech	Sponta-neously		
Verbal	None	Incomprehensible sounds	Inappropriate words	Confused	Orientated speech	
Motor response	None	Abnormal Extension to pain	Abnormal Flexion to pain	Withdraws from pain	Localises to pain	Obeys commands

Table 20.25   Glasgow coma scale

4.30   What is the diagnosis?

Left hemisphere primary intracerebral haemorrhage (stroke) causing right-sided hemiparesis. His anticoagulation with warfarin is probably responsible for the haemorrhage.

A stroke is defined as an acute episode of focal or global loss of cerebral function, lasting for more than 24 hours, with a presumed vascular cause. There are 3 main types: ischaemic (80%), intracerebral haemorrhage (15%) and subarachnoid haemorrhage (5%). The cause of ischaemic stroke is usually atherosclerosis leading to thrombosis or embolism of a cerebral artery but there are many rarer causes which should be considered in younger patients.

A TIA (transient ischaemic attack) is defined by stroke-like symptoms and signs that resolve within 24 hours. Usually they resolve within 20 minutes and some people would prefer to think of longer TIAs as strokes. Patients who have had a high risk TIA (ABCD 2 score ≥ 4) should have aspirin 300 mg and be referred urgently for specialist assessment and investigation within 24 hours of onset of symptoms, as there is a 6–12% risk of stroke within one week. Patients with crescendo TIAs (≥ 2 within a week) should be treated as being at high risk of stroke, even though their ABCD 2 score may be below 4.

Risk Factor	Category	Score
Age	Age ≥ 60 yrs Age < 60 yrs	1 0
Blood pressure	SBP ≥ 140 mmHg or DBP ≥ 90 mmHg Other	1 0
Clinical features	Unilateral weakness Speech disturbance (no weakness) Other	2 1 0
Duration	≥ 60 minutes 10–59 minutes < 10 minutes	2 1 0
Diabetes	Yes No	1 0

Table 20.26   Calculating the ABCD2 score

4.31   What investigations would you do?

- Blood tests include FBC, U&Es, glucose and lipid profile (preferably fasting), ESR, coagulation screen, 12 lead ECG (primarily to look for atrial fibrillation)

- CXR

- CT head scan – this should ideally be performed within 24 hours, or immediately in patients presenting with acute stroke if any of the following apply to them:

  o   On anticoagulant treatment

  o   A known bleeding tendency (e.g. haemophilia) or thrombotic tendency (e.g. Factor V Leiden deficiency)

  o   Decreased level of consciousness (GCS < 13)

  o   Unexplained progressive or fluctuating symptoms

  o   Papilloedema, neck stiffness or fever

  o   Severe headache at onset of symptoms

  o   A young patient with no obvious risk factors (where an atypical and treatable cause of stroke is more likely)

- Ultrasound carotid Doppler scanning is routine for all ischaemic strokes

- Cerebral angiography where arterial dissection is suspected

- Echocardiography is mandatory where embolic stroke is a possibility (particularly young patients)

4.32   What are the important risk factors for stroke?

- Hypertension
- Smoking
- Diabetes mellitus
- Family history
- Increasing age
- Previous strokes/TIAs
- Vascular disease elsewhere (peripheral vascular, ischaemic heart disease)
- Hyperlipidaemia (especially familial)
- Hypercoagulable state
- Alcohol abuse
- Malignancy

4.33   How would you manage this patient?

The management of haemorrhagic stroke and ischaemic stroke (thromboembolic) differ considerably.

In thromboembolic stroke:

Thrombolysis: patients presenting with an acute stroke within three hours from onset are eligible to receive thrombolysis with alteplase (recombinant tissue plasminogen activator) if no contraindication exists and haemorrhagic stroke has been excluded with urgent CT imaging. This is usually performed by physicians specialising in the management of stroke. The aim is to reduce the future level of disability but this comes with the added risk of intracerebral haemorrhage due to the treatment itself. Consider blood pressure reduction to 185/110 mmHg or lower in patients who are candidates for thrombolysis.

Acute stroke units are the single most effective intervention in stroke for reducing disability. These units are staffed by multidisciplinary teams consisting of doctors, nurses, physiotherapists, occupational therapists, speech and language therapists and dieticians all trained in the management of acute stroke. Management includes early mobilisation, aggressive rehabilitation, preventing complications and managing swallowing and nutrition.

Aspirin 300 mg is usually used acutely, with a long term dose of 75 mg onwards.

Lipid lowering drugs are used routinely as secondary prevention as they reduce the risk of future stroke.

Anticoagulation is usually required if the patient has atrial fibrillation or some other source of embolus, as well as in those patients whose stroke is caused by a systemic thrombotic tendency (e.g. cancer).

In haemorrhagic stroke:

All supportive aspects of care are the same as for ischaemic stroke but clearly thrombolysis, anticoagulation and aspirin are not used acutely. Referral to Neurosurgery is indicated where bleeding causes a mass effect that might improve clinical status if it were evacuated surgically. Investigations may be required (to establish the cause of bleeding) that are not required in the management of ischaemic stroke.

Anterior cerebral artery occlusion:

- Contralateral hemiplegia (leg most affected)
- Gait apraxia
- Urinary incontinence
- Lower limb sensory loss

Middle Cerebral artery occlusion:

- Contralateral hemiplegia (face and arm most affected)
- Homonymous hemianopia
- Contralateral sensory loss
- Dysarthria
- Dysphasia
- Non dominant symptoms – aphasia, neglect, constructional apraxia

Posterior cerebral artery occlusion:

- Homonymous hemianopia +/– macula sparing
- Contralteral hemiplegia
- Ataxia
- Visual agnosia
- Cortical blindness

Case 9 Answers

4.34   What is the likely diagnosis?

Vascular dementia classically presents with a 'stepwise' progressive loss in higher function. The stepwise progression suggests multiple cerebrovascular events and the patients often have vascular risk factors and may have parkinsonism (see question 3). Modern neuroimaging can show the cerebrovascular damage.

Alzheimers disease normally presents with a more steady slow deterioration of a range of cognitive abilities but mainly recent memory. Later in the disease severe problems with language and praxis (e.g. dressing, eating) develop. Pathologically it is characterised by the accumulation of amyloid plaques and neurofibrillary tangles in the cerebral cortex, leading to cell death.

4.35   How would you assess cognitive function?

Brief bedside examination of cognitive function is useful as a pointer to the degree of cognitive impairment but is crude and not to be relied on for diagnosis. The abbreviated mental test (AMTS) consists of ten questions to assess memory, calculation and orientation. Further, more detailed methods of assessment include the 30-point mini mental state examination (MMSE), 100 point Addenbrooke's cognitive assessment (ACE) and detailed formal neuropsychological testing providing increasing detail and accuracy respectively.

The AMTS is as follows:

1. Patient's age

2. Current year

3. Approximate time of day

4. Date of birth

5. Name of current place/location

6. Recall of address (e.g. 42 West Street, given at the start of the test)

7. Count from 20 to 1 backwards

8. Year WW2 ended

9. Name the job of two persons (e.g. a doctor and a nurse)

10. Name of current prime minister or monarch

4.36   How would you manage this patient?

The main aim would be to ensure that they are safe in their home environment and that support networks exist for when future problems develop (since this is a degenerative condition).

Issues that need attention include the patient's housing, mobility, walking aids, continence, toilet facilities, activities of daily living, carer support (respite), social services input, physiotherapy and occupational therapy. A social worker and community psychiatric nurse usually play key coordinating roles in all of this, together with the patient's GP and hospital consultant.

This applies to the management of all dementias but in the case of vascular dementia optimisation of vascular risk factors is required to try and slow future progression of cognitive decline, usually including the use of daily aspirin.

Case 10 Answers

4.37   What diagnosis do his symptoms suggest?

Motor neurone disease.

This is an idiopathic, progressive neurological disorder characterised by symptoms of wasting and weakness and a mixture of both upper and lower motor neurone signs, often in one or more limbs. There is no diagnostic test for motor neurone disease and therefore it can only be diagnosed based on clinical signs and negative investigations for other possible diagnoses. However nerve conduction studies and electromyography (NCS/EMG) play a key role in supporting the diagnosis.

MND can cause a progressive bulbar palsy (affecting CN IX to XII which lie within the medulla/bulb of the brainstem) presenting as 'nasal' speech, dysarthria and dysphagia. The tongue may be wasted, flaccid and weak with fasciculations.

MND carries a poor prognosis but riluzole may slow the progression of the disease, adding a few precious months to the patient's life. A multidisciplinary approach is required to provide therapy (eventually in the form of palliation). The prognosis is worse if there is bulbar involvement, as respiratory complications occur earlier.

4.38   What investigations would you perform?

A clinically very obvious case may only require:

- MRI of the cervical spine and brainstem (to exclude local brainstem pathology)

- NCS/EMG – showing acute 'denervation' of the lower motor neurones

Cases where the diagnosis is not clear often require:

- Lumbar puncture – to exclude inflammatory/malignant processes

- Muscle biopsy – to exclude primary muscle disease

- Blood tests for other conditions (e.g. myasthenia gravis)

4.39   How would you manage this patient?

- Counselling for both the patient and their family

- Physiotherapy

- Occupational therapy

- Speech therapist if speech involvement, as well as to assess swallow

- Nutritional support (NG feeding in the first instance/acute setting then to proceed to PEG if necessary with worsening of symptoms)

- Multidisciplinary team input – as above

Case 11 Answers

4.40   What is the diagnosis?

Migraine with aura and migraine without aura. Migraine is incredibly common affecting around 18% of women and 6% of men. It is most common in young women. There are many varieties of migraine but the 'common' variety is a moderate to severe, usually unilateral, throbbing headache lasting 4–72 hours. It is usually accompanied by nausea or vomiting, photophobia and phonophobia (heightened sensitivity to noise), and mechanosensitivity (aggravation by activity). Patients with migraine classically are unable to continue routine activities during an attack and often go to bed. Migraine is a great source of disability and financial burden (from sick leave).

Visual disturbance prior to the headache is the commonest type of aura (90%), but aura can take the form of any focal neurological symptom, motor, sensory, language etc. Auras typically spread or evolve over 5–20 minutes, distinguishing them from TIAs.

4.41   How would you manage this patient?

In a young patient with a typical history such as this no investigations are required. Being on the combined oral contraceptive pill increases the risk of stroke, as does having migraine with aura, and so patients with aura are advised to discontinue the COCP and use a non-oestrogen containing contraception instead.

Acute attacks of migraine are first treated with high dose non-steroidal s (NSAIDs) such as aspirin 900 mg or ibuprofen 600 mg dispersed in water to aid absorption. A pro-kinetic anti-emetic such as metoclopramide or domperidone is often given in addition. Alternative acute treatment when NSAIDs fail includes the triptans, which are specific migraine drugs not used in other pain disorders. They should be avoided where possible during auras and in vascular disease of any sort.

Where migraine is complex, frequent or sufficiently troublesome preventative drugs are usually used to reduce attacks. These are an ever increasing group of drugs that are taken daily and include tricyclic antidepressants, beta-blockers and some anti-epileptic drugs.

Case 12 Answers

4.42   What is the diagnosis?

Vasovagal syncope (a simple 'faint') is very common occurring in at least 25% of adults at some point in their lives. The importance of syncope in neurology is that it is often misdiagnosed as epilepsy, with disastrous social and personal consequences for the patient, not to mention the problem that treatment for epilepsy does not help and may make things worse.

The cause of vasovagal syncope (neurocardiogenic syncope) is unknown but patients are entirely normal in-between. It usually occurs in response to a trigger or circumstance, as seen in this scenario, and only rarely occurs in sitting or lying positions. Phlebotomy, micturition, coughing, pain, and prolonged standing still (e.g. in church) are other common examples. The mechanism is that of sudden and excessive vagal nerve activity causing a drop in heart rate and vasodilatation leading to a drop in blood pressure. This quickly leads to collapse and upon becoming horizontal on the ground, cerebral perfusion returns and the patient recovers, though feels tired. The presence of urinary incontinence and tongue biting can also occur in vasovagal syncope and so are not as reliable indicators of a seizure as previously thought.

4.43   What features suggest this is a faint rather than a seizure?

The patient is alert – patients recover quickly from faints but are often still drowsy or unresponsive when arriving in accident and emergency following a seizure.

The 'prodrome' – the symptoms before this faint are termed 'pre-syncope' and are very characteristic. They do not occur prior to seizures but some seizures can have similar symptoms. However, more typical seizure features usually follow.

The jerking movements – the brief jerks in the limbs are a result of cerebral hypoxia, termed 'convulsive syncope'. They are random in distribution, and only brief. They are often confused with the prolonged, rhythmical, violent tonic convulsions of a generalised epileptic seizure.

The history – all his blackouts occur in the standing position and in provocative situations such as hot weather.

Skin colour – patients with syncope of any sort are very pale before and after collapsing. Whilst patients can appear pale during a seizure it is often not as severe and cyanosis is more likely.

4.44   How would you manage this patient?

It is likely this man requires only reassurance, advice on avoiding provocative situations where possible and advice on getting to the floor when his symptoms begin, to avoid injury. However, the priority in all cases of syncope is to examine the patient for evidence of structural heart disease. Cardiac syncope, resulting from arrhythmia, is not benign and can result in sudden death. This is why an ECG is mandatory for transient loss of consciousness. A family history of sudden death or a history of heart disease requires specialist attention.

Syncope is often orthostatic or 'postural' where the blood pressure drops more slowly, on standing. This is more common in elderly patients on drugs that lower blood pressure or in patients with autonomic failure (e.g. diabetes). This can be difficult to treat.

References

Case 1

Meningitis: http://meningitis.org/health-professionals/hospital-protocols-adults

Case 2

Epilepsy: http://www.nice.org.uk/CG20

Case 3

Hughes AJ et al. (1992) UK Parkinson's Disease Society Brain Bank Criteria (*J neurol Neurosurg Psychiatry* 55: 181–4)

Case 4

C H Polman, BM J Uitdehaag (2000) Drug treatment of multiple sclerosis, *BMJ* 321: 490–494

Case 5–7

K W Lindsay, I Bone (2004) Neurology and Neurosurgery Illustrated, Churchill Livingstone, 4th Edition

Geraint Fuller (2008) Neurological Examination Made Easy, Churchill Livingstone, 4th edition

Case 7

Table 20.25 Glasgow Coma scale. Teasdale G, Jennett B, Assessment of coma and impaired consciousness. A practical scale. *Lancet* 1974, 2:81–84.

Case 8

Acute stroke and TIA clinical guideline
http://www.nice.org.uk/guidance/index.jsp?action=download&o=38877

Stroke Guidelines: http://www.rcplondon.ac.uk/pubs/books/stroke/stroke_guidelines_2ed.pdf

Case 9

Dementia NICE guidelines http://www.nice.org.uk/CG42

Case 10

Riluzole for motor neurone disease, BMJ. 2001 September 8; 323(7312): 573.

http://archive.student.bmj.com/issues/07/12/education/460.php

Case 11

Review: several drugs, especially triptans, are effective for pain relief in acute migraine. Oldman AD, Smith LA, McQuay HJ, Moore A. *Evidence-Based Medicine* 2002; **7**: 180; doi:10.1136/ebm.7.6.180

Case 12

http://emedicine.medscape.com/article/811669-overview

Recommended further cases:

- Internuclear ophthalmoplegia
- Charcot Marie tooth
- Myasthenia gravis
- HSMN
- Guillain Barre
- Peripheral neuropathy
- Holmes Adie pupil
- Argyll Robertson pupil
- Friedreich's ataxia
- Huntingdon's disease
- Myotonic dystrophy
- Syringomyelia/ syringobulbia
- Neurofibromatosis
- Subacute combined degeneration of the cord

Infectious diseases answers

Case 1: Answers

5.1   What additional information would you ask for in the history?

- Pre-travel immunisations
- Whether they took malaria prophylaxis for the duration of the trip
- Food history
- Any ill contacts

- Any contact with animals or exposure to insect bites

- Any exposure to freshwater

5.2   What is the differential diagnosis?

The patient is a returned traveller with a non-specific influenza-like illness with jaundice and altered mental state. The differential diagnosis is wide and includes

- Malaria

- Acute viral hepatitis

- Rift Valley fever

- Rickettsial disease

- Typhoid

- Leptospirosis

- Encephalitis/Meningitis

5.3   What should your immediate management be?

Administer intramuscular benzylpenicillin to cover bacterial meningitis which can be rapidly fatal – this covers the most common organisms namely streptococcus pneumoniae and neisseria meningitides. The patient needs admitting to hospital immediately for further tests and treatment.

5.4   What initial investigations would you perform?

- Urgent CT head – in a patient with reduced consciousness evidence of raised intracranial pressure may need urgent neurosurgical intervention

- Blood glucose – exclude hypoglycaemia causing reduced consciousness

- Microscopy of thick and thin blood films – three negative slides at least six hours apart taken over 48–72 hours are necessary to exclude malaria. Thick blood smears are optimal for detecting parasites, thin blood smears are used to identify species and estimate the degree of parasitaemia

- Serology for rapid diagnostic tests which detect parasite enzymes (LDH) and plasmodial DNA or antigen are now routinely performed in UK laboratories and have high sensitivity

- Blood cultures

- Full blood count – anaemia, leucopenia, thrombocytopenia

- Urea and electrolytes – renal impairment

- Liver function tests – hyperbilirubinaemia, elevated ALT/AST

- Serum save – for other serological tests if initial investigations unrevealing

- Urinalysis – proteinuria/haematuria in leptospirosis, rarely haemoglobinuria in malaria

- Chest X-ray – pulmonary oedema and acute respiratory distress syndrome (ARDS) are complications of severe Plasmodium falciparum malaria

5.5   While waiting for the results of the investigations what treatment should be commenced?

Treatment to cover bacterial meningitis and viral encephalitis should be started empirically – intravenous ceftriaxone and aciclovir.

5.6   What investigation is it now safe to perform?

A lumbar puncture should be performed to exclude meningitis/encephalitis.

5.7   What further treatment and management should this patient have?

The CSF findings are consistent with a traumatic tap. Acyclovir and ceftriaxone can be stopped. The patient has severe malaria and intravenous quinine should be started and continued until the patient is able to take oral quinine. A second drug should always be given with quinine, e.g. doxycycline, started when the patient can swallow. Length of treatment is usually seven days. Repeat blood films at 24, 48 and 72 hours after initiating therapy should be performed to ensure parasitaemia level is decreasing. Adequate fluid hydration is important, and monitor for complications such as hypoglycaemia, seizures, renal impairment, ARDS and secondary bacterial pneumonia.

Malaria is a parasitic infection transmitted to humans by the bite of the female Anopheles mosquito. There are four main species – P. falciparum, P. vivax, P. ovale, P. malariae. Falciparum malaria can progress to a life-threatening illness within hours. The non-falciparum species cause a similar febrile illness but are rarely fatal.

Case 2

5.8   What are the possible diagnoses?

The patient has a typical mononucleosis-like syndrome with fever, malaise, sore throat and lymphadenopathy. Common causes of this syndrome are

- Epstein-Barr virus (EBV) infection (glandular fever), but a rash is unusual with no prior administration of antibiotics

- Cytomegalovirus (CMV) infection

- Toxoplasmosis

- Streptococcal pharyngitis

- Primary HIV infection/ acute seroconversion illness

5.9   What other questions would you like to ask in the history?

- Sexual history

- History of intravenous drug use

- Blood transfusions or medical procedures abroad

- Drug history and allergies

- Foreign travel history

- Occupation

5.10   What is the likely diagnosis?

- Primary HIV infection – incubation period for symptomatic infection is usually two to four weeks but can be as long as ten months. Typical symptoms are as above with fever, nonexudative pharyngitis, lymphadenopathy, maculopapular rash and headache with aseptic meningitis. The illness is self-limited and usually resolves after 2 weeks. Antibodies to HIV appear shortly before or after the acute illness. Lethargy and fatigue can persist for several months. Lymph nodes decrease in size but a modest degree of adenopathy can persist.

5.11   What investigations would you request?

- HIV antigen/antibody testing. These fourth generation assays reduces the 'window period' where antibodies are not detectable by detecting HIV-specific p 24 antigen.

- Monospot test for heterophile antibodies in EBV and EBV specific antibodies if monospot is negative

- Serum sample for CMV and toxoplasmosis serology

- Full blood count – leucopenia, lymphopenia and thrombocytopenia suggest viral aetiology, atypical lymphocytosis in EBV

- Liver function tests – may be deranged in primary HIV infection, EBV, CMV

- Throat swabs for bacterial culture

5.12   How would you counsel her for an HIV test?

- Obtaining informed consent for HIV testing should be done in the same way informed consent is obtained for any other medical investigation. Main emphasis should be on the benefits of knowing their HIV status so treatment can be offered and details of how the results will be given (UK National Guidelines for HIV testing 2008). As with any other medical test, confidentiality should be maintained. Lengthy counselling is not necessary unless the patient specifically raises any other issues. Today HIV is a treatable illness and majority of those living with HIV infection remain well on treatment. Written consent is unnecessary but the offer of an HIV test and any relevant discussion surrounding it should be documented in the case record.

5.13   What should be the management now?

- Before giving a positive result, you should be certain of local specialist services available. Those testing positive HIV positive for the first time should be seen by a member of the local GUM/HIV team as soon as possible and preferably within 48 hours. More detailed post-test counselling will be provided then, including management of the current stage of disease and contact tracing.

- As in any 'breaking bad news' situation, the positive HIV test should be conveyed face-to-face with a clear and direct approach, in a confidential setting.

Case 3

5.14   What other questions would you ask in the history?

- When the rash first appeared

- Previous history of disseminated varicella zoster virus (VZV) infection (chickenpox)

- Past medical history or drug history that may cause immunosuppresion

5.15   What is the likely diagnosis?

- Herpes zoster ophthalmicus – caused by reactivation of VZV within the trigeminal ganglion. Lifelong latent infection is established in the sensory dorsal root ganglia after primary infection. Reactivation can occur along one or more dermatomes, most commonly thoracic or lumbar. Characteristic dermatome distribution of vesicles usually prevent diagnostic confusion. The herpes simplex virus rarely can cause similar segmental distribution.

5.16 **What is the significance of the vesicles on his nose and what is this sign known as?**

- Hutchinson's sign – it indicates involvement of the nasociliary branch of the first (ophthalmic) division of the trigeminal nerve. This branch innervates the cornea and nasal cavity. The patient is at high risk of corneal involvement (keratitis) which may threaten his sight.

5.17 **How would you manage the patient?**

- Antiviral therapy should be initiated within 72 hours of onset of rash to maximise benefits of treatment, namely earlier healing and prevention of complications, in this case keratitis and in patients older than 50 years, post-herpetic neuralgia. Oral aciclovir (800 mg five times a daily for 7–10 days) is well-tolerated. A newer related drug with better bioavailability and efficacy is now available, valacyclovir.

- The patient should be referred to the eye clinic the same day for assessment and adjunctive topical steroid therapy to prevent/control any corneal damage.

5.18 **What is the clinical syndrome he describes called? Is encephalitis a concern?**

Ramsay-Hunt syndrome (herpes zoster oticus) – a constellation of facial paralysis, ear pain, vesicles in the ipsilateral external auditory canal/auricle and loss of sensation of the anterior two-thirds of the tongue. This is shingles arising from the geniculate ganglion affecting the facial (seventh) nerve. Fifth, ninth and tenth cranial nerves are also frequently involved.

Zoster-associated encephalitis is more common in those with cranial or cervical dermatomal involvement. Other risk factors include two or more episodes of shingles in the past and impaired cell-mediated immunity. While normal hosts can develop VZV- encephalitis, majority of cases have been reported in immunosuppressed patients.

5.19 **What should you say to the patient?**

There is a risk of transmitting VZV infection to his wife. Although herpes zoster is not transmitted by droplet spread as in chickenpox, direct contact with his vesicular lesions to mucosal surfaces of household contacts may still result in transmission. While activation of latent infection in pregnant women is not problematic, disseminated primary infection is a risk to the mother and fetus. Varicella pneumonia is reported to be more severe, although not more frequent , in pregnant women. Intrauterine transmission can cause congenital varicella syndrome (pigmented rash, hypoplastic lower limbs, clubbed feet, chorioretinitis, optic atrophy and failure to thrive) in up to 2% of cases of maternal chickenpox before 20 weeks gestation. Neonatal chickenpox, which has a mortality rate of 25%, is a risk, with maternal chickenpox occurring one week pre- or post-delivery.

If the patient's wife has a convincing history of previous chickenpox or shingles, immune protection can be assumed and reassurance given. If there is uncertainty, the wife's susceptibility to varicella should be determined urgently. If she is varicella zoster-IgG negative she may be offered varicella zoster immunoglobulin.

Case 4

5.20 **What other questions should you ask?**

- Haemoptysis

- Fevers or sweats

- Ankle swelling, orthopnea, paroxysmal nocturnal dyspnoea

- Past medical history including previous chest infections, history of ischaemic heart disease

- Drug history including recent antibiotics

- Smoking history

- Full occupational history

- Any contact with tuberculosis

5.21   What are the differential diagnoses?

- Lung malignancy

- Pneumonia

- TB

5.22   What investigations would you do?

- Chest X-ray

- Full blood count – anaemia in malignancy, neutrophilia in infection

- Blood cultures

- Sputum for culture and acid-fast stain – at least three specimens with morning sputum samples having the highest yield

5.23   What should the management be?

As a definitive diagnosis has not been established and the patient is unable to produce good quality sputum, he should undergo induced sputum production with nebulised hypertonic saline or a bronchoscopy with bronchoalveolar lavage. Induced sputum is safer and less costly, but bronchoscopy may be advantageous in obtaining specimens to rule out malignancy. Although the clinical suspicion of tuberculosis is high anti-tuberculous therapy should ideally only be started once adequate culture specimens are available so sensitivities can be determined. Resistance, although still rare in the UK, is a serious problem.

5.24   What should be done prior to starting treatment?

He should be counselled about potential side effects. Rifampicin causes orange-red discolouration of the urine and other secretions. Isoniazid can cause peripheral neuropathy particulary in those with nutritional deficiency or alcoholism, pyridoxine is given to minimise this. Pyrazinamide can cause hyperuricaemia. All three can cause a rash and hepatic toxicity, the risk of which is increased with alcohol intake. His visual acuity and colour vision should be checked as ethambutol can cause optic neuritis.

5.25   What else should be done?

TB is a notifiable disease and the local health protection unit should be informed so that contact tracing can be initiated.

As he is smear-positive on his BAL but not sputum, he can be managed as non-infectious on a standard ward unless his sputum becomes smear-positive after bronchoscopy, there are other immunocompromised patients on the ward, or he is suspected of having drug-resistant TB eg contact with a case of known MDR-TB.

References

Case 1

1. Malaria Prophylaxis. Clinical Knowledge Summaries http://www.cks.nhs.uk/malaria_prophylaxis

2. Longmore M, Wilkinson I, Turmezei Tom, Cheung Chee. (7th Edition.) (2008) *Oxford Handbook of Clinical Medicine.* Oxford University Press. Oxford.

Case 2

1. Longmore M, Wilkinson I, Turmezei Tom, Cheung Chee. (7th Edition.) (2008) *Oxford Handbook of Clinical Medicine.* Oxford University Press. Oxford.

Case 3

1. Longmore M, Wilkinson I, Turmezei Tom, Cheung Chee. (7th Edition.) (2008) *Oxford Handbook of Clinical Medicine.* Oxford University Press. Oxford.

Case 4

1. Tuberculosis. Clinical diagnosis and management of tuberculosis, and measures for its prevention and control. Quick reference guide. Clinical guideline 33. March 2006. National Institute for Health and Clinical Excellence. http://www.nice.org.uk/nicemedia/pdf/CG33quickreffguide.pdf

2. Parker R, Sharma Asheesh. 2nd edition. 2005. *Crash Course General Medicine.* Mosby.

3. Longmore M, Wilkinson I, Turmezei Tom, Cheung Chee. (7th Edition.) (2008) *Oxford Handbook of Clinical Medicine.* Oxford University Press. Oxford.

Recommended further cases

- Notifiable diseases
- MRSA
- C. Difficile
- Sexually transmitted infections

Endocrinology answers

Case 1:

6.1   What is the likely diagnosis?

This is new onset diabetes presenting with diabetic ketoacidosis. Diabetes mellitus is a disorder caused by the lack or reduced effectiveness of endogenous insulin. It is characterised by raised blood glucose. It is a very common disorder. Type 1 Diabetes Mellitus is insulin dependent and type 2 non-insulin dependent. Diabetic ketoacidosis is an emergency complication of type 1 diabetes. Precipitating features are infection such as UTI, chest infection.

6.2   What investigations would you do?

- Venous blood glucose
- U&Es, amylase
- FBC

- Arterial blood gas

- Blood culture

- Urine culture/urine dipstick to look for ketonuria

- Chest X-ray

- ECG

6.3   How should you manage this patient?

- IV insulin – 6 units/hour, measure glucose hourly and aim for a fall of 3–6 mmol per hour. Once the blood glucose is < 12 mmol, reduce the rate to 3 units/hour and change over to 5% dextrose. (When blood glucose is < 6 mmol/l, reduce insulin infusion to 2 units/hr and change over to 10% dextrose. When glucose < 3 mmol/l, reduce insulin to 1 units/hr.) Never stop insulin when managing DKA in first 24 hrs.

- IV fluids – use normal saline:

Volume	Duration to give fluid
1L	30 min
1L	1 hour
1L	2 hours
1L	4 hours
1L	8 hours

Table 20.27   IV fluid regime for DKA

- Montior U&Es – if potassium > 5.5 mmol/L there is no need for replacement. Check in one hour.

- If potassium 3.5–5.5 mmol/L, add 20 mmol/L KCL to the bag of fluid and recheck.

- If potassium < 3.5 mmol/L, add 40 mmol/L KCL to the bag of fluid.

6.4   What are the complications of this?

- Cerebral oedema

- Gastric aspiration

6.5   What should you tell him?

Type 1 Diabetes is an autoimmune condition with both genetic and environmental factors. Most cases present before the age of 20 and it is caused because the B cells in the pancreas are destroyed and these are the cells which normally release insulin.

Diabetes is diagnosed on the basis of history (symptoms of polyuria, polydipsia and unexplained weight loss), plus:

- a random venous plasma glucose concentration ≥ 11.1 mmol/l

- or a fasting plasma glucose concentration ≥ 7.0 mmol/l

- or two-hour plasma glucose concentration > = 11.1 mmol/l, two hours after 75 g anhydrous glucose in an oral glucose tolerance test (OGTT)

If there are no symptoms then two readings are needed.

6.6   What will he need to do from now on?

- He will need to be on lifelong insulin
- He will need education about how to inject the insulin and how to self-monitor his blood sugars
- He will need information about hypoglycaemic attacks and also DKA
- He will need information about the complications of diabetes

6.7   What are the complications of this condition?

Microvascular complications:

- Diabetic retinopathy
- Diabetic neuropathy
- Diabetic nephropathy

Macrovascular complications:

- Cerebrovascular disease
- Cardiovascular disease
- Peripheral vascular disease

Case 2: Answers

6.8   What does this result mean?

A fasting plasma glucose of 6.1–6.9 mmol/L is termed impaired fasting glycaemia. This should be followed up with an oral glucose tolerance test to exclude diabetes.

6.9   What does this result mean?

This is not a positive glucose tolerance test. A result of 7.8–11.0 mmol/L is termed impaired glucose tolerance.

6.10   What is the management of this?

Having impaired glucose tolerance puts you at increased risk of cardiovascular disease and so the patient should have an assessment of his risk factors and yearly screening of his fasting plasma glucose.

Case 3: Answers

6.11   What is the initial management of type 2 diabetes?

- Diet modification
- Exercise
- If these fail, then medications
- Insulin as a final resort

6.12   What causes type 2 diabetes?

Type 2 diabetes usually has a late onset and is often associated with obesity. It is the result of a combination of insulin resistance and also impaired secretion of insulin. Patients do not usually require insulin but those not controlled by diet need oral hypoglycaemic agents.

6.13   What medication would you start for her?

Metformin – this is a biguanide. It increases glucose uptake. It does not cause weight gain as a side effect and so is used in obese people. It also does not tend to cause hypoglycaemia. It does cause gastrointestinal side effects such as nausea and diarrhoea.

6.14   What are the side effects of this?

Gliclazide is a sulphonylurea. These increase insulin secretion and can promote hypoglycaemic attacks and also cause weight gain.

6.15   What should the management be?

- Admit the patient to hospital
- 50 mls of 50% dextrose (or 100 ml of 20% dextrose)

This is a hypoglycaemic attack.

6.16   What are the symptoms of a hypoglycaemic attack?

Hypoglycaemia can be caused by too much insulin or too little glucose. Patients usually get warning signs and symptoms such as sweating, palpitations, hunger, dizziness, confusion, abnormal behaviour.

Case 4: Answers

6.17   What other questions would you ask her?

- Change in diet
- Change in appetite
- Medical problems – diabetes, thyroid problems
- Drug history
- Smoking and alcohol history
- Family history of any medical problems
- Any other symptoms

6.18   What is the likely diagnosis?

- Primary autoimmune hypothyroidism. Hypothyroidism is the clinical syndrome where the circulating levels of thyroid hormones are deficient. There is a higher incidence in women compared to men and it peaks in the fifth and sixth decades. Its onset is insidious and symptoms may go unnoticed for a very long time.

6.19   What investigations would you do?

- Thyroid function tests – free T3, T4 and TSH
- Thyroid peroxidase antibodies

6.20   What are the causes of this condition?

- Autoimmune thyroiditis – Hashimoto's thyroiditis, atrophic thyroiditis
- Subacute (De Quervain's thyroiditis) is typified by tender thyroid enlargement and transient thyrotoxicosis early in the illness.
- Riedel's thyroiditis
- Drug induced – thionamide drugs (carbimazole), propylthiouracil, amiodarone, lithium
- Iatrogenic hypothyroidism – following thyroidectomy, radioiodine eg for Graves, external beam radiotherapy to the neck
- Iodine deficiency
- Congenital dysgenesis, dyshormonogenesis

6.21   What other symptoms and signs can occur with this condition?

- Goitre
- Dry, scaly, thickened skin
- Alopecia
- Hoarse voice
- Anaemia
- Carpal tunnel syndrome, cerebellar ataxia, depression
- Bradycardia
- Angina
- Pericardial or pleural effusions
- Constipation
- Menorrhagia

6.22   How would you manage this patient?

- The patient will need replacement therapy with oral thyroxine for life with a starting dose of 25 micrograms daily. The dose should be titrated at regular intervals (every six to eight weeks) usually to a dose of 100 or 150 micrograms daily, aiming to restore serum TSH to the lower half of the normal range. (TSH should be checked six weeks after starting treatment or after changing the thyroxine dose).
- Starting dose and rate of titration are more cautious in the elderly and in patients with ischaemic heart disease as the increase in heart rate may precipitate worsening angina, MI or even death. Therefore a dose of 25 micrograms is commonly used, perhaps with a beta blocker.

Case 5: Answers

6.23   What other questions would you ask her?

- Any other symptoms

- Medical problems – heart problems, thyroid problems
- Drug history
- Family history of any medical problems
- Occupation – stressful job

6.24   What is the likely diagnosis?

Hyperthyroidism secondary to Graves' disease (80% of cases of hyperthyroidism). TSH receptor antibodies stimulate follicular cells in the thyroid gland, causing uncontrolled production of thyroid hormones.

6.25   What are the causes of this condition?

- Primary causes– Graves' disease, toxic nodule, multinodular goitre, Hashimoto's thyroiditis, iodine induced, excess thyroid hormone replacement, postpartum thyroiditis
- Secondary causes– pituitary or excess TSH hypersecretion, hydatiform mole, factitious

The components of Graves' disease are hyperthyroidism with goitre, eye changes, pretibial myxoedema.

6.26   What other clinical findings might you see?

- Diffuse goitre with bruit
- Sinus tachycardia
- Atrial fibrillation
- Sweating/warm peripheries
- Lid lag, lid retraction
- Proximal myopathy
- Swollen eyelids
- Chemosis
- Proptosis
- Ophthalmoplegia
- Diplopia
- Corneal involvement
- Sight loss
- Pretibial myxoedema
- Thyroid acropachy

6.27   What investigations would you request?

- Thyroid function tests
- Thyroid stimulating hormone receptor antibodies

6.28   **What treatment options are there for this patient and what are the side effects of these?**

- He should be referred to hospital care at diagnosis

- Medical treatment with anti-thyroid drugs- carbimazole (can cause agranulocytosis and so immediate attention must be sought if the patient develops sore throat, fever or mouth ulcers) or propylthiouracil. This can be used either as a block and replace regime, where a high dose is used to control the hyperthyroidism and thyroxine is given to prevent hypothyroidism (this is usually for 6–12 months), or the titration method where once euthyroidism is achieved with a high dose, a lower dose is given to keep the patient euthyroid. This is usually 18 months. Remission is about 50% after treatment stops.

- Beta-blockers

- Radioactive iodine – this is contraindicated in children, pregnancy and lactating women. It can worsen the eye condition in Graves' ophthalmopathy and is worse in smokers. Radioactive iodine causes hypothyroidism in almost 50 to 60% cases after its use. This effect is irreversible and the patient will need thyroxine supplement lifelong thereafter.

- Lugol's iodine

- Surgery subtotal thyroidectomy – can cause Hypothyroidism, recurrent thyrotoxicosis, hypoparathyroidism, recurrent laryngeal nerve injury

Case 6: Answers

6.29   **What is the likely diagnosis?**

Addison's disease – primary adrenocortical deficiency from the destruction of the adrenal cortex and so there are reduced levels of glucocorticoids, mineralocorticoids and sex steroids.

Addison's disease is associated with an increased incidence of:

- Hashimoto's thyroiditis

- Type I diabetes mellitus

- Graves' disease

- Premature ovarian failure

- Idiopathic hypoparathyroidism

- Pernicious anaemia

- Mucocutaneous candidiasis

- Vitiligo

- Alopecia

6.30   **What are the other causes of this condition?**

- Infection – tuberculosis, fungal infections (histoplasmosis)

- Autoimmune adrenalitis (most common cause in UK)

- Primary or secondary neoplasia

- Bilateral adrenal haemorrhage

- Enzyme defects e.g. 21 hydroxylase deficiency, 11b hydroxylase deficiency
- Iatrogenic – prolonged use of steroids followed by a sudden withdrawal, adrenalectomy

6.31   **What other clinical features would you expect to see associated with this condition?**

- Nausea, vomiting
- Anorexia
- Hypotension with postural drop
- Abdominal pain
- Diarrhoea
- Vitiligo

6.32   **What investigations would you do and what would you expect to see from the results?**

- Urea and electrolytes – hyponatraemia, hyperkalaemia, uraemia
- Plasma ACTH – > 80 ng per litre
- Serum renin – raised due to sodium depletion
- Aldosterone
- Blood glucose – hypoglycaemia
- Adrenal-cortical antibodies
- Abdominal X-ray – calcified adrenals of TB
- Chest X-ray – malignancy, TB

6.33   **Which tests will confirm the diagnosis?**

Synachten test – synachten is tetracosactrin, a synthetic analogue of ACTH and so stimulates cortisol secretion from a normal adrenal gland. Serum cortisol levels are taken at 0 min and 30 min post injection of synachten (250 micrograms). In healthy people, after the synachten is given the cortisol should rise, whereas in hypoadrenalism the patient can not raise their cortisol in response to synachten. Addison's can be excluded if the initial cortisol is > 140 nmol/L and the second cortisol is > 500 nmol/L.

A prolonged synachten test is similar to the short synachten test but a higher dose is given and it is repeated for three successive days. Primary adrenal insufficiency is diagnosed if the plasma cortisol is not increased as much as expected after the last dose. If the adrenal insufficiency is secondary to a pituitary deficiency in ACTH, then the cortisol is increased with this test.

6.34   **How will you manage this patient in an acute presentation?**

- IV access, IV fluids
- Since the entire adrenal cortex is destroyed, production of both cortisol and aldosterone is lost. Therefore the patient needs to be treated with oral hydrocortisone and fludrocortisone. (if vomiting, will need IV hydrocortisone)
- Patients should be advised to carry a steroid card and medicalert bracelet with them at all times
- Patient should be advised to increase dose of steroids in case of mild illness

Case 7: Answers

6.35   What is the likely diagnosis?

Acromegaly; this is a rare condition caused by excessive pituitary growth hormone production.

6.36   What are the causes of this condition?

Acromegaly results from excessive secretion of growth hormone, usually from a somatotroph pituitary adenoma. Excessive growth hormone and insulin-like growth factor (IGF 1) cause soft tissue expansion which causes enlargement of the extremities and coarsening of facial features. Metabolic effects are also prominent, especially insulin resistance and hypertension, and risk of cardiovascular and respiratory disease is substantially elevated.

The majority of patients with acromegaly present with pituitary macroadenomas, tumours greater than 1cm in diameter that typically expand outside the pituitary fossa and may cause headaches, hyperprolactinaemia, hypopituitarism, cranial nerve palsies, compression of optic chiasm causing visual field defects.

A useful aid in making the diagnosis of acromegaly is comparing old photographs with their present appearance.

6.37   What investigations would you do?

- Random GH & IGF1 are done as screening test
- Oral glucose tolerance test showing failure to suppress serum growth hormone
- MRI of pituitary – to look for a pituitary tumour

6.38   List other signs or symptoms that you would expect to see in this condition?

- Sweating
- Macroglossia
- Prognathism
- Interdental separation
- Hypertension
- Carpal tunnel syndrome
- Obstructive sleep apnoea
- Kyphosis
- Headache
- Bitemporal hemianopia
- Hypopituitarism

6.39   How would you manage this patient?

- Surgery – hypophysectomy (usually transphenoidal approach)
- Pituitary radiotherapy – only if surgery is contraindicated or if surgery fails
- Medical treatment with somatostatin analogue eg octreotide

- Dopamine agonist e.g. cabergoline, bromocriptine
- Growth hormone receptor antagonist e.g. pegvisomant

6.40   What are the complications of this condition?

- Hypertension
- Diabetes
- Ischaemic heart disease, heart failure
- Obstructive sleep apnoea
- Colon cancer and polyps – routine colonoscopy recom-mended

Case 8: Answers

6.41   What other questions would you ask her?

- Any muscle weakness
- Mood disturbance
- Loss of libido or impotence
- Medical problems
- Family history

6.42   What is the likely diagnosis?

Cushings syndrome – this is a set of clinical features as a result of high plasma cortisol levels. It is usually iatrogenic.

Causes are:

- Exogenous glucocorticoid exposure – iatrogenic secondary to steroids for example patients with Rheumatoid arthritis or respiratory problems, illicit drugs
- Endogenous glucocorticoid exposure – ACTH dependent: corticotroph pituitary adenoma (Cushings disease), ectopic ACTH syndrome
- ACTH independent: adrenal tumours

6.43   What other features are there in this condition?

- 'Moon' face
- Facial plethora
- 'Buffalo hump' Interscapular fat pad
- Purple striae
- Hirsutism
- Menstrual disturbance
- Loss of libido
- Lethargy
- Depression

- Psychosis

- Osteopenia impaired glucose tolerance.

6.44   What investigations would you do and what would you expect these to show?

- Midnight cortisol – cortisol will be high. Normally cortisol will be at a nadir (<50 nmol/L).

- 24-hour urinary free cortisol – cortisol will be high and diurnal variation is lost.

- Overnight (low dose) dexamethasone suppression test – dexamethasone is a synthetic steroid which normally suppresses ACTH and CRH secretion and hence cortisol secretion. If there is failed suppression then the patient has Cushing's syndrome.

Once Cushing's syndrome is confirmed the cause should be found by:

- Plasma ACTH – raised in ACTH dependent causes but will be undetectable in adrenal tumours which secrete excess cortisol as this will suppress the pituitary ACTH secretion.

- Low potassium – suggests ectopic ACTH production (found in 90%).

- High dose dexamethasone suppression test – in pituitary Cushing's the cortisol level falls by > 50% of basal values. If the cause is an ectopic tumour then the cortisol is not suppressed.

- Corticotrophin-releasing hormone test – exaggerated rise of serum cortisol occurs in 80% of pituitary Cushing's disease. Response in ectopic ACTH is extremely rare.

- Bilateral inferior petrosal sinus sampling (for plasma ACTH levels) – high central to peripheral ACTH levels are diagnostic of Cushing's disease.

- CT or MRI pituitary.

- Adrenal CT.

6.45   How would you manage this patient?

Surgery is the treatment of choice usually with a trans-sphenoidal approach. The aim is to render serum cortisol undetectable. Post-operative radiotherapy will be required if this is not achieved. Remission is achieved in 75–80% of cases.

Pituitary irradiation is now reserved for patients in whom surgery was not entirely successful or was contraindicated or unacceptable. Treatment may be necessary for several years but remission occurs in about 60% of cases.

Metyrapone or ketoconazole can be used to lower serum cortisol pre-operatively or as an adjuvant therapy. Metyrapone blocks cortisol synthesis and is effective within 2 hours. It may worsen hirsutism in women. Ketoconazole acts on the adrenal glands to inhibit cortisol and androgen secretion. Occasionally, bromocriptine may be used.

If the cause is due to the adrenals, then treatment is with bilateral adrenalectomy. Nelson's syndrome is a potential complication and pituitary irradiation is recommended as prophylaxis although not always successful.

References

Case 1, 2 &3

1. Longmore M, Wilkinson I, Turmezei Tom, Cheung Chee. (7th Edition.) (2008) *Oxford Handbook of Clinical Medicine*. Oxford University Press. Oxford.

2. Parker R, Sharma A. 2nd edition. 2005. *Crash Course General Medicine*. Mosby.

3. Type 1 diabetes: diagnosis and management of type 1 diabetes in adults. Quick reference guide. Clinical guideline 15. July 2004. National Institute for Health and Clinical Excellence. http://www.nice.org.uk/nicemedia/pdf/CG015adultsquickrefguide.pdf

4. Type 2 Diabetes. Full guideline. Clinical guideline 66. May 2008. National Institute for Health and Clinical Excellence. http://www.nice.org.uk/nicemedia/pdf/CG66FullGuideline0509.pdf

5. Type 2 Diabetes. Clinical Knowledge Summaries. http://www.cks.nhs.uk/diabetes_type_2

Case 4

1. Hypothyroidism. GP Notebook. http://www.gpnotebook.co.uk

2. Hypothyroidism. Clinical Knowledge Summaries. http://www.cks.nhs.uk/hypothyroidism

Case 5

1. Hyperthyroidism. Clinical Knowledge Summaries. http://www.cks.nhs.uk/hyperthyroidism

2. Hyperthyroidism. GP Notebook. http://www.gpnotebook.co.uk

Case 6

1. Addison's disease. GP Notebook. http://www.gpnotebook.co.uk

2. Klauer KM. Adrenal Insufficiency and Adrenal Crisis. Emedicine. http://emedicine.medscape.com/article/765753-overview

Case 7

1. Khandwala HM. Acromegaly. Emedicine. http://emedicine.medscape.com/article/116366-overview

2. Acromegaly. GP Notebook. http://www.gpnotebook.co.uk

Case 8

1. Adler GK. Cushing Syndrome. Emedicine. http://emedicine.medscape.com/article/117365-overview

2. Cushing syndrome. GP Notebook. http://www.gpnotebook.co.uk

Cases 1–8

Turner HE, Wass JAH (2003). *Oxford Handbook of Endocrinology and Diabetes*. Oxford University Press. Oxford.

Recommended further cases

- Conn's syndrome
- Phaeochromocytoma
- SIADH
- Diabetes Insipidus
- Hyper/hypoparathyroidism

Renal answers

Case 1: Answers

7.1   What is the differential diagnosis?

This includes other causes of acute abdominal pain

- Renal – stones, pyelonephritis, ureteric obstruction, acute renal infarction, renal abscess, renal rupture, renal tumour

- Ureteral tumour, testicular tumour

- Gastrointestinal – diverticulitis, appendicitis, bowel ischaemia, bowel obstruction, inflammatory bowel disease

- Cardiovascular – ischaemia, aortic aneurysm

- Prostatitis

7.2   What other questions would you ask about?

- Any previous episode like this – recurrence rates of renal stones can be high

- Any fever or weight loss

- Any urinary symptoms – low urine volume is associated with stone formation. Has there been any blood in the patient's urine?

- What is his diet like – enquire about high calcium intake, oxalate. Most stones are composed of calcium salts (60–80% are oxalate or phosphate)

- Drug history – medications such as vitamin D and calcium supplements and diuretics can be associated with stone formation

- Medical history – various diseases are associated with stone formations such as hyperparathyroidism, Crohn's disease, malabsorption, hypertension, gout, renal tubular acidosis. Are there any known kidney abnormalities such as ureteric strictures or obstruction.

- Family history of medical problems – there is a strong family history of stone formation

7.3   What is the most likely diagnosis?

- Renal colic should be suspected in any person that presents with abrupt onset of severe unilateral abdominal pain which originates in the flank or loin and radiates to the groin or testicles in men or labia in women. The pain is often associated with nausea and vomiting and microscopic haematuria. Peritoneal signs are absent and so this can rule out other causes for the pain.

  Independent predictors of acute renal colic are haematuria, loin tenderness, renal tenderness, duration of pain lasting < 12 hours, normal appetite and male sex. These in combination have a very high sensitivity and specificity in detecting renal colic. It is important to note, though, that haematuria can be absent in acute renal colic and is not in itself diagnostic.

- With the information about the patient eating lots of chocolate and drinking lots of tea this makes it a likely calcium oxalate stone.

7.4   What other investigations would you request?

- Urine dipstick – check for haematuria

- Urine microscopy, culture and sensitivity – to exclude UTI

- Bloods for urea, creatinine and electrolytes – important to know renal function as medications such as diclofenac can affect it if it is already reduced

- Bloods for calcium, phosphate and urate – may reveal hypercalcaemia in which case causes of this need to be investigated such as hyperparathyroidism. A high serum urate along with a radiolucent stone can support the diagnosis of a uric acid stone

- X-ray of kidneys, ureters and bladder – 90% of kidney stones are radio-opaque and contain calcium

- Renal ultrasound – this has the advantage that it is non-invasive. It will exclude hydronephrosis or hydroureter. However, small stones are difficult to diagnose.

- Intravenous urogram – this often used as a first line investigation for suspected ureteric stones. It may show degree of uteric obstruction and is the best imaging for defining the anatomy of the pelvicaliceal anatomy.

- Non-contrast helical CT – this is the gold standard, as it has the highest diagnostic accuracy. The availability is limited depending upon the hospital.

7.5   How should this patient be managed?

- Firstly it needs to be determined if the patient can be managed at home or needs to be admitted to hospital. In this case the patient should be admitted in view of his temperature to make sure there is no sepsis and his dehydration in order to get IV fluids.

- Analgesia and anti-emetic should be given – IM diclofenac 75 mg unless it is contraindicated. Another dose can be given after 30 minutes if needed. If this fails to control the pain then diamorphine can be given. IM metoclopramide 10 mg can be given.

- Intravenous fluids

- Collect urine to see if stone passed – the stone may pass spontaneously and if possible it should be captured in a sieve to send it off to the laboratory for analysis.

- Further management depends on the stone size and position. Stones less than 5 mm will spontaneously pass in more than 95% of cases and are usually managed expectantly. Intervention is required if:

- Solitary kidney

- Stone is too large to pass

- Infection occurs

- Stone fails to progress

- Social factors require a quick resolution (eg impending honeymoon)

Treatments include ureteroscopy (rigid and flexible), extracorporeal shockwave lithotripsy, percutaneous surgery, laparoscopic surgery, very rarely open surgery. In endoscopic surgery, if stones are small enough they can be removed with a basket, and if too large need to be broken up. The most commonly used devices are a pneumatic lithoclast, ultrasound or laser. Shock wave generators are either spark-gap, piezo-electric or electromagnetic. They only require sedation and no invasion of the body with any instruments but are less effective than surgery particularly for large stones (greater then 2 cm diameter).

Most stones are composed of calcium oxalate. Risk factors include low intake of fluids, hot environments, lots of exercise, flying.

7.6   What advice should you give this patient?

Drink plenty of fluids in future, aim for 2–3 L urine output in 24 hours. For people who experience their first episode of idiopathic calcium nephrolithiasis, limited evidence from a small five-year randomized prospective study supports increasing water intake (to produce a daily urine output of 2 litres or more) to prevent stone recurrence and to increase mean time of recurrence.

Encourage a balanced diet and as he had a calcium oxalate stone he will need to avoid calcium supplements, avoid oxalate-rich products such as rhubarb, nuts, cocoa, tea leaves and spinach. Dietary calcium does not need to be restricted.

Risk factors for calcium oxalate:

- Male sex
- Hyperoxaluria
- Hypercalciuria
- Hyperuricosuria
- Hypocitraturis
- Hypomagnesuria

Products with high urate content:

- Rhubarb 530 mg/100g
- Nuts 200–600 mg/100g
- Cocoa 625 mg/100g
- Tea leaves 375–1450 mg/100g
- Spinach 570 mg/100g

Case 2: Answers

7.7   What questions would you ask in the history?

- Duration of symptoms (longer indicates chronicity)
- History of fluid loss – vomiting, bleeding, diarrhoea, these would indicate an acute cause.
- History of sepsis – indicates an acute cause of the renal failure
- Past medical history – hypertension, diabetes, renovascular disease
- Previous stones or symptoms of bladder outflow obstruction
- Previous abdominal surgery
- Rashes, arthralgia, myalgia can indicate systemic disease
- Drugs such as nsaids and antibiotics can cause acute interstitial nephritis
- Nocturia – chronic

7.8   **What are significant features of hypovolaemia?**

Features with a diagnostic significance of hypovolaemia are dry axilla, postural pulse increment of 30/min, severe postural dizziness, postural hypotension > 20 mmHg systolic. Volume overload manifests as raised venous pressure and pulmonary crepitations.

7.9   **What is the diagnosis and what caused it?**

- Acute Kidney Injury (AKI, the term now used for acute renal failure). This can be split into pre-renal, renal and post-renal causes. Pre-renal causes include hypovolaemia such as occurs in massive haemorrhage, following burns, or dehydration; or in circulatory failure such as heart failure or shock. In this case a prolonged period of inadequate fluid intake in the face of severe emotional stress has caused the acute kidney injury.

- Renal causes are acute tubular necrosis (80% of cases), acute glomerulonephritis, drugs such as gentamicin, NSAIDs, ACE inhibitors, cisplatin, hepatorenal syndrome.

- Post-renal causes are obstructive lesions like stones, congenital conditions, prostatic hypertrophy. Malignancy is a common cause of obstruction: cancer prostate, bladder cancer in men and women, cancer cervix, cancer uterus/pelvic neoplasm.

7.10   **What other investigations should you do?**

- Electrolytes – hyperkalaemia, hyperphosphataemia and hypocalcaemia can occur

- Blood gas analysis and serum bicarbonate – to check for metabolic acidosis

- Creatine kinase and myoglobinuria – raised CK and myoglobinuria suggest rhabdomyolysis

- CRP and ESR – if raised may indicate inflammatory process such as SLE

- Serum immunoglobulins, Bence Jones protein and serum protein electrophoresis – to rule out myeloma

- Full blood count and coagulation studies – anaemia suggests a chronic or acute on chronic picture. Thrombocytopenia and red cell fragments suggest a thrombotic microangiopathy. DIC is associated with sepsis. Eosinophilia may be present in acute interstitial nephritis, cholesterol embolisation or vasculitis.

- Immunology – check ANA, dsDNA, ANCA to rule out SLE or other autoimmune disorders

- Hepatitis B, C or HIV – serology is required for dialysis

- Urine dipstick – haematuria and proteinuria suggest an acute glomerulonephritis. If protein +++ and blood +++ and normal size kidneys on renal US with elevated serum creatinine then urgent renal biopsy is indicated.

- Urine microscopy for cells, casts and crystals – red cell casts suggest glomerulonephritis, tubular cells or casts suggest acute tubular necrosis

- ECG – are there signs of hyperkalaemia? Check for signs of a MI or pericarditis

- Chest X-ray – is there any pulmonary oedema?

- Renal ultrasound – are there any signs of obstruction or reduced kidney size or asymmetry?

7.11   How should this patient be managed?

- Assess volume status

- Catheterise the patient

- Daily fluid balance chart and weight

- IV fluids

- Blood, sputum or urine cultures if sepsis suspected, and treat empirically with antibiotics

- Stop any nephrotoxic drugs – NSAIDs, ACEI, PPI (omeprazole, PPI can cause acute tubulointestinal nephritis)

7.12   What are the indications for dialysis?

- Hyperkalaemia > 7 mmol (if potassium remains above 6 mmol despite medical management then dialysis would be considered in an acute setting)

- Severe or worsening metabolic acidosis pH < 7.2

- Refractory pulmonary oedema

- Uraemic pericarditis

- Uraemic encephalopathy

Case 3: Answers

7.13   What other things would you want to know?

- Other medical problems – ischaemic heart disease, peripheral vascular disease, cerebrovascular disease, chronic heart failure, renal disease, multi-system diseases such as SLE

- Family history of kidney disease

- Medication history – any nephrotoxic drugs such as ciclosporin, long term NSAIDs

7.14   What is the likely diagnosis?

Chronic kidney disease – creatinine is not a reliable test to assess someone's renal function as it varies depending on factors such as a person's age, muscle mass, extrarenal loss of creatinine. The MDRD formula is used to assess eGFR in most laboratories as this equation is more accurate for eGFR < 60 ml/min. If the patient is Afro-Caribbean then there is a multiplication factor of 1.21

Males: = [1.23 × (140-age) × weight]/[creatinine]

Females: [1.04 × (140-age) × weight]/[creatinine]

Here is a table showing the values of eGFR:

Stage	GFR (ml/min per 1.73 m^2)	Description
1	> 90	Normal
2	60–89	Mild
3	30–59	Moderate
4	15–29	Severe
5	< 15	End stage kidney failure

Table 20.28   The values of eGFR

According to KDOQI classification, for Chronic Kidney Disease CKD 1 and 2 to be diagnosed there must be haematuria, proteinuria, scarred kidneys or abnormal renal US. If the renal US is normal and the urinalysis is normal (that is, there is no haematuria or proteinuria) then eGFR > 60 ml/min is normal and there is no Chronic Kidney Disease. An eGFR between 60–90 ml/min with no haematuria and no proteinuria with normal renal US is normal; it does not fulfil the criteria for CKD stage 2.

7.15   How would you investigate the cause of this?

- Full blood count

- Urinalysis – to check for blood

- Albumin: creatinine ratio (ACR)

- Serum calcium and phosphate

- Ultrasound kidneys – this should be done for those with evidence of progressive CKD

- A renal biopsy is required if there are normal-sized kidneys and proteinuria ≥ 100 mg/mmol (that is, proteinuria 1g/day) with no haematuria; OR if proteinuria ≥ 50 mg/mmol (that is, proteinuria 0.5 g/day) and non-visible haematuria (microscopic haematuria).

- Referral to a nephrologist – as progressive CKD

7.16   How can you manage this?

- Tight BP control is needed to reduce progression of CKD. As the patient has proteinuria/microalbuminuria he should be treated with an ARB or ACEI as these agents will have the dual action of reducing BP and reducing proteinuria for renoprotection.As there is hypertension with microalbuminuria, NICE recommends aiming for a blood pressure 120–129 systolic, < 80 diastolic.

- Advise him to reduce his alcohol intake, stop smoking, improve his diet and add anti-hypertensives to control his BP better.

Microalbuminuria is significant as the patient is diabetic, as it is a sign of underlying diabetic nephropathy.

- Ensure he is not on any nephrotoxic drugs. Avoid NSAIDs.

The key parameters that differentiate CKD from AKI (acute kidney injury) are

- Anaemia
- Small kidneys at imaging
- Renal bone disease
- Clinical tolerance of very severe uraemia

Erythropoietin can be used as treatment for anaemia in CKD patients. The main side effects include: hypertension, bone aches, flu-like syndrome, fistula thrombosis (rare), pure red cell aplasia.

In the UK approximately 70% of patients receive haemodialysis and the remainder CAPD. Ideally, a patient should be given the opportunity to choose dialysis modality according to lifestyle factors (employment, home environment), their capability and local resources.

References

Case 1

1. Renal colic. Clinical Knowledge Summaries. http://www.cks.nhs.uk/renal_colic_acute

2. Guidelines on Urolithiasis. European Association of Urology 2008. http://www.uroweb.org/fileadmin/user_upload/Guidelines/Urolithiasis.pdf

Case 2

1. Acute Kidney Injury. Renal Association Guidelines. http://www.renal.org/pages/guidelines/current/arf.php

Case 3

1. Chronic Kidney Disease. Clinical Knowledge Summaries. http://www.cks.nhs.uk/chronic_kidney_disease_not_diabetic

2. Chronic Kidney Disease. Renal Association Guidelines. http://www.renal.org/pages/guidelines/current/ckd.php

3. Chronic Kidney Disease. Quick reference guide. Clinical guideline 73. September 2008. National Institute for Health and Clinical Excellence. http://www.nice.org.uk/nicemedia/pdf/CG073QuickRefGuide.pdf

Recommended further cases

- Renal cancer
- Nephritic syndrome
- Nephrotic syndrome
- Polycystic kidneys
- Dialysis

Haematology answers

Case 1: Answers

8.1   What other symptoms would you enquire about?

- Radiation of pain
- Previous back pain
- Weight loss
- Fever
- Night sweats
- Presence of diarrhoea, faecal incontinence, rectal bleeding or slime
- Difficulty in passing urine

8.2   What is the differential diagnosis?

- Mechanical lower back pain should still be considered. However, the presence of pain not relieved by lying down is an "alarm symptom" that should alert you to the possibility of a serious underlying disorder.
- Malignancy with bony metastases (e.g. lung carcinoma as he is a smoker)
- Multiple myeloma (this commonly presents with back pain)
- Lower gastrointestinal malignant disease (this may cause lower back pain and could account for the change in bowel habit)
- Infections (e.g. discitis) – less likely, but cannot be dismissed completely
- Osteoporotic fracture

8.3   What investigations would you request?

- Full blood count (may reveal for example anaemia or a raised white cell count indicating infection or inflammation)
- ESR (as a screening test for inflammation, infection or malignancy)
- Urea, electrolytes
- Calcium (because of the presence of bone pain and the possibility of malignancy)
- Lumbar spine X-ray (justified by the presence of "alarm symptoms")

8.4   What action would you take now?

- Admit the patient to hospital urgently. He requires treatment of hypercalcaemia and urgent further investigation.
- Hypercalcaemia: remember 'bones (pain), stones (renal), moans (psychiatric problems) and groans (peptic ulcer)'

8.5   How should his hypercalcaemia be treated?

- Intravenous fluids (0.9% saline, 4–6 litres per 24 hours) to rehydrate. Careful monitoring of fluid balance is needed and a urine output of 100–150 mL/hour is a reasonable aim

- Loop diuretics (furosemide) should not be given routinely, but may be necessary if there is evidence of developing fluid overload

- A bisphosphonate such as disodium pamidronate will often be required to achieve normalisation of the serum calcium

8.6   What is the most likely diagnosis?

- Multiple myeloma. This would account for the hypercalcaemia, anaemia, renal failure and bony abnormalities.

- Multiple myeloma is a malignant neoplasm of plasma cells that arise in the bone marrow. It has an incidence of about 4 per 100,000 in the UK. It is more common in African-Americans and less common in Japanese and Chinese people. It is very rare before the age of 40 and has a median diagnosis at 69 years. It is more common in men. Bone destruction is a characteristic feature. This is because the osteoclasts cause bone resorption and bone formation by osteoblasts is inhibited. This leads to bone loss and osteolytic lesions, which predispose to pathological fractures. Bone pain is a common presentation, with symptoms of anaemia, infection and renal failure also being frequent.

Monoclonal gammopathy of uncertain significance is a condition which also causes a monoclonal band. Patients with this by definition have no "end organ" damage related to the paraprotein – they have a normal full blood count, no bony lesions, normal calcium and no paraprotein-related renal damage. Up to 3% of people over 70 have this and it is usually picked up as an incidental finding during investigations of another condition. No treatment is needed for this but these patients should be followed up as 1 per cent per year will go on to develop multiple myeloma. The mechanism of this is not known.

8.7   What further investigations should be performed after admission to hospital?

- An urgent renal ultrasound (this is a routine investigation in patients with renal failure, and is to exclude obstructive uropathy and seek evidence of prior undiagnosed renal abnormalities)

- MSU to exclude UTI (also routine in patients with renal failure)

- At least daily repeat of U&E and creatinine to monitor renal function

- Daily measurement of serum calcium until it has normalised

- Serum immunoglobulins and electrophoresis (to seek evidence of the presence of a serum paraprotein)

- Urine for Bence Jones protein (Bence Jones protein is monoclonal free urinary immunoglobulin light chain)

- Skeletal survey (to look for bony abnormalities in bones containing significant red marrow – skull, vertebral column, pelvis, upper humeri, upper femora)

8.8   What action should you take now?

- Referral to a haematologist

8.9   What additional tests is the haematologist likely to request to confirm the diagnosis?

- Bone marrow aspirate and trephine biopsy to look for the presence of a clonal increase in marrow plasma cells.

- B2 microglobulin. This is expressed on the surface of all nucleated cells and is elevated in multiple myeloma and reflects the tumour mass. It is the single most powerful predictor of survival in multiple myeloma patients. A value ≤ 4 mg/L implies a relatively good prognosis. A low serum albumin also occurs in advanced disease. An international prognostic system has been used which is based on serum B2 microglobulin and albumin levels. Patients with a serum B2 microglobulin > 5.5 mg/L and an albumin < 35 g/L have a poor survival.

8.10   What is the management of this?

- Supportive measures – analgesia often with opioids for the pain. Local radiotherapy will help if there are fractures or osteoporosis, rehydration for his renal impairment and hypercalcaemia, plasmaphoresis for hyperviscosity, broad spectrum antibiotics if there is infection

- For a patient of his age intensive therapy can be used and this involves corticosteroids and chemotherapy – combination chemotherapy produces higher response rates and improved survival.

NICE guidance on suspected referral for haematological cancers states that you should refer immediately patients:

- With spinal cord compression or renal failure suspected of being caused by myeloma

- With a blood count/film reported as acute leukaemia

8.11   What are common complications that can occur?

Pathological fractures, recurrent infections, renal failure, hypercalcaemia.

Case 2: Answers

8.12   What are possible differential diagnoses?

- Anaemia

- Respiratory disease – Asthma, COPD, chest infection

- Cardiac disease – heart failure, angina

- Anxiety

8.13   What other questions would you ask about in the history?

- Menstrual loss – heavy periods may cause iron deficiency anaemia

- Diet – vegan diet or poor quality diet can lead to B_{12} deficiency, folate deficiency can arise from a poor dietary intake

- Medical history – coeliac disease, inflammatory bowel disease, previous gastrectomy or other surgery, pernicious anaemia, malignancy, depression, heart disease or respiratory problems

- Drug history – anticonvulsants and other drugs can cause folate deficiency, medications for ischaemic heart disease, heart failure, respiratory problems

- Family history – known history of pernicious anaemia or associated diseases such as vitiligo, Hashimoto's disease, Addison's, cardiac or respiratory disease

- Alcohol intake – heavy alcohol intake can cause macrocytic anaemia

- Smoking history – may be associated with respiratory problems, maybe even lung malignancy

8.14   What other symptoms and signs would you look for?

- Cough, shortness of breath

- Swollen legs

- Fever

- Weight loss

- Headache

- Change in bowel habit

- Signs of anaemia – conjunctival pallor, koilonychias, glossitis, angular stomatitis

- Tachycardia

- Palpitations

- Angina

- Neurological problems

8.15   What investigations would you do?

- Full blood count and blood film – to look for anaemia, MCV and if evidence of megaloblastosis on blood film

- Thyroid function – to check her thyroid status

- Liver, bone and renal profile

8.16   What is the diagnosis?

Macrocytosis can be caused by megaloblastic erythropoiesis resulting from deficiencies of vitamin B_{12} or folate, or it can be from causes with a normoblastic bone marrow such as alcohol, liver disease, hypothyroidism. The raised lactate dehydrogenase indicates haemolysis of the red cells or ineffective erythropoiesis. The reticulocyte count is low, suggesting ineffective erythropoiesis.

- Folate deficiency

- B_{12} deficiency

8.17   What tests would you request now and what should you do whilst awaiting the results?

- Serum B_{12}

- Serum folate

- Start the patient on oral folate 5 mg/day and also vitamin B_{12} 1 mg on alternate days until no further improvement in symptoms, then 1mg every two months. (This is the regime if there is pernicious anaemia with neurological involvement). A deficiency of B_{12} can lead to demyelination of the brain and spinal cord (subacute combined degeneration). This produces demyelination of the posterior and lateral columns of the spinal cord which produces lower limb signs. This does not occur with folate deficiency, however, giving folate to someone with B_{12} deficiency may cause a worsening of the demyelination. Therefore patient should receive both folate and B_{12} replacement until the diagnosis is confirmed.

8.18   What should you do now?

- Serum gastric parietal cell antibodies

- Intrinsic factor antibodies

Schilling test – following an overnight fast the patient is injected with IM non-labelled vitamin B_{12} sufficient enough to saturate the body stores. The patient then has oral vitamin B_{12} which is labelled and the amount of excretion in 24 hours is measured. If this is abnormal then the patient is given labelled vitamin B_{12} orally with intrinsic factor and if the problem is due to intrinsic factor deficiency then this will be improved from before. This test is rarely used nowadays though.

8.19   What is the diagnosis?

- Pernicious anaemia – vitamin B_{12} is normally absorbed through the ileum, a process which depends on the presence of intrinsic factor which is secreted by gastric parietal cells in the stomach. Pernicious anaemia, which accounts for about 80% of all cases of megaloblastic anaemia, is an autoimmune gastritis that results in achlorhydia and the lack of intrinsic factor. The peak incidence is at 60 years of age and it is more common in women. It occurs more commonly in those with blood group A and in those with fair or prematurely grey hair and blue eyes. It may be associated with other autoimmune diseases, such as Addison's disease, Hashimoto's disease, vitiligo. Other causes of vitamin B_{12} deficiency are a vegan diet, partial or total gastrectomy and intestinal malabsorption.

8.20   What is the management of this?

- Treatment is with vitamin B_{12} injections 1 mg initially, six doses at intervals of three to four days, followed by maintenance injections of 1 mg a year for life every three months.

- Some units recommend an endoscopy should be done to confirm the gastric atrophy and to exclude a gastric carcinoma or polyps as these are more common in patients with pernicious anaemia.

Case 3: Answers

8.21   What are possible differential diagnoses?

- Idiopathic thrombocytopaenic purpura

- Leukaemia

- Bleeding disorder

- Drug induced purpura

- Idiopathic easy bruising

8.22   What other questions would you ask in the history?

- What are her periods like

- Any nose bleeds or bleeding from the back passage or haematemesis

- Any medical problems – hypertension, bleeding disorders, viral infections, autoimmune disorders, liver disease

- Family history of bleeding disorders

- Drug history – NSAIDs, warfarin, IV drugs

- Alcohol

- Sexual history

8.23   What other investigations would be useful to do?

- Fundoscopy – to check for retinal bleeding

- Full blood count – check for anaemia, thrombocytopenia

- Clotting screen to check for presence of a coagulopathy

- Blood film

- U&Es

8.24   What is the most likely diagnosis?

- Idiopathic thrombocytopenic purpura is a common disorder and is the most common cause of an isolated thrombocytopaenia without anaemia or neutropenia. In adults, it often has a chronic course. It is more common in women than men and may be primary, or seen in association with other disorders such as lymphoma or SLE. The autoantibody is usually IgG, directed against the platelet membrane which reduces the platelet lifespan to a few hours. Thrombocytopenia can be due to decreased production of platelets or decreased survival of platelets or both. The normal haemoglobin, white cell count, coagulation screen and blood film in this case make a diagnosis of cancer or haematological malignancy unlikely.

8.25   What should you do with this patient?

- Admit patient immediately to haematology unit

- Start prednisolone (1 mg/kg)

- She should NOT have any IM injections, aspirin or NSAIDs

- Ultrasound of the abdomen – to check for enlarged spleen, lymphadenopathy and any masses

- Bone marrow aspirate and biopsy – this should only be performed if there are atypical features such as failure to respond to first line treatment

8.26   What does this suggest?

The normal spleen size goes along with a diagnosis of ITP. Splenomegaly, if present, suggests an alternative diagnosis.

8.27   What is the further management of the patient?

- Steroids – to increase the platelet count, patients are often started on 1 mg/kg prednisolone a day with the dosage gradually being reduced after remission is achieved.

- Immunosuppression is usually second line treatment

- anti-D immunoglobulin, if available, can also be used in Rhesus (D) – positive patients

- Splenectomy is reserved for patients who do not respond to this or who do not want to take immunosuppression.

8.28   What should be given along with this to the patient?

Without a spleen susceptibility to infection by encapsulated bacteria such as streptococcus pneumonia, meninogococcus and Haemophilus influenza increases. Vaccination against these organisms should be offered to the patient pre-operatively and consideration given to lifelong prophylactic penicillin V (or erythromycin) on discharge.

Case 4: Answers

8.29   What questions would you ask?

- Any chest symptoms such as cough, shortness of breath

- Any diarrhoea or abdominal pain

- Any urinary symptoms

- Any lines inserted recently such as Hickman line

8.30   What investigations would you request?

- Full blood count with differential white cell count

- Urea and electrolytes

- Blood cultures

- Sputum cultures

- Stool culture – if diarrhoea

- Urinalysis

- Arterial blood gas if hypoxic

- Chest X-ray

8.31   What is the diagnosis?

Neutropenic sepsis – this is common after cytotoxic drugs as they cause myelosuppression with a consequent increased risk of infection. The chemotherapy kills normal cells as well as the malignant cells as it has a narrow therapeutic window. This can cause a pancytopenia as rapidly dividing bone marrow cells are characteristically affected.

8.32   How would you manage this patient?

- IV fluids

- Broad spectrum IV antibiotics according to local hospital policy. These should be started immediately without waiting for results of tests. It is important to cover Gram-negative organisms as these are associated with high mortality rates. Usually a beta-lactam broad spectrum antibiotic with or without an aminoglycoside are used. As the patient is hypotensive, dual antibiotic therapy would be usual. With a normotensive patient piperacillin/tazobactam may be used alone.

- Oxygen if needed

- If urine output is low then will need catheterising

- Daily bloods for biochemical profile and total and differential white cell count

- Consider GCSF to speed up neutrophil recovery

8.33   What should you do after the patient is stable?

- Inform the haematologist about the patient so they can adjust treatment accordingly

- Monitor for worsening signs of infection

8.34   What can be changed in the treatment?

- The antibiotics can be switched to a carbapenem such as meropenem

References

Case 1

1. AV Hoffbrand, PAH Moss and JE Pettit. 5th edition. 2006. *Essential Haematology*. Blackwell Publishing. 216–223.

Case 2

1. B_{12} and folate deficiency. Clinical Knowledge Summaries. http://www.cks.nhs.uk/anaemia_b_{12}_and_folate_deficiency

2. AV Hoffbrand, PAH Moss and JE Pettit. 5th edition. 2006. *Essential Haematology*. Blackwell Publishing. 44–57.

Case 3

1. Silverman MA. Idiopathic thrombocytopenic purpura. Emedicine. http://emedicine.medscape.com/article/779545-overview

2. AV Hoffbrand, PAH Moss and JE Pettit. 5th edition. 2006. *Essential Haematology*. Blackwell Publishing. .   281–283.

Case 4

1. Ramrakha P, Moore K. (Second edition) (2004). *Oxford Handbook of Acute Medicine*, Oxford University Press. Oxford.

Recommended further cases

- Leukaemia

- Lymphoma

- Iron deficiency anaemia

- Sickle cell and thalassaemia

- Haemophilia

- DIC

Musculoskeletal answers

Case 1: Answers

9.1   What are the differential diagnoses?

This presentation is typical of an inflammatory joint problem (sub-acute onset, polyarticular, joint swelling, prominent morning stiffness). Alternatives would include:

Inflammatory arthritis:

- Viral arthritis (Parvovirus arthropathy is relatively common, arthropathies can also occur with rubella, hepatitis A, B and C, CMV and EBV)
- Primary inflammatory arthritis
    - Rheumatoid arthritis
    - Psoriatic arthritis
    - Reactive arthritis
    - Connective tissue disease such as SLE
- Crystal arthritis
    - Gout – unlikely in a woman of this age
    - Pseudogout – unlikely in a woman of this age

9.2   What other questions would you ask?

- Any other joints involved and pattern of joint involvement (eg DIP inflammation, asymmetry of joint involvement seen in psoriatic arthritis)
- Pattern of stiffness – more than 30 minutes in the morning for inflammation, stiffening on rest in OA
- Extra-articular symptoms:
    - breathlessness may indicate pulmonary fibrosis, or pneumonitis, or anaemia or chronic disease
    - Sicca symptoms – dry eyes and dry mouth indicating Sjogren's syndrome(primary or secondary)
    - Eye inflammation: conjunctivitis, scleritis are seen in RA
    - Rashes – psoriasis, photosensitivity and butterfly rash of SLE
    - Raynauds – seen in RA and other collagenoses
- Ask about lower gastrointestinal symptoms as these may point towards reactive or enteropathic arthritis
- Ask about any genitourinary symptoms as these may indicate cervicitis or urethritis in reactive arthritis
- Ask about any rashes as these can be caused by disease such as psoriasis or be a drug side effect
- Systemic features of fever, night sweats and weight loss

- Impact of the disease on the patient and support at home

- Ask about family history of rheumatoid or psoriasis, other autoimmune conditions

9.3   What is the likely diagnosis?

Rheumatoid arthritis – this is a chronic systemic disease which primarily presents as a symmetrical deforming peripheral polyarthropathy, i.e. it presents as an insidious polyarthritis with inflammatory changes in the synovial membranes and articular structures leading to deformity. It affects between 0.5–1% of the population, with a male to female ratio of 1:3. The aetiology is multifactorial with a genetic component.

9.4   What joint deformities can you get in rheumatoid arthritis?

- Ulnar deviation

- Boutonniere deformity – flexion at the proximal IP joint and extension at the distal IP joint

- Swan neck deformity – hyperextension at the proximal IP and flexion at the distal IP joint

- Z thumb – flexion at the MCP and hyperextension at the IP joint

9.5   What investigations are indicated?

- ESR and CRP – raised during active inflammatory disease

- Rheumatoid factor – this is present in 70% of people with rheumatoid; high seropositivity is associated with systemic complications. RF is also positive in certain chronic infections – infective endocarditis, TB, viral infections such as glandular fever, other collagenoses such as Primary Sjogren's syndrome.

- Anti-cyclic citrullinated peptide antibody (Anti CCP). This is associated with erosive RA (up to 80% are positive for this). It has a higher specificity for diagnosing RA than Rheumatoid factor, is positive in rheumatoid negative patients, and high levels predict a worse prognosis.

- Full blood count – anaemia (normocytic)

- Other autoimmune antibodies if you suspect connective tissue diseases

- U&Es, LFTs, bone profile and calcium

- X-rays of the affected joints – to identify erosions

- Chest X-ray to exclude lung involvement

- Ultrasound or MRI of the joints. Ultrasound is increasingly performed in patients with early inflammatory disease. It is good at detecting synovitis and erosions before they are evident on X-ray.

9.6   What findings can you see on an X-ray of a badly affected joint in rheumatoid arthritis?

- Joint erosions

- Joint space loss

- Soft tissue swelling

- Joint deformity

- Periarticular osteoporosis

Here are figures showing a normal joint and then one affected badly with rheumatoid arthritis.

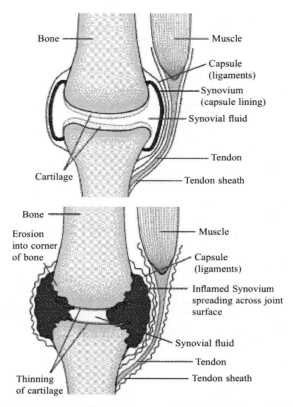

Figure 20.12   Normal and arthritic joints. Illustrations reproduced by kind permission of the Arthritis Research Campaign (www.arc.org.uk) from the Rheumatoid arthritis information booklet for people with rheumatoid arthritis.

9.7   What is the urgent management needed?

- Referral to the rheumatologist (to the early synovitis clinic.) This should not be delayed for any of the investigations.

- For pain relief offer her paracetamol or NSAIDs with PPI cover.

NICE recommends urgent referral for the following:

- More than one joint affected

- The small joints of the hands or feet are affected

- There has been a delay of three months or longer between onset of symptoms and seeking medical advice

9.8   What medication would be started for a newly diagnosed person with rheumatoid arthritis?

NICE recommends a combination of disease-modifying anti-rheumatoid drugs (DMARDS) including methotrexate and at least one other DMARD, plus short acting corticosteroid as first line treatment within three months of onset of persistent symptoms. This should only be commenced by the specialist.

DMARD	Side-effects
Methotrexate	GI upset, pneumonitis, raised liver enzymes, bone marrow suppression
Gold	Proteinuria, rash, bone marrow suppression
Penicillamine	Proteinuria, rash, bone marrow suppression
Sulfasalazine	Raised liver enzymes, GI upset, bone marrow suppression
Azathioprine	GI upset, bone marrow suppression
Ciclosporin	Renal impairment, Hypertension, bone marrow suppression
Cyclophosphamide	Infertility, bone marrow suppression

Table 20.29   DMARD side-effects

Case 2: Answers

9.9   What are the differential diagnoses?

- Frozen shoulder – adhesive capsulitis. Three phases may be described over a period of 18–24 months:

    1. Initial, gradual onset of diffuse and severe shoulder pain, typically worse at night with inability to lie on the affected side

    2. A stiff phase with less severe pain present at the end range of movement, global stiffness and severe loss of shoulder movement

    3. Finally, a recovery phase with a gradual return of movement

    Overall, global pain and restriction of all active and passive movements are present.

- Rotator cuff tear or tendinitis – rotator cuff tendinopathy is the most common cause of shoulder pain. Classically, pain is present over an arc of abduction, worse on active movement. Unless restricted by pain, the range of movement is generally almost full, unlike in frozen shoulder.

- Acromioclavicular disorders – pain, tenderness and occasionally swelling are localised to the acromioclavicular joint. There is restriction of passive horizontal adduction (flexion) of the shoulder, with the elbow extended across the body.

- Trauma

- Infection (rare)

- Referred pain – from neck, diaphragm, myocardial infarction

- Malignancy

9.10   What other questions would you ask?

- Occupation or whether the patient has done any heavy lifting recently

- Is there a painful arc of abduction – pain caused by supraspinatus tendinitis causes arc between 60 and 120 of abduction. If it is acromioclavicular arthritis, the arc is usually between 120 to 180 of abduction
- Medical problems such as recent stroke, any previous shoulder injuries or surgery
- Functional impact of this problem on his life
- Symptoms from elsewhere such as neck, upper limbs, chest
- Details of pain. Use the SOCRATES model: site, onset, character, radiation, associations, time duration, exacerbating factors and relieving factors, severity
- Does the pain occur just with movement or at rest and at night?
- Are there any systemic symptoms of fever, night sweats or weight loss?
- Drug history and allergies

9.11   What are the red flag symptoms to be worried about?

Red flag indicators include a history of cancer, any unexplained neurological deficit, any signs or symptoms of systemic disease, any lymphadenopathy, any palpable mass or bony tenderness around joint.

9.12   What muscle externally rotates the shoulder?

Infraspinatus.

9.13   What is the likely diagnosis?

Frozen shoulder.

9.14   What investigations should you request?

- Usually no further investigations are needed
- In view of his diabetes you may consider septic arthritis
- An ultrasound scan of his shoulder may be helpful, particularly if symptoms worsen

9.15   How should this patient be managed?

- Rest
- Analgesia such as paracetamol
- NSAIDs
- Physiotherapy
- Steroid injections into the shoulder joint if the above measures do not control things

Case 3: Answers

9.16   What is the differential of an acute monoarthritis?

- Reactive arthritis
- Gout
- Pseudogout

- Septic arthritis – this is an emergency
- Rheumatoid arthritis
- Psoriatic arthritis
- Trauma

9.17   What other questions would you ask?

- Recent trauma to the skin (anywhere) or infection
- History of gout or rheumatoid arthritis
- Known diabetes or leukaemia – predisposition to infection
- Preceding illness, e.g. GU or GI upset – reactive arthritis
- Alcohol use – gout more common in heavy drinkers
- Drug history – immunosuppressive drugs, steroids predispose to infection
- IV drug use – increases infection risk

9.18   What is the likely diagnosis?

Septic arthritis – this is infection of the joint and is commonly caused by gram positive organisms especially Staphylococcus aureus. There may be direct introduction of the organisms through a penetrating injury or they can occur spontaneously, probably due to haematogenous spread.

9.19   What investigations should you request?

- Aspiration of joint fluid for gram stain, culture and crystal analysis – this must be performed
- Bloods – FBC looking for leucocytosis which suggests sepsis
- ESR, CRP – high if inflammatory arthritis
- Urate – may be high in gout but not always
- U&Es – renal impairment may be present in gout
- Blood cultures – there may be an organism present indicating infection
- Urine culture, skin swab if septic lesions are apparent, throat swab, Anti-streptolysin O titre
- Viral screen to check if it is reactive arthritis or viral arthritis
- X-ray – can act as a baseline or may show acute changes. (Osteomyelitis if the history is greater than 10 to 14 days, otherwise just soft tissue swelling or elevated fat pads indicating an effusion)

9.20   How should you manage this patient?

- Emergency referral to the on-call orthopaedic or rheumatology service
- Commence treatment with broad spectrum IV antibiotics (according to the current microbiology guidelines for the hospital) covering staphylococci and streptococci once cultures have been sent. These can then be changed accordingly depending upon culture results. IV antibiotics for two weeks, then oral for six weeks.

- The joint should be aspirated to decompress the joint

Surgical drainage is indicated if aspiration is required more than three times per day, or if adjacent soft tissue is affected, or if there is no response to five days of aspiration plus antibacterial therapy or if the joint is difficult to aspirate.

Case 4: Answers

9.21   What other questions would you ask?

- Is pain worse after activity? OA symptoms are worse after activity and at end of the day
- Are any other joints involved?
- How severe are the symptoms? This will indicate need for surgery or not
- How much does it limit her lifestyle?
- Does the pain keep her awake?
- Medical problems such as diabetes or obesity, as these are associated with OA
- Family history. There is a genetic component to OA
- What is her occupation and what are her routine activities? These may predispose to OA

9.22   What is the likely diagnosis?

Osteoarthritis – disease of the synovial joints characterised by the loss of articular cartilage and overgrowth of the underlying bone. It is common and is age-related. It can affect any joint but the most commonly affected are the DIP of the hand and also the thumb carpometacarpal, the knees, hips.

Always remember to examine the hip when examining the knee.

9.23   What investigations should you do?

- Bloods. As OA is not a systemic disease the FBC, biochemical profile and immunology tests should all be normal
- Knee X-ray

9.24   What features on a knee X-ray characterise osteoarthritis?

- Joint space narrowing
- Osteophytes
- Subchondral bone cysts
- Sclerosis

Here are figures showing a normal joint, one mildy affected with OA and one severely affected with OA:

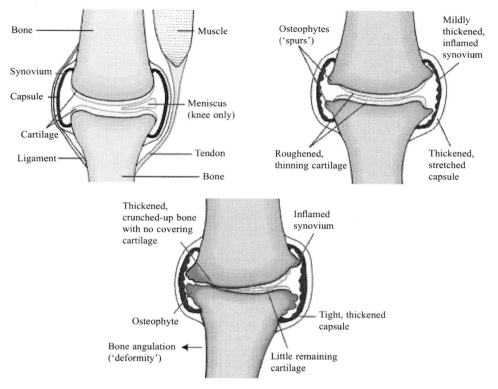

Figure 20.13   Normal joint, mild OA, severe OA. Illustrations reproduced by kind permission of the Arthritis Research Campaign (www.arc.org.uk) taken from the Osteoarthritis information booklet for people with arthritis.

9.25   What advice and treatment can you offer the patient?

- Education – reassurance that it is nothing sinister
- Exercise – this should be a core part of management despite age, comorbidity and pain. It helps to strengthen muscles and improve fitness
- Physiotherapy – to improve the range of motion of the legs and strengthen muscles
- Weight loss – to reduce the stress placed on the knees
- Better footwear – leather uppers, with plenty of room for the foot, shock-absorbing soles, medial arch support if flat feet
- Heat or cold packs on site of pain
- Analgesia with paracetamol and topical NSAIDs (although evidence is lacking for topical NSAIDs despite NICE guidance)

9.26   When should you refer for surgery?

NICE recommends that referral for surgery should be offered when:

- They have already been offered all the other core treatments
- The joint symptoms are having a substantial impact on their quality of life and are refractory to non-surgical treatment

Case 5: Answers

9.27   What other questions would you want to ask her?

- Drug history including steroids and anticonvulsants

- Medical history – hyperthyroidism, Cushing's syndrome, primary hyperparathyroidism, rheumatoid arthritis, malabsorption; as these are associated with osteoporosis

- Falls history – previous falls and circumstances around them, risk factors such as visual impairment, cognitive impairment, conditions affecting mobility such as stroke, Parkinson's, polypharmacy, frailty, urinary incontinence

- Family history of maternal hip fracture

- Previous fractures

- Any periods of immobility recently

- Alcohol

- Smoking

- Menstrual history – late menarche and early menopause before the age of 45 years is associated with osteoporosis

9.28   What things should you test when examining her for her falls risk?

- Assess gait and balance – use the up-and-go test by asking her to stand up from the chair without using her arms, walk 3 m, turn around and return to the chair and sit down. Also ask the patient to stand up and turn around 180 degrees, if they need more than four steps then further assessment is needed.

- Lying and standing blood pressure – to check for postural hypotension

9.29   What should you do at this stage?

- Request a DEXA scan

- Full blood count

- ESR, CRP

- Renal and liver profile

- Bone profile

- Thyroid function

- Serum electrophoresis and Bence Jones proteins

9.30   What are the indications for a DEXA scan?

There are many indications for doing a DEXA scan:

- A patient with a history of a low trauma fracture, age < 75

- An incidental X-ray finding of osteopenia or vertebral collapse or in the investigation of thoracic kyphosis or loss of height (if degenerative changes excluded)

- Postmenopausal women with family history of hip fracture

- If the patient has a low body mass index (BMI < 19 kg/m2 [in early NICE guidance])
- If the patient has received or requires long-term corticosteroid treatment (any dose)
- Oestrogen deficiency:
- in a patient with premature menopause (< 45 years of age)
- primary hypogonadism
- Conditions that predispose to secondary osteoporosis including:
  - malabsorption e.g. coeliac disease, inflammatory bowel disease
  - long-term treatment with anticonvulsants
  - anorexia nervosa
  - rheumatoid arthritis
  - chronic renal failure
  - hyperthyroidism
  - primary hyperparathyroidism
  - Cushing's syndrome
  - prolonged immobilisation

9.31   What does this mean?

This means that the woman has osteoporosis according the WHO criteria. This is the loss of bone density sufficient enough to cause fractures. The bone mineral composition is normal. It is given as a T-score of −2.5 which is defined as a bone mineral density more than 2.5 standard deviations below the mean of a healthy 25-year-old female peak bone mass.

9.32   What treatment should this lady be started on?

- Pain relief such as paracetamol for her wrist pain
- Bisphosphonates: alendronate should be commenced, assuming she has no contraindications or underlying metabolic bone disease
- Exercise
- Diet: calcium and vitamin D
- Stop smoking
- HRT also may be an option particularly for women with premature menopause, until they reach the age of about 50

Case 6: Answers

9.33   What are the differential diagnoses?

- Cellulitis
- Bursitis
- Gout – sodium monourate crystals

- Pseudogout – calcium pyrophosphate crystals

- Rheumatoid arthritis

- Seronegative arthritis

- Bunion

9.34 **What other questions would you ask in the history?**

- Medical history – psoriasis and myeloproliferative disorders both increase production of uric acid; renal impairment causes underexcretion of uric acid; previous attacks of gout

- Full drug history – diuretics and low dose aspirin can cause underexcretion of uric acid

- Pain – is it exacerbated by movement? Acute onset pain occurs in septic arthritis

- Systemically unwell – sepsis likely

- Recent genitourinary or diarrhoeal illness – reactive arthritis likely

- Impact on work and leisure activity

9.35 **What is the most likely diagnosis?**

- Gout – this is due to hyperuricaemia either due to overproduction or underexcretion by the kidneys. Monosodium urate crystals form within the joint.

9.36 **What investigations would you do to confirm this?**

- Bloods – serum urate, CRP, ESR, WCC – to check for inflammation and raised urate for gout

- Aspiration and polarised light microscopy of synovial fluid – to identify cause

- X-ray of joint

9.37 **What is the acute management of this?**

- Advise rest and leg elevation

- Keep the joint in a cool environment and use an ice pack

- Increase fluid intake

- NSAIDs such as diclofenac, indometacin or naproxen and continue until 48 hrs after the acute attack has resolved

- colchicine as an alternative

- Steroid injection – if sepsis has been excluded. Beware, patients with gout can get septic arthritis too!

9.38 **What other lifestyle changes would you advise this patient about?**

- Reduce alcohol intake

- Reduce diet of purine rich foods

- Weight reduction

- Stop smoking

- Stop medications that may contribute to gout

9.39   **What medication would you consider now and how would you tell the patient to take it?**

- Allopurinol should be started. This lowers the level of uric acid in the blood by inhibiting the enzyme xanthine oxidase (this catalyses the breakdown of hypoxanthine to xanthine and then from xanthine to uric acid). It is usually used when the patient has had two or more attacks within a year. It should be taken at a lose dose (100 mg) after food and the dose can be increased gradually until the serum uric acid result is less than 300 micromol/L.

- It should not be started during the acute attack as it can prolong the attack so it is usually started three to six weeks later, whilst the patient continues to take NSAIDs or colchicine

- If an acute attack occurs whilst on it, you should continue to take it while the acute attack is treated with either NSAID or colchicines.

- Starting allopurinol during an acute attack, or without NSAID or colchicine cover, can result in the development of severe polyarticular gout.

Case 7: Answers

9.40   **What are the causes of low back pain?**

- Structural – mechanical, prolapsed intervertebral disc, spinal stenosis, facet joint arthritis, spondylosis

- Infection – osteomyelitis, facet joint sepsis, discitis

- Inflammatory – sacroilitis, spondyloarthropathies

- Neoplasm

- Metabolic – osteomalacia, osteoporotic vertebral collapse, Paget's disease, hyperparathyroidism

- Referred pain

9.41   **What other questions would you ask?**

- Medical problems – psoriasis, IBD, Reiter's syndrome

- Family history of HLA-B27 conditions

- What makes pain better – if worse after inactivity indicated ankylosing spondylitis

- Is there any reduced movement of his back – common in ankylosing spondylitis

9.42   **What are the red flag signs of low back pain?**

- < 20 or > 55

- Taking steroids

- Non-mechanical pain

- Thoracic pain

- Unwell

- Past history of malignancy

- HIV

- Reduced weight

- Widespread neurology

- Structural deformity

- Also you should be aware of yellow flag signs which are psychological and social factors which can increase the risk of developing chronic back pain. These include:

  o Belief that bed rest is better than active treatment

  o Ongoing claims and compensation regarding back pain

  o Family problems

  o Financial problems

  o Negative attitudes or low mood

  o History of back problems and time-off

9.43   **What is the test that assesses lumbar flexion?**

Schoeber's test – this assesses lumbar flexion. You mark the position of the posterior iliac spine on the vertebral column and mark 5 cm below this mark and 10 cm above it. You then ask the patient to touch his toes, and if the distance increase between the two marks is < 5 cm then this indicates limitation of lumbar flexion.

9.44   **What is the likely diagnosis?**

Ankylosing spondylitis is a spondyloarthropathy which affects the spine and sacroiliac joints. There is a male:female ratio of 3:1. It is related to HLA-B27. Onset is usually in young adults. It is an enthesopathy – the site of insertion of the tendon, ligament or articular capsule into bone is affected.

9.45   **What other features are typical of ankylosing spondylitis?**

- Tender, swollen joints

- Failure to obliterate lumbar lordosis on forward flexion

- Osteoporosis

- Achilles tendinitis

9.46   **What extra-articular manifestations are associated with ankylosing spondylitis?**

- Pulmonary fibrosis

- Anterior uveitis

- Spinal fractures

- Aortic valve regurgitation

- Carditis

- Amyloidosis

9.47   **What investigations would you request?**

- Full blood count – leucocytosis

- CRP, ESR – raised

- Urea and electrolytes – before starting NSAIDs

9.48   What might you see on this?

- Bamboo spine, erosion and sclerosis of the sacroiliac joints

9.49   How would you manage this patient?

- Refer to a rheumatologist

- Advise exercise

- NSAIDs

- Physiotherapy

- NICE now recommend biologic treatments, e.g. anti-TNF for severe cases

Case 8: Answers

9.50   What is the likely diagnosis?

Polymyalgia rheumatic and temporal arteritis – granulomatous inflammation of the medium and large sized arteries, mainly affecting branches of the carotid artery. It almost exclusively affects people over 50 and affects women more than men.

9.51   What investigations would you do?

This is an emergency and time is crucial. Admit the patient straight away and treat immediately with steroids. Investigations should not delay this. The prompt initiation of steroids can lead to the return of vision in the affected eye and preserve vision in the non-affected eye. Blood tests would most likely reveal a high ESR and CRP, and perhaps anaemia.

9.52   How would you confirm the diagnosis?

Biopsy of the temporal artery is definitive, if a positive result is obtained. A negative result, however, may be a false reading due to the fact that skip lesions occur. That is, the vasculitic changes are partial rather than continuous along the artery. Doppler ultrasound looking for turbulent blood flow through an affected segment may improve the yield of positive results.

9.53   What should the treatment be?

- High dose steroids – 40 mg to 60 mg prednisolone daily for at least three months, plus oral bisphosphonate, calcium and vitamin D treatment to prevent osteoporosis.

- Regular monitoring of blood pressure and blood sugar is essential. The clinical team must maintain a high index of suspicion for infections during courses of high-dose steroid treatment as this may mask symptoms and signs of infection.

9.54   What can be done?

Steroid sparing drugs such as azathioprine or methotrexate can be used.

Case 9: Answers

9.55   **What are the differential diagnoses?**

- Scleroderma

- Subacute bacterial endocarditis

- Infective arthritis

- Lymphoma and leukaemia

- Drug reactions

- Thrombotic thrombocytopenic purpura

- Sarcoidosis

- Vasculitis

- Secondary syphilis

- Bacterial septicaemia

- Leprosy

- SLE

9.56   **What other questions would you ask?**

- Systemic features of fever, weight loss, tiredness

- Other skin manifestations – could be Sjogren's syndrome, Raynaud's phenomenon

- Any urinary symptoms or haematuria

- Any other chest symptoms such as haemoptysis, cough, shortness of breath, chest pain – consider pleuritis, pericarditis, pulmonary embolism

- Any swallowing difficulty – systemic sclerosis

- Any neurological or psychiatric symptoms

- Any eye problems

- Any other medical problems – previous DVTs (antiphospholipid syndrome)

- Drugs – could the symptoms be related to drugs?

- Obstetric history – recurrent miscarriages or antiphospholipid syndrome

9.57   **What is the likely diagnosis?**

SLE – multisystem disease of autoimmune origin. It is non-organ specific and can affect any system in the body. It is characterised by vasculitis and anti-nuclear antibodies. It is more common in women in a ratio of 10:1. It is multifactorial, the exact cause is unknown.

The American College of Rheumatology Classification system for SLE suggests a person may have lupus if they have 4 or more of the 11 criteria.

- Malar rash
- Discoid rash
- Photosensitivity
- Oral ulcers (oral or nasopharyngeal)
- Arthritis
- Serositis (pleuritis or pericarditis)
- Renal disorder
- Neurologic disorder (seizures or psychosis)
- Hematologic disorder
- Positive anti-nuclear antibody
- Anti-dsDNA or anti-Smith antibody (or positive antiphospholipid antibody or false positive serologic test for syphilis known to be + for at least six months and confirmed by fluorescent treponema pallidum antibody absorption test)

Table 20.30   SLE diagnosis criteria

The diagnosis of SLE is made if four or more of the manifestations are present, either serially or simultaneously, during any interval of observations.

9.58   What investigations would you do?

- Bloods – full blood count – normocytic anaemia, lymphopenia is characteristic of active SLE
- U&Es – renal impairment
- Urinalysis – dipstick to look for proteinuria, if positive request urgent 24 hour urine excretion of protein, if significant then urgent renal referral and biopsy required
- LFTs
- Autoimmune autoantibodies – ANA is positive in over 90% of patients with SLE but it is also positive in many other conditions and in the normal healthy population. Anti-dsDNA is more specific for SLE and can be helpful in monitoring disease activity. A variety of ENA (extractable extra nuclear antigens) may be seen in SLE and other connective tissue diseases. Anti Sm antibodies are very specific for SLE, anti-Ro and La occur in both SLE and Sjogren's syndrome, anti-histone indicate drug-induced SLE, anti-cardiolipin and lupus anticoagulant suggest antiphospholipid syndrome. Scl70 is suggestive of Sjogren's, Rheumatoid factor and anti CCP antibodies for rheumatoid arthritis, ANCA for vasculitis.
- ESR – raised, particularly if serositis eg. Pleuritis or pericarditis
- Complement – C3 and C4 usually reduced due to formation of immune complexes, gives an indication of disease activity
- Chest X-ray – to check for pleural and pericardial effusions, pulmonary fibrosis

9.59   How should she be managed?

- Mild disease may respond to rest, NSAIDs and the removal of any precipitating cause e.g. ultraviolet light, hormones, intercurrent infections
- Simple measures such as sun block creams, and prompt or prophylactic treatment of infection may prevent disease flares

- Hydroxychloroquine may help skin, joint and fatigue symptoms

Moderate disease severity requires steroid therapy with the dose being gradually reduced as the disease is controlled. Immunosuppressive agents such as azathioprine, methotrexate or mycophenolate may be added if steroid therapy and/or hydroxychloroquine is ineffective.

Cyclophosphamide or rituximab may be required for severe disease, particularly for renal or other life threatening organ involvement.

At all times, careful monitoring is required for treatment induced side effects.

Monitoring of levels of anti-dsDNA and treatment with steroids as soon as there is a significant rise in this marker may help to prevent relapse in many cases, without increasing the cumulative dose of steroid given.

References

Case 1

1. Rheumatoid arthritis. Clinical Knowledge Summaries. http://www.cks.nhs.uk/rheumatoid_arthritis

2. Rheumatoid arthritis. Quick reference guide. Clinical guideline 79. February 2009. National Institute for Health and Clinical Excellence. http://www.nice.org.uk/nicemedia/pdf/CG79QRGv2.pdf

3. Diagnosing Inflammatory Arthritis. Arthritis Research Campaign. http://www.arc.org.uk/arthinfo/medpubs/6532/6532.asp

4. Rheumatic Diseases: Serological Aids to Early Diagnosis. Arthritis Research Campaign. http://www.arc.org.uk/arthinfo/medpubs/6628/6628.asp

5. Rheumatoid arthritis. Arthritis Research Campaign. http://www.arc.org.uk/arthinfo/patpubs/6033/6033.asp

6. Table 20.29 DMARD side effects. – www.bnf.org

Case 2

1. Management of shoulder disorders in primary care. Arthritis Research Campaign. http://www.arc.org.uk/arthinfo/medpubs/6534/6534.asp

2. Frozen shoulder. GP Notebook. http://www.gpnotebook.co.uk

Case 3

1. Brusch JL. Septic Arthritis. Emedicine. http://emedicine.medscape.com/article/236299-overview

2. Andrew JG, Herrick AL, Marsh DR. 2000. *Musculoskeletal Medicine and Surgery*. Churchill Livingstone.

Case 4

1. Osteoarthritis. Quick reference guide. Clinical guideline 59. February 2008. National Institute for Health and Clinical Excellence. http://www.nice.org.uk/nicemedia/pdf/CG59quickrefguide.pdf

2. Osteoarthritis. Clinical Knowledge Summaries. http://www.cks.nhs.uk/osteoarthritis

3. Osteoarthritis. Arthritis Research Campaign. http://www.arc.org.uk/arthinfo/patpubs/6025/6025.asp

Case 5

1. Management of Osteoporosis. Quick reference guide 71. Scottish Intercollegiate Guidelines Network. http://www.sign.ac.uk/pdf/qrg71.pdf

2. Osteoporosis – secondary prevention including strontium ranelate: quick reference guide. Technology appraisal guidance 161. National Institute for Health and Clinical Excellence. http://www.nice.org.uk/nicemedia/pdf/TA161quickrefguide.pdf

3. Osteoporosis. Arthritis Research Campaign. http://www.arc.org.uk/arthinfo/medpubs/6531/6531.asp

Case 6

1. Gout. Clinical Knowledge Summaries. http://www.cks.nhs.uk/gout

2. An update on gout. Arthritis Research Campaign. http://www.arc.org.uk/arthinfo/medpubs/6624/6624.asp

Case 7

1. Ankylosing spondylitis. Clinical Knowledge Summaries. http://www.cks.nhs.uk/ankylosing_spondylitis

2. Low back pain. Arthritis Research Campaign. http://www.arc.org.uk/arthinfo/medpubs/6621/6621.asp

3. Ankylosing spndylitis. Arthritis Research Campaign. http://www.arc.org.uk/arthinfo/patpubs/6001/6001. asp

Case 8

1. Giant cell arteritis. Clinical Knowledge Summaries. http://www.cks.nhs.uk/giant_cell_arteritis#372612004

Case 9

1. Guidelines for referral and management of systematic lupus erythematosus in adults. American College of Rheumatology. 1999.

2. Bartels CM. Systemic lupus erythematosus. Emedicine. http://emedicine.medscape.com/article/332244-overview

3. Table 20.30 SLE Diagnosis criteria: http://www.reumatology.org/publications/classification/SLE/1982Revised_Criteria_Classification_SLE.asp?aud=mem

Recommended further cases

- Sjogren's syndrome
- Raynaud's phenomenon
- Systemic sclerosis (crest)
- Psoriatic arthritis

Dermatology answers
Case 1: Answers

10.1   What questions should you ask?

- How long has she had it?
- Is it getting worse?
- What treatment is she currently using and what she tried previously?
- What impact is acne having on her life? (acne is associated with anxiety, depression, social withdrawal, poor body image and poor self-esteem)
- What has prompted her to attend the surgery today and what are her concerns and expectations?

10.2   What are the differential diagnoses?

- Acne vulgaris

- Folliculitis

10.3   What is the likely diagnosis?

Acne vulgaris is very common; it is estimated that around 30% of teenagers have acne of sufficient severity to warrant medical therapy. It usually develops at puberty and is associated with an androgen-driven increase in sebum production in anatomically abnormal pilosebaceous units, which are located on the face, back and chest. It is thought that acne develops as a result of follicular plugging, sebum retention, overgrowth of Propionobacterium acnes and the release of inflammatory mediators.

10.4   How do you classify this condition?

- Mild acne predominantly consists of non-inflammatory comedones.

- Moderate acne consists of non-inflammatory comedones and inflammatory papules and pustules.

- Severe acne is characterized by the presence of nodules and cysts, as well as comedones, inflammatory papules and pustules.

- Acne conglobata (severe cystic acne with coalescing nodules, cysts and abscesses) and acne fulminans (acute onset severe cystic acne with suppuration and ulceration).

10.5   What should you tell the patient and how should you manage her condition?

Reassure her that acne is common and that most cases of adolescent acne clear spontaneously over time. There is no cure for acne but a variety of treatments are available.

10.6   What advice do you give?

Presently there is no good evidence that acne is related to diet.

10.7   She asks how to care for her skin. What do you advise?

Acne has nothing to do with not washing your face. However it is best to wash with a mild cleanser and warm water daily. Washing too often or too vigorously may make acne worse. Avoid excessive use of cosmetics and remove cosmetics every night with mild soap or cleanser.

10.8   What treatments are available and what would you offer this woman?

- Topical treatment: benzoyl peroxide, alone or with topical antibiotics, is good for inflammatory acne, retinoids are particularly useful for comedonal acne

- Oral antibiotics (erythromycin or a tetracycline)

- Oral contraceptive pills

- Isotretinoin (dermatologists only)

A combination of oral antibiotic and topical therapy is most appropriate for this patient.

10.9   What else should you tell her about treatment?

- Tell her that treatments can take up to two to three months to take effect.

- Ensure that she is fully aware of how to use the topical treatment.

- Explain that topical treatment can irritate the skin and that this may be ameliorated by reducing the frequency of application or by washing the product off after a few hours.

- Make her aware that tetracyclines and topical retinoids can cause photosensitivity.

- Advise that she should avoid pregnancy and breastfeeding whilst using topical retinoids and tetracyclines.

- Antibiotics can reduce the effectiveness of the oral contraceptive pill.

10.10   At what stage would you consider referral to a dermatologist?

You should refer acne:

- Immediately when acne is very severe

- Urgently when the patient has severe or nodulocystic acne and could benefit from oral isotretinoin, or for acne associated with severe social or psychological problems

- Routinely when patients are developing or at risk of developing scarring acne despite primary care therapies. In patients who have moderately severe acne that has failed to respond to two courses of oral antibiotics (minimum duration three months). Failure is probably best assessed by the patient

- Referral is also appropriate if there is diagnostic uncertainty

- If there is a suspicion of an underlying endocrine disorder then refer routinely to endocrinology or gynaecology

Case 2: Answers

10.11   What is the differential diagnosis?

- Seborrhoeic dermatitis

- Acne

- Rosacea

- Folliculitis

- Systemic lupus erythematosus

- Dermatomyositis

10.12   What is the diagnosis?

Rosacea is a common condition that affects adults over the age of 30 years. It is characterised by flushing, telangiectasia, papules and pustules located on the cheeks, nose, glabellar, forehead and chin. It usually spares the nasolabial fold and this feature can be helpful in differentiating rosacea from seborrhoeic dermatitis.

10.13   What are the subtypes of this condition?

- Erythematotelangiectatic (flushing, central facial oedema with/without telangiectasia)

- Papulopustular (persistent central facial erythema with papules and pustules)

- Phymatous (thick skin, irregular surface nodularities, enlargement)

- Ocular (dryness, itching, foreign body sensation, inflamed eyelids)

10.14   He asks you what makes this condition worse.

- Alcohol
- Caffeine
- Hot beverages
- Spicy food
- Stress
- Hot or cold environments
- Sun exposure
- Medications

10.15   What do you tell him?

Rosacea cannot be cured but long term treatments can be very effective. Treatment takes between four and eight weeks to become effective.

- Avoid precipitants
- Topical treatments
    - Metronidazole gel or cream
    - Azelaic acid
- Systemic antibiotics
    - Tetracyclines, erythromycin
- Laser therapy (erythematotelangiectatic disease)
- Other treatements
    - Isotretinoin (papulopustular rosacea)
    - Beta-blockers

10.16   What treatment do you offer next?

He should be commenced on a tetracycline antibiotic and the metronidazole gel changed to azelaic acid.

10.17   When should you refer?

- Uncertain diagnosis
- Papulopustular rosacea that has not responded to 12 weeks of oral plus topical treatment
- Rosacea associated with considerable psychological or social stress
- Ocular rosacea that is not responding to eyelid hygiene measures, ocular lubricants and oral tetracyclines; urgent referral is indicated if keratitis is suspected (eye pain, blurred vision, sensitivity to light)
- Refer phymatous disease to a dermatologist or plastic surgeon (if surgery is being considered)

Case 3: Answers

10.18   What is the differential diagnosis?

- Atopic eczema

- Seborrhoeic dermatitis

- Allergic contact and irritant dermatitis

- Dermatophytosis

- Psoriasis

10.19   What else should you ask?

- Does he have hayfever or asthma?

- Is there a family history of hayfever, asthma or eczema?

- What treatment has he been using?

- Does anything make the rash worse/better?

10.20   What is the most likely diagnosis?

Atopic eczema usually develops in childhood and is characterised by a chronic relapsing, pruritic, poorly defined rash with dry scale with a predilection for the flexures, neck, eyelids, forehead, face, wrists, and the dorsa of the hands and feet. It may be generalised in severe disease. It is common, affecting around 15–20% of children aged 7–19 years. It can have a significant impact on quality of life.

10.21   How should this condition be managed?

- Avoid irritants such as soap and detergents (including shampoo and bubble bath)

- Children should be offered a selection of unperfumed emollients to use every day for moisturising, washing and bathing. Leave-on emollients should be prescribed in large quantities (250–500 g weekly) and should be readily available at home and nursery/preschool or school.

- Topical steroids should be tailored to the severity of the child's eczema

  o Mild potency for the head and neck (flares may be treated with short duration moderate potency topical steroids)

  o Mild to moderate potency for sensitive sites such as the axillae and groin

  o Do not use super-potent steroids in children without seeking specialist dermatological advice

- Treatment of infection

- Education

  o Children and their parents/carers should be taught how to recognise infections and how to access appropriate treatment when a child eczema becomes infected.

  o Topical therapy; how much treatment to use, how often to apply, when and how to step up/step down treatment and how to treat infected eczema

10.22 What do you tell her?

- Features of bacterial infection are: weeping, pustules, crusts, eczema failing to respond to therapy, rapidly worsening eczema, fever and malaise.

- Features of viral infection (eczema herpeticum) are rapidly worsening eczema, painful eczema, clustered blisters, punched out erosions (depressed, ulcerated lesions 1–3 mm in diameter), fever, lethargy and distress.

10.23 What is the role of diet in atopic eczema?

The role of diet in atopic eczema is not clearly defined. Food allergy should be considered in children who have reacted previously to food with immediate symptoms or in children with moderate to severe atopic eczema that has not been controlled by optimum management.

10.24 What are the indications for referral?

- The diagnosis is, or has become, uncertain

- Management has not controlled the eczema satisfactorily as determined by the subjective assessment of the child, parent or carer

- Eczema on the face that has not responded to appropriate treatment

- The child or parent/carer may benefit from specialist advice on treatment application

- Contact dermatitis is suspected

- Eczema associated with significant social or psychological problems for the child or parent/ carer (e.g. sleep disturbance, poor school attendance)

- Eczema associated with severe and recurrent infections

Case 4: Answers

10.25 What is the differential diagnosis?

- Seborrhoeic dermatitis

- Atopic dermatitis

- Lichen simplex chronicus

- Psoriasis.

10.26 What specific questions should you include in the history?

- How long has he had it?

- Does he have any associated joint pain? (About 30% of patients with moderate to severe psoriasis will have associated psoriatic arthritis).

- Is he under a lot of stress? Can this be reduced?

- How much alcohol does he consume?

- What effect is it having on his personal and social life?

10.27 What is the most likely diagnosis?

Psoriasis is a common disorder affecting around 2% of the population. It can present at any age but it has a bimodal peak incidence in the 20s and 60s.

10.28 What types of this condition are there?

- Chronic plaque psoriasis

- Guttate psoriasis

- Palmoplantar psoriasis

- Inverse psoriasis (flexural psoriasis)

- Erythrodermic psoriasis

- Pustular psoriasis

10.29 What do you tell him about his condition?

- Psoriasis is not infectious and does not scar. It thought to have a genetic basis but this does not necessarily mean that his children will be affected.

- It is a chronic condition that can range from mild to severe.

- The course of disease is variable; it may follow an indolent course or be characterised by intermittent flares.

- It cannot be cured but there are various treatments available.

- Psoriasis can be exacerbated by stress and alcohol consumption.

10.30 What treatments are available and how would you treat this man?

Treatments can be broadly classified as topical, phototherapy, systemic therapies and biological therapies.

Topical therapy:

- Emollients

- Emollients with salicylic acid (useful for very scaly plaques but may irritate)

- Topical steroids (for face or flexural psoriasis only possible rebound on stopping)

- Tar preparations (helpful but messy)

- Dithranol (as short contact therapy useful for plaques on limbs. May stain clothes and bathroom)

- Vitamin D analogues (helpful, cosmetically acceptable; an irritant, so not suitable for facial or flexural psoriasis). Avoid in pregnancy or breast feeding. Do not exceed maximum dose

- Vitamin A analogues (can be an irritant, so not suitable for facial or flexural psoriasis. Avoid in pregnancy or breast feeding)

Phototherapy:

- UVB (usually narrow-band UVB)

- PUVA (UVA combined with oral psoralen)

Systemic therapy:

- Ciclosporin

- Methotrexate

- Acitretin
- Hydroxycarbamide (hydroxyurea)

Biological therapy:

- Etanercept
- Infliximab
- Adalimumab
- Ustekinumab

This patient has mild psoriasis and should therefore be treated with topical therapies.

10.31   He has not had a satisfactory response to treatment. What do you do next?

At this point it is appropriate to refer to a dermatologist.

Referral is appropriate where there is/are:

- Diagnostic uncertainty
- Need for further counselling and/or education including demonstration of topical treatment
- Failure of appropriately used topical treatment for a reasonable time (e.g. one month)
- Extensive disease
- Need for increasingly potent topical preparations
- Involvement of sites which are difficult to treat (e.g. face, palms, soles and genitalia)
- Need for systemic treatment
- Erythrodermic or pustular psoriasis (emergency referral)
- Adverse reactions to topical treatments
- Complications arising from a particular area of involvement
- Occupational disability or excessive time off work or school

Case 5: Answers

10.32   What is the differential diagnosis?

- Pemphigus vulgaris
- Bullous pemphigoid
- Erythema multiforme
- Dermatitis herpetiformis.

10.33   What is the most likely diagnosis?

Bullous pemphigoid is an acquired autoimmune non-scarring subepidermal blistering disease. It usually affects people over 70 years of age. There may be a prodromal rash (urticated plaques) for several weeks or months before the blisters appear. It may be localised or generalised and may involve the mucous membranes.

10.34   He asks you what causes it and if it is contagious. What do you tell him?

Bullous pemphigoid is not contagious. It is an autoimmune process where antibodies (part of the body's defence against infection) form against the structures anchoring the outer part of the skin to the deeper skin resulting in blister formation. The reason for this is unknown.

10.35   How will the diagnosis be confirmed?

- Serum antiepidermal antibodies (indirect immuno-fluorescence)
- Lesional skin biopsy (fresh blister) showing a subepidermal cleft with a mixed dermal inflammatory infiltrate with eosinophils
- Direct immunofluorescence of perilesional skin showing linear deposits of IgG and/or C3 at the basement membrane zone

10.36   Can the condition be cured?

No.

10.37   What treatments are available?

Bullous pemphigoid cannot be cured; however, there are a number of effective treatments available.

- Potent/super potent topical steroid (especially in localised disease but also appropriate for extensive disease initially)
- Antibiotics (tetracyclines), sometimes combined with nicotinomide
- Oral prednisolone
- Steroid-sparing agents (e.g. azathioprine)

10.38   How should this patient be managed?

- Seek expert advice for diagnosis and management
- Educate patient about bullous pemphigoid
- Aspirate larger blisters leaving the roof in place as a biological dressing
- If secondary infection is suspected, swab and treat with antibiotics
- Potassium permanganate soaks can be helpful for drying particularly weepy areas
- Potent or super-potent topical steroid to rash, blistered areas and erosions
- Non-adherent dressing where necessary, changed daily (involve practice/district nurse)
- Systemic agent as indicated

Case 6: Answers

10.39   What is the differential diagnosis?

- Atopic dermatitis
- Sub-acute nodular prurigo
- Scabies infestation

10.40   What questions would you ask him?

- Is anyone else in the house itching?

- Does anyone in the house have a rash?

- Has he been in contact with anyone with scabies?

10.41   What is the likely diagnosis?

Scabies is an infestation by the mite sarcoptes scabiei acquired through skin-to-skin contact with an infested individual, or in rare cases from objects such as clothes and bedding. It is characterised by intense pruritis and is classically associated with burrows in the web spaces. Often there are minimal cutaneous findings and the diagnosis is easily missed. It is therefore important to consider scabies in any patient with persistent generalised pruritis.

10.42   What should you tell the patient and how should you manage him?

- Explain that this is an infectious rash and has been acquired through close human contact with an infested individual.

- It can be treated with a cream or lotion and he and all household contacts must be treated simultaneously regardless of symptoms. Sexual contacts must also be treated.

- He needs treatment with permethrin or malathion.

10.43   How should the cream/lotion be applied?

- The cream should be applied to all areas of the skin including the face (also treat the scalp in children). It must be worked between the web spaces and under the nails. It must stay on the skin for 12 hours (permethrin) or 24 hours (malathion) before being washed off.

- When you wash your hands during this period the cream/lotion must be reapplied.

- Repeat the treatment once after seven days.

- Wash clothes and bedding the usual way so that fresh clothes and bedding are available when the treatment is washed off.

- It is not necessary to take a bath before treatment.

10.44   Is there any follow up needed?

- No follow up is usually required. Symptoms settle over a few weeks.

- Tell the patient to return if symptoms persist.

- If scabies has been acquired through sexual contact a sexual health screen is advised.

Refer if:

- The diagnosis is in doubt, or after two treatment failures.

- There is a history of risk behaviour for sexually transmitted infections (genitourinary medicine).

- There is an outbreak of scabies in an institution (e.g. school, prison, or nursing home); report to the local Health Protection Unit/Community Infection Control team.

Case 7: Answers

10.45   What is the differential diagnosis?

- Herpes zoster
- Bullous impetigo
- Zosteriform herpes simplex virus infection
- Cellulitis

10.46   What is the most likely diagnosis?

Herpes zoster is characterised by unilateral pain and a vesicular or bullous eruption limited to a dermatome. It is due to reactivation of dormant varicella-zoster virus in a sensory root ganglion. The majority of cases occur in people over 55 years of age. Other risk factors include malignancy and immunosuppression. It consists of a prodromal phase with paraesthesia or pain (pricking, stabbing, penetrating, lancinating or shooting) followed by an active phase with acute vesiculation for 3–5 days, then crusting (days to 2–3 weeks).

10.47   What do you tell him?

Yes, the blister fluid contains live virus and is capable of causing primary infection (chickenpox) in people who are not already immune, or zoster infection in immune-compromised hosts. Particular care should be taken to avoid exposure to pregnant women or immune-compromised individuals.

10.48   What treatment would you offer, if any?

This gentleman has presented in the active phase within 72 hours. He has active vesiculation and therefore should be treated with aciclovir. Herpes zoster will usually resolve spontaneously without treatment; however acyclovir can ameliorate and shorten the course of the disease.

10.49   What is the feared long-term complication of this condition?

Post herpetic neuralgia is a chronic neuropathic pain associated with herpes zoster. It is a source of considerable morbidity; elderly patients seem to be particularly vulnerable. Treatment with acyclovir may reduce the risk of post herpetic neuralgia.

10.50   What are the complications of ophthalmic zoster (herpes zoster in the ophthalmic division of trigeminal nerve)?

- Uveitis
- Keratitis
- Retinitis
- Optic neuritis
- Glaucoma
- Proptosis
- Cicatricial lid retraction and extraocular mucle paralysis. An ophthalmology consultation is mandatory.

Case 8: Answers

10.51   What else would you ask about the mole?

- Is the lesion itchy?
- Is the lesion painful?
- Has the lesion bled?
- Does it form a scab?

10.52   What is the differential diagnosis?

- Atypical naevus
- Superficial spreading melanoma

10.53   What is the likely diagnosis?

Malignant melanoma can occur at any age and the incidence is rising. Almost a third of cases occur under the age of 50 years. It is the second most common cancer among those aged 20–39 years, causing loss of more years of life than any other cancer. Early detection and excision is the only proven curative strategy. Several types of malignant melanoma are recognised: superficial spreading malignant melanoma, nodular melanoma, lentigo maligna, acral lentiginous and amelanotic melanoma.

10.54   What are the risk factors for this condition?

- Red hair and freckling
- Inability to tan (skin phototypes I and II)
- Sunburn
- Kindred (family history of melanoma)
- Moles: > 50 typical naevi
- Moles: multiple atypical naevi

10.55   What is the ABCD checklist?

Asymmetry

Border – the edges may be blurred, irregular or notched

Colour – uneven, different shades of brown, black and pink may be seen

Diameter – lesions greater then 6 mm

10.56   What is the weighted seven-point checklist for the clinical diagnosis of melanoma? Should you refer this patient urgently?

The weighted seven-point checklist should be used by all primary healthcare professionals in the assessment of pigmented lesions to determine referral.

- Major features are:
  - o   Change in size
  - o   Irregular shape

  o   Irregular colour

- Minor features are:

  o   Largest diameter 7 mm or more

  o   Inflammation

  o   Oozing

  o   Change in sensation

Suspicion is greater for lesions scoring three points or more (where each major feature scores two and each minor feature scores one). If there are concerns about cancer, any one feature is adequate to prompt urgent referral. Refer to a dermatologist or other suitable specialist with experience of melanoma diagnosis. Excision in primary care should be avoided. Do not biopsy pigmented lesions.

This patient should be referred urgently (national target for urgent referrals is currently two weeks).

10.57   What are the different types of this condition?

- Superficial spreading melanoma

- Nodular melanoma

- Lentigo maligna melanoma

- Acral lentiginous melanoma

- Amelanotic melanoma

10.58   What advice should you give patients to reduce the risk of getting skin cancer?

- In sunny weather seek shade between 11am and 3pm.

- Cover up: wear a hat that will protect your face, ears and neck. Wear long sleeves and long trousers rather than shorts. Use clothing that is tight weave that will block ultraviolet light.

- Wear sunscreen with an SPF of at least 15 that also provides UVA protection. Apply 30 minutes before anticipated exposure and reapply every two hours.

- Avoid sunbathing, sun beds and sun lamps.

- Keep babies out of the sun at all times. Protect older children with shade, clothing and SPF30+.

Case 9: Answers

10.59   What questions do you want to ask her?

- How long has it been present?

- Is it increasing in size?

- Is it itchy or painful?

- Has it ever bled or formed a scab?

10.60   What is the diagnosis?

Actinic keratoses are the most frequently encountered skin lesion. Risk factors include advancing age, fair skin and chronic sun exposure. Histologically they are characterised by partial thickness epidermal dysplasia. There is a small risk (around 0.2%) of progression to squamous cell carcinoma and they are therefore considered as precancerous lesions. For this reason treatment is recommended.

10.61   What treatments are available?

- Cryotherapy

- Diclofenac gel

- 5-fluorouracil cream (particularly useful if there are a large number of lesions)

- Imiquimod cream

- Photodynamic therapy (a chemical is applied to the lesion and then the lesion is illuminated with a certain wavelength of visible light)

- Curettage and cautery

10.62   What treatment would you recommend to this patient?

- Cyrotherapy. The patient should be warned that the treatment will sting and that it will become red and will occasionally blister (much like an oven burn). This will settle over a week or so and may leave a faint mark.

10.63   What do you advise on leaving the consultation?

- Photoprotection

- Skin self-examination

- To report back if the lesion does not resolve completely

Case 10: Answers

10.64   What is the differential diagnosis?

- Squamous cell carcinoma (SCC)

- Hypertrophic actinic keratosis

- Basal cell carcinoma

- Viral wart

- Seborrhoeic keratosis.

10.65   What is the most likely diagnosis?

Squamous cell carcinoma is a malignant tumour of keratinocytes. It is the second most common type of skin cancer in the UK. The majority of lesions are ultraviolet radiation-induced. SCCs are generally seen in people older than 55 years of age and occur on sun-exposed sites. SCCs can also occur in old scars, ulcers, burns and chronic wounds. They are associated with a low rate of distant metastasis.

10.66 What are the risk factors for this condition?

- Advanced age

- Fair skin

- Chronic ultraviolet radiation

- Ionising radiation

- Immunosuppression

10.67 What treatments options are available?

Surgical excision is the treatment of choice. Other options that may be appropriate include curettage and cautery, cyrotherapy and radiotherapy.

10.68 What do you tell him?

Yes, squamous cell carcinoma can be cured when they are detected early. If they are left untreated for too long they can spread to other parts of the body.

10.69 What factors are associated with a higher risk of recurrence and metastasis?

- Tumours on the lip, ears or non-sun-exposed sites

- Tumours arising in areas of previous injury

- Lesions greater than 2 cm in diameter

- Poorly differentiated lesions and perineural invasion

- Tumours greater than 4 mm in depth (histologically determined excluding surface keratin) or extending down to subcutaneous tissue

- Immunosuppression

- Local recurrent disease

10.70 Does he require urgent referral?

Yes, he should be referred urgently on the two-week wait rule. Any patient with a lesion suspected to be a SCC should be referred via this route.

10.71 What do you tell him?

- In sunny weather seek shade between 11 am and 3 pm.

- Cover up: wear a hat that will protect your face, ears and neck. Wear long sleeves and long trousers rather than shorts. Use clothing that is tight weave which will block ultraviolet light.

- Wear sunscreen with an SPF of at least 15 that also provides UVA protection. Apply 30 minutes before anticipated exposure and reapply every two hours.

- Avoid sunbathing, sun beds and sun lamps.

Case 11: Answers

10.72 What is the differential diagnosis?

- Basal cell carcinoma
- Sebaceous hyperplasia
- Adnexal tumour (tumour of the skin appendages)

10.73 What is the most likely diagnosis?

Basal cell carcinoma is a slow growing, locally invasive malignant skin tumour predominantly affecting Caucasians. Metastasis is very rare, limited to a number of case reports. It is the most common cancer in Europe, Australia and the United States.

10.74 What are the sub-types of this condition?

- Nodular
- Superficial (red/pink patch usually found on the trunk, very fine raised 'whipcord' edge, may be scale/crust on the surface)
- Infiltrative (yellow/white waxy patches with ill-defined edge and surface telangiectasia)

10.75 What do you tell the patient?

- The lesion is a basal cell carcinoma (it may be necessary to perform a biopsy first to confirm the diagnosis).
- This is a form of local skin cancer that can be cured and does not spread.
- It requires treatment otherwise it will continue to enlarge resulting in local destruction and ulceration.
- There are a variety of treatments available.

10.76 What are the treatments options for BCC?

- Excision (the treatment of choice for this patient)
- Moh's micrographic surgery (high risk BCC at cosmetically sensitive sites, an expensive technique involving excision of successive layers until histological confirmation of complete excision confirmed)
- Radiotherapy
- Curettage and cautery (low risk tumours only, operator dependent, higher chance of recurrence compared to excision)
- Cryosurgery
- Photodynamic therapy (superficial BCC only)
- Topical imiquimod (superficial BCC only)

10.77 What factors are associated with a higher risk of recurrence?

- Larger size
- Lesions on the central face, especially around the eyes, nose, lips and ears

- Poorly defined lesions

- Failure of previous treatments

- Histological features: subtype (morphoeic, micronodular, infiltrative) and perineural or perivascular invasion

- Immunosuppression may confer increased risk of recurrence

10.78   Does this patient require an urgent referral?

- No, where there is a suspicion that a patient has a basal cell carcinoma a non-urgent referral should be made.

- If the tumour involves a high risk site or in situations where local destruction is causing cosmetic disfigurement a semi-urgent referral is necessary.

- If there is diagnostic uncertainly an urgent referral may be appropriate.

- If there is concern about squamous cell carcinoma or melanoma an urgent two-week referral is indicated.

10.79   What are the risk factors for this condition?

- Ultraviolet radiation (sun exposure during childhood may be especially important)

- Increasing age

- Male sex

- Fair skin types (I and II)

- Immunosuppression

- Arsenic exposure

- Genetic predisposition

- Gorlin's syndrome (multiple BCCs, odontogenic keratocysts and skeletal abnormalities)

Following development of a BCC, patients are at a significantly increased risk of developing subsequent BCCs at other sites.

10.80   What advice do you give this patient on leaving the clinic?

- In sunny weather seek shade between 11 am and 3 pm.

- Cover up: wear a hat that will protect your face, ears and neck. Wear long sleeves and long trousers rather than shorts. Use clothing that is tight weave which will block ultraviolet light.

- Wear sunscreen with an SPF of at least 15 that also provides UVA protection. Apply 30 minutes before anticipated exposure and reapply every two hours.

- Avoid sunbathing, sun beds and sun lamps.

References

Case 1

1. Acne vulgaris. Clinical Knowledge Summaries. http://www.cks.nhs.uk/acne_vulgaris

Case 2

1. Rosacea. Clinical Knowledge Summaries. http://www.cks.nhs.uk/rosacea

Case 3

1. Atopic eczema in children: management of atopic eczema in children from birth up to the age of 12 years. National Institute for health and Clinical Excellence 2007

2. Atopic eczema. Clinical Knowledge Summaries. http://www.cks.nhs.uk/eczema_atopic

Case 4

1. Psoriasis – General Management. British Assocaition of Dermatologists. 2008. http://www.bad.org.uk/site/769/Default.aspx

Case 5

1. Wojnarowska F, Kirtstschig G, Highet AS, et al. Guidelines for the management of bullous pemphigoid. Br J of Dermatol 2002; 147: 214–221

Case 6

1. Scabies. Clinical Knowledge Summaries. http://www.cks.nhs.uk/scabies

Case 7

1. Shingles. Clinical Knowledge Summaries. http://www.cks.nhs.uk/shingles

Case 8

1. Skin cancer – suspected. http://www.cks.nhs.uk/skin_cancer_suspected

2. Improving outcomes for people with skin tumours including melanoma. 2006. National Institute for Health and Clinical Excellence. http://www.nice.org.uk/nicemedia/pdf/CSG_Skin_Manual.pdf

Case 9

1. Guidelines for the management of actinic keratoses, British Association of Dermatologists (2007)

Case 10

1. Motley R, Kersey P, Lawrence C. Multiprofessional guidelines for the management of the patient with primary cutaneous squamous cell carcinoma. Br J of Dermatol 2002; 146: 18–25

Case 11

1. Telfer NR, Colver GB, Morton CA. Guidelines for the management of basal cell carcinoma. Brit J of Dermatol 2008; 159: 35–48

Cases 1-11

1. Collier J, Longmore M, Scally P. 6th edition. 2003. *Oxford Handbook of Clinical Specialties.* Oxford.

Paediatrics answers

Case 1: Answers   ,

11.1   What are the main differential diagnoses?

- Possetting/reflux
- Gastroenteritis, usually associated with diarrhoea too.
- Overfeeding
- Pyloric stenosis
- Infection, particularly UTI
- Bowel obstruction, when vomiting is usually bilious

11.2   What else would you want to know in the history?

- More detail about the vomiting – frequency, relation to feeding, duration, colour, forcefulness, associated with coughing
- Any other associated symptoms such as fever, abdominal distension, stool colour and form
- Whether baby is bottle or breastfed, and how much feeding. At this age a normal baby will take around 150 ml/kg/day.
- Whether the baby's weight has been increasing (parent-held record)
- Whether there had been any problems during labour or post delivery

11.3   What is the most likely diagnosis?

Pyloric stenosis. This usually develops within the first three to six weeks of life. It is commonest in the first born, male child and there is familial clustering. There is hypertrophy of the pyloric muscle causing progressively worsening stomach outlet obstruction. Projectile vomiting is the classic symptom, but with no bile in the vomit, as the obstruction is proximal to the bile duct. The child is hungry afterwards. If diagnosis is delayed, there may be failure to thrive

11.4   What would you see during a test feed?

The majority of children have an olive-shaped mass palpable in the right upper abdomen, which you can feel contracting and relaxing under your fingers if you are patient. There may also be visible peristalsis of the dilated stomach in the epigastrium.

11.5   What other investigations might assist in making the diagnosis?

- Urea and electrolytes: hypokalaemia, hypochloraemia and raised bicarbonate are characteristic due to loss of stomach acid
- Blood gas – metabolic alkalosis
- Ultrasound – muscle thickness ≥ 3 mm thickness or canal length $>$ or $= 16$ mm

11.6   Outline the management.

- Refer to paediatricians
- Keep nil by mouth and correct dehydration and electrolyte disturbance with IV fluids
- Surgery (Ramstedt's pyloromyotomy) is curative

Case 2: Answers

11.7   What are the differential diagnoses?

- Febrile seizure

- Epilepsy, but not possible to diagnose this until there have been three episodes or more

- Infection, especially meningitis, but child would be ill

- Hypoglycaemia: DEFG ('Don't Ever Forget Glucose')

- Brain injury, especially associated with child abuse, but this most commonly presents in early infancy

- Poisoning, especially tricyclics

11.8   What questions would you ask in the history?

- What was the seizure like and how quickly did the child recover? Atypical febrile seizures are > 5–10 minutes, focal, or associated with prolonged reduced conscious level.

- Was there any change in her behaviour before the seizure started?

- Has the child been unwell recently?

- Any rash (especially non-blanching?)

- When did she last eat (particularly if hypoglycaemic, as this tends to occur with fasting?)

- Is there a family history of seizures, particularly with fever?

- What was her previous developmental status: if abnormal, there may be an underlying neurological condition?

- Were there any problems during her pregnancy and birth?

11.9   What should your immediate management be?

- Assess airways to ensure patency

- Assess her breathing

- Check her pulse and blood pressure

- Check blood sugar

- Check AVPU (and later Glasgow Coma Scale). AVPU is a 4-point scale used in the rapid assessment of the neurological status of children. A (lert), responding to V(oice), responding to P(ain) and U(nresponsive).

11.10   What is the most likely diagnosis?

Febrile convulsion – these are benign, generalised convulsions occurring in children febrile due to an infection or inflammation outside the central nervous system in a child who is otherwise neurologically normal. They occur between the ages of six months to five years. They must leave no underlying or residual abnormality and usually last less than ten minutes.

11.11   What further investigations are required?

If the child has fully recovered then there is no need for any further investigations, unless the fit is atypical (see above). However, if the child is still unwell then conditions such as UTI and meningitis need to be excluded, and a lumbar puncture considered.

11.12   Outline your management and the advice you would give to the parents.

- Immediate management is to treat conservatively

    o   Monitor neurological status until recovered

    o   Anticonvulsants for any further prolonged seizures (lorazepam IV)

    o   Treatment of any underlying infection e.g. UTI, otitis media

- Reassurance and education:

    o   Advice about temperature control:

        ▪   Paracetamol

        ▪   Stripping off

        ▪   Encouraging air flow to reduce fevers.

        ▪   Tepid sponging is of possible value, but if excessively used can encourage shivering and thus heat generation.

        ▪   Paracetamol can be given prior to MMR vaccine

    o   Advice about seizure:

        ▪   Putting the child in the recovery position.

        ▪   Call for an ambulance if the fit is focal or lasts ten minutes with no signs of stopping. Fits lasting longer than 30 minutes are more dangerous to the child.

        ▪   If complex or prolonged recurrent seizures occur, then buccal midazolam or rectal diazepam can be precribed for home use.

    o   Advice about the prognosis:

        ▪   Risk of recurrence is about 30%

        ▪   The risk of epilepsy with a simple febrile seizure is 1.5–2.5%. If there is a complex seizure then it is 4–6%. Risk increases with family history of epilepsy, fever of short duration before the seizure, complex seizure and neurological abnormalities or developmental delay before the onset of febrile seizure.

Case 3: Answers

11.13   What are differential diagnoses for short stature?

- Familial short stature

- Constitutional delay in growth and puberty

- Chronic disease, e.g. renal, gastrointestinal or liver disease, severe asthma, cystic fibrosis

- Endocrine causes, especially. hypothyroidism, GH deficiency, panhypopituitarism

- Psychosocial causes

11.14 What further questions would you ask?

- What is his exact height? Has his height always been short for his age or is it falling off? How tall are his parents?

- Does he have any medical problems? Chronic diseases can cause growth failure

- What is his appetite like?

- Has his weight been stable?

- Was pregnancy normal? Was there congenital infection, or placental problems?

- Was his birth normal? Was his birth weight normal (intrauterine growth retardation (IUGR)? Were there any problems post delivery?

- Developmental milestones

- Problems at home or school

- Family dynamics e.g parental depression, substance misuse

- Does he have any other siblings and if so how tall are they?

- Family history of any medical problems such as malabsorption or dysmorphic syndromes

11.15 What clinical examination would you focus on?

- Anthropometry: his height and weight should be accurately measured and plotted on a culturally-appropriate growth chart. Sitting height should be measured and plotted, to detect any disproportion between trunk and limb length.

- Dysmorphic features should be sought, e.g of achondroplasia or Russell-Silver syndrome.

- Signs of puberty: if there are none, then he will not yet have entered his pubertal growth spurt, and will continue on his childhood growth rate. He will thus gradually sag below his peers in height.

11.16 What is the mid-parental height?

This is an indicator of the genetic growth potential of a child. It is based upon a calculation involving the parent's height – short parents are likely to have short children. There is an adjustment based on sex.

It is calculated by adding the parent's height together, then dividing by 2. If it is a girl then you subtract 7 cm, and if a boy you add 7 cm.

For him it is $[(155 + 145)/2] + 7$ cm = 157 cm.

11.17 What is the likely diagnosis?

There are two differentials to consider: familial short stature and constitutional delay in growth and puberty. They can also coexist. Both parents are short, and there are no signs of puberty.

- Familial short stature – this is the commonest cause of short stature. Before this can be diagnosed other causes need to be ruled out and the growth needs to be plotted on growth charts to check that there is a steady growth and that there is no crossing of centiles.

- Constitutional delay in growth and puberty – if there are no signs of puberty by this age.

11.18 What investigations would you do?

- Plot a detailed growth chart (collect all data from parent-held record)

- X-ray to determine bone age (compares with standards published in radiological atlases, such as Gruelich-Peil or Tanner and Whitehouse).

- Thyroid function tests (hypothyroidism)

- U&Es, LFTs (looking for occult renal or liver failure)

- Urine dipstick (occult renal problems)

- Full blood count (anaemia associated with malabsorbtion or iron deficiency from dietary inadequacy)

- Other investigations tailored to the history and examination, e.g. coeliac antibodies

11.19   What are the management options?

- No treatment is needed but reassurance to him and his parents.

- His growth should be plotted on growth charts regularly every six months to calculate his growth velocity. Use the formula: (later height − present height)*2 to annualise. In the prepubertal child it should be > 4 cm/year. A low growth velocity should prompt further endocrine investigations.

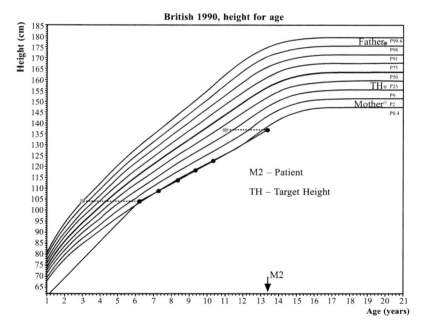

Figure 20.14 Growth chart: growth chart from a child with constitutional delay in growth and puberty. Note that the bone age (squares) is delayed by more than 2 years from the chronological age (circles). Father and mother's height and target height have also been plotted. (courtesy of Dr Colin Melville and Stafford Hospital)

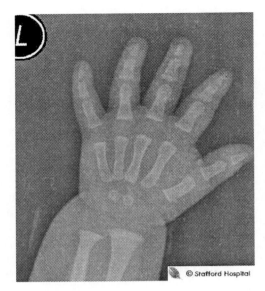

Figure 20.15 Bone age 1: left wrist X-ray in an infant. Note that very few of the carpal bone ossification centres are visible. (courtesy of Dr Colin Melville and Stafford Hospital)

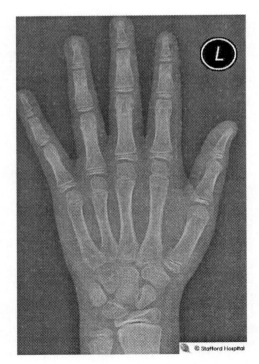

Figure 20.16 Bone age 2: left wrist X-ray in an adolescent. Note that all the carpal bone ossification centres are now visible. However, the epipheses are not yet fused, showing that some further growth is possible. (courtesy of Dr Colin Melville and Stafford Hospital)

Case 4: Answers

11.20   What is failure to thrive and what are the main causes?

Failure to thrive means that the person is not growing or gaining weight in a healthy way. It is detected by serial measurements of weight on the growth chart. After initially regressing towards the mean, children by six months of age have usually found their genetic centile and track this thereafter if healthy. However, there is considerable variation. A fall across two standard deviations is clinically significant.

There are a huge number of potential causes, with weight loss being a general manifestation of chronic or acute severe disease.

- Malnutrition – worldwide, inadequate food intake is the commonest cause, and this still affects deprived UK communities. It can also result from global delay, behavioural feeding disturbance or physical feeding problems, such as cleft palate
- Gastro-oesophageal reflux disease, with 'lost' calories through regurgitation
- Malabsorption, such as cow's milk protein intolerance or Coeliac disease
- Chronic medical problems such as cystic fibrosis, hypothyroidism, renal failure, congenital heart disease, malignancy
- Child abuse, especially neglect
- Social problems, such as severe poverty and deprivation

11.21   What other history would you make specific enquiry about?

- The child's appetite
- Food intake: time and content of liquids and solids , amount eaten
- Any feeding problems: food refusal, swallowing difficulties/choking
- Any diarrhoea or vomiting
- Any significant infections, for example chest or ENT
- Birth weight, and any problems during pregnancy or perinatally
- Family and social history
  - Interaction at home with family, particularly mother. Maternal depression can interfere with feeding. General condition of child, especially if well cared for.
  - Who else is at home?
  - Any stresses at home with finances or work
  - Are there any other siblings, and if so how are they?
  - Has the child or family had any other involvement with other services such as social services in past?
- Physical examination to check no underlying problem or evidence of malnutrition, such as dysmorphic features, anaemia, jaundice, cyanosis, clubbing, oedema, lymphadenopathy, temperature, rickets

11.22   What investigations would you request?

- Five-day dietary assessment. Parents keep a diary of all food eaten. Dietitian's computer works out intake relative to RDA for CHO, protein, fat, vitamins, minerals

- Dipstick of urine: to exclude UTI, glycosuria

- Bloods for FBC (including film), ferritin (folate and b12 if macrocytic)

- U&Es and LFTs (occult renal and liver disease)

- Thyroid function tests

- Coeliac disease antibodies – anti-endomysium, anti-gliadin, tissue transglutaminase

- Sweat test for cystic fibrosis

- Urine metabolic screen

- Many other tests as clinically indicated e.g. chromosomes if developmentally delayed with dysmorphic features

11.23   What is the diagnosis and how can this be confirmed?

- Coeliac disease. This is a gluten-sensitive enteropathy. It is the most common cause of generalised malabsorption in Western Europe with an incidence of 1 in 1000. The incidence is highest in childhood with peak age 0–5 years. It is associated with HLA-B8. There is an increased incidence in people with Down's syndrome, autoimmune thyroid disease and insulin dependent diabetes. There is an increased risk of small bowel malignancy in particular lymphoma with Coeliac disease and the risk of this is reduced by maintaining a gluten-free diet.

- Traditionally the diagnosis is confirmed with serial small bowel biopsies. First jejunal biopsy usually reveals a completely flat mucosa (subtotal villous atrophy).

- A second biopsy taken 9–12 months later should show re-establishment of normal mucosa.

- Another biopsy following the reintroduction of gluten (gluten challenge) with biopsy taken three months later, or earlier if symptoms develop (should show villous).

- Many experts now feel that subtotal villous atrophy on a single biopsy plus a high titre of initial antibodies that falls rapidly on a gluten-free diet is sufficient to confirm the diagnosis.

11.24   What is the treatment?

Gluten free diet for life – no wheat, oats, barley or rye. With the gluten-free diet the symptoms should resolve. They should be referred to the dietician to give them help in following this diet.

Case 5: Answers

11.25   What are the differential diagnoses?

- Henoch schönlein purpura

- Meningococcal septicaemia

- Idiopathic thrombocytopaenic purpura

- Acute leukaemia

- Child abuse

11.26   What other questions would you ask?

- Is this child well or ill? HSP and ITP occur in well children, whilst if the child is ill meningococcal disease, leukaemia or child abuse should be considered

- Any fever?
- Any joint pain or swelling, abdominal pain or haematuria?
- Any headache, photophobia, neck stiffness or tiredness?
- Any social issues?
- Any history of trauma?
- Is he up-to-date with his immunisations? (Hib and pneumococcal septicaemia can present in a similar way to MCD)
- Any contact with infections recently?

11.27   What is the likely diagnosis?

Henoch schönlein purpura – this is a condition characterised by widespread vasculitis of medium-sized arteries. It classically affects children 3–8 years, and is more common in boys. In 50% there may be evidence of Group A streptococcal infection (strep. throat). There are skin, renal, gastrointestinal and joint manifestations. The rash characteristically affects the buttocks and shins. Affected gut can act as a trigger for intussusception.

11.28   What examination would you do?

- Check the child is not ill-looking. May suggest meningococcal disease or leukaemia
- Check the rash is non-blanching (tumbler test)
- Check child is responding appropriately. 'Frozen watchfulness' in child abuse
- Systems examination, especially for distribution of rash, joint involvement

Investigations may include:

- Blood pressure monitoring
- Urine dipstick and MSU, looking for haematuria and proteinuria
- U&Es – check for renal function
- FBC (anaemia, high or low white cell count, platelets) and film (exclude blast cells)
- Coagulation, which may indicate DIC in meningococcal disease
- ASO titre and throat swab

11.29   What is the treatment?

- HSP is usually self-limiting and does not need any treatment. The child should have bed rest and be allowed up to toilet only, until the rash is settling.
- If blood pressure is elevated with haematuria and proteinuria he should be referred to hospital. If this does not settle, then referral for specialist renal investigation may be required (glomerulonephritis).
- Confirm that the child can keep food and drink down: this may require admission.
- If there are any complications then referral to the paediatricians is needed. These include:
  o Raised BP
  o Renal involvement (haematuria and proteinuria)
  o GI bleeding

- ○ Vomiting

- ○ Intussusception

- ○ Joint pain and swelling preventing weight-bearing

Case 6: Answers

11.30   What is the likely diagnosis?

Nocturnal enuresis – this is more common in boys than girls. It occurs in 15% of five-year-olds and is still present in 3% of 15-year-olds.

11.31   What advice can you give them?

- Reassurance that many otherwise completely normal children have this problem

- Do not have any drinks just before sleeping

11.32   What is the management?

- Bedwetting alarm (this requires support, e.g. in a nurse-led clinic)

- Rewarding successful behaviour (dry nights) with star charts

- Medications such as desmopressin are more useful for trips away, as the problem tends to recur as soon as the medication is stopped

- Most children will grow out of it even with no treatment

Case 7: Answers

11.33   What other questions would you ask about in the history?

- Has the cough present been present all the time (recurrent vs, chronic persistent, though it may be difficult to tell in the early stages)?

- Any diarrhoea and/or vomiting?

- Any other forms of infection (ear, throat, urine, skin, joint, CSF)?

- Any other medical problems?

- Any family history of medical problems (familial, e.g. asthma, and genetic disease, e.g. CF?)

- What previous investigations have been done (CF screening is now universal in the UK) and what were the results?

- Vaccination history (this dramatically alters the likelihood of specific infections, and needs to be taken into account when doing laboratory tests of immunity)

11.34   What are your differentials?

- Cystic fibrosis

- Immunodeficiency, particularly severe combined immuno-deficiency (SCID)

- Gastro-oesophageal reflux disease, particularly complicated by recurrent aspiration, which occurs more often if the child has neurological problems.

11.35   What investigations would you request?

- Growth chart (plot all data from parent-held record)

- Review chest X-rays and get a Consultant Radiologist's opinion on these

- Full blood count and film (lymphocyte count $< 1 \times 109/l$ is associated with SCID)

- Sweat test (cystic fibrosis)

- Total immunoglobulins (low in agammaglobulinemia)

- NPA, urine, stool and throat cultures (looking for specific organisms)

11.36   What is the diagnosis?

Cystic fibrosis – this is an autosomal recessive disorder. The CF gene lies on the long arm of chromosome 7 and the commonest mutation is in the F508 resulting in the omission of one phenylalanine amino acid from the CF transmembrane conductance regulator protein encoded by the gene. Patients with CF have either no CFTR or a defective CFTR in the cell membrane of affected tissues. In the Caucasian population it has a carrier frequency of one in 20 and an incidence of one in 2000. It was previously diagnosed in infants and toddlers, who presented with meconium ileus, recurrent chest infections or failure to thrive. The neonatal screening programme now picks up most cases.

11.37   Outline your further management.

- Repeat sweat test to make sure it is definitely CF

- Offer genetic counselling to the family

- Physiotherapy and prophylactic antibiotics

- Ensure vaccinations are up to date

- Pancreatic supplementation

- Vitamin supplements

- Dietary advice (high calorie diet because of the high metabolic demands of chronic infection and increased work of breathing)

- Give them information about the condition such as the leaflet at http://www.patient.co.uk/health/Cystic-Fibrosis.htm

Case 8: Answers

11.38   What other questions would you ask?

- Is he ill? (The patient usually will be, in septic arthritis or osteomyelitis)

- Can he weight-bear, and if not when did this occur?

- Any previous history of bone or joint problems, and any other joints involved (JCA or tumour will have more prolonged symptoms)?

- Any family history of bone or joint problems?

- What is his weight (especially slipped upper femoral epiphysis)?

11.39 What are the differential diagnoses?

- Trauma (e.g. bruising/haemarthrosis)

- Perthes disease (usually younger boys)

- Slipped upper femoral epiphysis (usually in overweight, older patients)

- Transient synovitis (reactive arthritis)

- Septic arthritis

- Osteomyelitis

- Osteosarcoma

- Acute leukaemia

- Haemophilia (causes haemarthrosis in boys)

- Rheumatic fever, but this tends to cause a migratory arthritis or arthropathy, and follows a sore throat

- Pre-rash Henoch-Schonlein purpura

- Still's disease (more chronic, with fever, evanescent rash +/– palpable lymph nodes/liver/ spleen)

11.40 Why is the hip held in this position?

To minimise stretching of the inflamed hip joint capsule, which is painful.

11.41 What investigations would you request?

- Full blood count and differential white cell count, film (white count elevated in infection/ inflammation. Film may show blast cells)

- Inflammatory markers ESR and CRP

- Ultrasound of hips, looking for effusion

- X-ray of hips and knees, looking for structural changes of SUFE or Perthes'. Changes of osteomyelitis take more than seven days to appear

- Urine, stool and throat culture: looking for infections associated with reactive arthritis

- Bone scan may be helpful if septic arthritis is suspected

11.42 What is the most likely diagnosis?

Perthes' disease. This is avascular necrosis of the femoral head. It occurs mainly in boys between four and eight years. It presents with pain and limping, usually affecting one hip.

11.43 What is the management of this condition?

The goal of treatment is to create a spherical well-covered femoral head.

- Initially, bed rest and traction if pain is severe

- Physiotherapy to maintain hip movements

- Initial restriction of activities. Surveillance with X-ray. If it worsens then surgery may be needed

References

Case 1

1. Pediatrics, pyloric stenosis. Emedicine. http://emedicine.medscape.com/article/803489-overview

Case 2

1. Pediatrics, febrile seizure. Emedicine. http://emedicine.medscape.com/article/801500-overview

2. Febrile seizure. Clinical Knowledge Summaries. http://www.cks.nhs.uk/febrile_seizure

3. Feverish illness in children. Quick reference guide. Clinical guideline 47. May 2007. National Institute for Health and Clinical Excellence. http://www.nice.org.uk/nicemedia/pdf/CG47QuickRefGuide.pdf

4. UTI in children. Quick reference guide. Clinical guideline 54. August 2007. National Institute for Health and Clinical Excellence. http://www.nice.org.uk/nicemedia/pdf/CG54quickrefguide.pdf

Case 3

1. Constitutional Growth Delay. Emedicine. http://emedicine.medscape.com/article/919677-overview

Case 4

1. Failure to thrive. Emedicine. http://emedicine.medscape.com/article/985007-overview

2. Coeliac disease. Emedicine. http://emedicine.medscape.com/article/932104-overview

Case 5

1. Henoch schonlein purpura. Emedicine. http://emedicine.medscape.com/article/984105-overview

Case 6

1. Enuresis. Emedicine. http://emedicine.medscape.com/article/1014762-overview

.2. Bedwetting. Clinical Knowledge Summaries. http://www.cks.nhs.uk/bed_wetting_enuresis

Case 7

1. Cystic fibrosis. Emedicine. http://emedicine.medscape.com/article/1001602-overview

Case 8

1. Perthes disease. Emedicine. http://emedicine.medscape.com/article/1248267-overview

2. Oxford Handbook of Clinical Specialties. Judith Collier, Murray Longmore, Peter Scally. 6th Edition. 2003

Cases 1–8

1. Collier J, Longmore M, Scally P. (6th edition) (2003). *Oxford Handbook of Clinical Specialties*, Oxford.

2. Lissauer T, Clayden G. (3rd edition) (2007). *Illustrated Textbook of Paediatrics*. Mosby International Limited. Elsevier.

Recommended further cases

- Slipped upper femoral epiphysis

- Croup

- Bronchiolitis

- Asthma in children

- Intussuseption

- UTI

Psychiatry answers

Case 1: Answers

12.1   What is the likely diagnosis?

Depression.

12.2   What are the symptoms you should ask about in this condition?

NICE recommends using the ICD10 classification for diagnosing and assessing the severity of depression. Major Symptoms include:

- Persistent sadness or low mood

- Loss of interests or pleasure

- Fatigue or low energy

If any of the above have been present most days for most of the time for at least two weeks then ask about the following symptoms:

- Increased or poor appetite

- Disturbed sleep

- Poor concentration or attention

- Low self confidence or self-esteem

- Pessimistic views of future

- Guilt or self-blame

- Self harm or suicidal thoughts

Mild depression is classified by at least two of the major criteria and at least two of the other symptoms above. These need to be present for at least two weeks and the person will still be able to function despite difficulty with work and ordinary activities.

Moderate depression is classified by at least two of the major criteria and at least three, preferably four of the other symptoms present for at least two weeks. The person will have symptoms to a marked degree and will have difficulty with work, social and domestic activities.

In severe depression all three of the major criteria should be present and at least four of the others, some of which are of severe intensity. The symptoms should be present for at least two weeks, but if they are severe and very rapid in onset then the diagnosis can be made before two weeks. Severe depression can be then further classified depending on psychotic symptoms – delusions, hallucinations or stupor.

In General Practice, two screening questions are used: 'During the last month have you often been bothered by feeling down, depressed or hopeless?' and 'During the last month have you often been bothered by having little interest or pleasure in doing things?'

Suicidal risk must always be assessed in every patient.

12.3   What signs might you pick up from this patient in the consultation?

- Poor eye contact

- Tearful

- Emotionally flat

- Very anxious

12.4   What are risk factors in the history you should ask about?

- Recent bereavement, job loss or similar changes in circumstances

- Previous depression or mental health problems

- Significant physical illness

- Family history of mental health problems

- Previous deliberate self-harm or suicide attempts

- Any abuse

- Frequent attendance at GP or A&E or multiple symptoms

- Chronic pain syndrome

12.5   What are other causes of low mood?

- Alcohol and substance misuse

- Iatrogenic prescribed drugs – Beta-blockers, benzodiazepines, steroids

- Medical conditions – Parkinson's, cancer, hypothyroidism, Cushing's syndrome, CVA, MS, anxiety, post-traumatic stress disorder, grief reaction

- Mood disorders – dysthymia, cyclothymia, bipolar disorder

- Schizoaffective disorder

- Secondary to psychiatric disorder

- Anxiety

- Eating disorders

- Adjustment disorders

- Personality disorders

- Psychotic disorders

- Dementia

12.6   What investigations may be needed sometimes to exclude other differential diagnoses?

Investigations can help to exclude other medical or substance-related problems, and can also act as a baseline before treatments are commenced.

- Urea and electrolytes, liver function tests
- Full blood count – check for anaemia, raised WCC in infection, high MCV with alcohol misuse
- Thyroid function to exclude hypothyroidism

12.7   What is the management of her depression and does she need urgent referral?

This patient meets the criteria for moderate depression. For moderate depression first line treatment is with an SSRI, usually fluoxetine or citalopram. Sertraline is used in people with a recent MI or unstable angina. Psychological treatment should be offered to those that do not want medication. NICE recommends psychological treatment should be considered as first line. For moderate depression, even if the patient wants medication, ideally short-term psychological input is first line treatment. The options need to be discussed fully with the patient and their choice taken into account.

Severe depression should be treated with a combination of both antidepressants and CBT.

In mild depression for people who do not want an intervention, or for people who you think may recover without intervention, then watchful waiting is an approach where a follow up should be arranged normally in two weeks. Antidepressants are not recommended as the risk-benefit ratio is low. Usually simple counselling or problem solving is used, and exercise is also used for mild depression. If mild depression persists after other interventions, or is associated with medical or psychological problems, or if there is past history of moderate or severe depression, then you can consider the use of antidepressants.

Urgently refer to a specialist mental health service if:

- The person is actively suicidal or has a current suicide plan
- The person presents a considerable risk to other people
- There is severe agitation accompanying severe symptoms
- There are psychotic features (delusions, hallucinations)
- There is evidence of severe self-neglect

12.8   You start the patient on citalopram. What should you tell the patient about the medication?

- Risk of discontinuation/withdrawal symptoms (fluoxetine and citalopram have fewer of these)
- Potential side effects
- Delay in onset of action; the duration for which the medication needs to be taken; when and how to take the medication

12.9   The patient is not deemed to be at risk of suicide. When do you need to review her again?

As she is not at high risk of suicide or under 30, she can be seen after two weeks and then regularly every two to four weeks. If she is under 30, she would be monitored closely in the early stages for restlessness, agitation and suicidality.

12.10   The patient had been on citalopram at the optimal dose for a month but is still not getting better. What can be done now?

Switching to a different antidepressant. Choices for a second antidepressant include a different SSRI or mirtazipine.

When switching between selective serotonin reuptake inhibitors (SSRIs), the first SSRI should be withdrawn before the second SSRI is started. After stopping fluoxetine, a different SSRI should not be started until four to seven days later, as it has a long half-life and active metabolites.

For more information on switching between other types of antidepressant see the clinical knowledge summaries on depression.

Beware of the risk of serotonin syndrome when a combination of serotonergic antidepressants are used. Features of this include confusion, delirium, sweating, shivering, myoclonus and changes in blood pressure.

12.11   Three months later she comes to see you for one of her reviews and she is feeling a lot better. She asks if she can stop taking the medications. What should you do?

NICE recommends that for moderate or severe depression then antidepressants should be taken for at least six months after remission.

In patients that have had two or more depressive episodes in the recent past and experienced significant functional impairment during these episodes, it is recommended to be on antidepressants for two years.

Case 2: Answers

12.12   What is the likely diagnosis?

Schizophrenia.

This is a major psychiatric disorder characterised by psychotic symptoms that change their behaviour, effect, perceptions and thoughts. Everyone has a different unique experience of schizophrenia.

People often present with delusions or hallucinations. About 1% of the population will suffer with an acute episode of schizophrenia in their lifetime. Men tend to develop it three to four years earlier than women. The peak age is late teens, early 20s for men and late 20s for women. The patient often lacks insight and so history may come from a friend or relative.

The most important risk factor is having a family history of schizophrenia. Others are being from a socially disadvantaged background, social isolation, drug misuse, birth complications, time of birth (more common in those born in late winter and early spring).

12.13   What are the differential diagnoses?

- Temporal lobe epilepsy
- Illicit drugs – cocaine, amphetamines, cannabis
- Dementia
- Schizoaffective disorder
- Personality disorders
- Acute confusional state
- Depression with psychotic symptoms
- Mania
- Brain damage, brain tumour
- Stroke
- Endocrine causes – Cushing's

12.14   What are Schneider's first rank symptoms?

One or more of these symptoms is suggestive of schizophrenia.

- Auditory hallucinations in the form of a running commentary
- Hearing own thoughts spoken out aloud
- Hearing voices referring to self in the third person
- Somatic hallucinations
- Thought broadcasting
- Thought insertion, withdrawal and interruption
- Delusional perception
- Feelings, impulses or actions are experienced as made or influenced by external agents (passivity of affect, impulse or volition)
- Somatic passivity

Positive symptoms – presence of abnormal mental process

- Hallucinations – false perceptions that occur in the absence of a real external stimuli
- Delusions – fixed beliefs that are unshakable
- Formal thought disorders – loosening of associations like derailment, 'knight's move thinking'

Negative symptoms reflect the absence or reduction of mental function that is normally present. They are harder to treat and persistent.

- Poverty of speech – talk less spontaneously
- Flattening of affect – express less emotion
- Avolition/apathy – less energy, drive, interest
- Social isolation

Initial presentation of schizophrenia is usually with positive symptoms.

12.15   This patient is male and has some negative symptoms. What are other poor prognostic factors?

- Early or insidious onset
- Male sex
- Negative symptoms
- Family history of schizophrenia
- Significant psychiatric history
- Drug or alcohol misuse
- Social isolation, low social class

12.16   What should this man's management be?

Early referral to an early intervention service is needed for the first acute presentation. If there is a high risk of harm to themselves or others then assessment should be within 24 hours. If out of hours, speak to the crisis team. If treatment with anti-psychotics is needed you should discuss this with a specialist first. CBT should be offered to all patients with schizophrenia.

12.17   What kind of medication is first line treatment?

Typical anti-psychotics are not recommended by NICE. First line treatment is with atypical anti-psychotics such as olanzapine, risperdione, amisulpride. Clozapine is for treatment-resistant schizophrenia.

Patients should be given information on the benefits and side effects of the medication and be able to discuss this with the medical practitioner. The decision to start medication should be made in partnership. Side-effects include akathisia and weight gain.

12.18   What things will you need to check regularly in patients with schizophrenia?

- Urine/blood glucose
- Blood pressure
- Weight
- Healthy diet and exercise
- Smoking cessation
- CHD risk annually
- Ask about adverse effects such as tardive dyskinesia, extrapyramidal symptoms, sexual dysfunction (LUNSERS scale)
- Bloods
- ECG
- Ask about alcohol and drugs

People with schizophrenia are at an increased risk of suicide, cardiovascular disease, respiratory disease, obesity and alcohol and drug use.

12.19   When should you consider referral?

Consider referral if:

- The person is at increased risk of harm to themselves or others (referral should be urgent).
- They are showing symptoms of relapse (some people have very specific 'relapse signatures', which should be documented in the care plan).
- They are not responding well to treatment.
- They are not taking their treatment, or you suspect this is the case.
- They have intolerable adverse effects (e.g. weight gain, movement disorder or diabetes).
- They require a second opinion.
- They have just joined the practice (for formal assessment and development of a care plan).
- The features of the episode differ from those of previous episodes.
- You suspect they are misusing alcohol or drugs. (Or, consider direct referral to local drug or alcohol services).
- You feel that you cannot meet the individual's needs.
- The family or carer is not coping.

Case 3: Answers

12.20   What is the differential diagnosis?

- Anorexia nervosa
- Bulimia nervosa
- Atypical eating disorders
- Binge eating

12.21   What questions should you ask the patient?

- Do they think they have an eating problem?
- Do they worry excessively about their weight?
- Ask about their current weight expressed as the body mass index
- What methods they use to control their weight
- Do they binge eat?
- Do they make themselves sick?
- Do they use laxatives?
- Do they exercise excessively?
- Other psychiatric illnesses
- Menstrual history
- General medical history
- Medication history
- Family history of eating disorders

12.22   Who should GPs screen for eating disorders?

- Young women with a low BMI
- Patients with weight concerns who are not overweight
- Women with menstrual problems and amenorrhoea
- Patients with GI symptoms
- Patients with physical signs of starvation or repeated vomiting
- Children with poor growth
- Young people with type 1 diabetes and poor treatment adherence

Morgan et al (1) devised a series of screening questions for possible cases of anorexia or bulimia.

The SCOFF questions:

- Do you make yourself Sick because you feel uncomfortably full?
- Do you worry you have lost Control over how much you eat?
- Have you recently lost more than One stone in a three-month period?

- Do you believe yourself to be Fat when others say you are too thin?

- Would you say that Food dominates your life?

*One point for every "yes"; a score of > = 2 indicates a likely case of anorexia nervosa or bulimia.

12.23   You think that this is anorexia nervosa. What is the diagnostic criteria for this?

Anorexia ICD-10 criteria:

- Low body weight (BMI ≤ 17.5 kg/m2)

- Self-induced weight loss

- Overvalued ideas of fatness

- Endocrine disturbances – amenorrhoea

Mean age of onset is 16–17.

Bulimia nervosa is recurrent binge eating and then compensatatory behaviour such as vomiting, purging, exercise and fasting. BMI is > 17.5 and menses are normal. Mean age of onset is 18–19.

12.24   What kind of physical problems and findings may be present?

Possible physical features of anorexia nervosa include:

- Amenorrhoea

- Cold intolerance

- Bradycardia

- Emaciation

- Dry skin

- Hair changes e.g. lanugo, hair loss from the scalp

- Hypothermia

- Hypotension

- Ankle oedema

- Osteoporosis

- Enlarged salivary glands (usually parotids)

- Morbidity and mortality from coronary heart disease is increased

12.25   What are these caused by?

Dental erosion is a common problem and is due to the frequent exposure of the dental enamel to gastric acid. Teeth may become discoloured and change shape. There may also be tooth sensitivity and high levels of dental caries. Callouses on the back of the hand (Russell's sign) are caused by self-induced vomiting.

12.26   What electrolyte disturbance may you find?

Fluid and electrolyte disturbances may occur as a result of laxative or diuretic abuse. The most common are dehydration, hypokalaemia, hypochloraemia, and alkalosis. Hypokalaemia is potentially life-threatening, and so severe hypokalaemia is an indication for hospitalisation.

12.27 How should this girl be managed?

Psychological treatment is used for anorexia nervosa – cognitive analytical therapy, cognitive behavioural therapy, interpersonal psychotherapy, family interventions. Outpatient psychological treatment should be at least six months' duration. Medication should not be used for the sole or primary treatment of anorexia nervosa. 0.5 kg weight gain weekly is the target in outpatient settings, 0.5–1 kg in inpatient settings. If vomiting the patient should be advised to avoid brushing after vomiting and to rinse with a non-acid mouthwash after vomiting to reduce an acid oral environment.

Referral of all people with an eating disorder to secondary care is recommended.

Case 4: Answers

12.28 What questions should you ask someone who has tried to commit suicide?

- Circumstances of the incident, what happened and when and how and why
- Did they intend to kill themselves?
- Was it planned or impulsive?
- How do they feel now?
- Do they still wish they were dead?
- Do they have any more plans to kill themselves again?
- Background to the attempt, how have things been last few months, previous attempts, relationships, work
- Personal, medical and family history
- Use of alcohol or drugs
- Do you feel your life is not worth living?
- Did the patient leave a suicide note?
- Did they make plans such as leaving a will?
- Did they take measures to avoid discovery?
- Did they speak about this to anyone else?

12.29 What are the risk factors for suicide?

- Male > female
- Increased with age
- Serious medical condition
- History of deliberate self-harm
- Depression
- Schizophrenia

- Personality disorder

- Bipolar disorder

- Previous suicide attempts

- Social isolation

- Alcohol or drug dependence

- Early parental loss

- Neglect or abuse as child

- Certain professions, e.g. doctors

- Financial or other social crisis

- Physical illness, especially chronic painful disorders

- Recent admission or discharge from psychiatric care

12.30   His paracetamol level comes back above the normal treatment line. What factors can cause you to be on the higher treatment line?

Patients who are on enzyme-inducing drugs such as phenytoin, carbamazepine, rifampicin, or who have a history of alcohol excess can be on the higher treatment line.

12.31   What should the management of this patient be?

Patients who present within 24 hours of suspected paracetamol overdose should receive gastric lavage followed by activated charcoal, 50 g.

Patients with levels on or above the normal treatment line should be given N-Acetylcysteine. The effect is to enhance glutathione stores and to promote the elimination of paracetamol metabolites. It is given as:

- 150 mg/Kg in 200 ml of 5% dextrose over 15 minutes; then

- 50 mg/Kg in 500 ml of 5% dextrose over 4 hours; then

- 100 mg/Kg in 1 litre of 5% dextrose over 16 hours

Patients allergic to this may be given methionine.

12.32   What should be done?

If the acute management of paracetamol poisoning is ineffective and fulminant hepatic necrosis ensues then liver transplantation is life-saving.

The indications for liver transplantation are:

- Acidosis (pH < 7.3), or

- All of the following:

  o   PT > 100 sec

  o   Creatinine > 300 mcg/l

  o   Grade 3 encephalopathy (or worse)

References

Case 1

1. Depression: management of depression in primary and secondary care. Quick reference guide. Clinical guideline 23. April 2007. National Institute for Health and Clinical Excellence. http://www.nice.org.uk/nicemedia/pdf/CG23quickrefguideamended.pdf

2. Depression. Clinical Knowledge Summaries. http://www.cks.nhs.uk/depression

Case 2

1. Schizophrenia. Quick reference guide. Clinical guideline 82. March 2009. National Institute for Health and Clinical Excellence. http://www.nice.org.uk/nicemedia/pdf/CG82QuickRefGuide.pdf

2. Schizophrenia. Clinical Knowlege Summaries. http://www.cks.nhs.uk/schizophrenia

Case 3

1. Eating disorders. Quick reference guide. Clinical guideline 9. January 2004. National Institute for Health and Clinical Excellence. http://www.nice.org.uk/nicemedia/pdf/cg009quickrefguide.pdf

2. Eating disorders. Clinical Knowledge Summaries. http://www.cks.nhs.uk/eating_disorders

3. Morgan JF et al. The SCOFF questionnaire: assessment of a new screening tool for eating disorders. BMJ. 1999 Dec 4; 319(7223): 1467–8

Case 4

1. Self harm. Quick reference guide. Clinical guideline 16. July 2004. National Institute for Health and Clinical Excellence. http://www.nice.org.uk/nicemedia/pdf/CG016QuickRefGuide.pdf

2. Posioning or overdose. Clinical Knowledge Summaries. http://www.cks.nhs.uk/poisoning_or_overdose

Recommended further cases

- Bipolar disease
- Anxiety
- Phobia
- Personality disorders
- Mental Health Acts

General surgery answers

Case 1: Answers

13.1   What are the differential diagnoses?

- Fibroadenoma
- Benign cyst
- Breast cancer

13.2   What other questions should you ask her?

- Has the lump changed since she noticed it?

- What does it feel like?

- Is it tender?

- Are there multiple lumps or just one?

- Has she noticed any change with her menstrual cycle?

- Are there any other lumps?

- Any skin changes?

- Any nipple discharge – colour, amount, blood stained, milky?

- Menstrual history

- Medical history

- Family history – breast and ovarian cancer

- Gynaecology history

- Medications

- Other symptoms to suggest malignancy such as breathlessness, bone pains, weight loss

13.3   What is the likely diagnosis?

Fibroadenoma – benign non-tender discrete lumps within the breast. They are usually smooth and very mobile (breast mouse) and are common in women between ages of 20–30.

13.4   What investigations should you do?

- Ultrasound – in women > 35 years old mammography is the standard investigation. However, it is not as useful in women < 35 because the breast stroma is dense.

- Fine needle aspiration or needle core biopsy

All women with breast conditions need a triple assessment – clinical examination, radiological imaging and tissue biopsy.

13.5   What should the management be?

- Most fibroadenomas do not need excision. If the lump was > 4 cm or she was > 40 then it should be excised.

- Reassurance to the patient that this is a benign lump and there is no danger to her from this. She should be reviewed in three to six months again.

- Encourage regular self examination

Breast cancer is the commonest malignancy in women in the UK. Risk factors:

- Genetics – BRCA1 and BRCA2 (linked to ovarian cancer also)

- First degree relative with breast cancer

- Early menarche

- Late menopause

- Nulliparity

- HRT

On examination there may be a hard, irregular mass and also skin dimpling or tethering, nipple inversion, peau d'orange, ulceration. Imaging and biopsy is again needed. Treatment depends on patient choice and also on the tumour.

Case 2: Answers

13.6   What other questions would you ask him?

- Onset of dysphagia – sudden onset at time of eating suggests a bolus obstruction, progressive dysphagia is commonly associated with malignancy

- Pain on swallowing, what started first difficulty swallowing foods or liquids

- Food sticking

- Retrosternal pain

- Vomiting

- Regurgitation

- Weight loss

- Tiredness, shortness of breath

- Smoking and alcohol history

- Medical history – peptic ulcers, malignancy, coeliac disease, achalasia, oesophageal stricture

13.7   What is the likely diagnosis?

- Oesophageal cancer – more common in males than females (3:1) and rare in those under 50 years old. It is associated with alcohol and smoking, Barrett's oesophagus and achalasia. Squamous cancers are more common in the upper and middle thirds of the oesophagus with adenocarcinoma more common in the lower third. Spread is via lymphatics and the blood. Progressive dysphagia is a presenting symptom along with anaemia and weight loss.

13.8   What investigations would you do?

You should refer this patient under the two-week wait referral for suspected upper GI cancer. NICE recommends that patients should be urgently referred if they present with:

- Dysphagia

- Unexplained upper abdominal pain and weight loss, with or without back pain

- Upper abdominal mass without dyspepsia

- Obstructive jaundice

Investigations required are:

- Barium swallow – to outline the lesion and anatomy

- Endoscopy – to identify histology and biopsy

- CT scan – to look for metastases and local extension of disease (staging)

13.9   What should the management be?

- Radiotherapy is the treatment of choice for upper third tumours

- If surgery is deemed appropriate then oesophagectomy is done (Ivor Lewis resection)

- Stenting/balloon dilatation for obstruction relief and surgery only for curative resection (consider laparoscopic and open treatment)

The prognosis for oesophageal carcinoma is dependent on the site of the tumour. Approximate 5-year survival figures are:

- Upper third tumours have a 20% 5-year survival

- Middle third tumours have a 6% 5-year survival

- Lower third tumours have a 15% 5-year survival

The prognosis also depends on:

- Tumour size and site

- Depth of invasion

- Node metastases

- Widespread metastases

- Tumour grade

- Lymphocytic response

- General health of the patient

Case 3: Answers

13.10   What other questions would you ask?

- Pain – site, onset, character, radiation, associations, time, exacerbations, severity

- Any weight loss, her weight (BMI)

- Other symptoms – bowels and urinary system

- Medical problems – previous gallstones

- Diet – fatty foods

13.11   What are the differential diagnoses?

- Acute cholecystitis

- Biliary colic

- Ascending cholangitis

- Perforated duodenal ulcer

- Acute pancreatitis

- Hepatitis

- May be respiratory cause such as pneumonia or PE

- Sometimes can be cardiac cause with referred pain

13.12   What is Murphy's sign?

The examiner places his or her hand on the right upper quadrant of the abdomen and presses in at the same time as asking the patient to take a deep breath. If the test is positive the patient catches their breath as a swollen tender gallbladder moves down with the liver and reaches the area of the examiner's fingers.

13.13   What is the diagnosis?

Acute cholecystitis – acute inflammation of the gallbladder caused by gallstones in 90% of cases. Bile contains bile salts, cholesterol and phospholipids, and if the concentrations of these vary then different gallstones can form.

Gallstones are common in people with the Fs – Female, Fair, Fat, Fertile, Forty, (low) Fibre diet

13.14   What investigations would you do?

- Full blood count – white cells will normally be raised

- U&Es – to check renal function

- Liver function tests – abnormal LFTs indicate more severe inflammation. Raised bilirubin and alkaline phosphatise suggests biliary obstruction

- Abdominal X-ray – may show stones (only 10%)

- Consider chest X-ray

- Consider ECG

- Ultrasound – may show gallstones, thickened gallbladder wall and status of the common bile duct

13.15   What is the management?

- Conservative management keeping patient nil by mouth, IV fluids, analgesia with IV pethidine and antibiotics. Patient is to stay off fatty food and receive dietary advice.

- Discharge the patient once stable and list for elective cholecystectomy after six weeks when infection should have fully resolved. (Some units have a policy of removing the gallbladder acutely within 5 days of the onset of symptoms).

13.16   Why do patients with acute cholecystitis have an elective cholecystectomy when symptoms have settled down, whilst patients with appendicitis need an urgent appendicectomy?

This difference is due to the differing blood supply of the gallbladder and the appendix. The appendix is supplied by the appendicular artery which is an end artery and so if this artery is thrombosed then the entire blood supply to the appendix is lost and gangrene will result. In contrast the gallbladder receives its blood supply from more than one vessel and the liver bed, and so gangrene of the inflamed gallbladder is rare.

13.17   What are the complications of cholecystitis?

The complications of cholecystitis include:

- Empyema of gallbladder

- Perforation of the gallbladder

- Perihepatic abscess

Other problems associated with gallstones include:

- Stone in CBD, cholangitis, obstructive jaundice, Mirizzi syndrome
- Mucocoele
- Pancreatitis
- Gallstone ileus

Case 4: Answers

13.18 What are the differential diagnoses?

- Inguinal hernia
- Femoral hernia
- Saphena varix
- Lymph nodes
- Psoas Abscess
- Varicocoele
- Hydrocoele of processus vaginalis
- Hydrocoele of spermatic cord

13.19 What other things would you ask about?

- Medical problems – cough, constipation, previous hernias
- Family history of hernias
- Any urinary symptoms
- Any abdominal pain
- Vomiting

13.20 What is the diagnosis?

Inguinal hernia. Any hernia is a protrusion of intra-abdominal contents through a defect in the abdominal wall. There are two main types of inguinal hernia, indirect and direct. Indirect hernias go through the internal ring with the spermatic cord and go though the whole inguinal canal. They constitute about 75% of inguinal hernias. Direct inguinal hernias make up the other 25% of inguinal hernias, and originate medial to the internal ring through a weakened or torn posterior wall of the inguinal canal. Inguinal hernias tend to be more common on the right side.

Always ask the patient to try to reduce the hernia themselves when lying on the couch, as this is less likely to cause them pain.

13.21 How can you distinguish a direct inguinal hernia from an indirect one?

Although it is possible to distinguish between the two, the initial treatment is the same. If you can reduce the hernia then occlude the internal ring (situated just one cm above the mid-point of the inguinal ligament, which is halfway between the anterior superior iliac spine and the pubis tubercle) with one or two fingers. Ask the patient to cough. If there is still a bulge it is likely to be a direct hernia coming out medially whereas an indirect hernia will be controlled.

You should always examine the other side and look for previous surgery, especially appendectomy, as this increases the risk of a hernia on that side.

Feature	Direct Inguinal	Indirect Inguinal	Femoral
Sex	M > F	M > F	F > M
Pathogenesis	Acquired	Congenital or acquired	Acquired
Age	Adults	Children and adults	Middle-aged
Reduction	Spontaneously on lying down	Does not reduce immediately	Does not reduce spontaneously
Relation to pubic tubercle	Above and medial	Above and medial	Below and lateral
Control by pressure over deep ring	No	Yes	No
Strangulation risk	Rare	Moderate	High

Table 20.31   Table showing the features of common hernias

13.22   What is the management of this?

Due to the risk of complications of the hernia such as incarceration, obstruction and strangulation it is best to repair the hernia surgically. This can be done either laparoscopically or by open surgery. It is recommended that all inguinal hernia repair is done using mesh to reduce recurrence. If there are recurrent or bilateral hernias then laparoscopic repair may be recommended.

13.23   The patient had an open mesh repair carried out. What advice should be given to the patient post-op?

- No driving in the first week or activities which may weaken the repair (especially heavy lifting)

- Gradual increase in activity over the next few weeks before returning to normal activities.

- Return to work about four to six weeks if in a heavy occupation. Desk workers can return after one to two weeks.

Case 5: Answers

13.24   What are the differential diagnoses?

- Ectopic pregnancy

- Miscarriage

- PID

- Appendicitis

- Ruptured ovarian cyst

- Salpingitis

- Crohn's disease

- Perforated ulcer

- Pyelonephritis

- UTI

- Renal colic

- Pancreatitis

- Cholecystitis

- Mesenteric adenitis

- Constipation

13.25   What other questions would you ask?

- Pain – site, onset, character, radiation, associations, time, exacerbations, severity

- Loss of appetite

- Vomiting

- Constipation

- Last menstrual period – any chance she may be pregnant?

- Sexual history – previous STIs

- Vaginal discharge

- Medical problems

13.26   What is the likely diagnosis?

Acute appendicitis – inflammation of the appendix caused by obstruction of the lumen by lymphoid hyperplasia or a faecolith.

Initially the inflammation causes visceral pain which is central (since appendix is part of midgut in embryological terms). As it increases and involves the parietal peritoneum, which has somatic innervation, the pain localises to the right iliac fossa.

13.27   What is Rovsing's sign?

Pressing in the left iliac fossa causes pain in the right iliac fossa. This is usually indicative of appendicitis. (It is not an absolute test and not diagnostic).

13.28   What investigations would you do?

- Full blood count – white cell count will be high

- U&Es – to assess dehydration

- Pregnancy test – to exclude pregnancy

- Amylase – to exclude pancreatitis

- Urine dipstick and MC&S – to exclude UTI

- Abdominal X-ray if the diagnosis is in doubt, although X-rays should be avoided in young people if possible

- CT scans can show an inflamed appendix and associated free fluid, but to give an even higher radiation dose CT scan is not a good diagnostic tool unless the appendicitis is perforated or an abscess has formed. It is still a clinical diagnosis

- Pelvic ultrasound – can show free fluid and tubo-ovarian changes

- Diagnostic laparoscopy

13.29 What is the management of this?

- Keep nil by mouth

- Analgesia with IM pethidine and anti-emetics

- IV fluids

- IV antibiotics (metronidazole)

- Appendicectomy (open or laparoscopic)

Case 6: Answers

13.30 What is the differential diagnosis?

- Left-sided bowel cancer

- Diverticular disease

- Colitis (inflammatory bowel disease)

- Haemorrhoids

13.31 What other questions would you ask?

- Bowel habit – is this normal or has there been a recent change, is blood seen only wiping bottom or is the blood mixed with stool, and what colour is it? Dark blood is usually from the sigmoid colon or above, if it is mixed with stool this is usually above the sigmoid colon, blood with mucus could be inflammatory bowel disease or colorectal cancer, mucus and no blood is typical of irritable bowel syndrome.

- Medical problems – history of piles, malignancy, inflammatory bowel disease

- Family history of bowel cancer

- Drugs – Warfarin, NSAIDs

- Diet

- Other symptoms – weight loss, bone pain

13.32 What is the likely diagnosis?

Colorectal cancer is the second most common cause of cancer in the UK. The presentation depends upon the sight of the cancer. It spreads by direct invasion and via the lymphatics, blood and also by seeding across the peritoneal cavity. It is staged according to the Duke's classification.

Stage A – confined to the bowel wall, 80% 5-year survival

Stage B – extends through the bowel wall, 60% 5-year survival

Stage C – lymph node metastases, 30% 5-year survival

Stage D – distant metastases, 10% 5-year survival

Be aware of the TNM classification also as this is used widely.

13.33   What investigations should you request?

This patient should be urgently referred under the two-week wait. Here are the referral guidelines from NICE.

Refer urgently patients:

- Aged 40 years and older, reporting rectal bleeding with a change of bowel habit towards looser stools and/or increased stool frequency persisting six weeks or more

- Aged 60 years and older, with rectal bleeding persisting for six weeks or more without a change in bowel habit and without anal symptoms

- Aged 60 years and older, with a change in bowel habit to looser stools and/or more frequent stools persisting for six weeks or more without rectal bleeding

- Of any age with a right lower abdominal mass consistent with involvement of the large bowel

- Of any age with a palpable rectal mass (intraluminal and not pelvic; a pelvic mass outside the bowel would warrant an urgent referral to a urologist or gynaecologist)

- Who are men of any age with unexplained iron deficiency anaemia and a haemoglobin of 11 g/100 ml or below

- Who are non-menstruating women with unexplained iron deficiency anaemia and a haemoglobin of 10 g/100 ml or below

PR exam can detect 25% of tumours.

- Full blood count – to check he is not anaemic

- Urea and Electrolytes

- Liver Function Tests – to check if any metastatic involvement of liver

- CEA

- Faecal occult blood

- Proctoscopy and rigid sigmoidoscopy (can detect 50% of tumours)

- Flexible sigmoidoscopy

- Barium enema

- CT scan

- CT colonography – this is like a colonoscopy but for patients who cannot have a barium enema or have difficult anatomy

75% of tumours are on the left side of the colon (50% are below the rectal sigmoid junction and 25% are at the lower rectum). That is why PR and rigid sigmoidoscopy is important at the outpatient clinic for assessment.

13.34   What is the management of this?

- Biopsy for histology

- Colonoscopy to exclude synchronous tumours or polyps

- CT staging of chest and abdomen (if not already carried out)

- Sigmoid colectomy when diagnosis confirmed (done open/laparoscopically)

- Depending on staging (age and histology) will have radiotherapy and chemotherapy. Radiotherapy for sigmoid rectal lesion and chemotherpay for colonic lesion

- Also advice on stoma depending on whether primary anastomosis possible

- Also colonic stenting for palliative case to relieve obstruction

Case 7: Answers

13.35   What are the differential diagnoses?

- Small bowel obstruction – vomiting starts earlier, pain is higher in the abdomen, less distension

- Large bowel obstruction

- Bowel cancer

- Gastric outlet obstruction

- Hernia

13.36   What questions would you ask?

- When did vomiting start?

- Any weight loss?

- Site of pain and how long has the abdomen increased in size

- Nature of vomitus – bilious, profuse, frequent vomiting suggests small bowel obstruction, faeculent and intermittent suggests large bowel obstruction

- Medical problems – previous abdominal surgery (adhesive obstruction), bowel conditions, malignancy

13.37   What is the diagnosis?

- Small bowel obstruction – the patient has all the features of acute intestinal obstruction: abdominal pain, constipation (absolute for flatus as well as faeces), vomiting and abdominal distension.

Causes of small bowel obstruction can be divided into:

Dynamic:

- Extra mural: adhesions, hernia, tumour, volvulus.

- Mural: intussusceptions, strictures, inflammatory (Crohn's Disease). Primary tumours of the small bowel are uncommon but should be considered.

- Luminal: gallstone ileus, impacted faeces, meconium in neonates.

- Severe large bowel obstruction, especially proximally, can present as a small bowel obstruction (when the ilea-ceacal value is incompetent).

- Bowel sounds are usually hyperactive, but if the bowel becomes very distended can sound "tinkling".

Adynamic:

- Paralytic ileus, (may be associated with local sepsis)

- Mesenteric vascular occlusion

These are usually associated with absent or reduced bowel sounds.

13.38   What investigations would you do?

- Full blood count – to see if the white cell count is raised

- U&Es – to check for dehydration

- Chest X-ray – air under the diaphragm

- Abdominal X-ray – dilated bowel, air/fluid levels. In small bowel the valvulae conniventes completely cross the lumen, whilst in large bowel the haustral folds do not cross the lumen fully.

- CT scan

Here is an X-ray of a large bowel obstruction:

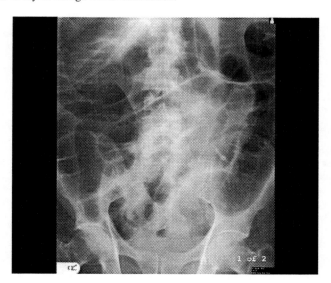

Fig 20.17   X-ray of large bowel obstruction (courtesy of Dr John Asquith)

13.39   What is the management?

- Reassure patient that it is nothing sinister

- Pain relief with morphine

- "Drip and suck"
- Rehydrate with IV fluids if dry
- Pass NG tube to aspirate gastric contents

13.40 When would you consider surgery?

- Unexplained small bowel obstruction in the absence of previous abdominal surgery, likely to be congenital band adhesion, internal hernia or tumour
- Severe abdominal pain (the bowel may be ischaemic and need urgent release). The use of strong analgesics instead of surgery is dangerous.
- If symptoms not resolving after a period of conservative treatment (48 hours)
- Diagnosis of a situation that needs surgical correction

Case 8: Answers

13.41 What are the differential diagnoses?

- Abdominal aortic aneurysm
- Perforated duodenal ulcer
- MI
- Pancreatitis

13.42 What other questions would you ask?

- Medical history – hypertension, heart disease, hypercholesterolaemia, Marfan's syndrome
- Family history of AAA
- Smoking
- Drugs

13.43 What is the likely diagnosis?

AAA leak/rupture – an aneurysm is an abnormal dilatation of an artery. Abdominal aortic aneurysms are often asymptomatic and an incidental finding. An abdominal aortic aneurysm (AAA) is defined as an enlargement of the aorta of at least 1.5 times its normal diameter or greater than 3 cm diameter in total. Most AAAs occur in the lower part of the abdominal aorta, below the kidney (infra-renal). Main risk factors for AAA include increasing age, high blood pressure, smoking and family history of AAA.

13.44 What is the management?

- Urgent group and save and cross match 10 units of blood plus fresh frozen plasma and platelets and full resuscitation
- Notify theatre and anaesthetic staff and vascular team immediately
- Establish IV access with two large bore cannulae and catheterise
- IV resuscitation with fluids – (permissive hypotension with systolic BP not more than 100 mmHg)

- ECG to exclude MI; amylase to exclude pancreatitis
- Also need to check patient's general health and warn the relatives about maximum of 50% survival. If poor health the chance of death is higher
- Plan urgent CT scan to assess diagnosis and operability (supra-renal inoperable)
- If patient too unstable, probably not going to survive
- Also consider emergency endovascular repair
- Also check any family members for screening

A thoracoabdominal aneurysm can involve either the ascending or descending thoracic aorta and the abdominal aorta. It can be asymptomatic but severe chest, back and abdominal pain can occur, and this means expansion or impending rupture. CT scan can show the extent of the aneurysm. Type A dissection of the ascending aorta has a very poor outcome and needs surgery. Type B dissection of the descending aorta can be treated with conservative blood pressure control.

Case 9: Answers

13.45 What other questions would you ask?

- How far can he walk on the flat before getting the pain (walking distance) – a long history of reduced walking distance suggests atherosclerotic disease (chronic ischaemia)
- Any pain elsewhere in thigh or buttocks – site where pain occurs can indicate the level of the disease:
  - Calf – femoropopliteal
  - Thigh – iliofemoral
  - Buttock – aortoiliac
- Any pain at rest? This indicates severe disease (critical ischaemia)
- Smoking history/cholesterol problem
- Other medical problems – angina or MI, AF, COPD, TIAs or CVAs, Diabetes
- Family history of similar problems or vascular disease
- How much is it affecting his life?

13.46 What are the differential diagnoses?

- Peripheral vascular disease – intermittent claudication
- Spinal stenosis – this will not ease with rest and may be worse. Flexion of the spine relieves the pain caused by spinal stenosis

13.47 What is Buerger's angle test?

A normal limb can be lifted to 90 degrees without there being any change in colour. However, an ischaemic limb blanches when lifted above the horizontal and the angle at which this occurs is called Buerger's angle. If this is less than 20 degrees it means there is severe ischaemia. If the limb is then hung over the edge of the bed or couch it turns from white to pink and then to a dusky red-purple colour and this is called Buerger's sign.

13.48 What are the signs/symptoms of acute ischaemia?

- Pale
- Pulseless
- Perishing cold
- Paraesthesia
- Painful
- Paralysis

Acute limb ischaemia is an emergency and can be caused by thrombosis, emboli, trauma, graft/angioplasty occlusion. Treatment depends upon the severity and cause and can include embolectomy, thrombolysis, angioplasty and surgery.

13.49 What is the diagnosis in this patient?

PVD – intermittent claudication. This is due to lack of blood/oxygen supply to meet the demand of the muscles in the calf. (Analogy of "angina" of the calf muscle). Most commonly the affected segment is a diseased portion of superficial femoral artery with either tight stenosis or occlusion.

13.50 What investigations would you do?

Ankle-brachial pressure index – this involves taking the brachial blood pressure and then the lower limb pressure. It is a simple method for quantifying the severity of the arterial occlusion in the leg. Normally the pressures are about the same. Peripheral arterial disease is present if the ABPI is < 0.95.

$$ABPI = \frac{Ankle\ pressure\ (DP\ or\ AT)}{Brachial\ pressure}$$

Brachial pressure is used as a normal reference as this artery is less affected by arteriosclerosis. That is why diabetics have calcified arteries and hence give falsely elevated readings.

13.51 How would you manage this patient?

In an acute ischaemic leg angiography should be arranged as soon as possible. This will show the cause of the acute problem and determine the need for and type of urgent treatment.

For this patient conservative management is appropriate as symptoms resolve spontaneously in one third of patients.

- Encourage him to stop smoking and lose weight
- Check his cholesterol and start statins if needed
- Encourage regular exercise to open and develop the collateral circulation. This will increase the claudication distance over time
- Emphasize the need to take great care not to injure the leg since healing is generally poor
- Optimise his hypertension and diabetic drug therapy
- Symptomatic treatment with either naftidrofuryl 200 mg tds daily, which may alleviate symptoms and improve pain-free walking distance in moderate disease; or cilostazol, a phosphodiesterase inhibitor. This is licensed for use in intermittent claudication to improve

walking distance in patients without peripheral tissue necrosis and who do not have pain at rest

- Follow up patients regularly ›
- Duplex to confirm the level of disease

13.52 What options are available if these measures do not work?

- Angiogram and percutaneous transluminal angioplasty – stenosis and complete occlusion can be recanalised
- Surgery – only for disabling symptoms or critical ischaemia

Here is a digital subtraction angiogram which shows popliteal artery occlusion in the right leg:

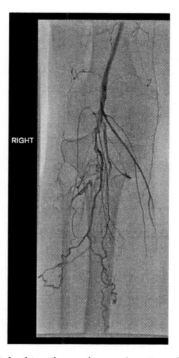

Figure 20.18   Digital subtraction angiogram (courtesy of Dr John Asquith)

13.53   What is critical ischaemia?

This is when a limb has rest pain for at least two weeks' duration or tissue loss caused by arterial disease. Features are rest pain, gangrene and ulceration. The ABPI is severely reduced (< 0.5) or there is an absolute occlusion pressure of less than 45 mmHg

References

Case 1

1. Fibroadenoma. GP Notebook. http://www.gpnotebook.co.uk

Case 2

1. Management of oesophageal and gastric cancer. A national clinical guideline 87. June 2006. Scottish Intercollegiate Guidelines Network. http://www.sign.ac.uk/pdf/sign87.pdf

Case 3

1. Gladden D, Cholecystitis. Emedicine. http://emedicine.medscape.com/article/171886-overview

Case 4

1. Laparoscopic surgery for inguinal hernia repair. Technology appraisal 83. September 2004. National Institute for Health and Clinical Excellence. http://www.nice.org.uk/nicemedia/pdf/TA083publicinfoenglish.pdf

Case 5

1. Craig S. Appendicitis. Emedicine. http://emedicine.medscape.com/article/773895-overview

Case 6

1. Lower GI Cancer – suspected. Clinical Knowledge Summaries. http://www.cks.nhs.uk/gi_lower_cancer_suspected

2. Referral guidelines for suspected cancer. Quick reference guide. Clinical guideline 27. June 2005. National Institute for Health and Clinical Excellence. http://www.nice.org.uk/nicemedia/pdf/CG027quickrefguide.pdf

Case 7

1. Ansari P, Intestinal Obstruction Merck Manuals 2007. http://www.merck.com/mmpe/sec02/ch011/ch011h.html

2. Small bowel obstruction. www.surgical-tutor.org.uk

3. Large bowel obstruction. www.surgical-tutor.org.uk

Case 8

1. Tan WA. Abdominal aortic aneurysm, rupture. Emedicine. http://emedicine.medscape.com/article/416397-overview

Case 9

1. Diagnosis and management of peripheral arterial disease. A national clinical guideline 89. October 2006. Scottish Intercollegiate Guidelines Network. http://www.sign.ac.uk/pdf/sign89.pdf

Cases 1–9

Kontoyannis A. 3rd edition (2008). *Crash Course: Surgery*. Mosby.

Recommended further cases

- Diverticulitis
- Haemorrhoids
- Arterial and venous ulcers
- Varicose veins

Obstetrics and gynaecology answers

Case 1: Answers

14.1   How often should women have their smears?

Women are invited for screening when aged 25. Between the ages of 25–49 women should have smears at three-yearly intervals. Women aged 50–64 should have smears at five-yearly intervals.

14.2   What is dyskaryosis?

Dyskaryosis is the cytological term used to describe nuclear changes in cells picked up on the smear test. These include changes in the nuclear size and shape. It can be graded according to the severity of these changes and also the ratio of the nucleus to the cytoplasm, with the higher ratio indicating more severe dyskaryosis. It can be classified as mild, moderate and severe.

14.3   What should the management be now?

Referral for colposcopy. Both moderate and severe dyskaryosis require colposcopy referral. For mild dyskaryosis the smear should be repeated in six months' time. Colposcopy is a test used to visualise the transformation zone of the cervix. This is the area which undergoes metaplastic change from columnar to squamous epithelium. Colposcopy allows us to see abnormal cells and determine their extent, and allows biopsies to be taken.

14.4   What questions would you ask the patient to elicit any risk factors for cervical cancer?

- Does she smoke?
- Is she sexually active?
- How many sexual partners has she had? The higher the number the greater the risk
- Age at first sexual intercourse – higher risk if early
- Is there a family history of cervical cancer

14.5   What do these findings mean?

Abnormal tissues stain white with acetic acid because the abnormal cells have high density nuclei which take up the acetic acid more than normal cells. Abnormal cells have less glycogen than normal cells and so stain less well and remain pale when iodine is applied.

14.6   What does this mean?

CIN is the histopatholigical term that describes abnormal proliferation of the squamous epithelium of the transformation zone of the cervix. This can be graded depending upon what thickness of the epithelium (in thirds) has become dysplastic. In CIN 2 this means that up to two thirds of cells in the affected area of her cervix are abnormal. She will require treatment for this. Treatment is with large loop excision of the transformation zone. This involves excision of the abnormal transformation zone using a diathermy loop. It is usually done with local anaesthetic in an outpatient setting. The aim of treatment is to try and avoid progression to invasive cancer.

14.7   When should she have a follow up smear?

She should have a follow up smear at six months and then 12 months after treatment. She will then need a cervical smear annually for the next nine years. The same applies if she had CIN 3.

If a woman had treatment for CIN 1, she would need a smear at six months, 12 months and 24 months after treatment. If all these tests were normal, she could return back to routine screening – every three to five years, depending on her age.

Case 2

14.8   What are the differential diagnoses?

- Pelvic inflammatory disease
- Endometriosis
- Irritable bowel syndrome
- Psychosexual disorders
- Fibroids
- Ovarian cyst
- Interstitial cystitis (painful bladder syndrome)
- Back-related problems

14.9   What is the likely diagnosis?

Endometriosis – classic symptoms of dysmenorrhoea, dyspareunia and pelvic pain. It is a common condition in which endometrial glands and stroma are located outside the endometrial cavity. It is a benign condition and occurs in about 10–25% of women in their reproductive years. The exact aetiology is not known but several theories exist such as retrograde menstruation, coelomic metaplasia and lymphatic spread. The most common sites are the ovaries and the uterosacral ligaments. There is a poor correlation between symptoms and laparoscopic findings and a great variety in symptoms. It is strongly associated with infertility.

14.10   What investigations would you order to confirm the diagnosis?

Ultrasound and laparoscopy (gold standard). Ideally histology should be taken to confirm the diagnosis. Positive histology confirms the diagnosis, however, negative histology does not exclude it.

14.11   What is the management?

- Treatment is to help alleviate symptoms, stop progression of the disease and to improve fertility.

- This can be either medical or surgical. Medical options include analgesia such as NSAIDs, hormonal treatment such as progestogens and the contraceptive pill (create pseudopregnancy) or GNRH analogues (this inhibits ovulation and so stimulation of the endometrial deposits) and danazol (creates pseudomenopause). Use of danazol and GNRH analogues are usually restricted to six months. The lesions of endometriosis regress in pregnancy and the menopause, and so the treatments try to mimic this. The levonorgestrel intrauterine system can also be used to reduce endometriosis associated pain.

- Surgical options can be conservative or radical. Conservative surgery can be performed through laparoscopy or at laparotomy and involve using diathermy or laser ablation or excision of the endometriotic deposits. Radical surgery is for those women in which other options have failed and no longer desire fertility and is with total abdominal hysterectomy with bilateral salpingo-oophorectomy. Young women may need HRT after this.

Case 3

14.12   What other questions would you ask in the history?

- When else does she get the incontinence?

- Is there any urgency?

- Is there any dysuria?

- Is there any frequency or nocturia or other urinary symptoms?

- How much does she drink daily, what does she drink and at what times of day?

- Obstetric history including parity, type of delivery, pregnancy and labour complications

- Medical history – previous gynaecological surgery, other gynaecological problems, cough, asthma, COPD, Diabetes

- Any bowel symptoms

- Smoking history

- Occupation history – does this involve heavy lifting or other stress?

- How many pads is she having to use, how often is she wet?

- How much is it affecting her life at work and at home?

A patient who gives a history of stress incontinence can still have detrusor instability also.

14.13   What is the likely diagnosis?

Urinary incontinence is the involuntary loss of urine which can be objectively demonstrated and is a social problem. The most common cause of this is genuine stress incontinence and this woman has it. Genuine stress incontinence is where the intravesical pressure exceeds the maximal urethral pressure in the absence of detrusor contractions. It increases with age and is also associated with increasing parity and genital prolapse, pelvic floor surgery and also post-menopause.

14.14   What investigations would you do to confirm this?

- Urine dipstick and midstream MSU – to exclude UTI

- Post-micturition ultrasound scan to exclude retention with overflow

- Urodynamic studies – cystometry is probably the single most useful test

14.15   What is the management at this stage?

- Conservative management – lifestyle change, reduced weight, stop smoking, avoid drinking tea and coffee

- NICE recommends three months' pelvic floor exercises

14.16   What would you do now?

Arrange for urodynamic studies.

14.17   What does this mean and what is the importance of confirming the diagnosis?

This means that the woman has genuine stress incontinence. This is very important, as if she had detrusor instability then this could be made worse by surgery. The woman can now have surgery to correct the problem, and this involves either colposuspension or a tension-free vaginal tape procedure.

Case 4

14.18 What are the differential diagnoses?

- Ectopic pregnancy

- Miscarriage

- PID

14.19 What other questions would you ask in the history?

- Last menstrual period

- When did the pain start and what has been its course?

- Loss of consciousness

- What is the pain like, does it radiate anywhere? Shoulder tip pain?

- Any pv discharge?

- What contraception does she use?

- Medical history – previous PID, previous ectopics, previous miscarriages, previous gynaecological surgery, endometriosis, last cervical smear

- Drug history

- Sexual history

14.20 What is the likely diagnosis?

Ectopic pregnancy – this is when the products of conception implant outside the endometrial cavity. The most common site is in the ampulla of the fallopian tube. The condition occurs with an incidence of one in every 300 to 1000 deliveries in the UK. There is usually amenorrhoea (six weeks on average) followed by bleeding and pain. However patients can be asymptomatic. There may be a history of previous ectopic pregnancy, previous tubal surgery or pelvic surgery, IVF, PID or endometriosis.

It is essential that GPs and other clinicians consider the diagnosis of ectopic pregnancy in any woman of reproductive age who complains of acute abdominal pain. Therefore they should have a pregnancy test.

14.21 What investigations would you want to do?

- Urine pregnancy test

- Serum Beta HCG – a value of > 1000IU should show an intrauterine pregnancy on a transvaginal scan and > 6500IU on a transabdominal scan

- Full blood count

- Transvaginal ultrasound – to demonstrate an intrauterine pregnancy or not

- Laparoscopy

14.22 What do you do now?

- Urgent referral to gynaecology for further tests.

A positive pregnancy test in the absence of an intrauterine pregnancy should always be considered an ectopic until proved otherwise.

14.23 What are the options?

Management depends on the overall clinical picture. If the patient is shocked or collapses then she will need urgent resuscitation and surgery with laparotomy.

Expectant – if the diagnosis is in doubt and the patient is stable then laparoscopy can be delayed until two Beta hCG tests have been taken 48 hours apart. In a viable pregnancy the level will double, if there is a miscarriage then it will fall, and if it is an ectopic then the level will plateau or rise but not double, and then the patient can be booked for laparoscopy.

Medical – methotrexate can be given to the woman IM or by injection directly into the ectopic, prostaglandins can also be given.

Surgical – this can be either with salpingectomy (removal of the tube) or salpingotomy. If the contralateral tube is healthy then salpingectomy is the preferred option, if other tube is damaged then salpingotomy is used.

If the patient has had methotrexate or the tube has been conserved, then it is crucial to measure hCG levels and check they are falling.

14.24 What is the best option for her then?

Medical treatment – in her case as the patient is haemodynamically stable and the ectopic is < 3.5 cm, medical management is the best option.

There is a risk of recurrence and so the woman should be advised that if she becomes pregnant again she should present early (five to six weeks) to ensure that it is an intrauterine pregnancy.

Case 5

14.25 What are causes of this?

- Miscarriage
- Ectopic pregnancy
- PID

14.26 What is the likely diagnosis?

Spontaneous miscarriage is the loss of a pregnancy before 24 weeks gestation. It is most common in the first trimester and it occurs in 10–20% of clinical pregnancies. If the cervical os is open or products of conception are passed then the miscarriage is inevitable. This woman has had a missed miscarriage – this is when the fetus has died before 24 weeks gestation but has not been lost from the uterus.

14.27 What investigations should you do?

Transvaginal ultrasound.

14.28 What does this mean?

Crown-lump length more than 6 mm means a fetal heart should be visible on transvaginal ultrasound in all cases of viable pregnancy. This result means that there is a missed miscarriage.

14.29 What are the management options?

- Expectant – wait and see, woman will need follow-up scans to confirm the uterus is empty

- Medical – mifepristone followed 48 hours later by misoprostal

- Surgical – evacuation of retained products of conception

14.30 What things are important to explain to the woman?

- Offer counselling and support.

- Reassure her that she has done nothing wrong and that this would have happened and nothing that she did, such as heavy lifting, could have caused it. In most cases a cause is not found. Explain that most women will go on to have a normal, healthy pregnancy.

- Explain that most are due to sporadic chromosomal abnormalities.

- Counsel on contraception as this may be needed.

Case 6

14.31 What are the differential diagnoses?

- Placental abruption

- Placenta praevia

- Excessive show

- Vasa previa

14.32 What is the likely diagnosis?

Placental abruption – this is partial or complete premature separation of the placenta prior to the baby's birth. It occurs in about one in 80 deliveries.

14.33 What are risk factors for it?

- Trauma

- Hypertension

- Multiple pregnancy

- Increasing age

- High parity

- Previous placental abruption

- Smoking

- Drugs

- Lower social class

14.34   What investigations should she have?

- FBC

- Group and save/cross match

- Rhesus status

- Urea and electrolytes and liver function tests

- CTG

- Ultrasound scan

Never carry out a PV exam until placenta praevia has been excluded.

14.35   What are the features of a normal CTG?

Feature	Reassuring	Non-reassuring	Abnormal
Baseline heart rate	110–160 bpm	100–109 or 161–180 bpm	< 100 or > 180 bpm
Variability	5 bpm	< 5 bpm for > 40 minutes	< 5 bpm for > 90 minutes
Accelerations	Present	Uncertain significance if absent when CTG is otherwise normal	Uncertain significance if absent when CTG is otherwise normal
Decelerations	Absent	Early or variable	Late, variable with abnormal features

Table 20.32   Features of a normal CTG

14.36   How should this woman be managed?

Placental abruption causing maternal or fetal compromise requires delivery. In this case management involves:

- Assess ABC

- Insert Central Venous Pressure line, IV line, urinary catheter keeping urine output > 30 ml/hour

- Get urgent cross-match 4–6 units, clotting time, FBC, fibrinogen

- Administer analgesia

- Give bloods and fluids as indicated from CVP, try to maintain haematocrit > 30%, aim to keep systolic blood pressure above 100 mmHg

- Monitor fetal heart sounds with CTG

If abruption is severe enough to cause fetal demise, vaginal delivery is preferred as the complications of serious coagulation defects are less dangerous than with LSCS. There is a danger that a consumption coagulopathy may develop with hypofibrinogenaemia. If this occurs, give fresh whole blood, FFP or pure fibrinogen. Sometimes excessive fibrinolysis may occur. Also, acute renal failure may occur if there has been extensive haemorrhage.

14.37 How does Placental abruption differ from placenta praevia?

Feature	Abruption	Placenta praevia
Pain	Constant	Painless
Obstetric shock	Actual amount of bleeding may be a lot more than vaginal loss	Obstetric shock is in proportion to the amount of vaginal loss
Uterus	Tender and tense (woody hard)	Non-tender
Fetal lie and presentation	Normal	Abnormal
Fetal heart	Distress/absent	Normal

Table 20.33   Placental abruption vs placenta praevia

Patients that have had antepartum haemorrhage are at risk of a postpartum haemorrghage.

Case 7

14.38 What is the likely diagnosis?

Pre-eclapmsia – this is pregnancy-induced hypertension with proteinuria ≥ 0.3 g in 24 hours, with or without oedema. It is a multisystem disorder with about 5/1000 maternities in the UK suffering with severe pre-eclampsia. Severe pre-eclampsia is severe hypertension with a diastoilic blood pressure ≥ 110 mmHg on two occasions or systolic blood pressure ≥ 170 mmHg on two occasions and also significant proteinuria (at least 1g/litre). Risk factors include hypertension, multiple pregnancy, previous pre-eclampsia, age > 35, family history, primips. The woman can be asymptomatic but can also present with headache, visual disturbance (flashing lights), right upper quadrant pain or epigastric pain and facial swelling. The only cure for pre-eclampsia is delivery.

14.39 What other investigation would you do?

- Bloods for FBC, U&E, LFTs, uric acid – uric acid can increase in severe pre-eclampsia and this correlates with a poorer outcome for both the mother and baby. Falling platelets are associated with worsening pre-eclampsia, as are raised transaminases and a high haematocrit

- CTG

14.40 What syndrome does this constitute?

HELLP syndrome – this comprises haemolysis, elevated liver enzymes and low platelets

14.41 How should this patient be managed?

- This is an obstetric emergency and the consultant obstetrician, senior anaesthetist and senior midwife should all be informed. The only treatment is delivery.

- The woman should be admitted and have IV access established.

- Bloods for group and save.

- Urinary catheter inserted and accurate fluid input and output charted. Oral anti-hypertensive – labetalol or nifedipine.

- Magnesium sulphate to reduce risk of eclampsia – the Magpie study demonstrated that the use of magnesium sulphate to women with pre-eclampsia reduces the risk of eclampsia.

- Caesarean section in view of the fetal distress illustrated by the CTG.

- Blood pressure should be managed if the systolic blood pressure is over 160 mmHg or diastolic above 110 mmHg. This can be with labetalol, nifedipine or hydralazine.

Eclampsia is fitting secondary to pre-eclampsia. About 44% occur postnatally. Management involves:

- ABC

- Turn onto the side to avoid aortocaval compression.

- IV magnesium sulphate 4 g loading bolus dose over five to ten minutes, then infusion of 1 g/hr maintained for 24 hours after the last seizure.

It is important to measure the respiratory rate and check the patellar reflex every 15 minutes as magnesium can depress neuromuscular transmission.

It may be necessary to continue on anti-hypertensives for at least three months after delivery, depending upon the blood pressure. The GP should make sure they check the blood pressure and also check for proteinuria at the six weeks postnatal appointment. If the blood pressure is still high or there is still proteinuria then further investigation is needed.

Case 8

14.42 What kind of questions would you ask?

- Was it planned pregnancy?

- How does she feel about this and her partner also?

- Any previous pregnancies?

- Does she smoke?

- Does she drink alcohol?

- Any medical problems?

- Any medical problems in the family?

- When was her last period?

14.43 What would you check whilst she is in the surgery?

- Weight

- Blood pressure

- Urine

14.44 What advice should you give to the woman now?

- Start folic acid 0.4 mg daily

- Avoid vitamin A supplementation

- Stop smoking and drinking alcohol – advise women to avoid drinking alcohol in the first three months of pregnancy. If they choose to drink advise them to drink no more than one to two UK units once or twice a week, and to avoid getting drunk and binge drinking.

- Avoid foods like soft cheese, unpasteurised milk (risk of listeria), raw meats (risk of toxoplasmosis) and shellfish (risk of food poisoning)
- Arrange appointment with the midwife

14.45 What information should you tell her?

NICE guidance recommends that the combined test of nuchal translucency, beta HCG and pregnancy-associated plasma-protein A should be offered to all woman between 11 weeks and 13 weeks 6 days. Depending on the risk result from this then she can have further tests to diagnose problem. The high risk cut-off is one in 300. Currently the triple test is used, which is alpha feto protein, unconjugated oestriol and human chorionic gonadotrophin.

14.46 How many appointments should a nulliparous woman have in an uncomplicated pregnancy?

NICE recommends that there should be ten appointments for nulliparous women and seven for parous women.

Case 9

14.47 What questions would you ask in the history?

- What are her preferences for contraception?
- Why now?
- Any medical problems – migraine with aura, breast cancer, blood clots, hypertension?
- Family history of any medical problems – breast cancer, stroke, clots?
- Drug history
- Smoking history

14.48 What are the recommended options from NICE?

To use a long-acting reversible contraceptive – all these methods (Implanon, IUD, IUS, injections) are more cost-effective than the combined oral contraceptive pill even at one year of use.

14.49 What should you tell her about this?

It is a combined oral contraceptive pill containing oestrogen and progesterone. It is a tablet taken for 21 days, and then there is a seven-day pill free interval. It needs to be taken at the same time everyday and there is a 12-hour window. It works by inhibiting ovulation. Most common pill is Microgynon 30.

UKMEC 4 criteria – pill should not be used:

- Smoking aged $\geq$ 35 and smoking $\geq$ 15 a day
- Obesity $\geq$ 40 kg/m2
- Current or past history of venous thromboembolism
- Historical or current ischameic heart disease
- Migraine with aura
- Current breast cancer
- Blood pressure systolic $\geq$ 160 mmHg and/or diastolic $\geq$ 95 mmHg

Ideally the pill should be started on the first day of the period but it can be started up to and including day five without the need for additional contraception. So she can start taking it now. It can be started at other times in the cycle provided there is certainty that she is not pregnant, but additional contraceptive precautions such as condoms are required for the first seven days.

14.50   What other important points should you discuss with her?

- Missed pill rules (see figure below)

- Diarrhoea and vomiting

- Increased risk of thromboembolism and breast cancer and cervical cancer, stroke

- Antibiotics – patient needs extra protection whilst on them, and for seven days after

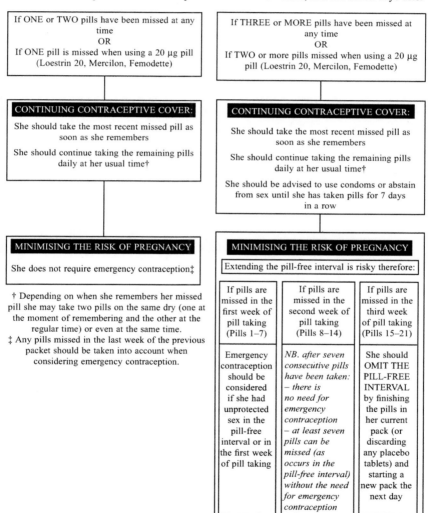

Figure 20.19   Missed pill rules: Reproduced from Figure 1, *Advice for women missing combined oral contraceptive pills* **from the** *Faculty of Family Planning and Reproduction Health Care Clinical Guidance First Prescription of Combined Oral Contraception* **July 2006 (updated January 2007).**

14.51   What should you check while she is with you in the surgery?

Blood pressure and weight.

Case 10

14.52   What are the possible causes?

- Physiological
- Candida
- Bacterial vaginosis
- Trichomonas vaginalis
- Chlamydia
- Gonorrhoea
- Foreign body
- Cervical polyps
- Genital tract malignancy

14.53   What else should you ask about?

- When did it start
- Duration
- Colour
- Consistency
- Odour
- Associated symptoms
- Sexual history
- Contraceptive history
- Medical history

14.54   What is the likely diagnosis?

Bacterial vaginosis – this is a non-sexually transmitted infection. There are diagnostic criteria for this called the Amsel criteria:

- pH > 4.5
- Clue cells
- White discharge
- Fishy odour (with addition of 10% KOH to discharge)

Three out of four of these are needed.

14.55   What are risk factors for this?

- High number of sexual partners

- Early age of first intercourse

14.56 What should you tell her?   ,

It is not a sexually transmitted disease. It is the commonest type of infective vaginal discharge.

14.57 How do you treat it and what advice should you give?

Metronidazole 400 mg bd for seven days, or metronidazole 2 g stat. Treatment of male partner is not needed. Other treatment regimes involve metronidazole gel, clindamycin cream or oral clindamycin.

References

Case 1

1. NHS Cervical Screening Programme. http://www.cancerscreening.nhs.uk/cervical/index.html

Case 2

1. Endometriosis. Clinical Knowledge Summaries. http://www.cks.nhs.uk/endometriosis#

2. The Investigation and Management of Endometriosis. Green-top Guideline No. 24. October 2006. Royal College of Obstetricians and Gynaecologists. http://www.rcog.org.uk/files/rcog-corp/uploaded-files/GT24InvestigationEndometriosis2006.pdf

Case 3

1. Urinary incontinence. Quick reference guide. Clinical guideline 40. October 2006. National Institute for Health and Clinical Excellence. http://www.nice.org.uk/nicemedia/pdf/word/CG40quickrefguide1006.pdf

Case 4

1. Management of Tubal Pregnancy. Green-top Guideline No. 21. May 2004. Royal College of Obstretricians and Gynaecologists. http://www.rcog.org.uk/files/rcog-corp/uploaded-files/GT21ManagementTubalPregnancy2004.pdf

Case 5

1. The Management of Early Pregnancy Loss. Green-top Guideline No. 25. October 2006. Royal College of Obstetricians and Gynaecologists. http://www.rcog.org.uk/files/rcog-corp/uploaded-files/GT25ManagementofEarlyPregnancyLoss2006.pdf

Case 6

1. Antepartum haemorrhage. http://www.patient.co.uk/doctor/Antepartum-Haemorrhage.htm

Case 7

2. Pre-eclampsia and eclampsia. http://www.patient.co.uk/doctor/Pre-eclampsia-and-Eclampsia.htm

3. The Management of Severe Pre-eclampsia/eclampsia. Guideline No. 10(A). March 2006. Royal College of Obstetricians and Gynaecologists. http://www.rcog.org.uk/files/rcog-corp/uploaded-files/GT10aManagementPreeclampsia2006.pdf

4. Hypertension in pregnancy. Clinical Knowledge Summaries. http://www.cks.nhs.uk/hypertension_in_
pregnancy

Case 8

1. Antenatal care. Routine care for the healthy pregnant woman. Quick reference guide. Clinical guideline 62.
March 2008. National Institute for Health and Clinical Excellence. http://www.nice.org.uk/nicemedia/pdf/
CG062QuickRefGuide.pdf

Case 9

1. First Prescription of Combined Oral Contraception. Clinical Effectiveness Unit July 2006. Faculty of
Family Planning & Reproductive Health Care Clinical Guidance. http://www.ffprhc.org.uk/admin/uploads/
FirstPrescCombOralContJan06.pdf

2. Long-acting reversible contraception. Quick reference guide. Clinical guideline 30. October 2005. National
Institute for Health and Clinical Excellence. http://www.nice.org.uk/nicemedia/pdf/cg030quickrefguide.
pdf

3. Contraception. Clinical Knowledge Summaries. http://www.cks.nhs.uk/contraception

Case 10

1. The management of women of reproductive age attending non-genitourinary medicine settings complaining
of vaginal discharge. Journal of Family Planning and Reproductive Health Care 2006; 32(1): 33–42.

2. Vaginal discharge. Clinical Knowledge Summaries. http://www.cks.nhs.uk/vaginal_discharge

Case 1–10

Panay N, Dutta R, Ryan A, Broadbent JAM. 1ˢᵗ edition. 2004. *Crash Course Obstetrics and Gynaecology*.
Mosby.

Recommended further cases

- Menorrhagia
- Small for gestational age
- Emergency contraception
- Ovarian and uterine cancer
- HRT and menopause
- Placenta praevia

Orthopaedics answers

Case 1

15.1   What other questions would you ask in the history?

- More details about the pain – site, onset, character, radiation, associated factors, time,
exacerbating factors and severity
- Ability to move the joint

- Other systemic features, e.g weight loss, pyrexia
- Any history of trauma to the knee?
- Other medical problems
- Drug history

15.2   What are the potential differential diagnoses?

- Osteomyelitis
- Sickle cell crisis causing a bone infarction
- Septic arthritis
- Cellulitis

15.3   What is the likely diagnosis?

Acute Osteomyelitis. This is an infection of the bone that is rapid in onset and usually severe. It is commonly a disease of childhood. The most common causes are post-trauma, post-surgery and acute haematogenous. The infection usually begins in the metaphysis. Organisms which are commonly involved include staphylococcus aureus, staphylococcus epidermis and pseudomonas, and also haemophilus in under-fives. Untreated the infection can spread until it erodes the surrounding bone. Areas of dead bone can occur called sequestrum, and new bone can then arise due to perforation of the cortex by pus elevation of the periosteum and subperiosteal new bone formation. The new bone formation is called involucrum.

15.4   What antibiotics should be started?

Antibiotics that cover the most likely organisms in the hospital and area should be started. As staphylococcus aureus is a usual culprit they should cover this. The microbiologist should be asked for advice. Flucloxacillin 500 mg four times daily and ampicillin 500 mg four times daily should be started. This should be intravenous initially, usually with bone-penetrating meds as well, such as fucidin, gentamicin, rifampicin.

15.5   What other investigations would you do to confirm this?

- X-ray of leg. This may show only soft tissue swelling for the first two weeks. Periosteal new bone formation is visible by the end of the second week. Later, the cortex becomes rarefied and ragged, and a sequestrum may be visible
- Ultrasound guided aspiration of pus, and gram stain and culture. This relieves symptoms by relieving pus under pressure, and also identifies organisms present
- Bone scan – this is useful at all stages of osteomyelitis. It can demonstrate increased osteoblastic activity, which appears as a hot spot. Areas of dead bone may appear as cold areas on scan.
- MRI scan

15.6   How should this patient be managed?

There are four principles of treatment:

- General supportive therapy – adequate analgesia to ease the child's distress. If the patient is dehydrated then they should have IV fluids
- Splintage
- Antibiotics – these will be needed for two to three months as a minimum. Some experts advocate continued antibiotics for anything up to 9–12 months

- Drainage – if there are signs of deep pus or the systemic signs do not improve within 48 hours then the abscess should be drained. Smaller amounts of pus should be drained via a needle, under ultrasound guidance and under anaesthetic. Many experts advocate early surgery to avoid bony destruction and growth plate damage and to relieve pain. Osteomyelitis can be a very serious life threatening condition if not treated aggressively.

Case 2

15.7   What other questions would you ask in the history?

- Mechanism of injury – was it a tackle from front, behind or side, did the knee twist?
- How quickly the swelling occurred – immediate implies haemarthrosis and ligament injury, late implies effusion and meniscal injury
- Has he been able to weight-bear on that leg since injury?
- Any giving way or clicking?
- Medical history – previous knee injuries or operations
- Drug history

15.8   What are the potential differential diagnoses?

- Anterior cruciate ligament injury
- Posterior cruciate ligament injury
- Medial or lateral collateral ligament injury
- Meniscal tear
- Patella dislocation
- Fracture of the tibial plateau
- Osteochondral fracture of the femoral condyle

15.9   What is the likely diagnosis?

Anterior cruciate ligament injury – the anterior cruciate ligament limits forward movement of the tibia on the femur and is often ruptured in sporting injuries in which there is a twisting movement or tackle which pushes the upper part of the tibia forwards.

15.10   What investigations would you do?

- X-ray of the knee. Look for haemarthrosis and lipo haemarthrosis. The latter implies bony injury
- MRI of the knee

15.11   How should this patient be managed?

- Conservative – removal of blood with an arthroscopy
- Physiotherapy – this will build up his hamstrings and quadriceps
- ACL complete rupture in an adult does not heal. Symptoms may not be intrusive and therefore surgery may not be warranted. In an acute situation surgery is avoided to minimise the chance of stiffness that can occur with early intervention.

- If there are persistent symptoms (giving way, pain) then ACL reconstruction may be warranted. The ACL is reconstructed from a bone-patellar tendon graft, hamstring graft or synthetic graft.

Case 3

15.12   What other questions would you want to ask him?

- Details about the back pain and leg pain – site, onset, character, radiation, associations, time, exacerbations, severity
- When did he last pass urine and open his bowels? Does his bladder feel full?
- Has he had any urine dribbling or leakage?
- Does his backside and genital area feel normal, can he tighten his anus?
- Any unilateral or bilateral motor and/or sensory abnormality? This and the above three points are red flag symptoms that must be asked about
- Any previous back problems or operations?
- Medical problems – malignancy, arthritis
- Drug history – steroids

15.13   What are the potential differential diagnoses?

- Cauda equina syndrome
- Spinal cord compression
- Prolapsed disc
- Mechanical low back pain
- Lumbar fracture
- Malignancy

15.14   What is the likely diagnosis?

- Cauda equina syndrome – the cauda equina is formed by nerve roots caudal to the level of spinal cord termination. Cauda equina syndrome is a combination of low back pain, unilateral or usually bilateral sciatica, saddle sensory disturbances, bladder and bowel dysfunction, and there may be lower extremity motor and sensory loss. It is a medical emergency and immediate referral for investigation and treatment is required to prevent permanent neurological damage.
- The patient in this case is exhibiting low back pain, painless urinary retention, and lower limb motor and sensory loss.

15.15   How should this patient be managed?

- Admission urgently to hospital
- Refer to the spinal surgeons
- Urinary catheterisation to prevent further distension and relieve the bladder
- Urgent MRI spine to assess for cauda equina compression

15.16 What should happen next?

This patient has cauda equina syndrome – retention. This needs to have urgent decompression within 24 hours. The prognosis is worse if there is cauda equina syndrome with painless urinary retention and complete saddle and genital sensory deficit. Even with surgery there may still be some permanent neurological disturbance of the bladder and bowel.

Case 4

15.17 What other questions would you ask in the history?

- Any sensory or motor symptoms?

- Any other injuries when fell?

- Any previous falls?

- Medical problems

- Drug history

- Family history

- Social history – does she live alone, how does she manage normally with daily activities, does she have a good support network?

15.18 What are the potential differential diagnoses?

- Colles fracture

- Galaezzi fracture – fracture of the lower radius with dislocation or subluxation of the distal radio-ulnar joint

- Scaphoid fracture can occur with this mechanism, but usually in younger age groups

15.19 What is the likely diagnosis?

This is a Colles fracture – transverse fracture of the distal end of the radius. Features of the dinner fork deformity include:

- Dorsal angulation of the distal fragment

- Dorsal displacement of the distal fragment

- Radial deviation of the hand

- Supination

- Proximal impaction

It is important to assess distal neurovascular status. The median nerve can be compromised in this injury.

15.20 How should this patient be managed?

Basic principles for the treatment of any fracture are:

- Reduction of the fracture with anaesthesia and analgesia

- Stabilisation to maintain reduction until healing occurs. This can be either conservative, most commonly with a plaster cast immobilising the joint above and below the fracture. Operative treatment is always required for open fractures and displaced intra-articular fractures. In this case using a plaster cast is fine, and this should be checked the next day to ensure that there is no undue swelling.

- Rehabilitation

- Advise the patient to keep her fingers moving – this avoids chronic regional pain syndrome type 1 (reflex sympathetic dystrophy) in which the hand becomes blue, stiff and cold as a result of disturbance to the sensory and autonomic supply of bone and blood vessels.

- Review in fracture clinic in seven to ten days, with repeated exercise to monitor for loss of reduction.

Operative management of this fracture can include fixation with K wires and plaster splintage. There are some advocates of external fixation or open reduction and internal fixation with a locking plate.

15.21   The patient asks what other complications she may get and when she should expect the fracture to have healed fully?

- Median nerve damage

- Rupture of the extensor pollicis longus

- Malunion

The fracture should be able to come out of plaster in about six weeks. Full union can take three to six months, and full bony remodelling can take up to a year.

Case 5

15.22   What other questions would you ask her?

- Sensory or motor deficits

- Other injuries

- Medical history – previous fractures, osteomalacia, diabetes, osteoporosis, vision, physical activity

- Drug history – steroids, benzodiazepines

- Family history of fractures

- Alcohol use

- Smoking

- Weight

15.23   What is the diagnosis?

- Fractured neck of femur – this can be classed as either intracapsular or extracapsular and displaced or non-displaced. In a displaced intracapsular fracture the blood supply to the femoral head can be completely cut off, which can lead to avascular necrosis, non-union or both. In a fully displaced intracapsular fracture the femoral head lies freely within the aceatbulum making accurate reduction difficult.

- Extracapsular fractures do not disrupt the blood supply, so treatment is by fixation for example with dynamic hip screws.

15.24 What investigations would you do?

- X-ray of left hip – to check for fracture

15.25 How should she be managed?

- Treatment of the fracture depends on the type of fracture sustained and the age of the patient.

- All fractures of the femoral neck are best treated with an operation.

- Completely displaced fractures in the elderly at risk of avascular necrosis are treated by a prosthetic replacement (for example a hemiarthroplasty).

- Reduction and internal fixation is preferred in younger and very active patients and in patients with little displacement. Ideally this should be done as soon as possible after the fracture, particularly in young patients requiring reduction and fixation (ideally within six to eight hours).

Case 6

15.26 What is the diagnosis?

Compartment syndrome.

After trauma such as fracture, pressure in myofascial compartments increases. This pressure can exceed the venous capillary pressure and will cause a loss of venous outflow from the compartment. If left untreated, the tissue swelling results in reduced tissue perfusion and in turn, tissue ischaemia. This causes further swelling, a further increase in pressure, and a further reduction in capillary blood flow. The damage is irreversible after four to six hours. Eventually, the dead muscle fibroses and shortens, and an ischaemic contracture results.

Tibial fractures are the commonest cause of compartment syndromes. The clue in this case is the pain being out of proportion to the injury.

15.27 What are late features of compartment syndrome?

These are features of an ischaemia plus:

- Pallor

- Pulselessness

- Paralysis

- Coolness and loss of capillary return

15.28 How should this patient be managed?

- The backslab should be removed and the limb fully exposed and elevated – this prevents further constriction

- The compartment pressure should be measured using a slit catheter (this is not often done, and clinical suspicion often drives surgical compression)

- Fasciotomy to decompress all the myofascial compartments

15.29 How long should the wound be left open?

Following fasciotomy, the wound should be left open until the swelling subsides. The wound can then be closed or the defect grafted.

Case 7

15.30   What other questions would you ask in the history?

- Pain – site, onset, character, radiation, associated factors, time, exacerbating factors, severity

- More details about tingling – where specifically it is in the hand. This can help narrow down the nerve distribution

- Any injury to her hand or arm or neck?

- Past medical history – diabetes, pregnancy, rheumatoid arthritis, hypothyroidism, trauma, these are all associated with carpal tunnel syndrome

- Family history of any medical problems

- Occupation

- Drug history

15.31   What are the possible differential diagnoses?

- Carpal tunnel syndrome

- C6/7 radiculopathy

- Tendon disorders

- Demyelinating disease

- Other neuropathy

15.32   What is the diagnosis?

Carpal tunnel syndrome results from compression of the median nerve as it enters the tunnel created by the flexor retinaculum. When this space is reduced, pain and tingling along the median nerve distribution occurs. The median nerve provides sensation to the volar aspect of the thumb, index finger, middle finger and lateral half of the ring finger. This causes tingling in these fingers. The median nerve supplies the lateral two lumbricals, opponens pollicis, abductor pollicis brevis and flexor pollicis brevis (LOAF). If the carpal tunnel is longstanding or very severe then there may be muscle wasting over the thenar eminence and weakness.

Conditions that predispose to this include diabetes mellitus, hypothyroidism, pregnancy, rheumatoid arthritis, acromegaly, trauma.

The tests done in the examination are used to support the diagnosis. Tinel's test is when the volar aspect of the wrist is tapped and this produces tingling/paraesthesia in the median nerve distribution. Phalen's test is when hyperflexion for one minute reproduces the symptoms.

15.33   What further tests can be done to confirm the diagnosis?

EMG and nerve conduction:

- A delay in the terminal latency of the motor unit action potential from abductor pollicis brevis

- A delay in conduction across the carpal tunnel

15.34   How should you manage this patient?

Carpal tunnel syndrome may resolve spontaneously.

- Patient reassurance

- Rest

- Night-time splints
- Local steroids

If these measures fail then she should have surgical treatment with complete division of the flexor retinaculum and decompression of the tunnel. The operation is successful in approximately 80% of patients.

Case 8

15.35 What should the doctor do?

Check the airway and check the cervical spine immobilisation. Any abnormalities must be treated as they are found.

15.36 What should happen now?

The doctor should assess the patient's breathing. Any abnormalities must be treated as they are found. Appropriate monitoring must be commenced.

15.37 What should the doctor do now?

Assess the circulation. Any abnormalities must be treated as they are found.

IV access must be gained and bloods taken for FBC, U&E, G&S, clotting and glucose. Warmed Hartman's solution or similar crystalloid should be commenced intravenously.

15.38 What should be done now?

Assess disability and neurological status.

15.39 What should be done now?

Take chest, c-spine and pelvic X-rays.

15.40 What should be done next?

Expose the patient and check for any other injuries including pelvic instability.

The measures above make up the primary survey ABCDE which is part of the ATLS protocol. This system prioritises interventions so that life-threatening injuries are treated first. The 'golden hour' is the first hour after the injury and it is during this time that complications of trauma manifest clinically.

15.41 What should be done next?

Secondary survey – this is a head to toe examination of the patient.

15.42 How should this be managed?

- Analgesia
- Leg splintage and elevation
- Fracture reduction
- Fracture fixation
- IV broad spectrum antibiotics – metronidazole and cefuroxime
- Wound debridement and irrigation

Follow the ATLS protocol to avoid missing any life-threatening injury.

References

Case 1

1. King RW. Osteomyelitis. Emedicine. http://emedicine.medscape.com/article/785020-overview

Case 2

1. Hubbell JD. Anterior Cruciate Ligament Injury. Emedicine. http://emedicine.medscape.com/article/89442-overview

Case 3

1. Qureshi NH; Cauda Equina. Emedicine. http://emedicine.medscape.com/article/249203-overview

Case 4

1. Hoynak BC, Hopson L. Fractures, Wrist. Emedicine. http://emedicine.medscape.com/article/828746-overview

Case 5

1. Femoral fractures. http://www.patient.co.uk/doctor/Femoral-Fractures.htm

Case 6

1. Wallace S, Goodman S, Smith DG. Compartment Syndrome, Lower Extremity. Emedicine. http://emedicine.medscape.com/article/1270542-overview

Case 7

1. Ashworth N. Carpal Tunnel Syndrome. Emedicine. http://emedicine.medscape.com/article/327330-overview

2. Carpal tunnel syndrome. Clinical Knowledge Summaries. http://www.cks.nhs.uk/carpal_tunnel_syndrome

3. Carpal tunnel syndrome. Arthritis Research Campaign. http://www.arc.org.uk/arthinfo/medpubs/6523/6523.asp

Case 8

1. Dries D. Initial Evaluation of the Trauma Patient. eMedicine. http://emedicine.medscape.com/article/434707-overview

Cases 1–8

1. Dandy DJ, Edwards DJ. 4th edition. 2003. *Essential Orthopaedics and Trauma*. Churchill Livingstone.

ENT answers

Case 1: Answers

16.1   **What are the differential diagnoses?**

- Acute otitis media
- Otitis externa

- Mastoiditis
- Aural foreign body
- Referred pain from throat

16.2   What is the likely diagnosis?

Acute otitis media (AOM) – this is infection of the middle ear, characterized by the presence of a middle ear effusion associated with an acute onset of symptoms and signs of middle ear inflammation.

16.3   What would your management plan be?

- Simple analgesia (paracetamol +/– NSAIDs)

Antibiotics should NOT be prescribed in the first instance as 80% will recover in three days.

16.4   What are the potential complications of AOM?

- Chronic otitis media with effusion
- Mastoiditis
- Hearing loss
- Tympanic membrane perforation
- Otitis externa
- Cholesteatoma

16.5   Should Peter be referred for ventilation tube insertion?

No.

The latest NICE guidance advises that surgery should be reserved for patients with persistent bilateral otitis media with effusion (OME) over a period of three months with a hearing level in the better ear of 25–30 dBHL averaged at 0.5, 1, 2 and 4 kHz.

16.6   Is there any other treatment that Peter may benefit from?

Hearing aids.

NICE do not recommend the use of 'topical or systemic antihistamines, topical or systemic decongestants, topical or systemic steroids, homeopathy, cranial osteopathy, acupuncture, dietary modification, including probiotics, immunostimulants, massage' in the treatment of OME.

Case 2: Answers

16.7   What are the differential diagnoses?

- Coryzal illness
- Pharyngitis
- Tonsillitis
- Infectious mononucleosis

16.8   What is the likely diagnosis and how would you manage it?

- Acute tonsillitis

- Analgesia, good fluid intake

> Antibiotics are not routinely used for sore throat/tonsillitis unless there is concern about the clinical state of the patient. Some use the Centor criteria to determine which patients are more likely to have Group A beta-haemolytic streptococcal pharyngitis (GABHS). If the patient has three or more of the criteria (tonsillar exudates, tender anterior cervical lymph nodes, absence of cough, history of fever) the chance of the patient having GABHS is between 40% and 60%, so the patient may benefit from antibiotic treatment. Conversely, absence of three or four of the signs suggests that there is an 80% chance that the patient does not have the infection.

16.9   What has happened and what is the management of this?

She has developed a left peritonsillar abscess (quinsy).

Management is by drainage of the abscess per-orally under local anaesthesia, either via needle aspiration or incision. This is usually performed by an otolaryngologist. The patient will usually require hospitalisation for analgesia, intravenous antibiotics and fluids for 24 to 48 hours.

16.10   What advice should you give her?

Recurrent attacks of acute tonsillitis are an indication for a tonsillectomy.

The SIGN guidelines say that indications for tonsillectomy include:

- Sore throats that are due to tonsillitis

- Five or more episodes of sore throat per year

- Symptoms for at least a year

- Episodes of sore throat are disabling and prevent normal functioning

16.11   What are the main complications of tonsillectomy?

Pain, bleeding, post operative infection. The risk of bleeding is generally quoted as 4%. 1% of patients will require a second operation for persistent bleeding following tonsillectomy.

Case 3: Answers

16.12   What otological symptoms would you ask about?

- Hearing loss

- Tinnitus

- Otalgia

- Otorrhoea

'Vertigo' is a term used by patients (and doctors!) to encompass a very wide range of symptoms and it is therefore essential that you strictly define exactly what the patient is experiencing. Vertigo in a neuro/otological sense means the sensation of movement and is not a feeling of light-headedness, which is more accurately termed pre-syncope.

With accurate history taking, the diagnosis for most 'dizzy' patients will become evident before you begin your examination.

16.13   What examinations would you perform?

- Otoscopy – this will often be normal even with an otological cause but problems such as cholesteatoma and otitis media should be excluded.

- Neurological – many causes of vertigo are central in origin and it is therefore essential that a full systemic and cranial neurological examination is performed.

- Cardiological (including carotid surgery).

- Audiometry – specific labyrinthine causes of vertigo may also cause hearing loss and audiograms can therefore give important clues as to the aetiology of the problem.

16.14   What could the diagnosis be and what specific test could be done to diagnose it?

Benign Paroxysmal Positional Vertigo (BPPV).

This can be diagnosed by the Dix-Hallpike test. This involves moving the patient through a set series of positions and observing whether nystagmus is present in certain positions. It relies on the movement of otoconia through the semi-circular canals eliciting nystagmus.

16.15   How can this condition be treated?

The aim of treatment is to move the otoconia from the semicircular canal where they cause symptoms to the utricle. There are a variety of different methods for this, the commonest being the Epley manoeuvre. This involves moving the patient's head (and body!) through a variety of positions, holding each one for between one and five minutes. If correctly performed, the procedure has a fair chance of success but may need to be repeated to ensure full resolution of symptoms.

Some patients will also benefit from vestibular rehabilitation exercises to allow compensation of any underlying vestibular weaknesses.

Case 4: Answers

16.16   What specific questions would you ask her?

- History of previous epistaxis
- Recent URTI
- Recent trauma
- Past medical history
- Drug history
- Smoking and alcohol
- Allergies

16.17   What is the site of the majority of epistaxes?

Kiesselbach's plexus – a network of blood vessels in the anterior portion of the nasal septum.

16.18   What are the causes of epistaxis?

There are many causes, the more significant of which are listed:

Local:

- Trauma (including picking!)
- Foreign body
- Inflammation (URTI, rhinitis, etc.)
- Drugs (e.g. cocaine)
- Anatomical deformities
- Tumours

Systemic:

- Hypertension
- Drugs (e.g. aspirin, warfarin)
- Bleeding disorders
- Connective tissue diseases

16.19   How should this patient be managed?

- Assessment of airway, breathing and circulation
- Ask the patient to sit up and tilt their head forward and to apply direct pressure to the alar region of the nose with the thumb and index finger
- Apply an ice pack to the forehead
- Maintain this position for 20 minutes

If the bleeding is not controlled after this time:

- Bloods for full blood count, coagulation profile and cross-match if needed.
- IV access and IV fluids if there is significant haemorrhage.
- Pack the nose. There are many devices for this, the method most commonly employed without access to specialist equipment is anterior packing with either a Merocel® nasal tampon or Rapid Rhino® balloon pack.
- The patient should be referred to the ENT department for further management. The pack is usually left in situ for 24 to 48 hours before removal. At this stage, it may be possible to cauterise the bleeding point, often with silver nitrate.

References

Case 1

1. Acute otitis media. Clinical Knowledge Summaries. http://www.cks.nhs.uk/otitis_media_acute

2. Diagnosis and management of acute otitis media in primary care. Quick reference guide 66. Scottish Intercollegiate Guidelines Network. 2003. http://www.sign.ac.uk/pdf/qrg66.pdf

3. Surgical Management of Otitis Media with Effusion in Children. Quick reference guide. Clinical guideline 60. February 2008. National Institute for Health and Clinical Excellence. http://www.nice.org.uk/nicemedia/pdf/CG60quickrefguide.pdf

Case 2

1. Management of sore throat and indications for tonsillectomy. Quick reference guide 34. 1999. Scottish Intercollegiate Guidelines Network. http://www.sign.ac.uk/pdf/qrg34.pdf

2. Sore throat. Clinical Knowledge Summaries. http://www.cks.nhs.uk/sore_throat_acute

3. Respiratory tract infections – antibiotic prescribing. Quick reference guide. Clinical guideline 68. July 2008. National Institute for Health and Clinical Excellence. http://www.nice.org.uk/nicemedia/pdf/CG69QRG.pdf

Case 3

1. Epistaxis. GP Notebook. www.gpnotebook.co.uk

Case 4

1. Chang AK. Benign positional vertigo. Emedicine. http://emedicine.medscape.com/article/791414-overview

Cases 1–4

1. Collier J, Longmore M, Scally P. (6th Edition) (2003). *Oxford Handbook of Clinical Specialties*. Oxford.

2. (7th Edition) 2008, Scott-Brown's Otorhinolaryngology, Head and Neck Surgery. Hodder Arnold.

Recommended further cases

- Laryngitis
- Ménières disease
- Otitis externa

Urology answers

Case 1: Answers

17.1   **What are the differential diagnoses?**

This condition is referred to as haematuria. It can be either visible to the eye (macroscopic) or invisible and seen on dipstick urinalysis (microscopic). It has recently been suggested that rather than using macroscopic and microscopic, the terms should be visible and invisible haematuria. Macroscopic haematuria is associated with more serious pathology. Macroscopic haematuria has a risk of 20–25% of cancer (bladder, prostate and renal) and the risk of developing cancer in patients with microscopic haematuria is about 4%. Painless haematuria may be the only symptom of an underlying malignancy.

Differentials include:

- Bladder cancer
- Bleeding from the prostate (benign or malignant)
- Renal carcinoma
- UTI

- Bladder stones
- Glomerulonephritis
- Haemoglobinuria
- Drugs such as rifamipicin
- Food such as beetroot

17.2   What other questions would you ask the patient?

- Amount of bleeding, where in the stream, how long and whether it has cleared up. Type of blood seen (fresh, clots, altered)
- Urinary symptoms such as frequency, nocturia, urgency, dysuria, urinary stream
- Medical problems – previous urological problems or operations, renal disease, hypertension
- Drug history – rifamipicin, anticoagulants
- Occupation: dye industry, leather industry, chemicals, rubber, paint, textiles – working in these industries is associated with an increased risk of bladder cancer
- Does he smoke? (Increased risk of bladder cancer)
- Any other symptoms such as weight loss

17.3   What is the likely diagnosis?

Bladder cancer – second most common urological malignancy. It commonly presents with painless macroscopic haematuria with transitional cell cancer being the most common type (90%). Staging is with the TNM system. Histological grading is divided into three – well differentiated, moderately differentiated and poorly differentiated.

17.4   What investigations would you request?

- Urine dipstick – to exclude UTI
- Urine cytology – particularly good at suggesting a poorly differentiated tumour or carcinoma-in-situ
- Urine culture and sensitivity – if dipstick suggests an infection
- Full blood count – to assess blood loss and effects of renal failure if found to be present
- Clotting if on warfarin
- U&Es – to assess renal function
- Biochemical profile – to assess evidence of bone or liver metastases
- X-ray kidneys, ureters and bladder
- Ultrasound – for renal cancers, hydronephrosis and to check the state of the bladder
- CT urogram (which has replaced intravenous urogram) – to assess function and anatomy of urinary tracts (not always required)
- Flexible cystoscopy – to assess the bladder

17.5   What should your management be?

All patients with bladder cancer should be managed by urologists who are part of the multidisciplinary team of the cancer network.

Cancer target referral guidelines state that urgent referral is required if the patient is:

- Of any age with painless macroscopic haematuria

- Aged 40 years and older, and presents with recurrent or persistent urinary tract infection associated with haematuria

- Aged 50 years and older, and is found to have unexplained microscopic haematuria

- With an abdominal mass identified clinically or on imaging that is thought to arise from the urinary tract

The definitive diagnosis is made on biopsy usually by a rigid cystoscope or resectoscope under anaesthesia. It is important to include bladder muscle on this as muscle invasion is the single most important prognostic factor of bladder cancer.

17.6   What is the management of this?

Management depends upon the grade and stage of the tumour. In this case transurethral resection of the tumour and a single instillation of a chemotherapeutic agent (usually mitomycin C) given into the bladder within 6–24 hours of resection significantly reduces the incidence of recurrent disease. The patient will then need follow up surveillance with cystoscopy.

Intravesical chemotherapy is used for intermittent risk tumours and intravesical BCG for high risk tumours (T1, Grade 3 and carcinoma-in-situ). Invasive cancer will need either radical cystectomy and urinary diversion or radical radiotherapy possibly with chemotherapy pre-treatment. Metastatic cancer will require chemotherapy – MVAC (methotrexate, vinblastine, doxorubicin, cisplatinum) if the patient can withstand it, but prognosis is poor.

Case 2: Answers

17.7   What are the differential diagnoses?

- UTI

- Urethral syndrome

- Bladder stones

- STI

17.8   What other questions would you ask her in the history?

- Medical problems such as diabetes, pregnancy

- Drugs

- Any foreign bodies or catheter used in past

- Sexual history

- General urological symptoms

- Whether she has a prolapse

17.9   What is the likely diagnosis?

Urinary tract infection – this is very common in women as they have a short urethral length which allows easy bacterial colonisation of the bladder.

17.10   What investigations would you request?

- Urine dipstick – look for positive nitrites and leucocytes, leucocyte esterase test detects pus cells, nitrate reductase test detects bacteria that reduce nitrates to nitrites

- Urine microscopy if dipstick positive, $> 10^5$ bacteria/high field indicates UTI

- If chlamydia is suspected a polymerase chain reaction on initial void urine should be obtained (not necessary in this case)

17.11   What medication would you give?

Antibiotics should be given according to local advice set by knowing general bacterial sensitivities. It is usual to start with an antibiotic that will cover the most likely organisms which can be changed depending on results of the urine MC&S. Trimethoprim was popular but 50% of isolates are resistant and at the moment co-amoxiclav is the first choice.

Further investigations are only needed if there are three or more episodes in women or a UTI in a man. This includes bloods for U&Es, ultrasound of the urinary tract including a post-micturition residual, X-ray KUB. In some circumstances a micturating cystogram, CT scan, DMSA or MAG3 renogram may be required.

Causes of bacterial UTI:

- E. coli (most common cause in both sexes)

- Klebsiella spp

- Pseudomonas aeruginosa

- Staphylococcus saprophyticus

- Serratia spp

- Enterococcus faecalis

- Staphylococcus epidermis

- Proteus mirabilis

If recurrent infections which are not due to E. coli infection, particularly with a Proteus infection, consider the possibility of a Staghorn calculus.

17.12   What advice can you give her to reduce UTIs in the future?

Prevention is better than cure.

- Wear cotton underwear

- Wipe from front to back after micturition or defecation

- Drink plenty of fluids including cranberry juice

- Empty the bladder after intercourse

- Wash the genital area regularly with water, but avoid perfumes and talcum powder

- Pass urine regularly

- Avoid wearing pants in bed

- Avoid constipation

Risk factors for complicated UTI:

- Functional or structural abnormality

- Drug resistant organisms
- Pregnancy
- Diabetes
- History of stone disease
- Urinary tract instrumentation
- Immunosuppression
- Haematuria
- Male sex
- Old age

Case 3: Answers

17.13 What are the differential diagnoses?

- Acute epididymo-orchitis
- Testicular torsion
- Appendicitis
- Torsion of the hydatid of Morgagni
- Haematocoele
- Testicular tumour
- Strangulated femoral or inguinal hernia

17.14 What other questions would you ask in the history?

- Details about the pain – onset, type of pain, radiation, relieving factors
- Previous problems with testicles
- Sexual history – previous STIs
- Any urethral discharge?
- Previous UTIs
- Any nausea or vomiting – associated with strangulated hernias
- Systemic features of fever, rigors – can occur in epididymo-orchitis

Duration of pain is very important. A history of over 24 hours means that, even if it is torsion, the testicle will have infarcted beyond redemption. Survival of the testicle is rare after 12 hours and any time interval of less than six hours should generally lead to surgical exploration unless very certain that it is an infection. Torsion may have been preceded by previous episodes of pain that settled spontaneously within a few hours.

17.15 What test can be used to help differentiate between torsion of testis and epididymo-orchitis?

- Prehn's sign – scrotal elevation relieves pain in epididymitis but not in torsion. It is not reliable and any doubt may require scrotal exploration

- Colour Doppler ultrasound may be helpful, but may appear to indicate blood flow when there is none

17.16   What investigations should you do if infection is suspected?

- Full blood count – get leucocytosis

- Blood cultures – to check for infective organisms

- Urine dipstick plus MSU if needed

- Polymerase chain reaction on first part of urinary stream for chlamydia

If there is any doubt about the possibility of torsion, scrotal exploration should be performed and you should not wait for the results of the tests above.

17.17   What is the management?

Doxycycline for 14 days, treatment of his sexual partner, bed rest and scrotal elevation.

Case 4: Answers

17.18   What are the differential diagnoses?

- Benign prostatic hypertrophy

- Prostate cancer

- Prostatitis

- Urethral stricture

- Multiple myeloma

- Any neurological condition e.g. spinal cord compression, CVA, Parkinson's disease

17.19   What other questions would you ask in the history?

- Any family history of prostate cancer

- Any hormone use – increased testosterone use

- Any haematuria

- Any bone pains elsewhere

17.20   What is the likely diagnosis and what investigations would you do to confirm it?

Prostate cancer – this is the most common cancer in men and is more common in elderly males. Early prostate cancer can produce no specific symptoms so most men present with lower urinary tract symptoms of benign prostatic hypertrophy.

- PSA – higher the value above normal increased likelihood of prostate cancer. If the PSA is very high, the prostate feels malignant and particularly if there is evidence of bone metastases, no further investigations may be needed

- Transrectal ultrasound of the prostate with biopsy

- Bloods – check for uraemia, bone (evidence of bone metastases) and liver biochemistry (some hormonal treatments damage the liver and so base line tests are needed)

- Urine microscopy – to rule out UTI and prostatitis
- CT scan and/or MRI to check for metastases if the disease is localised and radical treatment is intended (either radical radiotherapy, brachytherapy or prostatectomy)
- Bone scan if PSA is greater than 20 or there is evidence of bone metastases

17.21   What does this mean?

PSA is not specific enough to detect prostate cancer. Although a normal range for men 60–69 is PSA ≤ 4.0 it is possible to have prostate cancer at much lower readings. This gentleman's PSA is a lot higher and indicates more than an 80% chance of prostate cancer. The higher the PSA the more likely the chance of prostate cancer being present.

17.22   What else can cause elevated PSA values?

- UTI
- Acute or chronic prostatitis
- Urinary retention
- Catheterisation
- Ejaculation
- DRE (very small effect and clinically not usually relevant)
- TURP/Biopsy
- BPH

17.23   What is the management of this?

Refer urgently patients under the 2-week cancer guidelines for suspected prostate cancer:

- With a hard, irregular prostate typical of a prostate carcinoma. Prostate-specific antigen (PSA) should be measured and the result should accompany the referral. (An urgent referral is not needed if the prostate is simply enlarged and the PSA is in the age-specific reference range).
- With a normal prostate, but rising/raised age-specific PSA, with or without lower urinary tract symptoms. In patients compromised by other comorbidities, a discussion with the patient or carers and/or a specialist may be more appropriate. Generally a life expectancy of over 10 years is considered necessary to justify screening for prostate cancer.
- With symptoms and high PSA levels.

17.24   How are prostate cancers graded?

The Gleason grading system is used and this defines five histological patterns or grades with decreasing differentiation. The primary and secondary pattern, i.e. the most prevalent and the second most prevalent pattern, are added to obtain a Gleason score or sum. The Gleason score has been modified such that Gleason pattern one and two are no longer used. The lowest Gleason score now possible is six.

Gleason scores of eight to ten are associated with worse prognoses. Gleason score 7 has an intermediate prognosis and tumours with Gleason scores of six are associated with lower progression rates after definitive therapy.

17.25   What would the management of this be?

If this patient has bone metastases, he would be initiated on hormonal treatment. This can be using anti-androgens, LHRH agonists or bilateral orchidectomy. Orchidectomy is less used these days due to patient preference, but it is the first choice treatment in incipient spinal cord compression or renal failure due to involvement of the ureters as it has the most rapid onset of action. Chemotherapy is used in men who have failed hormonal treatment. Bisphosphonates for pain relief (IV zoledronic acid is the only bisphosphonate shown to be effective in these circumstances). Palliative radiotherapy to the prostate or a painful secondary may also be required.

References

Case 1

1. Urological cancer – suspected. Clinical Knowledge Summaries. http://www.cks.nhs.uk/urological_cancer_suspected

2. Guidelines on Bladder Cancer. Muscle-Invasive and Metastatic bladder cancer. 2009. European Association of Urology. http://www.uroweb.org/fileadmin/tx_eauguidelines/2008/Full/Muscle-Invasive_BC.pdf

3. Non-muscle invasive bladder cancer. 2009. European Association of Urology. http://www.uroweb.org/fileadmin/tx_eauguidelines/2009/Full/TaT1_BC.pdf

Case 2

1. Lower urinary tract infection. Clinical Knowledge Summaries. http://www.cks.nhs.uk/urinary_tract_infection_lower_women

2. Guidelines on Urological Infections. 2009. European Association of Urology. http://www.uroweb.org/fileadmin/tx_eauguidelines/2009/Full/Urological_Infections.pdf

Case 3

1. Guidelines on Urological Infections. 2009. European Association of Urology. http://www.uroweb.org/fileadmin/tx_eauguidelines/2009/Full/Urological_Infections.pdf

Case 4

1. Guidelines on prostate cancer. 2009. European Association of Urology. http://www.uroweb.org/fileadmin/tx_eauguidelines/2009/Full/Prostate_Cancer.pdf

2. Prostate cancer. Quick reference guide. Clinical guideline 58. February 2008. National Institute for Health and Clinical Excellence. http://www.nice.org.uk/nicemedia/pdf/CG58QuickRefGuide.pdf

Cases 1–4

Dawson C, Whitfield HN. 2nd edition. 2006. *ABC of Urology*. Blackwell Publishing.

Recommended further cases

- Testicular torsion

- Benign Prostatic Hypertrophy (BPH)

Ophthalmology answers

Case 1: Answers

18.1   What are the differential diagnoses of red eye?

- Subconjunctival haemorrhage

- Conjunctivitis

- Keratitis

- Iritis

- Episcleritis

- Scleritis

- Acute glaucoma

18.2   What further questions would you ask her?

1. Any history of trauma?

   - Subconjunctival haemorrhage – although this can be spontaneous (more common if anticoagulated or hypertensive)

   - Corneal foreign body or corneal abrasion

2. Any itching?

   - Allergic conjunctivitis – especially if history of asthma, eczema or hayfever

   - Itching can also be present in blepharitis and dry eye

3. Type of discharge?

   - Watery – viral conjunctivitis

   - Mucoid – allergic conjunctivitis

   - Mucopurulent bacterial, chlamydial or gonococcal conjunctivitis

4. Concurrent sore throat, tender preauricular lymph nodes, cough?

   - Suggestive of viral conjunctivitis

5. Recent contact with someone else with a red eye?

   - Suggestive of viral or bacterial conjunctivitis

6. Contact lens wearer?

   - Possible bacterial keratitis

7. History of cold sores/localised vesicular skin rash?

   - Herpes simplex keratitis

8. Photophobia

   - Iritis

   - May also be present with corneal pathology

9. Type of pain

    - Irritation, grittiness, itching – conjunctivitis,

    - Burning, stinging and localised pain – keratitis,

    - Generalised discomfort – episcleritis,

    - Deep boring pain, tender globe, pain on eye movement – scleritis,

    - Severe pain with associated headache and nausea/vomiting – acute glaucoma

10. Reduced vision?

    - Can occur with keratitis, iritis and scleritis depending on severity

    - Acute glaucoma

11. Haloes of light?

    - May occur with acute glaucoma

12. Systemic disease?

    - Rheumatoid arthritis – dry eye, keratitis, scleritis

    - Ankylosing spondylitis or psoriatic arthritis – iritis

    - Inflammatory bowel disease – iritis

18.3   What is the likely diagnosis in this case?

Infective conjunctivitis – inflammation of the conjunctiva due to infection. It can be caused by bacteria or viruses. In this case, the sticky discharge is suggestive of bacterial conjunctivitis. The most common bacterial causes are Haemophilus influenzae, Staphylococcus aureus, Streptococcus pneumoniae and Moraxella catarrhalis.

18.4   How would you treat this patient?

Most cases of bacterial conjunctivitis are self-limiting and resolve within five days (viral conjunctivitis takes about three weeks to resolve). If the patient is a contact lens wearer, care must be taken to exclude an infective keratitis and contact lenses must not be worn until conjunctivitis is better.

Symptomatic relief can be achieved with cold compresses applied to the eyelids and infected secretions should be removed with cotton wool soaked in cooled boiled water. Advice should be given to avoid contagion risk. This includes not sharing towels and pillows and ensuring good hand hygiene.

Topical antibiotics can be prescribed to speed recovery and prevent re-infection. These include antibiotic drops, for example chloramphenicol applied every two hours, or an ointment such as fusidic acid or chloramphenicol may be used.

18.5   What features would make allergic conjunctivitis more likely?

- Usually bilateral and concurrent (infective causes may infect one eye and then the other)

- Often itchy as well as sore

- Clear mucoid/watery discharge

- History of eczema, asthma or hayfever

- Subtarsal conjunctival swelling gives rise to a lumpy appearance indicating papillae. If large and chronic these may give appearance of cobblestones

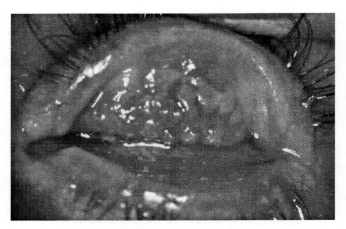

Figure 20.20 Subtarsal cobblestone papillae in allergic conjunctivitis (courtesy of Mrs Hannah Sharma)

18.6   Describe the main features of other causes of red eye.

- Allergic conjunctivitis (as above)
- Subconjunctival haemorrhage
    - Possible history of trauma, anticoagulated or hypertensive but may be idiopathic and spontaneous
    - Can occur in severe viral conjunctivitis
    - Usually unilateral, minimal discomfort, normal vision
    - Blood seen beneath the conjunctiva
- Keratitis – inflammation of the cornea
    - Maybe bacterial (usually contact lens related)
    - Viral (e.g. Herpes simplex infection causing dendritic ulcer)
    - Marginal (peripheral ulceration related to blepharitis or autoimmune disease)
    - Often unilateral, painful eye which may also be photophobic
    - Vision may be reduced or normal
    - Eye will be injected, and may be possible to see white/grey infiltrate on cornea
    - Fluorescein drops will demonstrate any corneal epithelial defect from ulceration including a dendritic pattern if Herpes simplex
- Iritis (anterior uveitis) – inflammation of the iris
    - Usually unilateral, red, painful, photophobic eye
    - Vision may be reduced
    - Circumcorneal injection
    - If very severe may have hypopyon
    - Small pupil, may be irregular if recurrent episodes of iritis

- Episcleritis – inflammation of the episclera (layer overlying sclera but below conjunctiva)
  - Usually unilateral, red, uncomfortable eye
  - Vision normal
  - Wedge-shaped area of injection (may have nodule within)
- Scleritis – inflammation of the sclera
  - Usually unilateral, severe boring pain with tender globe and pain on eye movement
  - Vision may be reduced or normal
  - Deep red injection with bluish hue
- Acute glaucoma – drainage angle closes acutely causing sudden rise in intraocular pressure
  - Unilateral severe pain with associated headache, nausea and vomiting
  - Blurred vision
  - Injected eye
  - Hazy cornea
  - Shallow anterior chamber
  - Mid-dilated unreacting pupil

18.7   What examinations should you do for all patients presenting with a red eye?

- Measure visual acuity (with distance glasses if necessary, and if the visual acuity is worse than 6/6 get the patient to look through a pinhole also)
- Look at eyelids – any blepharitis, eyelid redness or swelling
- Conjunctival redness – diffuse injection, circumcorneal injection, wedge-shaped injection, subconjunctival haemorrhage
- Look at cornea – white/grey spot (ulcer) present in bacterial keratitis, cloudy in acute glaucoma
- Instill fluorescein – will stain corneal abrasion, bacterial ulcer and dendritic (branching) ulcer in herpes simplex
- Assess anterior chamber – shallow in acute glaucoma; there will be hypopyon in severe iritis or endophthalmitis; hyphaema following trauma
- Pupil size – fixed, mid-dilated pupil in acute glaucoma, there may be constricted in iritis or irregular shape if recurrent iritis

Case 2: Answers

18.8   What are the differential diagnoses?

- Central retinal artery occlusion (CRAO)
- Branch retinal artery occlusion (BRAO)
- Central retinal vein occlusion (CRVO)
- Branch retinal vein occlusion (BRVO)

- Vitreous haemorrhage

- Retinal detachment

- Ischaemic optic neuropathy

- Age-related macular degeneration (AMD)

- Temporal arteritis

18.9   What other things would you check in the history?

- Details of loss of vision

  o   Type of visual loss

     ■   Whole visual field – CRAO, CRVO, vitreous haemorrhage

     ■   Central visual field – wet AMD

     ☛   Part of visual field – BRAO, BRVO, retinal detachment

  o   Preceding flashes or floaters

     ■   Vitreous haemorrhage, retinal detachment

  o   Preceding trauma

     ■   Vitreous haemorrhage, retinal detachment

  o   Previous episodes, e.g. amaurosis fugax

     ■   Suggests vascular cause

  o   Associated symptoms

     ■   Temporal pain/tenderness, scalp tenderness, jaw claudication, weight loss, malaise – temporal arteritis

- Past ocular history

  o   Myopia – retinal detachment

  o   Diabetic retinopathy – vitreous haemorrhage

- Vascular risk factors

  o   Diabetes

  o   Hypertension

  o   Hypercholesterolaemia

  o   Smoking

  o   Family history

  o   Previous CVA, TIA, MI, known AF

18.10   What is the diagnosis in this case?

Central retinal artery occlusion showing pale non-perfused retina with cherry red spot.

18.11   What is the management?

Cardiovascular examination including blood glucose (BM), blood pressure, pulse, auscultation of the heart for any murmurs, auscultation for carotid bruit, palpation of temporal arteries for tenderness and pulsatility.

A focussed history should be taken to assess the likelihood of temporal arteritis as a possible underlying cause. If associated symptoms of temporal arteritis are present, blood should be sent for urgent FBC, ESR, CRP. If temporal arteritis is felt to be a likely cause for visual loss, the patient should be referred urgently to eye casualty where high-dose steroids will be commenced.

If temporal arteritis is felt to be unlikely and visual loss has occurred within 12 hours, immediate referral to the eye casualty is appropriate. Here, measures may be taken to try to restore the arterial circulation via massage of the globe, paracentesis of the anterior chamber or intravenous acetazolamide. These are however only rarely of any benefit. To reduce future vascular risk, the patient may benefit from being started on aspirin and should be referred for an echocardiogram and carotid Doppler ultrasound scan to identify any locations for thrombus formation.

Case 3: Answers

18.12   What is the differential diagnosis?

- Posterior vitreous detachment (PVD)
- Retinal tear
- Retinal detachment
- Migraine

18.13   What else would you ask in the history?

- Preceding trauma
  - o   PVD, retinal tear or detachment
- Dark shadow/curtain in peripheral visual field
  - o   Retinal detachment
- Past ocular history
  - o   Previous retinal tears requiring laser treatment or surgery for retinal detachments
- Family history
  - o   Migraine, retinal detachment
- Specific symptoms of migraine
  - o   Known migraine sufferer
  - o   Prodrome, progression of fortification spectrum, headache, nausea or vomiting

18.14   What factors predispose to an increased risk of retinal detachment?

- Myopia
- Family history of retinal detachment
- Trauma
- Previous retinal tear

- Retinal detachment/tear in fellow eye
- Previous ocular surgery

18.15 How does a retinal detachment develop?

The vitreous pulls the retina creating a tear through which fluid from the vitreous passes and separates the inner neuro-retina from the underlying outer retinal pigment epithelium.

18.16 What is the management?

Urgent referral to the eye casualty. An assessment will then be made as to whether the macula is detached or not. If the macula is still on, urgent surgery will be performed to reattach the retina and the prognosis for vision is good. If the macula is already off, surgery will be carried out in the next week or two as the outcome will be the same as if surgery were carried out immediately. The prognosis for good vision is worse.

References

Case 1

1. Red eye. Clinical Knowledge Summaries. http://www.cks.nhs.uk/red_eye

Case 2

1. Graham RH, Ebrahim SA. Central Retinal Artery Occlusion. eMedicine. http://emedicine.medscape.com/article/1223625-overview

Case 3

1. Larkin GL. Retinal detachment. Emedicine. http://emedicine.medscape.com/article/798501-overview

Cases 1–3

James B, Chew C, Bron A. 10th edition. 2007. *Lecture Notes Ophthalmology.* Blackwell Publishing.

Judith Collier, Murray Longmore, Peter Scally (2003). *Oxford Handbook of Clinical Specialties,* 6th Edition. Oxford.

Khan PT, Shah P, Elkington AR (4th Edition) 1999. *ABC of Eyes.* Wiley Blackwell.

Recommended further cases

- Cataracts
- Refractive errors
- Diabetic and hypertensive retinopathy
- Age related macular degeneration
- Squint
- Glaucoma

Communication skills and ethics answers

Case 1: Answers

19.1   What are the key points when breaking bad news?

Breaking bad news is something that needs to be done carefully. There is a protocol called SPIKES which can be used as a strategy.

- Setting – privacy is a key part of where to break any bad news and it is important to minimise other distractions also. You should ask the patient if they would like anyone else to be present with them when you break the news. Make sure that you listen to the patient.

- Perception – before you say anything you should ascertain what the patient knows about the current situation and what he has already been told. You should take note of the language used by the patient as they speak and try to use the same language when you address them.

- Invitation – not all patients want to know everything and so it is vital that you check what they want to know, for example by asking, 'How much information would you like me to give you about your diagnosis and treatment?'

- Knowledge – before giving the bad news you should give a warning shot such as 'Unfortunately I have some bad news to tell you.' You should use similar language to the patient, avoid the use of jargon and scientific words and give information in small parts.

- Empathy – this helps to validate the patient's feelings

- Strategy and summary – check the patient has understood what you have told them and summarise things. Allow them to ask questions and formulate an action plan.

Case 2: Answers

19.2   What questions would you ask her?

- Is she currently sexually active and if so has she been using any protection?
- If she has a partner and if so how old they are
- How many sexual partners has she had
- Do her parents know she is here and that she wants to be on the pill?
- Will she tell them or let you tell them?
- Medical problems
- Drug history
- Family history of medical problems

19.3   What things do you need to check to deem her Gillick competent?

It is important to involve children and young people as much as possible in decisions about their care. All people aged 16 and over are presumed in law to have the capacity to consent to treatment unless there is evidence against this.

Children in this age group are not deemed to be automatically legally competent to give consent. The courts have determined that such children can be legally competent if they have 'sufficient understanding and maturity to enable them to understand fully what is proposed'. This is known as Gillick competence and is based upon the case of Gillick v West Norfolk & Wisbech HA in 1986. The term Fraser competency is also used in this respect (Lord Fraser was the judge who ruled on the case).

If, however, a competent child under the age of 16 is insistent that their family should not be involved, their right to confidentiality must be respected, unless such an approach would put them at serious risk of harm.

The following points are important when assessing competence to prescribe the pill in someone under 16:

- Check she understands your advice and its implications

- You cannot persuade her to tell her parents or get her permission to allow you to inform her parents about this

- The girl is likely to have sexual intercourse with or without the contraception

- She communicates her thoughts to you

- She is able to weigh up the risks and benefits about taking the pill

- She can retain the information you give her

- Her physical or mental health is likely to suffer unless she receives such advice or treatment

- It is in the best interests of the patient to receive such advice or treatment without parental knowledge or consent

19.4   How should you handle this situation?

Patients have a right to expect that information about them will be held in confidence by their doctors. You are not able to divulge any information about seeing her daughter or to even acknowledge that you have. You must inform her mother that her daughter is a patient and therefore you have to respect her confidentiality. You can tell her that she should discuss things with her daughter and if they want to then come and see you together then that is fine.

Case 3: Answers

19.5   What concerns does this raise and how should you best address them?

- You must protect patients from risk of harm posed by another colleague's conduct, performance or health. Patient safety must be paramount at all times

- If you have concerns then you must take the appropriate steps straight away so that the concerns are investigated and patients protected if necessary

- You should try and address your concerns with your colleague directly first

- You can discuss things with someone impartial such as the MDU or your educational supervisor

19.6   What should you do now?

You should now talk to your consultant and address the issue seriously as patient care is being compromised.

Case 4: Answers

19.7   What would you do in this situation?

Giving a gift is a common and socially acceptable way of people saying thank you. In this situation the patient knows the doctor well and she has made it clear that the gift is to say 'thank you for your help' over the unfortunate period she has had. In this situation the doctor should accept the gift, as it acknowledges the patient and will make her feel good. Refusing the gift may risk upsetting the patient and endangering the doctor-patient relationship.

19.8   What is the guidance that governs accepting gifts from patients?

The General Medical Council in its document 'Good Medical Practice' provides guidance about doctors receiving gifts.

- Paragraph 72c states that you must not encourage patients to give, lend or bequeath money or gifts that will directly or indirectly benefit you.

- Paragraph 74 states that you must act in your patients' best interests when making referrals and when providing or arranging treatment or care. You must not ask for or accept any inducement, gift or hospitality which may affect or be seen to affect the way you prescribe for, treat or refer patients. You must not offer such inducements to colleagues.

Many trusts have policies on accepting gifts from patients and set an upper limit value. It is generally agreed that accepting money is not acceptable and the GP contract states that GPs must keep a register of gifts exceeding a value of £100.

19.9   What kind of reasons would make it inappropriate to accept gifts?

- Monetary gifts are not acceptable

- If you feel the patient is trying to influence you or get better care or special treatment by doing it

- When it may be perceived by others that it may influence your care to the patient

- When it makes you feel uncomfortable, such as very personal gifts

- When accepting gifts may lead to receiving more gifts which are more costly

References

Case 1

1. Baile WF, Buckman R, Lenzi R, Glober G, Beale EA, Kudelka AP. (2000) SPIKES—A Six-Step Protocol for Delivering Bad News: Application to the Patient with Cancer. *The Oncologist*, Vol. 5, No. 4, 302–311.

Case 2

1. GMC 0-18 years: guidance for all doctors. General Medical Council. http://www.gmc-uk.org/guidance/ethical_guidance/children_guidance/index.asp

2. GMC Confidentiality. General Medical Council. http://www.gmc-uk.org/guidance/news_consultation/confidentiality_guidance.asp

Case 3

1. GMC Good Medical Practice. General Medical Council. http://www.gmc-uk.org/guidance/good_medical_practice/index.asp

2. GMC Raising concerns about patient safety. General Medical Council. http://www.gmc-uk.org/guidance/current/library/raising_concerns.asp

Case 4

GMC Good Medical Practice. General Medical Council. http://www.gmc-uk.org/guidance/good_medical_practice/index.asp

Recommended further cases

- Confidentiality
- Organ donation
- Ending life

Index

Titles in the Essential Clin... Series

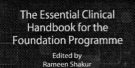

The Essential Clinical Handbook for the Foundation Programme

Edited by
Rameen Shakur

January 2010

425 pages

Paperback

ISBN 978-1-906839-09-3

£24.99

Unsure of what clinical competencies you must gain to successfully complete the Foundation Programme? Unclear on how to ensure your e-Portfolio is complete to enable your progression to ST training?

This up-to-date clinical handbook is aimed at current foundation doctors and clinical medical students and provides a comprehensive companion to help you in the day-to-day management of patients on the ward. Together with this it is the first handbook to also outline clearly how to gain the core clinical competencies required for successful completion of the Foundation Programme. Written by doctors for doctors this comprehensive handbook explains how to successfully manage all of the common cases you will face during the Foundation Programme and:

- Introduces the Foundation Programme and what is expected of a new doctor especially with the introduction of Modernising Medical Careers

- Illustrates clearly the best way to manage, step-by-step, over 150 commonly encountered clinical diseases, including NICE guidelines to ensure a gold standard of clinical care is achieved.

- Describes how to successfully gain the core clinical competencies within Medicine and Surgery including an extensive list of differentials and conditions explained

- Explores the various radiology images you will encounter and how to interpret them

- Tells you how to succeed in the assessment methods used including DOP's, Mini-CEX's and CBD's.

- Has step by step diagrammatic guides to doing common clinical procedures competently and safely.

- Outlines how to ensure your ePortfolio is maintained properly to ensure successful completion of the Foundation Programme.

- Provides tips and advice on how to start preparing now to ensure you are fully prepared and have the competitive edge for your CMT/ST Application.

The introduction of the e-Portfolio as part of the Foundation Programme has paved the way for foundation doctors to take charge of their own learning and portfolio. Through following the expert guidance laid down in this handbook you will give yourself the best possible chance of progressing successfully through to CMT/ST training.

LEARNING MEDIA

www.bpp.com/learningmedia